A COMPANION TO
THE BOOK OF MARGERY KEMPE

A COMPANION TO
THE BOOK OF MARGERY KEMPE

EDITED BY

John H. Arnold and Katherine J. Lewis

D. S. BREWER

First published 2004
D. S. Brewer, Cambridge
Reprinted in paperback 2010

Transferred to digital printing

ISBN 978-1-84384-030-5 hardback
ISBN 978-1-84384-214-9 paperback

D. S. Brewer is an imprint of Boydell & Brewer Ltd
PO Box 9, Woodbridge, Suffolk IP12 3DF, UK
and of Boydell & Brewer Inc.
668 Mt Hope Avenue, Rochester, NY 14620, USA
website: www.boydellandbrewer.com

A CiP catalogue record for this book is available
from the British Library

Library of Congress Catalog Card Number: 2004 018213

This publication is printed on acid-free paper

Contents

Illustrations

for
FELICITY RIDDY

Acknowledgements

The editors would like to thank all of the contributors to this volume for their professionalism and their scholarship. Editing this book has been interesting and rewarding, and never a chore; who could ask for more from one's fellow academics? We are very grateful to Caroline Palmer for her support for this project from its earliest stages, and for her useful ideas and comments as the book has progressed. Finally, to our teacher and dedicatee, we say 'thank you' – for her enduring encouragement for our labours, her generous intellectual energy, and her example both as a scholar and as a friend.

Notes on Contributors

John H. Arnold

John H. Arnold is Senior Lecturer in History at Birkbeck College, University of London. He researches medieval religion and culture, and has published articles on medieval literacy, gender and heresy. He is author of *History: A Very Short Introduction* (Oxford University Press, 2000) and *Inquisition and Power: Catharism and the Confessing Subject in Medieval Languedoc* (University of Pennsylvania Press, 2001). He is currently completing a book on lay belief in medieval Europe.

P. H. Cullum

P. H. Cullum is Head of History at the University of Huddersfield. She has published widely on hospitals and charity in late medieval England, and has interests in female piety and clerical masculinity. She is co-editor (with Katherine J. Lewis) of *Holiness and Masculinity in the Middle Ages* (University of Wales Press, 2004).

Isabel Davis

Isabel Davis is Lecturer in English Literature at the University of Warwick. She is working on aspects of gender and especially masculinity in late medieval English literature and culture. Currently she is writing a book on masculinity and life writing in the later Middle Ages.

Allyson Foster

Allyson Foster is a postgraduate student in English at the Graduate Center at the City University of New York. Her Masters thesis considers the reception of Margery Kempe and Catherine of Siena in early modern England, particularly in relation to extracts from their works that appeared in print. Research interests include female mysticism, late medieval and early modern women's literary culture, and early print culture.

Jacqueline Jenkins

Jacqueline Jenkins is Associate Professor in the Department of English at the University of Calgary. Her research areas include the Middle English lives of St Katherine of Alexandria, manuscript production and late medieval women's reading habits, and vernacular devotional literature, especially the writings of Julian of Norwich. She is currently completing a monograph, provisionally entitled *Gender and Social Identity in Guild Celebrations of St Katherine in Late Medieval Bath*.

Katherine J. Lewis

Katherine J. Lewis is Lecturer in History at the University of Huddersfield; she is the author of *The Cult of St Katherine of Alexandria in Late Medieval England*

(The Boydell Press, 2000) and several articles which explore the relationships between saints' cults and ideologies of femininity and masculinity. She is currently writing a book on ideas of gender in later medieval England for Routledge (forthcoming 2005).

Kate Parker

Kate Parker is an Associate Tutor in Medieval History at the University of East Anglia. She is presently working on her Ph.D. thesis concerned with the political relationships within and beyond the town of King's Lynn between 1370 and 1420. Her interest in the borough began when she moved to Lynn with her husband in 1986. She graduated from UEA in 2000.

Kim M. Phillips

Kim M. Phillips is Senior Lecturer in History at the University of Auckland. She is the author of *Medieval Maidens: Young Women and Gender in England, 1270–1540* (Manchester University Press, 2003), and co-editor of *Sexualities in History: A Reader* (Routledge, 2002) and *Young Medieval Women* (Sutton, 1999). She is currently writing *Sexual Histories: Western Sexualities from the Ancient to the Postmodern*, with Barry Reay, and developing projects on gender and medieval material culture, and on sexualities in later medieval representations of the East.

Sarah Salih

Sarah Salih is Senior Lecturer in English Literature at the University of East Anglia. She is the author of *Versions of Virginity in Late Medieval England* (D. S. Brewer, 2001) and co-editor of *Gender and Holiness: Men, Women and Saints in Late Medieval Europe* (Routledge, 2002) and of *Medieval Virginities* (University of Wales Press, 2003). She is currently working on a study of medieval paganities.

Claire Sponsler

Claire Sponsler is Professor of English at the University of Iowa, where she specialises in late medieval literature and culture, particularly drama. She is the author of numerous essays and of the books *Drama and Resistance: Bodies, Goods and Theatricality in Late Medieval England* (University of Minnesota Press, 1997), *East of West: Crosscultural Performance and the Staging of Difference*, co-edited with Xiaomei Chen (Palgrave St Martin's, 2000), and *Ritual Imports: Performing Medieval Drama in America* (Cornell University Press, 2004).

Diane Watt

Diane Watt is Professor of English at the University of Wales, Aberystwyth. She is the author of *Amoral Gower: Language, Sex, and Politics* (University of Minnesota Press, 2003) and *Secretaries of God: Women Prophets in Late Medieval and Early Modern England* (D.S. Brewer 1997); editor of the collection *Medieval Women in Their Communities* (University of Wales Press, 1997); and co-editor of two volumes of essays, *Decentring Sexualities: Politics and Representations beyond the Metropolis* (Routledge, 2000) and *The Arts of Seventeenth-Century Science* (Ashgate, 2002).

Barry Windeatt

Barry Windeatt is Professor of English in the University of Cambridge, and a Fellow of Emmanuel College. His Penguin Classics translation of *The Book of Margery Kempe* (1985) has played a key role in the modern revival of interest in Kempe, and his annotated edition of the Middle English text of *The Book* has just been reprinted by Boydell & Brewer. He has also edited an anthology, *English Mystics of the Middle Ages* (1994), and is working on a major reappraisal of the literature of mysticism in medieval England.

Abbreviations

BMK	S. B. Meech and H. E. Allen, eds, *The Book of Margery Kempe*, EETS original series 212 (London, 1940)
EETS	Early English Text Society
Goodman, *World*	Anthony Goodman, *Margery Kempe and Her World* (London, 2002)
Lochrie, *Translations*	Karma Lochrie, *Margery Kempe and Translations of the Flesh* (Philadelphia, 1991)
Staley, *Dissenting Fictions*	Lynn Staley [Johnson], *Margery Kempe's Dissenting Fictions* (University Park, PA, 1994)

All quotations from *The Book of Margery Kempe* are taken from the EETS edition and cited by chapter and page number within the text (e.g. 40: 97). Unless otherwise specified the quotation is taken from Book I; quotations from Book II appear as follows (II, 8: 241). In some instances we have included both single and double quotation marks around a quotation from the *Book* – this is in order to convey that the quotation in question is entirely direct speech within the text.

All quotations are given in Middle English with translations provided only for obscure vocabulary or spellings.

Preface

JOHN H. ARNOLD AND KATHERINE J. LEWIS

The Book of Margery Kempe, often described as the first autobiography in English, was probably written in the late 1430s and presents an account of the visionary encounters and conversations with Christ experienced by a woman from a prosperous urban mercantile family, who lived in Lynn in Norfolk. It details her attempts to follow a life of intense spirituality while living in the world, rather than withdrawing from it as an anchoress or nun, and describes the approbation and criticism which she received as a result. The single manuscript preserving the *Book* was in the library of Mount Grace (the Yorkshire Carthusian monastery) during the late Middle Ages, but following the tumultuous events of the sixteenth century it was lost from view and knowledge until the twentieth century. Before its rediscovery Margery Kempe was known solely through two printed editions of extracts excerpted from the *Book*, which were published in the early sixteenth century.

The last couple of decades have seen a veritable boom in the field of 'Margery Kempe studies'; from being a text that, as Barry Windeatt's essay here shows, aroused largely negative and dismissive responses in its earliest commentators, the *Book* has attained canonical status, appearing as a set text on undergraduate English courses, and functioning as an important primary source on History courses. The editor of the only previous collection of essays dedicated to Margery Kempe noted that interpretations of the *Book* had been, to date, 'largely harsh and negative', but the scholarship of the last twelve years since these words were written has been much more positive and has forced a widespread recognition of the text's importance and utility.[1] In this respect interest in the *Book* has been and continues to be firmly rooted in a wider flourishing scholarship devoted to the lives and experiences of medieval women, as well as medieval ideologies and practices of gender. As a result the allure of Margery Kempe's *Book* to medievalists has very often been rooted in the rare access it provides to the 'marginal voice' of a lay medieval woman. Paradoxically, this allure has now rendered her anything but marginal: there are three modern critical editions of the text available (in addition to the original Early English Text Society edition), as well as translations, and excerpts from it (either in the original or translation) often appear in anthologies too. There have been five scholarly monographs on the *Book*, plus a great variety of articles and essays, and an edited collection.[2] There

---

[1] Sandra J. McEntire, *Margery Kempe: A Book of Essays* (New York, 1992), p. ix.
[2] See the bibliography of works on Margery Kempe at the end of this volume for details.

is also a website which seeks to locate Margery Kempe and the *Book* within its 'cultural and social matrix' through providing access to the material culture of her world, in the form of digital resources.[3] Moreover, Margery Kempe has also entered into more popular realms; her life as described in the *Book* has been dramatised, both as a play and on BBC Radio 4 and it has also been rewritten as a novel.[4] Why, then, a new set of essays?

Despite, indeed perhaps because of, the wealth of existing accounts and analyses of Margery Kempe and her *Book*, there is certainly room for another collection devoted to her. A key rationale of *A Companion to the Book of Margery Kempe* is to complement the existing, almost exclusively literary, scholarship on the *Book* with work that draws on more historical analysis. This is not to suggest a rejection of existing literary and theoretical insights into the work and its author: this volume includes essays written by literary scholars, and others written by historians who are attuned to the *Book*'s status as a textual production, with all the advantages and constraints which this imposes upon our understanding of it and the events which it describes. Both of the editors of this volume are historians and, as such, our aim in putting the collection together has been to attempt to shift concentration away from the *Book* as a unique textual product and Margery as 'author', towards a greater consideration of the text as a source for and of its period. Some might argue that a historicising or contextualising approach is necessarily a reactionary one, and, indeed, historians have often made rather simplistic use of the *Book*; some having perceived it as a window onto late medieval England through which they had a clear and unmediated view of the lives of its inhabitants. There has also been a tendency to cherry-pick episodes from the *Book* to provide illustration for particular arguments about the nature of belief and devotion or the role and experiences of women, with no acknowledgment of the ways in which representation of the episodes that the *Book* presents may well be dictated more by considerations of genre and discourse than by what 'actually' happened, or by 'real' events at all (not least because there is absolutely no corroborative documentary evidence for the vast majority of what is described within the *Book*). Such considerations render inherently problematic straightforward identification of the *Book* and its protagonist as 'representative' or 'illustrative'. However, we believe that informed contextualisation of the *Book* serves to enhance an understanding of its nature and contents as well as providing a path into the culture and society of late medieval England. By this means these essays serve both as an introduction to some of the *Book*'s key themes and as material which we hope will stimulate readers (both those who are already familiar with the *Book* and those who are not) to formulate their own approaches to this extremely important text.

---

3   'Mapping Margery Kempe' created by Sarah Stanbury and Virgina Raguin http://www.holycross.edu/departments/visarts/projects/kempe/ (consulted 16 June 2004).

4   Roger Howard, *The Tragedy of Mao and Other Plays* (Colchester, 1989), pp. 41–56 for the play 'Margery Kempe', which was written in 1977 and first produced the following year. The BBC adaptation was written by Alison Joseph and originally broadcast in five daily parts on *Woman's Hour* from 2–6 October 2000 (with thanks to Liz Lewis for this reference). Robert Glück, *Margery Kempe* (London and New York, 1994).

Barry Windeatt (whose translation of the *Book* has done a great deal to bring it to a wider audience) provides an introduction to the collection by describing early twentieth-century reactions to the *Book* on its rediscovery and then exploring key trends which have influenced more recent scholarly analysis both of the text and its protagonist. He then turns to consider an aspect of the *Book* which continues, he argues, to 'resist or repel modern assessment'; namely Margery's 'lifetime of conversations with Christ', arguing that 'all else included in the *Book* is significant but secondary'. This is an impression which one would not gain from early writing about the *Book* which judged these conversations 'inauthenic' or found them embarrassing and downplayed (or even excised) them as a result. Nor does it emerge from some modern critical writing with its emphasis on the peripheral details which the *Book* provides about Margery's life. Reconsidering the ways in which the *Book* resembles a variety of narrative forms while resisting easy categorisation, Windeatt concludes with the bold assertion that Margery's inner voices should be central to interpretations of the *Book* and read as 'an insight into her own mentality'.

Broadly speaking, the next five essays explore some of the wider social or cultural contexts which provide settings for the *Book* and which inform its contents and their presentation. Kim Phillips's essay takes both a social and cultural historical approach in its attempt to find 'an appropriate framework' for Margery's life in terms both of lived experiences and the meanings which were attached to these. While recognising that the *Book* cannot be used as simple biographical material, Phillips begins by comparing its presentation of Margery's life to the common patterns which emerge from documentary evidence for the lives of contemporary women of elite urban status. By focusing on the key stages of upbringing, occupation, marriage and motherhood Phillips argues that the *Book* 'can help to illuminate our understanding of women and life cycle'. She then turns to examine the *Book* in relation to medieval paradigms of female life cycle, in particular the 'maid, wife, widow' formula and compares textual representations of these to be found in a variety of texts (romances, saints' lives, courtesy literature) with the representation of Margery. Phillips notes that the *Book*'s divergence from these models is not simply a matter of genre, and her analysis emphasises that, both in terms of the social and cultural means that we can use to frame Margery's life, it is as important to consider what is left out, as what is included.

During her analysis Phillips highlights the extent to which representations of female and male life cycle were used to underpin models of gender which rendered a woman's identity dependent upon a man's. This issue is also addressed by Isabel Davis in an essay which locates the *Book* within medieval constructions of patriarchy. This is a setting that has been considered by several previous commentators on Margery Kempe, but Davis's analysis adds a new layer by focusing on ideologies both of femininity and of masculinity. Reading the *Book* in relation to Hoccleve's contemporaneous 'Ballade to Sir John Oldcastle' and its construction of hegemonic and subordinate versions of masculinity, Davis investigates patriarchy 'not simply as a deplorable inequality between the sexes but as a complex set of compromises between women and men, and also between men and other men'. For example, Davis discusses the ways in which Kempe (as author) presents a glamorised account of Margery's marriage to the Godhead which draws on romance models to use patriarchal fantasies of feminine docility and obedience 'for her own ambitious and challenging ends'. She also highlights the ways in which Margery is seen to take advantage of gender inequalities between men of different status, and between men and God, to authorise her own position. Much analysis of the *Book* has focused on what it can tell us about women's bodies, but Davis concludes by suggesting that the question of men's bodies in the *Book* remains unexplored and would benefit from further consideration.

Kate Parker's essay draws on her considerable knowledge of medieval Lynn to 'describe the activities of Margery's social milieu in the late fourteenth and early fifteenth centuries'. She describes the geographical position and economic status of the town, as well as its religious and intellectual background and presents comparative evidence for the lives of women in medieval Lynn. Parker's essay (in combination with Phillips's) reminds us that Margery Kempe was a member of an elite social group within a wealthy and powerful town. This immediately problematises identification of her as 'marginal'; for, as Parker shows, in her travels Margery was able to draw on a network of hospitality and support derived from her mercantile background and contacts, and her personal status as the daughter of a five-times mayor of Lynn. Parker traces the impact of national events that led to a shift in the political climate of Lynn and the downfall of Margery's father and identifies this as a crucial precursor to Margery's visionary experiences and the composition of the *Book*. In this respect the public humiliation which Margery experienced is central for 'Margery's descriptions of the town's disparagement of her own spiritual manifestations mirror that endured by her friends and family'.

Several times within the *Book* public disparagement and criticism of Margery take the form of accusations of heresy. In his essay John Arnold points out that historiographical opinion usually clears Margery of the charge of heresy, but frequently identifies and celebrates her, nonetheless, as a dissenter; a woman who challenges the various forms of ideological oppression with which male authority figures seek to control and contain her. Arnold questions this approach by asking 'what is the nature of dissent, and what is the nature of the orthodoxy – social, political or religious – from which it demurs?' Scholars have frequently sought to link the *Book* and certain aspects of Margery's presentation within it to contemporary anxieties about Lollardy, but Arnold notes that, while the Norwich heresy trials of 1428-31 might provide a context for the composition of the *Book* in this respect, the atmosphere at the time of the events depicted was actually quite different. Moreover, he notes the ways in which 'Lollard' or 'heretic' could be a catch-all accusation in this period and suggests that Margery also aroused suspicion in other ways, identifying hermeneutics as a key issue: 'the problems that people had, in the context of religious fears, of deciding on how to "read" the interior person from the exterior shell'.

For many centuries, the only way in which people could read Margery at all was through the printed extracts from her *Book* published in the early sixteenth century, given the title *A Shorte Treatyse of Contemplacyon*, and this provides the focus for Allyson Foster's essay. The *Treatyse* effectively elides 'any trace of the outspoken, boisterous, independent Margery that is presented in her *Book*'. Foster argues that the reshaping of Margery's *Book* to focus on Christ's words to her can shed important light on the text's place in early modern piety and literary practices. Rather than focusing solely on what the *Treatyse* fails to do, she highlights the importance of considering what it does do, and why. Foster places her analysis of the *Treatyse* firmly into the setting of late medieval and early modern interest in devotional literature and the particular popularity of such texts among a female readership. In 1521 the *Treatyse* appeared alongside extracts taken from the life of another female visionary, Catherine of Siena, and Foster presents a comparison of both texts to show the ways in which Margery's revelations can be seen engaging in a dialogue with Catherine's to present a model of the mixed life for lay readers. The *Treatyse* demonstrates that far from being dismissed or forgotten in this period, Margery Kempe was apparently recognised as a visionary of some stature whose writings were deemed fit to be read alongside those of an acknowledged saint.

The next three essays have a different emphasis in their approaches as they consider the influence of particular textual models and discourses upon Margery's self-fashioned identity and the *Book*'s retelling of her experiences. Leading on from Foster's piece, Jacqueline Jenkins's remains within the setting of devotional reading and literate practices to re-examine the complex issue of Kempe's ability to read; a subject upon which scholars have often speculated in the past. Jenkins's outlines the varying abilities that could be encompassed in the term 'literate' and the ways in which literacy could be attained by a woman of Margery's status. She also considers the meanings attached to the act of reading and the ownership of books in the later Middle Ages. Focusing on the list of devotional works which Margery had read to her by a priest Jenkins's argues that far from the priest instructing a passive listener, 'Margery "cawsyd" her reader to become familiar with previously unfamiliar devotional works. In other words, she led, he followed.' Moreover, this list of books is not included at random, but in order that the *Book* can convey certain messages about Margery; on the one hand providing a context for understanding why Margery conducts herself in the way that she does, and on the other constructing a legible sign of her devout identity.

Reading matter was not the only means by which medieval lay people had access to devotional narratives and Claire Sponsler's essay argues that in order to understand Margery's piety we need to examine drama and dramatic texts more closely 'not least because Margery's own spiritual expression – as described in the *Book* – is emphatically theatrical'. Medieval East Anglia had a particularly rich performance tradition and Sponsler recounts the evidence for specific plays and other performance activities both here and in the other places Margery visited, in order to give an idea of the sorts of traditions and dramatic paradigms to which she had access. Certain of Margery's visions, particularly of the Passion of Christ, are clearly seen to be predicated on dramatic re-enactments of these, such as are preserved in the York and Towneley cycles. Thus the *Book* provides evidence both of the impact of such performances upon Margery and her appropriation of them in the service of her own spiritual self-definition, and Sponsler argues that Margery uses her body as a performative vehicle in order to make this manifest. The essay concludes by suggesting that dramatic models provided a means for the *Book* to integrate orthodox and more questionable practices in its representation of Margery while still retaining ecclesiastical approval for her way of life.

Both Jenkins's and Sponsler consider the influence of female models upon
Margery and the *Book*, considering Bridget of Sweden and Mary Magdalene
respectively. Female models are also the concern of Diane Watt's essay as she
examines Margery Kempe's self-representation as a prophet. Such a role may
seem an extraordinary one for her to have undertaken, but Watt illustrates the
ways in which the *Book* fits comfortably into a much wider discourse of female
prophetic utterance. Bridget of Sweden was a particularly important exemplar in
this respect as Kempe engaged with current affairs both religious and political.
The incidents described in chapter 25 where Margery becomes involved in a dispute between the clergy and laity in Lynn, and other instances where she prophesies on issues of importance to her home town, serve both to confirm her
supernatural abilities and to emphasise the status of religious authority in Lynn.
Watt also explores instances where Margery's prophesies touch on national and
international issues and controversies. Contrary to the views expressed in some
recent scholarship Watt argues that 'Kempe's prophetic interventions . . . reveal
her real interest and involvement in political events and current affairs.' By this
token the historical events which underlie the *Book* and which are sometimes
referred to within it are absolutely crucial to the meaning of the text and the ways
in which it constructs Margery's prophetic identity.

Taken together these three essays all emphasise the differing ways in which
the *Book* seeks to present Margery as a holy woman, and even as a prospective
saint. The next two essays continue this theme by considering the *Book* alongside
certain practices which have come to be associated in particular with women's
experiences of religion and spirituality. The body has often been identified as the
means by which women, denied access to other forms of religious expression
and experience, could create their own intimate relationships with God, and, in
so doing, gain recognition as holy individuals in the eyes of others. Sarah Salih
begins her essay with a survey of the scholarship which has established this
argument as almost canonical within Medieval Studies, noting the extent to
which the characterisation of women's piety as physical was ideologically
informed. The main part of the essay is taken up with an exploration of the bodily practices in which Margery engages in the *Book*, observing that 'unlike the
majority of medieval holy women, Margery aspires to a purely interior piety'.
Bodies are central to the *Book* but Salih argues that Margery's performance of
ascetic piety is located in the early years of her conversion, and that she subsequently begins to eschew this in favour of less physical forms of piety. Slander
and public criticism come to substitute for bodily suffering as do practices
which Salih labels 'social asceticism': taking care of an old woman in Rome and
then her own debilitated husband. Even the most distinctive and controversial
aspect of Margery's physical piety – her crying – is seen to be diminished as the
Book shows Margery moving towards less bodily forms of devotion. In this way
Salih uses the *Book* to emphasise that ' "Feminine bodily piety" was never a
monolithic phenomenon' and makes a strong case for the ways in which
Margery appropriates a certain, affective model of piety, but transforms it in performance.

The same case could be made for Margery's appropriation and performance
of the model of lay charity, as P. H. Cullum's essay shows. The chief duties of

a Christian in this respect were encapsulated in the formula of the Seven Works of Mercy, both Spiritual and Corporal, and this provided an oft-reiterated blue-print for pious aidworking in late medieval England. Lay people had various means at their disposal in order to carry out these Works but Cullum notes that the practices of charity could be fraught with tension and ambivalence and that this is reflected in the *Book*. Charity is another area in which Margery's experiences are often likened to the hagiographic accounts of holy women such as Frances of Rome. Although there are similarities, Margery is much less given to acts of extravagant almsgiving than they are, and her charitable practices are rather more parochial and conformist as a result. Overall Cullum argues that Margery strongly prioritises the Spiritual over the Corporal Works of Mercy, praying for people rather than giving them material assistance: 'Almsgiving may be described as the kind of thing that she did as an unregenerate soul, in her earlier and more conventional life.' This emphasis therefore serves as part of a strategy which highlights Margery's difference from and elevation over the 'average' lay people who appear in the *Book*.

Finally Katherine Lewis turns to the issue of the *Book*'s intention for Margery, which, it has often been stated, was to instigate and/or confirm her status not simply as holy, but as a saint. Much of the scholarship on Margery in this respect has drawn comparisons between the *Book* and the lives of other saints and holy women to demonstrate the debt it owes to hagiographic models. The fact that Margery did not subsequently come to be recognised or venerated as a saint is often attributed to failures within the text, or to Margery's imperfect or improper performance of sanctity. Taking a different approach Lewis suggests that we should interpret Margery's failed sanctity not solely, or even chiefly, from the perspective of her life, but rather from the setting in which her cult would have operated, considering exactly who it was that late medieval English people identified and venerated as saints, and why they did not come to count Margery among their ranks. The pattern of saint making which this essay identifies establishes that, despite the popularity of saints' lives as reading matter and exemplary inspiration, the fundamental criterion by which most English people recognised sanctity in an individual was through their performance of miracles. No matter how holy her life, without miracles Margery would have little chance of being identified as a saint after her death.

Some of the contributors here are well-established commentators on Margery Kempe, while others present their first published work in this area. Choice of topics was governed by a wish both to revisit aspects of the *Book* that have received a considerable degree of scholarly attention (such as issues of literacy and the bodily nature of women's piety) as well as to present analyses of contexts that have received less or no attention (such as the politics of Lynn and ideologies of masculinity). As editors we have not dictated a 'party line' to our contributors in their approaches to the *Book*. For instance, some of the essays employ Lynn Staley's distinction between 'Margery' the central character of the *Book*, and 'Kempe' its author, while others (including both editors) deliberately do not. As a result this volume does not present a collective or univocal interpretation of any aspect of the *Book* or of Margery Kempe, nor is the coverage which it provides intended to be exhaustive; indeed, there are many other areas, both in terms of text and context, that await further consideration. What follows is a selection of essays that provides interpretive settings, synthesises existing scholarship and presents original analysis which we hope will provoke further dialogue about Margery Kempe and her fascinating text.

Introduction: Reading and Re-reading
The Book of Margery Kempe

BARRY WINDEATT

> Sum dissolute personys, supposyng it was Mar. Kempe
> of Lynne, seydyn, þat sche myth esily heryn þes wordys
> in-to repref: 'A, þu fals flesch, þu xalt no good mete
> etyn!' . . . & þus it sprong [sprang up] in-to a maner of
> prouerbe a-ȝen hir . . . rehersyd in many a place wher
> sche was neuyr kyd ne knowyn . . . Sche askyd hem yf
> þei had any knowlach of þe persone whech xulde a [who
> was supposed to have] seyd þes wordys? þei seyd,
> 'Nay for-soþe, but we haue herd telde þat þer is swech a
> fals feynyd [pretending] ypocrite in Lynne whech seyth
> sweche wordys, & leeuyng of gret [coarse] metys, sche
> etith þe most delicyows & delectabyl metys þat comyn on
> þe tabyl!' (II, 9: 243–4).

Quite a sensation was caused by the rediscovery in the 1930s of a manuscript of
the full text of *The Book of Margery Kempe*, which its chief protagonist might have
relished. *The Times* of 30 September 1936, for instance, hailed its first publication
as 'more unexpected and more important than the discovery of the "Morte
d'Arthur" at Winchester'. Prior to that, Margery Kempe had been known only
through a brief selection of devotional material from her text published by
Wynkyn de Worde in 1501, and reprinted in 1521 by Henry Pepwell, who mis-
leadingly described the author as 'a devoute ancres'.[1] The owner of the manuscript, Colonel William Butler-Bowdon, descended from an old Catholic gentry
family, also wrote in *The Times*: 'the manuscript has lain in a bookshelf in the
library of Pleasington Old Hall, Lancashire . . . ever since I can remember', and
he further recalled how in 1934 he had taken it to the Victoria and Albert
Museum, where it was later identified by Hope Emily Allen as 'Margery
Kempe's lost autobiography'.

In 1936 Butler-Bowdon's own lightly modernized text ('A Modern Version') of
what it entitled *The Book of Margery Kempe* duly appeared, but he relegated to an
appendix the longer of the two prefaces, the concluding prayers, and thirteen chapters which largely consist of Kempe's colloquies with Christ, explaining: 'Except to

---

[1] For further discussion of the early printed material see Allyson Foster's essay in the present
volume.

those particularly interested in it, the great amount of mystical matter would probably prove wearisome.'[2] Before the modernization was published, in a long letter
to *The Times* on 27 December 1934, Allen characterized the text as the recovery of an
unusually immediate personal witness and testimony: 'It was said regretfully (not
long ago) by a distinguished historian that in the Middle Ages old ladies did not
write their reminiscences. The reminiscences of a medieval old lady have lately
come to light.' In this earliest assessment the *Book*:

> is found to be crammed with highly interesting narratives of real life . . . It does
> give remarkably elevated spiritual passages, but they are interspersed with
> others highly fanatical . . . a neurotic strain runs through her religious
> life . . . Her earnest desire to set down everything just as it happened brings us
> many narratives full of unconscious humour . . .

Already present here are what were to prove very persistent strands in twentieth-
century perceptions of the *Book*, whereby its subject is characterized as providing
uniquely direct access to the realities of daily life in medieval England but is also
marked out as disturbed and disturbing. And that the *Book* may be sometimes unin-
tentionally amusing has licensed a continuing condescension in modern assessment of an author whose candour and apparent absence of self-consciousness could
result in such a loss of control over her text's effect on its audience.

While registering the drama and romance in the rediscovery of a 'long-lost
autobiography' in English by such an early woman writer, the first reviews and
notices of the *Book* suggest not only fascination but also embarrassment and disappointed expectations. The *Book*'s very vividness in making real the sense of an
individual presence and a voice has always seemed to provoke responses as much
to Kempe's personality as to her book more broadly; a personality variously
experienced by modern readers (as by her contemporaries) as tiresome, unrea-
sonable and attention-seeking. Although *The Listener* felt 'it would have been
wonderful to have met her on a bus', *The Evening Standard* (under the caption
'Tears, Idle Tears') declared that 'Margery was certainly queer, even in a queer
age.' Stemming from that early misdescription of Margery Kempe as an
anchoress, expectations had been raised that another major English mystical text
had come miraculously to light. It hardly helped that a review in *Light*, the official organ of spiritualists in Britain, claimed Margery for one of their own as a
clairvoyant, if Evelyn Underhill could declare in *The Spectator*: 'There is very little
in Margery Kempe's book which can properly be described as mystical.'[3] Even
R. W. Chambers's introduction to the modernized version observed that 'to those
who had hoped to find a new *Scale of Perfection* Margery's book must be, from
certain points of view, painful . . .'.[4] The most disappointing and enduring comparison was always with Julian of Norwich. Looking back in 1961, Dom David
Knowles wrote that at its rediscovery the *Book* was 'recognized as at once a godsend
and a disillusionment', and proceeded to give the by-then customary valuation of

---

2   *The Book of Margery Kempe 1436, A Modern Version*, ed. W. Butler-Bowdon (London, 1936), p. 16.
3   For these early reviews, see George Burns, 'Margery Kempe Reviewed', *The Month* 171
    (1938): 238–44.
4   Butler-Bowden, *A Modern Version*, p. 6.

Kempe as an historical source ('invaluable information on contemporary religious and social conditions'); as a case study for 'the student of religious sentiment or psychology', while demoting her from any contemplative canon ('clearly not the equal of the earlier English mystics') and setting up the usual unflattering and unwinnable competition with Julian of Norwich ('more homely, perhaps, and even more comprehensible, but of an altogether coarser mould').[5]

It is noticeable that early reviewers, absorbing their disappointment over what Margery Kempe might have been as a great mystic, dwell instead on her narrative's power to summon up the life of its times. Writing in the *Morning Post* Graham Greene discounted the *Book*'s religious significance but instead enthused: 'Nowhere else can we find so vivid a picture of England in the early years of the fifteenth century... her book is a kind of Froissart of civil life ... she had a sense of *this* world.' Such a novelist's praise of Kempe's value as an historical witness can serve to represent a persistently romantic aspect of the *Book*'s reception, viewed as a window into its times. While sidestepping the question of what judgement to pass on Kempe's spiritual worth, the 1936 introduction – in common with many early notices – sees the *Book*'s main value in the light thrown on fifteenth-century life by what it carefully calls 'a biography, or autobiography'. Few other earlier commentators were restrained by any such caution from reading the *Book* as an 'autobiography', while from the earliest commentaries onwards the interpretation of Kempe's self-account was entangled – and not to her advantage – with the developing contemporary vogue for psychiatric analysis. One clerical reviewer refers to 'the prejudice which her terrible hysteria ... must create'.[6] Another clerical reviewer – for whom her cryings have all the appearance of 'violent hysteria' – sees her revelations as exhibiting 'not only a supreme and amazing egotism but also that even more unattractive quality of "possessive amorousness" which would seem to be a special failing of hysterical devotion'. Such egotism includes Kempe's being assured that she will bypass purgatory – upon which the reviewer comments coolly: 'This last assurance is of doubtful orthodoxy, and we incline to think that Margery's soul would require at least a short interval in the place of purification.'[7] Yet more damaging to perceptions of Kempe's psychology, as supposedly available for analysis through her text, was Hope Emily Allen's return to what she had already termed Kempe's 'highly fanatic' aspect and 'neurotic strain' in the damning tones of her 'Prefatory Note' to the Early English Text Society edition of the Middle English original in 1940. Here Allen writes: 'I would call her a minor mystic ... she was petty, neurotic, vain, illiterate, physically and nervously overstrained; devout, much-travelled, forceful and talented', and in assembling their apparatus 'the editors of this volume ... will aid the professional psychologist who later will doubtless pronounce at length on Margery's type of neuroticism ... I intend my notes to be a study in Margery's suggestibility'.[8]

5 David Knowles, *The English Mystical Tradition* (London, 1961), pp. 139, 142.
6 Herbert Thurston, 'Margery the Astonishing', *The Month* 168 (1936): 446–56.
7 Justin McCann, 'The Book of Margery Kempe', *Dublin Review* 200 (1937): 103–16, esp. 110, 113–14.
8 *BMK*, pp. lxiv–lxv.

Despite the excitement and attention prompted by its rediscovery, it is no great exaggeration to say that *The Book of Margery Kempe* then fell subject to an uneasy neglect that lasted for the best part of forty years.[9] The Early English Text Society edition appeared in wartime and could have neither the impact nor the appeal of the 1936 modernization. Nonetheless, it remained the only available text of the Middle English original for nearly sixty years. Butler-Bowdon's modernization was reprinted by Oxford University Press in its World's Classics series in 1954 (with the relegated materials restored to their proper places in the sequence), but this version eventually went out of print. Although the EETS edition remained available, and much of its erudite commentary, establishing chronologies, connections and parallels, is likely to remain definitive, some of its exploration of Kempe's possible 'suggestibility' has served her reputation less well. Before the 1980s, if *The Book of Margery Kempe* was read and studied, it was as a quarry for instances and anecdotes to illustrate the social and religious history of medieval England, or as an awkward appendage to studies of the medieval English mystics often directed to a devout readership. There always seems something headshakingly hopeless about Margery Kempe's walk-on parts as an also-ran in these mystic stakes.

From the 1980s onwards has come a revival of both academic and broader interest, with a Penguin Classics translation, a number of monographs, a fast-growing secondary literature of critical and contextualizing readings, and some new editions of an author, who is often now referred to as 'Kempe' in preference to the 'Margery' of earlier commentators.[10] This recent scholarly work on the *Book* has naturally reflected the preoccupations of its own late twentieth-century times, and much of it has been very properly concerned with assessing the implications of Kempe's exceptional status as a woman in her particular historical moment who feels impelled to create a book in the vernacular. There has been valuable work on Kempe's excluded and marginal status, as a woman dependent on the literacy of the clergy, yet implicitly contesting the misogyny of male clerical stereotyping of women's minds and bodies.[11] 'Experience, though noon auctoritee / Were in this world, is right enough for me / To speke . . .' as Chaucer's Wife of Bath begins her prologue, and Kempe's ambivalent relationship with clerical authority has been a focus of study, in view of the tensions created by the special claims to which she is

[9] This neglect may be observed in the modest number of published items on the *Book* listed in the bibliographical essay by John C. Hirsh, 'Margery Kempe', in A. S. G. Edwards, ed., *Middle English Prose: A Critical Guide to Major Authors and Genres* (New Brunswick, 1984), pp. 109–19. See also Stanley Hussey, 'The Rehabilitation of Margery Kempe', *Leeds Studies in English*, NS 32 (2001): 171–94.

[10] For monographs devoted to the *Book*, see especially Clarissa Atkinson, *Mystic and Pilgrim: The Book and the World of Margery Kempe* (Ithaca, NY, 1984); Lochrie, *Translations*; Staley, *Dissenting Fictions*; Goodman, *World*. For recent editions, see Lynn Staley, ed., *The Book of Margery Kempe*, TEAMS Medieval Institute Publications (Kalamazoo, Michigan, 1996); Barry Windeatt, ed., *The Book of Margery Kempe*, Longmans Annotated Texts (Harlow, 2000); Lynn Staley, ed., *The Book of Margery Kempe*, Norton Critical Editions (New York, 2001).

[11] Karma Lochrie, '*The Book of Margery Kempe*: The Marginal Woman's Quest for Literary Authority', *Journal of Medieval and Renaissance Studies* 16 (1986): 33–55; Sarah Beckwith, 'Problems of Authority in Late Medieval English Mysticism: Agency and Authority in *The Book of Margery Kempe*', *Exemplaria* 4 (1992): 171–200.

persuaded by her experience.[12] Her *Book* shows Kempe challenged by clerics who see her as usurping the male clerical monopoly on preaching; it also represents her as winning those arguments by sufficiently asserting her own orthodoxy at a time of heightened sensitivity to heresy because of Lollard activity. The devout woman author's need to establish her own authority in wary negotiation with clerical authority has prompted some modern analyses of Kempe as an 'illiterate' author, who professedly could not read or write, and of the nature of her responsibility for a text dictated once and then subsequently copied out again in conferral with a clerical amanuensis.[13] Along with this has come much more recognition of the carefully, even artfully, constructed nature of reportage and self-presentation in a text written down decades after the events recounted.[14] As an 'historical' witness, the *Book* has come to seem as ambivalent as any other 'literary' text. Invaluable too have been those recent studies that have enlarged the topic of Kempe's 'suggestibility' by illuminating the contexts, inspirations and role models in the contemporary literature and culture of devotion.[15]

Yet the modern focus on Margery Kempe's quest to establish the authority of her own experience in negotiation with ecclesiastical authorities, while attending to some of the more stagey sequences of the *Book* (chapters 51–54), has underplayed the duller, but more frequent and equally significant evidence of just how much support, understanding and tolerant openness characterized Kempe's reception by clerics. Although the clerical establishments at Canterbury and York show prejudiced hostility towards her (chapters 13, 52), she receives a commendably fair hearing and treatment from a splendidly testy archbishop of York. The bishop of Norwich bears 'meekly and patiently' with her loud cries during a sermon of his at Lynn (69). Archbishop Arundel of Canterbury, the bishops of Lincoln and Worcester, the abbot of Leicester, a papal legate, various Norwich clerics of some repute, as well as numerous humbler clerics on her travels and at home in Lynn, show her the respectful consideration of listening to what she has to say and taking it seriously, in some cases over many years. In Leicester, as is also partly the case in Yorkshire, her troubles are instigated by over-zealous secular authorities, jumpy about her possible connection with Lollard activity.[16] But while Kempe is accused of Lollardy in as widely separate places as London, Canterbury, the Midlands and Yorkshire, it is at least as significant that she does not suffer greater challenge on account of some of the ostensible overlaps between

---

[12] Janette Dillon, 'Holy Women and their Confessors or Confessors and their Holy Women?', in Rosalynn Voaden, ed., *Prophets Abroad: The Reception of Continental Holy Women in Late-Medieval England* (Cambridge, 1996), pp. 115–40.

[13] John C. Hirsh, 'Author and Scribe in *The Book of Margery Kempe*', *Medium Aevum* 44 (1975): 145–50; R. C. Ross, 'Oral Life, Written Text: The Genesis of *The Book of Margery Kempe*', *Yearbook of English Studies* 22 (1992): 226–37.

[14] Lynn Staley [Johnson] 'The Trope of the Scribe and the Question of Literary Authority in the Works of Julian of Norwich and Margery Kempe', *Speculum* 46 (1991): 820–38.

[15] Roger Ellis, 'Margery Kempe's Scribe and the Miraculous Books', in Helen Phillips, ed., *Langland, the Mystics and the Medieval Religious Tradition* (Cambridge, 1990), pp. 161–75. Devotional contexts and models are also explored by Sarah Salih and Patricia Cullum in this volume.

[16] The *Book*'s relationship to Lollardy and dissent is revisited in John Arnold's essay.

Lollard assumptions and her singular lifestyle as a woman who constantly speaks of and with God. Remarkably, she records no serious challenge to her as a Lollard at home in East Anglia, where Lollard networks were being uncovered and prosecuted in her day.[17] Nor has the sympathetic recent focus on Kempe as a marginalized and excluded figure quite accounted for the inclusion afforded her by an assured bourgeois social status that Kempe herself proudly asserts and exploits.[18] She deals easily and unsubserviently with everyone from prelates down; she recalls dining with bishops, abbots, great ladies, and indirectly reveals her dealings with Henry IV's half-sister, the countess of Westmorland (54). By dwelling on her supposed marginalization and her eccentricity, a certain modern preference for reading and teaching narratives about heroic underdogs may risk implicitly accepting some of her medieval detractors' strategies for regarding her as marginal. Similarly, the zeal with which recent commentators have stressed the supposed limits to how far an illiterate Kempe may be regarded as exercising authorship over her dictated book risks muting this medieval woman's voice more insidiously but effectively than medieval clerics succeeded in doing. The well-to-do mayor's daughter, who set off on pilgrimage to Palestine accompanied by her maid, was not socially and materially marginalized (however much her otherworldly attitudes may have self-marginalized her), just as her evident civic pride in her home town and its parish church are consistent with a marked absence of any sustained moralizing critique of failings in her contemporary society from a spiritual perspective. Her specific criticisms of unbecoming conduct in episcopal households (16, 45) only serve to underline Kempe's unspoken larger conservatism – despite all her noisy disruptiveness – in social and political terms. In spiritual terms too: for modern explorations of parallels between the *Book* and other contemplative literature have implicitly diminished a sense of the uniqueness of her testimony. Yet notions of her suggestibility need not reduce Kempe to a mere consumer and mimic of contemplative texts or just a spirited practitioner of the role-play prompted by affective devotion.[19] When Kempe mentions to Richard Caister some spiritual classics she knows, 'Hyltons boke, ne Bridis boke, ne Stimulus Amoris, ne Incendium Amoris' (17: 39), it is not simply to list her devout reading for its own sake. Margery Kempe's project is bolder: she measures her experience against these classics only to assert her superior authority and originality, claiming that her own inward confabulations with the divine, if only she could express them, are unmatched by any such texts she ever heard read, in speaking of the love of God.

Despite so many exceptionally insightful contextualizings, significant aspects of *The Book of Margery Kempe* still resist or repel modern assessment. If Margery Kempe is no longer read as 'a kind of Froissart of civil life' or somewhat naively viewed as opening a clear-glass window for us onto medieval England, she seems no nearer to being read for that greater part of her text that disappointed

[17] Norman P. Tanner, ed., *Heresy Trials in the Diocese of Norwich, 1428–31* (London, 1977).

[18] Margery's social and family background is explored in detail by Kate Parker in this volume, while Isabel Davis considers the gendered dimensions of this, both with respect to femininity and masculinity.

[19] Jacqueline Jenkins's and Claire Sponsler's essays argue for Margery's active and creative response to devotional writing and drama respectively.

and embarrassed when it was first rediscovered. In an appropriately postmodern spirit, much modern writing about the *Book* ignores the centre for the margins, averting its gaze from what its author might have regarded her text as being centrally concerned to put on record: her lifetime of conversations with Christ. Compared with this wholly extraordinary and justifying inward experience, all else that is included in the *Book* is significant but secondary, as is implicit in the design and proportions of the work as a narrative in which any passing challenges and peripheral irritations are overcome. It is in recording a recurrent dialogue with the divine that the *Book* finds its continuity and structure as a self-account. Viewed as a whole, the *Book* dissolves a linear historical narrative in order to convey what is central to Kempe's experience in a continuing colloquy with Christ, to which a conventional chronology is of no consequence. These prayerful dialogues, reported as if verbatim in the present tense, are often unassigned to particular periods in Kempe's career. Near the beginning of her narrative Christ instructs Kempe to leave her 'byddyng of many bedys [prayers]' after six o'clock and give herself over to 'thynk swych thowtys as I wyl putt in þi mend . . . þan schalt þow ly stylle & speke to me be thowt [by thought], & I schal ȝefe to þe [give to thee] hey medytacyon and very contemplacyon' (5: 17). Indeed, Kempe has already hinted at how her inward meditations go hand in hand with colloquy with the divine, reporting 'hy contemplacyon day be day & many holy spech & dalyawns of owyr Lord Ihesu Cryst boþe a-for-noon & aftyrnoon' (13: 29). For Kempe, these interchanges are so centrally important ('I xal beleuyn þat every good thowt is þe speche of God' [59: 146]) that the most significant continuum in her text takes the form of a book of prayers, a kind of stream of consciousness reported through the inward dialogue between her own prayers and those divine locutions which she intuits through prayer, intuitions often more innovative than her visions.[20] To look more closely at how the *Book* defines, classifies and categorizes these prayers – as various brief types of interchange seeking and understanding divine guidance, as prophetic revelation, contemplative visualizings, and more extended colloquies with Christ – is to reclaim one neglected but crucial key to the structure and unity of the *Book*.

Not only in the early chapters, but also throughout the *Book*, Margery Kempe tells of Christ answering her prayers with instructions and reassurances, so that a narrative of recollected actions is embedded within Kempe's constant experience of inner uncertainty and fearful forethought from which, through prayerful interchange with Christ, her decisions and reactions are shown to follow. Christ tells her she must fast on Fridays (9) and later tells her 'wyth gret swetnesse' how to exploit this fasting in negotiating with her husband (11: 24–5). Christ answers in direct speech to her reported prayer and dictates the reply she should give to Bishop Repingdon of Lincoln (15). Christ instructs her to introduce herself to Richard Caister at Norwich (17), gives instructions for her return from Jerusalem (30), tells her not to be governed by a certain Norwich anchorite (43), tells her to wear white clothes (44), or to visit

---

[20] See also Barry Windeatt, ' "I use but comownycacyon and good wordys": Teaching and *The Book of Margery Kempe*', in Dee Dyas and Roger Ellis, eds, *Approaching Medieval English Anchoritic and Mystical Texts* (forthcoming).

Denny abbey (84), to stop eating meat (5), to resume eating meat (66), among many other injunctions in divine locutions which Kempe hears and records. Narratives of stressful episodes (like her time in the Holy Land or other travels and times of confrontation) depict her course of action as evolving out of frequent inward dialogue with Christ ('Sithyn, as þis creature was in contemplacyon, owyr Lord warnyd hir in hir mende þat sche xuld not seylyn in þat schip' [28: 66]). Frequent speeches by Christ throughout the text urge Kempe not to be afraid (for example 10: 22; 26: 62; 30: 75; 39: 96; 42: 100), acting out a repeated drama between inward uncertainty and resolution, and so positioning the text's focus less on outward tribulation than on the inner life that transcends it. It is a recurrent device of the *Book* that chapters close with climactic reports in direct speech of Christ's utterances (for example chapters 13, 32, 56, 63), variously endorsing and confirming Kempe's actions and prayers in what has just preceded.

The significance that attaches to such divine locutions in the *Book* is reflected in the pervasive care with which they are defined and attributed. In many cases the text simply records that 'Our Lord seyd', and conversations with Christ are woven into the unceremoniously domestic circumstance of daily life ('and þan owr Lord seyd to hir as sche lay in hir bed . . .' [71: 171]). Elsewhere the *Book* typically troubles to note that Christ answered or said 'to her mind', and spoke or answered 'to her thought'. One divine locution begins when Christ 'answeryd to hir mende & seyde' and concludes after he 'had thus swetly dalyed [conversed] to hir sowle' (38: 92–3), but if not all the definitions are consistent, the *Book* consistently views the classification of such speeches as significant. The import of divine locutions is such that they are often presented in direct speech where the prayer by Kempe to which they respond is merely reported or described. Divine communication 'to her soul' frequently indicates an especially pressing message ('þe spiryt of God seyd to hir sowle, "Helde þis for a gret myracle . . ." ' [9: 22]). Throughout the *Book* there is a vividly spatial sense of the soul as a capacious space into which Christ, Mary and some saints may be welcomed for conversation. As she tells Richard Caister, 'sum-tyme þe Fadyr of Hevyn dalyd to hir sowle as pleynly and as veryly as o frend spekyth to a-noþer be bodyly spech' (17: 39), while on other occasions 'owyr Lady spak to hir mend' (17: 39) or 'aperyng to hir sowle bad hir' (66: 162), or various saints 'aperyd to hir sowle & tawt hir' (17: 39). Throughout Kempe understands herself as being inwardly taught by Mary, Christ and God, whose colloquies with her are variously described as teaching (21: 50; 41: 98; 83: 201), a persuasive aspect of their authority, and of Kempe's in receiving such teaching. Much later, assorted saints reportedly 'spokyn to þe vndirstondyng of hir sowle . . . & answeryd to what þat sche wolde askyn of hem, & sche cowde vndirstond be her maner of dalyawns whech of hem it was þat spak vn-to hir' (87: 215). To be in conversation with otherworldly interlocutors – even to interrogate them, as here – evidently becomes part of Kempe's consciousness and hence part of the texture of her *Book*.

One outcome of such prayerful interrogations is Margery Kempe's role as a local prophet, which is evidently the most successful and acceptable aspect of her vocation in her own times, for her triumphs in prophecy make her useful to her community.[21] Powers of prophetic intuition also prove useful in enabling Kempe to control various clerics (by confronting them with their secret sins or otherwise proving her superior information). A number of chapters record those prayerful exchanges in which Christ provides her with the necessary information ('Owyr Lord Ihesu seyd to hir spirite, "Dowtyr, be not abaschyd for þis man, he schal levyn & faryn rygth wel"' [23: 54]). Some testimonies to the accuracy of her 'felyngys' are stressed to have been assembled together by theme rather than in chronological order, so as to offer a kind of dossier on her success as a prophet (25: 58), but while there is some suggestion that her revelations came thickest at a particular period (21: 48), she represents herself as cast in a prophetic role by her society throughout much of the text. With some consistency the *Book* reserves the term 'felyng', and less often 'revelacyon', to describe these prayerful intuitions through which Kempe is enabled to perform the role of prophet ('as owyr Lord schewyd to hir be reuelacyon & bad hir tellyn hym, þat he wist wel þerby hir felyngys wer trewe' [33: 83]). Such 'felyngys' enable Kempe to satisfy those seeking prophetic insight into the future health or otherwise of the sick, the destination of their souls, whether certain strangers are to be trusted, and even some forms of weather forecasting ('þe wederyng fel as sche felt be reuelacyon' [42: 101]). Her prophetic revelations, about herself and others, are several times declared too extensive to allow more than a selective report ('vn-possibyl to writyn al þe holy thowtys, holy spechys, and þe hy reuelacyons whech owr Lord schewyd vn-to hir, bothyn of hir-selfe & of oþer men & women' [59: 144]). Unwelcome revelations prompt her to disbelieve her own prophecies and be punished with delusions (59). A compulsion to see her prophecies proved right evidently becomes a continuing psychological burden. It is also the determining factor in structuring episodes so as to demonstrate her prophetic insights being validated by outcome: as narrated, the recovery from illness of her supporter Alan of Lynn has less significance in itself than in validating her prophetic insight that they would speak together again (70). Throughout she implies – and sometimes acknowledges with feeling (24: 55) – that a prophetic role is forced on her much against her will by her companions. For the ease of measuring prophecies against outcomes puts on trial Kempe's effectiveness as a prophet – and hence by implication her whole vocation – in an anxious confrontation of her outward circumstances and her inward life in colloquy with Christ.

Less troublesome because more inwardly directed are her visualizings of her imaginative participation in the narrative of Christ's life. Although in the early days she needs to ask for a cue (' "Ihesu, what schal I thynke?" Ower Lord Ihesu answeryd to hir mende, "Dowtyr, thynke on my Modyr . . ." ' [6: 18]), for much of the text, and by implication for much of her career, her inward life is preoccupied with an activity often termed by the *Book* 'contemplacyon', as when she tearfully witnesses the Adoration of the Magi, 'beheldyng al þe processe in contemplacyon' (7: 19), or seems in devout imagination to move about in a contemplative inner landscape ('Sithyn sche went forth in contemplacyon . . .' [80: 191]). During her

---

[21] On Kempe as a prophet see Diane Watt, *Secretaries of God: Women Prophets in Late Medieval and Early Modern England* (Cambridge, 1997), ch. 2, and Diane Watt's essay in the present volume.

visits to the Holy Places the processes of her imaginative perceptions are carefully
defined: in the church of the Holy Sepulchre she weeps 'as þow sche had seyn
owyr Lord wyth hir bodyly ey . . . Befor hir in hyr sowle sche saw hym veryly þe
contemplacyon . . . Beforn hir face sche herd and saw in hir gostly sygth þe
mornyng of owyr Lady . . .' (28: 68). Yet other accounts introduce a slightly
guarded note about quite precisely what she saw: 'Þan sche thowt sche saw
owyr Lady in hir sowle' (29: 71); she 'beheld how owr Lady was, hir thowt, in
deying' (73: 175); 'Than on a nyth sche say in vision how owyr Lady, hir
thowt . . . askyd mete for hir' (38: 93). Such reservations are tokens of a shrewd
modulation that often underlies the presentation of Kempe's inner life. By the late
point in her narrative at which Kempe's various devout reactions to the Holy
Week liturgy are recounted, the scrupulous attention to her forms of vision cannot but suggest a highly developed alertness to this aspect of her understanding.
As Kempe goes in procession with others on Maundy Thursday 'sche saw in hir
sowle' the Virgin, Mary Magdalene and the Apostles, and then 'sche be-held wyth
hir gostly eye' how Mary parted from Jesus (73: 174). Similarly, during a Palm
Sunday procession 'it semyd to hir gostly sygth as þei sche had ben þat tyme in
Ierusalem' (78: 184). There is a recurrent concern to note how perceptions come to
her 'gostly sygth' and 'gostly vndirstondyng', or that 'sche saw wyth hir gostly
eye' (85: 208). The same is true of auditory phenomena, as when she records hearing an exchange between the Virgin Mary and St John ('The creatur herd as clerly
þis answer in þe vndirstondyng of hir sowle as sche xulde vndirstondyn o man
spekyn to an-oþer' [81: 195]), or how St John the Evangelist hears her confession
in Rome ('sche saw hym & herd hym in hire gostly vndirstondyng as sche xuld a
do an-oþer preste be hir bodily wittys' [32: 81]).

As these last instances imply, there is a pervasive concern to convey the substance and intensity of spiritual perception through the vividly corporeal and
concrete lifelikeness with which Margery Kempe experiences that perception.
Witnessing the Good Friday liturgy at an Easter Sepulchre occupies her mind
completely with the Passion of Christ 'whom sche behelde wyth hir gostly eye
in þe syght of hir sowle as verily as thei sche had seyn hys precyows body betyn,
scorgyd, & crucifyed wyth hir bodily eye, whech syght & gostly beheldyng wrowt
be grace so feruently in hir mende' (57: 140). At the Palm Sunday procession she
'beheld hym in hir gostly syght as verily as he had ben a-forn hir in hir bodily syght'
(78: 185), and after the unveiling of the crucifix 'hir thowt þat sche saw [Christ] as
verily in hir sowle wyth hir gostly eye as sche had seyn be-forn þe Crucifixe wyth
hir bodily eye' (78: 187). Contemplating the Passion a little later she emphasizes
how 'sche sey swech gostly syȝtys in hir sowle as freschly & as verily as ȝyf it had
ben don in dede in hir bodily syght' (79: 190), just as at Candlemas 'hir mende was
raueschyd in-to beholdyng' the Presentation in the temple 'as verily to hir gostly
vndirstondyng as ȝyf sche had be þer in hir bodily presens' (82: 198). The *Book*
groups together three visions that occur during a form of sleep – an angel shows
her the Book of Life, she sees Christ's dead body being mutilated, and she feels
Christ's toes – but it is the spiritual nature of the two latter, almost bathetically sens-
ory and physical visions-in-sleep that is underlined (85: 208). In the context of the
Book's practice as a whole, Kempe carefully distinguishes spiritual from physical
experiences, for she 'felt many gret comfortys, boþe gostly comfortys & bodily

comfortys' (35: 87), and she acknowledges what are identifiably bodily tokens (sounds and melodies, heat in her breast, white specks before her eyes [35]), even though she comes to see spiritual significance in some of them (chapters 35, 78). If by 'Hyltons boke' Kempe meant the first book of his *Scale of Perfection*, she would have been schooled there, as in other meditative literature, on the need to distinguish bodily tokens. Indeed, her account of Italian housewives' devout reactions to a Jesus doll puts some distance between that and her own current devotion (30: 78). On various occasions Kempe represents herself as having moved beyond bodily and earthly things to the spiritual ('Sche had forȝetyn alle erdly thyngys & only ententyd to gostly thyngys' [73: 174]; 'þan was hir mende al holy takyn owt of al erdly thyngys & set al in gostly thyngys' [78: 187]). This often takes the form of a devoutly heightened suggestibility that is reminded of Christ and his Passion by sights seen in the street (a male baby, a handsome man, a beast being beaten) or may be prompted to spiritual parallels by the bodily and literal. Far from confusing spiritual and bodily, or diminishing the spiritual by describing it in bodily, material terms, Kempe may be observed in her practice striving to distinguish spiritual and bodily, and to understand one more clearly in relation to the other. In a retrospect on her experience at the close of her first book, Kempe stresses the burdensome responsibility of interpreting her understandings, and acknowledges the need to distinguish þe bodily and spiritual by candidly admitting the difficulty: 'For sumtyme þat sche vndirstod bodily it was to ben vndirstondyn gostly . . .' (89: 220).

To this understanding an important contribution is made by those extended colloquies with Christ that in 1936 were banished to an appendix, because they are the most sustained developments of the pattern of Margery Kempe's dialogue with the divine that runs throughout the text, and address some of the work's most besetting preoccupations, foregrounding the nature of the text as a record of inward development. Thus, very early in the account of her conversion comes a chapter mostly taken up with a lengthy speech by Christ after he has 'ravished her spirit', with the key assurances that: her sins are forgiven and she will never enter hell or purgatory; and that she will triumph over her foes and have the ability to answer every cleric; and the instruction that she must give up eating meat but receive communion every Sunday (5). Here, in the first long inward address to her by Christ she receives fundamental assurances that underpin her subsequent life and is encouraged to pursue the singularity that will antagonize her society. In the midst of her first set of travels round England comes another lengthy address that Christ speaks 'in her mind' undertaking to safeguard and sustain her (14). After she has become pregnant again and laments her loss of virginity, she hears 'in her spirit' a further chapter-length speech in which Christ praises her, assures her that her sins are forgiven, that she is especially beloved and shall have eternal life (22). Such extraordinary undertakings receive their fulfilment in the sequence (35–36) where her marriage to the Godhead in a church in Rome is recorded in part through her hearing of divine locutions. Home again in Lynn, preached against and almost friendless, she receives an exceptionally lengthy address (64–66) in which Christ describes back to Kempe her good deeds (65), reassuring her that no cleric can justly speak against her or teach her better than Christ does (presumably through such colloquies). The placing of this consoling inward exchange with Christ at one of the very lowest points in her outward life within her society only sustains the vivid reality in the *Book* of an inner world, illuminated and directed by dialogue with Christ, which makes the outer world of time and place something less real and substantial. Rather later in the sequence – for thematic reasons, despite being vaguely dated to the period when she first had her 'cries' – is a long 'gostly dalliaunce' in which Christ explains why he will not agree to her request to stop her crying (71). Finally, in a sequence of chapters at the close of the first book (84, 86–88), Christ offers his thanks to Kempe ('owre Lord spak to þe sayd creatur whan it plesyd hym, seying to hyr gostly vndirstondyng . . .' [86: 209]). In an adroit positioning of voice and authority, this allows the *Book* to represent Christ rather than Kempe (who nevertheless reports Christ) as recollecting, celebrating and endorsing many aspects of Kempe's contemplative life. It is Christ who gratefully recalls for the record some of Kempe's praiseworthy achievements in her inward life, while promising her rewards and endorsing the writing of her book, in a way that draws together many themes of the chapters already devoted to his addresses to Margery Kempe in the course of the *Book*.

It is the key place and function of these confabulations with Christ, his father, his mother, and various saints, that work to move the *Book* outside conventional generic classifications. The *Book* may patchily resemble such other genres as saint's life or pilgrimage narrative, yet the generic contribution of these is subsumed and modified within the continuum of a book of prayers. Here is a saint's life dictated by the would-be saint, constructing sainthood for herself through her own reported dialogues with a supportive Christ, and so shifting the centre of the genre towards an uneasy hybrid of 'autohagiography'.[22] It is the *Book*'s elusion of generic classification that is cumulatively most revealing, as with its popular modern byline: 'the first autobiography in English'. The *Book* fails to include so much of what has come to be expected in an autobiography, while including so much of its subject's directly reported inner life and thoughts over many years of her life. The *Book*'s longer preface candidly admits that it does not follow any chronological order, and in practice the text is unselfconsciously indifferent to conventional sequentiality, leaving it to each reader's experience to determine what does order a narrative that records in retrospect, long after the event, what Kempe believed it spiritually beneficial to record. The *Book* is not set out as a chronological record in which the passage of time is accorded any significance in itself, reflected in the form of the writing, or even much noticed. Since Kempe has already been assured of salvation, there is no concern to plot out a narrative that demonstrates spiritual progress, and since outward history is largely irrelevant, occurrences need only be located in relation to her own inner story (so chapters may open: 'whan owyr Lord had forȝouyn hir hir synne, as is wrete be-forn' [15: 32]; 'whan þe seyd creatur had first hyr wondirful cryis' [77: 181]). Other people's names are irrelevant, if the focus is upon the spiritual import of their actions: Kempe seems unconcerned to name her enemies any more than her friends, and there is some attempt, not carried through, to conceal the name of Lynn as the scene of events. As to naming foreign places accurately, it is beneath

---

[22] Margery Kempe's status as a putative saint is considered in Katherine Lewis's essay.

a would-be contemplative's notice ('for sche stodyid mor a-bowte contemplacyon þan þe namys of þe placys' [II, 4: 233]). Even her own surname emerges indirectly and belatedly (II, 9), and she makes no attempt to ask for her readers' prayers. All this may derive from the caution of her clerical amanuensis, but it also points to how she placed the emphasis on the inward. Yet rather than measuring Kempe's text against anachronistic comparisons, it is time to allow the seeming strange-nesses and omissions of the *Book* to establish the text to us on its own terms. Rather than matters of regret, Kempe's indifference to outward time, dates and chronology, and the highly individual structure of her book, are to be celebrated as aspects of the intimate record of an inward life. The way in which the *Book* does not match sustainedly with any single genre is mimetic of how Kempe's own way of life could never fit comfortably with established roles and lifestyles:

> . . . I must beware
> In Rome the pilgrim's more besetting sin,
> Which made poor Mistress Kempe so hard to bear,
> God's holy howler-monkey from King's Lynn,
> Too much engrossed in Margery Kempe to spare
> A page to the great city she was in . . .
>
> (A. D. Hope, 'A Letter from Rome')[23]

Within its structure, the *Book* conflates several narrative trajectories. There is the narrative of conversion, followed eventually by a frenetic mid-life story of flight from domesticity and matrimony into a restless devotional lifestyle, suc-ceeded by a lengthy anticlimax of living at home again, in poor health and seem-ingly short of cash. Since the book appears to begin as a conversion narrative, it can have little to say about childhood and passes over that in silence.[24] The begin-ning (perhaps revealingly abrupt) is with her marriage because that is also an important ending – of the virginity whose loss comes to seem to Kempe an abid-ing disadvantage to her contemplative vocation. However, the *Book* then deals sketchily with the first twenty years of her married life (actually half the time-span covered by the narrative), only concerned with experience that complements her later vocation. In effect, much of the narrative of events dwells on the experi-ence of just five hectic years (c.1413–c.1418), after Kempe secures agreement with her husband to end sexual relations and embarks on her pilgrimages around England, to Jerusalem, Rome, Santiago, and in England again. Once returned to Lynn, the last twenty years of Kempe's life are treated at least as much as a nar-rative of spiritual reflection as of events, with some of that spiritual narrative belatedly acknowledged to originate from before her pilgrimage years (85: 208). Such a trajectory has the mis-paced earlier spurt, the seeming lack of follow-through and the lapse into repetition that is true enough to actual lives and does not make for a shapely narrative. However, this trajectory is framed and interpol-ated by sequences of Kempe's devout meditations that might indicate the *Book*

---

[23] *A. D. Hope: Selected Poems*, ed. Ruth Morse (Manchester, 1986), pp. 61–2. 'A Letter from Rome' was written 1958–62.
[24] Kim Phillips's essay considers this issue in greater depth.

was planned to find its unity over its whole length in the contemplation of Christ's life: there are some early chapters on contemplation of the Nativity (6–7), an account of Kempe's visits to the Holy Places near the middle of her text, with meditations prompted by the Holy Week observances towards the close. But to note that Kempe's reflections on Holy Week themes jumble the biblical events into almost their reverse order (Good Friday, 57; Maundy Thursday, 73; Palm Sunday, 78; and then the Passion sequence, 79–81; to be followed by the Presentation in the temple, 82) is only one pointer to the way that Kempe's text has passed beyond predictable narrative sequences, whether of Christ's life or her own, and follows a course determined more by her contemplative understanding than autobiographical concerns.

But what models of autobiography would have been available for emulation by Margery Kempe and her advisers? The most immediate parallel for autobiographical narrative perhaps lay in the experience of confession itself. Among the few literary models would be Richard Rolle's *Incendium Amoris* and 'Seynt Brydys boke' (two of those texts which Kempe recalls having read to her). However, the revelations of St Bridget of Sweden, mediated through amanuenses, no longer read like a personal account of the self, while her *Liber Celestis* makes *The Book of Margery Kempe* seem by comparison a highly structured and tightly interconnected narrative. If St Bridget's spiritual example was more closely imitable by Margery Kempe than her text, Rolle's construction of himself in his writing may have been more of an influence on the mode of her *Book*. From the *Incendium* Kempe would know the heady example of a text where non-linear, wavelike explorations of contemplative rapture and moral reflection are interleaved with passages vividly projecting the personality of its idiosyncratic author as a passionately striving but fallen exile from heaven. The *Incendium*'s significance may also have lain in what it ignored as irrelevant. Here was a prayerfully personal contemplative text, often implicitly autobiographical and sometimes explicitly so, but quite unconcerned to narrate a developing experience and an unfolding life through any conventional apparatus of chronological order, date or models of progress. In the *Incendium*, as in the *Book*, the impetus of a driven self shapes the text around those interactions with the divine that are the cornerstone of the life, and the conviction of a personal calling and special divine favour allow for an unusually intense but partly dehistoricized projection in the text of a self at prayer. The *Book*'s longer preface recalls how – perhaps wary of their likely control – Kempe resisted various clerics' recommendations that she should 'makyn a booke of hyr felyngys and hir revelacyons' (or in the shorter preface 'hir tribulacyons and hir felingys' [Proem: 6]). When Christ does eventually command her to have her book written, he orders a significant extension of its subject matter ('hyr felyngys & revelacyons & þe forme of her leuyng' [Proem: 3–4]), which exploits a reminiscence of Rolle's English epistle to an anchoress, *The Form of Living*, in order to endorse Margery Kempe's mode of meditative life as the focus of her book. Its subject is a manner of living ('in party þe leuyng' [Proem: 2]); her habitual way of life, rather than a 'life' or *vita*.

Yet as the *Book* records, her inner life is in itself often testing and anguishing, and there develops a deep sense of separation between the demands of that inner world and of her society. There is a strong emphasis, stronger later rather than earlier in the text, on what cannot be communicated (78: 187; 80: 191; 87: 214), of the daunting difficulty of interpreting what she apprehends, and her longing at times not to have the pain and trouble her revelatory experience brings ('þe drede þat sche had of hir felyngys was þe grettest scorge þat sche had in erde' [89: 220]). In a profusion of inner experience professedly too frequent to write down entirely or even to remember, Kempe does not give a linear shape in her text to the contemplative progress that she implies. Her text represents intermittently, but does not narrate in sequence, the developing devotion from the Manhood to the Godhead that she claims ('vn-to þat tyme þat it plesyd owr Lord to ȝeuyn hir vndirstondyng of hys invndirstondabyl Godhed . . . mor sotyl in vndirstondyng þan was þe Manhod' [85: 208–9]), although it certainly bears witness to the spiritualizing attention with which she comes to view all outward life. Her claim at her mystical marriage in Rome to have had as yet no experience of the 'dalyawns of þe Godhede' (35: 86) does not square with her earlier account to Richard Caister of her conversations with the Trinity (17), but the text's later passages do show suffusedly an increasing awareness of the Father, as too of the Holy Ghost. Yet it would be unwise to assume that the absence of some kinds of spiritual experience and expression necessarily mean that Kempe lacked such experience, rather than that she was cautious about recording and claiming it. The *Book*'s longer preface records how she made one of her intended amanuenses swear never to divulge the contents of her text during her lifetime, probably because Kempe made a sharp distinction between the edifying exhortations and moralizing tales which constituted her daily conversation with her contemporaries and the contents of this private inner journal, which presumably records those matters Kempe represents herself as only divulging to sympathetic clerical advisers. To take one example: 'Sche tolde hym [the English friar in Rome] of hir maner leuyng, of hir felyngys, of hir reuelacyons . . . & how owyr Lord dalyed to hir sowle in a maner of spekyng' (31: 79).

It is time to read Margery Kempe's inner voices as a projection of her own spiritual understanding of divine interaction with her, and hence as an insight into her own mentality. If Kempe's earlier twentieth-century readers (often professional religious) were embarrassed by reportedly divine speeches which they could not accept as authentic mystical illuminations from God, more recent academic interpreters – if they have noticed the prayers and locutions at all – have judged them adversely on their stylistic and imaginative originality: not so much the Holy Ghost as some ghost-writer from among Kempe's clerical circle.[25] If Kempe's candour leads her to report Christ foretelling an earthquake, declaring (most improbably) that every word written in St Bridget's revelations is true, or even declaring (unsustainably as it turns out) that the truth of St Bridget's book will be proved true through Kempe's example (20), that is a token of Kempe's understanding. Some of the more startling divine assurances of her own worth that Kempe receives – not least that Christ loves her more than Mary Magdalene (74) – are so extraordinarily unlikely that they are to be read not so much literally

---

[25] The exception is the excellent chapter 'Conversations with Christ', in Santha Bhattacharji's insightful *God is an Earthquake: The Spirituality of Margery Kempe* (London, 1997), to which I am indebted.

(or censoriously) than as part of the *Book*'s record of her inward life. In contemporary 'discernment of spirits' such locutions, with all their unevenness of content and tone, might have been read as the soul's report of what it had understood itself to hear, mediated through the soul's own capacity to apprehend the answer to its question. Kempe's dialogues with Christ record an inward debate with her own understanding of the divine demands upon her, a debate which, by the time the *Book* was composed, had come to form the continuum of how she views her experience.

Compared with this inward spiritual reality in communication with the divine, all outward worldly and social experience must seem a repetitive, essentially meaningless cycle of irritations, frustrations and challenges. The *Book* records a number of painful inner dialogues where, although she dare not go against a divine injunction, Kempe correctly foresees that she will be accused of some hypocritical, time-serving change of course. Her sadly indignant anecdote ('A, þu fals flesch . . . !') about how her imputed hypocrisy had become a proverb and she a byword, as far outside Lynn and East Anglia as London, is an intriguing pointer to her possible contemporary reputation and its burden, or at least to how she saw herself and others' views of her. Steadfast to her inner voices despite their periodic contradictoriness, she loses credibility, status and friends, and the *Book* chronicles an increasingly painful and absolute divide between her inner and outer worlds: '& sche stably & stedfastly beleuyd þat it was God þat spak in hir sowle' (87: 215). Viewed as it is from within the continuum of her inner life, Margery Kempe's record of her outward life will seem variously bitty, petty and largely shapeless – for what shape or purpose could outward life any longer have, except as a distraction?

1

Margery Kempe and the Ages of Woman

KIM M. PHILLIPS

> Whan þis creatur was xx 3er of age or sumdele mor, sche
> was maryed to a worschepful burgeys and was wyth
> chylde wyth-in schort tyme, as kynde wolde [as nature
> would have it]. (1: 6)

Margery Kempe's account of her life begins abruptly. This opening statement
sweeps aside the earlier life stages – childhood and youth – rendering invisible
almost the first third of Margery's life. Such erasure of early years is unconventional within the genre of medieval spiritual biography, but then Margery Kempe
differed from the norm in many respects. The work also avoids close adherence
to models of life-cycle narrative available to medieval writers, such as the 'maid,
wife, widow' configuration, or the well-worn structure of the 'ages of man'. This
essay surveys medieval paradigms of life cycle, considers what we can know of
women's lives at different ages, and examines Margery's *Book* in an attempt to
find an appropriate framework for her life.

There are two main approaches one can take to the study of medieval life
stages. Studies informed by cultural history examine the languages and iconog-
raphy used in medieval texts and visual arts to represent the human life course,
in order to determine the *meanings* attached to human ages. This is part of cultural history's wider project of reading 'for meaning – the meaning inscribed by
contemporaries'.[1] The aim is to describe and explain the distinctive features of
medieval life structures and the connotations of the different phases, rather than
applying present-day models. Social-historical studies trouble themselves less,
as a rule, with differences between past and present definitions and representations. Taking the life stages as read, they attempt to describe the *experiences*
attached to each stage through documentary research. This essay will consider
both models, comparing them with the evidence of Margery's book.

Every study associated with Margery Kempe must make some remark about the
Book's authorship. My views are, in brief: (1) There was a real Margery Kempe, and
she was heavily involved in producing the work of which the surviving manuscript
is a copy; (2) The scribes who assisted her in the production of the book did not simply take down her dictation but played an important role in shaping the text and

---

[1] Robert Darnton, *The Great Cat Massacre and Other Episodes in French Cultural History* (New
York, 1984), p. 5. Cultural history is, however, difficult to define in a way which pleases all
practitioners, and many would provide a different gloss.

on occasion wrote in their own voice; (3) Margery's *Book* was probably not, as has been recently suggested, written 'by clergy, for clergy, and about clergy' for the purposes of clerical reform,[2] because if it were it would have probably followed orthodox models of hagiography more closely, and also because if this is a kind of elaborate forgery its authors surpassed Chaucer, Langland, Lydgate, Gower and every other then-popular author in the creation of a compelling fictional heroine; and (4) I will follow Sarah Salih's logic of avoiding the distinction between the fictional 'Margery' and 'Kempe' her author. 'If there is a distinction between 'Kempe' and 'Margery' it is not that between author and character, but between the writing and written selves of autobiography. Their difference is not total.'[3] Moreover, given that Margery constructs herself as a writer distinct from her character or narrative subject, we are dealing with three entities – 'Margery' the character, 'Kempe' the writer, and 'Margery Brunham Kempe of Lynn', the historical subject to whom we have least access.[4] 'Margery' will alternate with 'Margery Kempe' in what follows for stylistic rather than meaningful reasons, and the work is treated neither as a straightforward presentation of lived experience nor as pure fiction, but as a conscious and collaborative construction of a holy woman's life.

It is useful to sketch a short chronology of Margery's life, paying attention to her ages at key turning points and stages.[5] Given the haphazard chronology of the *Book* it is often impossible to be exact about her age at specific points in the narrative, but estimations can be made. Born in or slightly before 1373 in Bishop's (now King's) Lynn, the daughter of John Brunham and an unnamed mother, Margery's early life was of unusually high comfort and privilege within urban society. Her father's occupation of powerful offices in Lynn, including his multiple stints as mayor and MP, largely coincided with his daughter's childhood and youth.[6] Through these formative years, Margery developed a strong notion of herself as the daughter of an influential man. Also at some point during her first twenty years, Margery committed the sin which would later so torment her (1: 6–7). Unlike male spiritual autobiographers from Augustine to Guibert of Nogent, Margery avoids making her youthful transgression a key element of her autobiography. Male medieval life writing tends to make much of early waywardness, if only to heighten the drama of later conversion to a more spiritual life.[7]

---

2 Sarah Rees Jones, 'A *peler of Holy Cherch*: Margery Kempe and the Bishops', in Jocelyn Wogan-Browne et al., eds, *Medieval Women: Texts and Contexts in Medieval Britain: Essays for Felicity Riddy* (Turnhout, 2000), pp. 377–92 (p. 391).

3 Sarah Salih, *Versions of Virginity in Late Medieval England* (Cambridge, 2001), pp. 171–2. The distinction between 'Kempe' and 'Margery' originates with Staley, *Dissenting Fictions*, see esp. p. 3.

4 Salih, *Versions of Virginity*, pp. 172–3.

5 Goodman, *World*, provides the most recent discussion of Margery's life and material context. See also Charity Scott Stokes, 'Margery Kempe: Her Life and the Early History of Her Book', *Mystics Quarterly* 25 (1999): 9–67.

6 John Brunham was mayor of Lynn in 1370, 1377, 1378, 1385 and 1391, and Member of Parliament in 1364–65, 1368, 1376, 1379–80, 1382–83 and 1384. He also served terms as alderman of the Trinity Guild, coroner, justice of the peace, and chamberlain. *BMK*, Appendix III.ii; Michael D. Myers, 'A Fictional-True Self: Margery Kempe and the Social Reality of the Merchant Elite of King's Lynn', *Albion* 31 (1999): 377–94 (380–1).

7 St Augustine, *Confessions*, trans. R. S. Pine-Coffin (Harmondsworth, 1961), bks 1–8; John F. Benton, ed., *Self and Society in Medieval France: The Memoirs of Abbot Guibert of Nogent (1064? – c. 1125)*, (New York, 1970), bk. 1, chs 1–19.

Margery's early twenties were a time of considerable change and crisis: marriage, pregnancy, childbirth, madness, and her first visionary experiences. The years between her recovery at twenty-one or twenty-two and her mid-thirties were strongly marked by worldly concerns. In addition to almost constant pregnancy and childbearing (most of her fourteen children must have been born during this time), it was a time of materialistic pride, ambition, and failure.

It was probably at around thirty-five that Margery heard the heavenly melody which made her leap out of bed, and instigated her fervent wish for celibacy (3: 11). The next few years were marked by sexual struggle as she tried to persuade her husband to become chaste and took to wearing a hair shirt, but after two years found herself once more prey to lust, and was subject to temptations for three years. She was at most thirty-eight when she approached, and was rebuffed by, a man in church (4: 14). In her late thirties Margery began her travels within England, and publicly presented herself as an exceptionally devout woman, gifted with visions. Probably in 1411 she conceived of the desire to undertake pilgrimage to the three great holy sites, and Jesus first asked that she adopt white clothing (15: 32). John Kempe had by this time agreed to live in chastity, and certainly by the age of forty Margery's sexual and reproductive life was ended (11: 23; 15: 33).

From her late thirties to late fifties Margery led a highly active and adventurous life, at forty travelling to Jerusalem (where she picked up her habit of loud crying or screeching) and Rome (where she temporarily re-adopted white clothes, experienced mystic marriage to the Godhead, and discovered the spiritual pleasures of poverty). Following her return to England in 1415, she completed her trilogy of major pilgrimages with a short trip to Santiago in 1417. Difficulties arose that year, when she was repeatedly accused of and examined for heresy. She began to suffer from numerous ailments, one of which she claims lasted eight years (56: 137). Lustful thoughts returned to plague her, with visions of men's members and fantasies of prostitution (59: 145). Yet it was also an important period in her education. Her priest read to her from the Bible, St Bridget of Sweden's revelations, Hilton's *Stimulus Amoris*, Rolle's *Incendium Amoris* and others (58: 143). Towards the end of this time John Kempe was injured in a fall, and Margery took on the role of nursemaid to punish herself for her former lust for his body (76: 179). In 1431, when Margery was about fifty-eight, her husband and son died (II, 2: 225). The writing of the first draft of Book I may have begun by the late 1420s.[8]

At or around sixty, in 1433, Margery travelled to Danzig with her daughter-in-law, and as a by-now decidedly elderly woman endured a final year of adventure. She was physically frail (her confessor worried about her sore feet, she struggled to keep up with her companion on pilgrimage from Stralsund to Wilsnack, and for some years she had been falling asleep in church [e.g. 85: 206]), yet managed to travel great distances by foot, cart and horse and was still greatly afraid for her chastity. On the way from Aachen to Calais she would get young women to share her bed, to help ward off potential rapists (II, 7: 241). The last years of her life, from the mid-1430s, were spent composing the two parts of

8   Stokes, 'Margery Kempe', pp. 40–1.

her *Book*, and the final act for which she is known was to enter the Guild of the Trinity at Lynn in 1438. She was listed again in the guild's records in 1439, and lived, therefore, until at least the age of sixty-six.[9] With this, her last known act, Margery expressed the two recurrent themes of her life: her devotion, and her pride in family status and sense of connection to her father.

Margery never divides her life into clear segments. While there are key events which she seems to regard as turning points, such as her post-partum illness, her first revelation, and her husband's agreement to celibacy, she does not find any age-scheme a particularly useful explanatory mode for the changes of her life. Still, four stages stand out. The first twenty years, from c.1373 to 1393, mark her suppressed childhood and maidenhood; the next fifteen to twenty were defined by marriage, sexuality, worldly cares and the transition to holy life; from forty to around sixty she attained her maturity, with the culmination of her active life and fulfilment of major spiritual goals; and the fourth and last age, up to her death sometime after 1439, represent her old age, in which her increasing physical frailty is more significant than the loss of her husband. Indeed, Christ tells Margery that he regards her as a widow because of her chastity, some years before her husband's death (65: 161). The four ages of Margery Kempe do not match up with the major models available, and which the next sections will discuss.

Women's Life Cycle

Social historians have borrowed the term 'life cycle' from social science disciplines such as anthropology and sociology, which in turn had borrowed it from the biological sciences, to regularise perceptions of the life span. Some sociologists have since jettisoned the term, in favour of the supposedly less loaded 'life course', arguing that 'life cycle' presupposes the existence of set developmental stages (for example, childhood, adolescence, young adulthood, middle age and old age), and does not allow for the possibility of different experiences between individuals, or between cultures, or historical periods.[10] While such questions raise relevant methodological problems for social historians, the latters' focus has been more on sketching the experiences associated with the life phases, which, for medieval women, were also heavily bound up with marital status. Their work can help us establish what a 'normal' life for a woman of Margery Kempe's social status, location and time might have looked like. As we know comparatively little about the particular conditions of women in Bishop's Lynn it is valid to bring in evidence from different parts of England to compile a picture of some common patterns of life for women of elite urban status.[11]

While the childhood of English burgesses' daughters has not yet been studied at any length, one important element would have been their education or

---

9   *BMK*, Appendix III.i.
10 For a sample of a large literature see Alice Rossi, 'Life Span Theories and Women's Lives', *Signs* 6 (1980): 4–32; Alan Bryman et al., eds, *Rethinking the life cycle* (Houndmills, 1987); Patricia Allatt et al., *Women and the Life Cycle: Transitions and Turning Points* (New York, 1987).
11 For women in late medieval Lynn see Kate Parker, below, pp. 67–8; Goodman, *World*, pp. 59–61.

upbringing. This should be understood in broader terms than modern schooling, for while some girls in towns attended school probably most did not.[12] Their upbringing included religious education, ability to work with textiles and carry out a range of household tasks, conduct appropriate to their status and some familiarity with books and their contents.[13] For some girls – possibly including Margery – this familiarity went no further than 'phonetic reading', the ability to pronounce aloud words on a page. Many Latin liturgical books owned by bourgeois families would have been 'read' in this way. Others were taught to read with understanding in English, and some were also taught to write in English. French does not seem to have been a very important language for late medieval English townspeople.[14] Perhaps more important than reading or writing by individuals was their opportunity to participate in textual communities. Books were read aloud, discussed and quoted: in all, this was still a strongly oral culture. Blunt terms such as 'literate' and 'illiterate' are totally inadequate in conveying the layers of late medieval literacy and orality.[15] As Diana R. Uhlman has argued, Margery's *Book* may be seen as inverting the modern privileging of literacy over orality, gaining authority by the very process of 'making readers see the *Book* as the [spoken] words of Margery Kempe'.[16] Modern scholars' quest for women's literacy may have blinded them to a world in which the oral and written interacted in a way now difficult to imagine, which was largely 'phonocentric', and where a relationship such as that between speaker and scribe could produce a level of authorial validity which was greater than the sum of its parts. Women, in particular, may have gained more authority through employing the aid of a male (especially a clerical) amanuensis, than they could have ever gained through sole authorship. In secular spheres too, mercantile and gentle women often used secretaries for letter writing, even when they had orthographic abilities.[17]

Most English girls, whether of similar background to Margery or not, experienced a stage between the end of childhood, at around twelve, and adulthood, usually (although not always) marked by consummated marriage. We could call this youth, or adolescence, although 'maidenhood' is more useful as a way of avoiding modern connotations and incorporating gender. Daughters of the urban elite would spend their period of maidenhood in one of four contexts: living in the parental home, living away from home in service, serving under conditions of indentured apprenticeship, or undergoing novitiate in a nunnery.

---

[12] Caroline M. Barron, 'The Education and Training of Girls in Fifteenth-Century London', in Diana E. S. Dunn, ed., *Courts, Counties and the Capital in the Later Middle Ages* (Stroud, 1996), pp. 139–53.

[13] Felicity Riddy, 'Mother Knows Best: Reading Social Change in a Courtesy Text', *Speculum* 71 (1996): 66–86; P. J. P. Goldberg, 'Girls Growing Up in Later Medieval England', *History Today* (June, 1995): 25–32; Kim M. Phillips, *Medieval Maidens: Young Women and Gender in England, 1270–1540* (Manchester, 2003), pp. 62–71.

[14] M. B. Parkes, 'The Literacy of The Laity', in his *Scribes, Scripts and Readers: Studies in the Communication, Presentation and Dissemination of Medieval Texts* (London, 1991), pp. 275–97 (pp. 287–90).

[15] As further discussed by Jacqueline Jenkins below, pp. 114–16.

[16] Diane R. Uhlman, 'The Comfort of Voice, the Solace of Script: Orality and Literacy in *The Book of Margery Kempe*', *Studies in Philology* 91 (1994): 50–69.

[17] Phillips, *Medieval Maidens*, p. 68.

The last accounted for proportionately few girls. Marilyn Oliva's work on late medieval East Anglian nunneries has shown that nearly three-quarters of nuns within the Norwich diocese were drawn from the gentry, of whom the great majority (64 per cent of the total number) were from the lower or 'parish' gentry. Twenty per cent derived from urban social groups, but most of these women were found in a single location – Carrow priory in the Norwich suburbs. Most East Anglian nuns were professed between the ages of fifteen and seventeen, with a trousseau worth £5–7, which would be affordable for some among the urban elite.[18] On the basis of this evidence it would have been possible for Margery to have become a nun in her teens, but this was not a common choice for girls of her background.

Apprenticeship might seem an unlikely option for a maiden of Margery's status, but it is clear that in fact many female apprentices were drawn from middle- or upper-middle-status backgrounds. Of six surviving indentures, two girls are listed as daughters of a 'gentleman' or 'squire', two are daughters of merchants or burgesses, and one appears to be of substantial yeoman background.[19] Some London merchants made provision in their wills for their daughters' apprenticeships.[20] Most opportunities for female apprenticeship were found among the London silkwomen, and certainly a maiden from Bishop's Lynn could have travelled the distance to London to enter a new life in the silk industry. Margaret Bishop arrived from Seaford in Sussex in 1378, Eleanor Fincham travelled to London from Norfolk in 1447, and Elizabeth Eland journeyed from Lincolnshire in 1454.[21] Other girls took up apprenticeships closer to home, even in their fathers' households.[22] Peter Fleming has discussed female apprentices in Bristol in the early to mid-sixteenth century, finding records of enrolment for fifty-six girls between 1532 and 1542, out of a total of nearly 1,500 male and female enrolments. Female apprenticeship was thus overwhelmingly outweighed by male, in Bristol as elsewhere, but it was not unheard of, with an average of five to six girls being enrolled each year.[23] The Bristol evidence does not pre-date 1532, however, so it is unknown whether these figures represent a fourteenth- and fifteenth-century pattern. Margery was not apprenticed, but had her circumstances been slightly different – if her father had not been so prominent in Lynn society, or if she had been orphaned, for example – such a step would not have been inconceivable.

---

[18] Marilyn Oliva, *The Convent and the Community in Late Medieval England: Female Monasteries in the Diocese of Norwich, 1350–1540* (Woodbridge, 1998), pp. 45–61.

[19] Norfolk Record Office, Hare MSS 2091; Public Record Office E 210/1176; Corporation of London Record Office, Misc MSS 1863; Richard Goddard, 'Female Apprenticeship in the West Midlands in the Later Middle Ages', *Midland History* 27 (2002): 165–81, supplies transcripts and translations of two girls' indentures from fourteenth-century Coventry, 179–81. The sixth is Westminster Abbey Muniments 5966.

[20] Barron, 'Education and Training of Girls', pp. 144–5; Eileen Power, *Medieval Women*, new edn (Cambridge, 1997), p. 49.

[21] WAM 5966; NRO Hare Mss 2091; PRO E210/1176.

[22] Two girls were apprenticed to a (male) pursemaker in fourteenth-century Coventry: Goddard, 'Female Apprenticeship'; Agnes Hecche, an armourer, was trained by her father in an unofficial sort of apprenticeship in late fourteenth-century York: Heather Swanson, *Medieval Artisans: An Urban Class in Late Medieval England* (Oxford, 1989), pp. 71, 116.

[23] Peter Fleming, *Women in Late Medieval Bristol*, The Bristol Branch of the Historical Association, Local History Pamphlets no. 103 (Bristol, 2001), pp. 9–11.

It was far more common to send daughters into service than into apprentice-ships. One of the keys to understanding service in medieval England is to realise that it was not generally viewed as a lowly or shameful occupation. Like peas-ant, artisan, gentle and noble families, burgess parents commonly sent their sons and daughters into other households.[24] Servants were often of similar status to, or slightly below, their masters and mistresses. Outside of court society or the great households of the nobility, however, there was a tendency for servants to be young and unmarried. Jeremy Goldberg sums up the institution perfectly: it 'appears unhelpful to identify servants as a "class"; rather, they may more use-fully be described in life-cycle terms'.[25] Burgess daughters would probably have usually gone into other high-status urban households. Their tasks would have covered the range of activities engaged in by women within the household: that is, not only domestic service and childcare, but participation in the by-industries by which women brought extra income into the household (such as brewing, and textile work), and assistance with the major economic activity of the household. Margery is not known to have spent any part of her youth in service, yet the role of maidservant played an important part in her imaginative life, as an appropri-ately worshipful and feminine activity. She imagines herself as the handmaiden of St Anne, assisting at the birth of the Virgin and helping to nurture the Virgin to the age of twelve, and of the Virgin before and during the latter's parturition and at Christ's Passion (6: 18; 79: 190; 81: 195). In her forties she served a poor woman in Rome for six weeks as a penitential act, at the command of her confessor, but this service was a spiritual duty rather than a life-cycle experience (34: 85).

At home Margery would have engaged in tasks similar to those of the female servants, aimed at simultaneously boosting the labour force of the household and preparing her for adulthood and marriage. There is nothing to indicate that youth was a time primarily of leisure or formal education for teenaged girls. Maidens of numerous parishes, however, took part in 'maidens' guilds' or stores – the near-est thing late medieval English society had to female youth groups.[26]

As relatively small numbers of elite urban women remained unmarried, the dominant adult female roles on offer were those of wife and mother, often followed by widowhood and sometimes by remarriage.[27] Life as an adult bourgeoise was thus marked by important responsibilities as household manager and mother,

---

[24] Jennifer Kermode, *Medieval Merchants: York, Beverley and Hull in the Later Middle Ages* (Cambridge, 1998), p. 98. Goldberg shows that urban maidens usually entered service: P. J. P. Goldberg, *Women, Work, and Life Cycle in a Medieval Economy: Women in York and Yorkshire, c. 1300–1520* (Oxford, 1992), ch. 4. It is still unclear, however, whether service was a fully acceptable occupation for daughters of the urban *elite*. Goldberg suggests that in the later fifteenth century, at least, fewer girls of high urban status were living away from home, and links this to economic pressures associated with recovering populations, pp. 261, 275. For gentry and aristocratic daughters in service see Phillips, *Medieval Maidens*, pp. 109–20.

[25] Goldberg, *Women, Work, and Life Cycle*, p. 158.

[26] Katherine L. French, 'Maidens' Lights and Wives' Stores: Women's Parish Guilds in Late Medieval England', *Sixteenth Century Journal* 29 (1998): 399–425; Phillips, *Medieval Maidens*, pp. 185–94.

[27] Perhaps 10 to 20 per cent of European women between 1250 and 1800 never married: Judith M. Bennett and Amy M. Froide, 'A Singular Past', in Bennett and Froide, eds, *Singlewomen in*

assistance with the primary craft or business of the household, and also very often by independent economic activities. Burgesses' wives were technically not supposed to trade in their own right, but in many cities such as London, Bristol and Exeter they could take on *femme sole* status, allowing them to trade as though they were single.[28] It is not clear if women could enjoy official *femme sole* privileges in Lynn, but Kate Parker's research reveals a small number of prominent married women who carried on independent business dealings, rather as Margery Kempe seems to have done (2: 9).[29] Although women were very rarely admitted to the franchise in medieval English towns, and were not entitled to full guild memberships, they were active in a very extensive range of economic activities.[30]

Margery's marriage at a little over twenty was not unusual for medieval urban Englishwomen, and, in general, English society seems to have viewed marriage as unsuitable for girls above the age of consent before they reached an adequate level of maturity. This unwritten code could be broken when considerable financial or political gains could be made through a girl's early marriage, or when she was an orphan. We do not know how much say, if any, Margery had over the choice of her husband, although she mentions the 'many delectabyl thowtys, fleschly lustys, & inordinat louys to hys persone' she had felt in the early years of their marriage (76: 181). Although later in their marriage Margery looked down on John, the match would have been viewed as an excellent linkage of two of the most prominent local families.[31] In many English cities merchant daughters experienced exceptional upward social mobility, marrying into the gentry or nobility, and it is intriguing to imagine Margery as a gentlewoman.[32] As a mother, Margery's fourteen children made for a large family by burgess standards, yet such family sizes were not unheard of. Conservative counting of children based on will evidence suggests an average mercantile family size of three to four children, but it is thought that ten or eleven children may have been common. Some London merchants had up to twenty-three offspring, but such cases would almost certainly involve more than one wife.[33] Like most women, Margery probably had to endure the death of one or more of her children, but

---

the *European Past, 1250–1800* (Philadelphia, 1999), pp. 1–37 (p. 2). Such figures are too general to have much meaning in the present context, except to support the impression that marriage was a normal part of most women's life cycles.

28 Mary Bateson, ed., *Borough Customs*, 2 vols, Selden Society 18, 21 (London, 1904–6), 2, pp. 227–8; Caroline M. Barron, 'The "Golden Age" of Women in Medieval London', *Reading Medieval Studies* 15 (1989): 35–58 (pp. 37–39); Fleming, *Women in Late Medieval Bristol*, p. 7; Maryanne Kowaleski, 'Women's Work in a Market Town: Exeter in the Late Fourteenth Century', in Barbara A. Hanawalt, ed., *Women and Work in Preindustrial Europe* (Bloomington, IN, 1986), pp. 145–64 (p. 146).

29 Parker, p. 68, below.

30 Goldberg, *Women, Work, and Life Cycle*, ch. 3; Kowaleski, 'Women's Work in a Market Town'; Maryanne Kowaleski and Judith M. Bennett, 'Crafts, Guilds, and Women in the Middle Ages: Fifty Years after Marian K. Dale', in Judith M. Bennett et al., eds, *Sisters and Workers in the Middle Ages* (Chicago, 1989), pp. 11–25.

31 Myers, 'Fictional-True Self', p. 393; Parker, below, pp. 00–00.

32 Kermode, *Medieval Merchants*, p. 111.

33 Ibid., pp. 72–3; Thrupp, *Merchant Class*, p. 198.

the only anxiety she reveals relating to pregnancy is that it makes her feel less worthy of heavenly reward than virgins (21: 48). Burgess wives would have also had a degree of responsibility for the male and female servants who would almost certainly have formed part of their *familia* (as Margery did, 2: 10), and in many cases for apprentices too.

Middle age entailed a range of experiences for elite urban women. Some remained in their first marriage, carrying on with the raising of their younger children while perhaps at the same time becoming grandmothers. Margery mentions the birth of a grandchild *perhaps* when she was in her fifties, but the date is unclear, and this may not have been her first grandchild (II, 1: 223). Some women were widowed, and remarried, especially if they had minor children. The majority of widows, however, seem not to have remarried.[34] Kermode finds that in fourteenth- and fifteenth-century York it was common for merchants to die between the ages of forty-five and sixty, though the not inconsiderable proportion of 20 per cent lived past sixty in the fifteenth century, and overall 79 per cent predeceased their wives.[35] Given the English preference for companionate marriage, some bourgeois widows were still enjoying vigorous middle age when their husbands died while others were entering their senior years. London citizens' widows who did not remarry were required by city custom to maintain their deceased husbands' households and businesses, including seeing any apprentices through to the end of their contracts, and several of the brief biographies edited by Barron and Sutton provide examples of burgess widows energetically carrying on the household interests after their husbands' deaths.[36] The experience of advanced old age has been little studied among this social group, so it is difficult to say at what age burgess women became 'elderly' in the eyes of contemporaries.[37] Margery became relatively frail in her sixties, yet still able to travel long distances and endure physical effort. Studying inquisitions post mortem, Josiah C. Russell found 10.6 per cent of the adult population of landholding groups to be over sixty – the age he defines as marking the onset of old age – in 1401–25. Given that most of these landholders would have been men, and that women who survived to forty often lived longer than men, it is possible that a larger proportion than this of the female landed elite lived into their seventh decade and beyond.[38]

While Margery Kempe's *Book* is first and foremost an account of an aspirational spiritual journey, it also offers tantalising glimpses of one woman's life.

---

[34] Perhaps two-thirds of urban widows did not remarry: Kowaleski, 'History of Urban Families', p. 56; Barbara A. Hanawalt, 'Remarriage as an Option for Urban and Rural Widows in Late Medieval England', in Sue Sheridan Walker, ed., *Wife and Widow in Medieval England* (Ann Arbor, 1993), pp. 141–64.

[35] Kermode, *Medieval Merchants*, pp. 86–7.

[36] Caroline M. Barron, 'Introduction: The Widow's World', in Caroline M. Barron and Anne F. Sutton, eds, *Medieval London Widows, 1300–1500* (London, 1994), pp. xxiv–xxv.

[37] Joel T. Rosenthal, *Old Age in Late Medieval England* (Philadelphia, 1996), and Shulamith Shahar, *Growing Old in the Middle Ages: 'Winter Clothes us in Shadow and Pain'*, trans. Yael Lotan (London, 1997), offer general studies.

[38] Josiah C. Russell, 'How Many of the Population were Aged?', in Michael M. Sheehan, ed., *Aging and the Aged in Medieval Europe* (Toronto, 1990), pp. 119–28 (pp. 123–5, 126).

Even if the work cannot be used as straightforward biographical evidence, reading it in conjunction with a wider body of recent scholarship relating to women of similar backgrounds can help illuminate our understanding of women and life cycle. Conversely, by getting a sense of what the *Book* could have discussed but leaves out, we gain a clearer insight into the choices the authors have made in constructing the text.

The Ages of Woman

A cultural-historical study of medieval lives must pay much closer attention to the terminology of life stages and their representations. A primary aspect of such study is the gendered nature of human life courses. This has been recognised in studies of the so-called 'ages of man' theme, study of which is fundamental to existing cultural histories of age in medieval society. Medieval literature, natural philosophy, medicine, cosmology, art and other discourses frequently employed the idea that man's life follows a set pattern, with specific mental and physical attributes associated with each stage. While different authors, according to period and genre, used varying models – the three ages, the four ages, the six, the seven, the eight or the ten ages of man – each followed a similar basic pattern. Infancy, childhood and youth (*infantia, pueritia, adolescentia*) were associated with bodily heat and energy, learning, lusts and ill-discipline; middle adulthood, maturity or middle age (*iuventus*) with strength and wisdom; late adulthood, old age and decrepitude with steady decline and the approaching grave (*gravitas, senectus, senium*).[39] As Elizabeth Sears writes, medieval thinkers 'understood the periodization of life to be an issue'. Their interest was connected to thinking about the Fall and the introduction of ageing into human life, and to broader examination of God's ordering of the world. 'To discover the harmonious pattern of human development was to learn something vital about man and, by extension, about the universe. It was also to gain insight into the purpose of life and, thus, into kinds of conduct which might ensure the well-being of body and soul.'[40] It is significant, then, that women were generally excluded from the scheme, as this is an illustration of the deeply androcentric nature of medieval cosmology.[41]

There are a handful of representations of the ages which include women, and even some which take the female as paradigmatic, yet these are very much the exception.[42] It was not until the sixteenth century that the ages of woman became

---

39 J. A. Burrow, *The Ages of Man: A Study in Medieval Writing and Thought* (Oxford, 1986); Elizabeth Sears, *The Ages of Man: Medieval Interpretations of the Life Cycle* (Princeton, 1986).

40 Sears, *Ages of Man*, pp. xvi, 3.

41 Mary Dove, *The Perfect Age of Man's Life* (Cambridge, 1986), p. 25; Kim M. Phillips, 'Maidenhood as the Perfect Age of Woman's Life', in Katherine J. Lewis, Noël James Menuge and Kim M. Phillips, eds, *Young Medieval Women* (Stroud, 1999), pp. 1–24 (pp. 2–3).

42 See the feminised description of the four seasons in M. A. Manzaloui, ed., *Secretum Secretorum: Nine English Versions*, EETS original series 276 (Oxford, 1977), pp. 55–8, 153–5, 346–9, 572–4.

an important artistic and legal theme, and even then was limited to particular artists and regions. The ages of man theme is sometimes treated as though it was the only way medieval people could conceptualise the life cycle. It is undoubtedly important, but not overwhelmingly so. Certainly, it seems to have meant little or nothing to Margery Kempe and her scribes.

Alternative models, however, existed for women. These were organised not around a framework of ages, but of familial, marital or sexual conditions. There are three dominant structures: 'virgin, continent (or widow) and married (or wife)', 'daughter, wife and widow' and 'maid, wife and widow'. The first of the models is concerned not with life cycle so much as degrees of chastity and the three-fold rewards of heaven.[43] When 'maiden', 'wife' and 'widow' are applied to Margery they usually carry connotations of chastity-degrees, rather than age: for example ' "Why gost þu in white? Art þu a mayden?" . . . "Nay, ser, I am no mayden; I am a wife" ' (52: 124); ' "þu art a mayden in þi sowle" ' (22: 52); ' "þu hast þi wil of chastite as þu wer a wedow, thyn husbond leuyng in good hele" ' (65: 161). The second framework, of 'daughter, wife and widow', emphasises a woman's familial relationships. These terms are often used in legal documents such as manor court rolls and urban customals. One sometimes finds the term 'sister' rather than 'daughter' in customals, and 'sister' refers to women generally in guild records.[44] Christ addresses Margery as 'dowtyr' throughout the *Book*, but his word has spiritual connotations.

These tripartite models of the female state are more reminiscent of the 'three orders' of *oratores*, *bellatores* and *laboratores* than of the ages of man, and they encapsulate the virtues and functions of womanhood. The 'maid, wife, widow' structure often collapses matters of life cycle and sexual state so that it is difficult to distinguish one from another. A poem on the incarnation summarises the conditions of woman:

> Of womanhede, lo, thre degres there be:
> Widowehede, wedlocke, and verginnitie.
> Widowehede clamed heauen, her title is this:
> By oppressions that mekelie suffrethe she,
> A[nd] wedlocke by generacion heauen hires shuld be,
> And virgins clame by chastite alone.
> Then God thought a woman shoulde set them at one
> And cease ther strife,
> For Marie was maden, widowe, and wife.[45]

Maidens, wives and widows each have their own claims to heaven, according to the author: maidens through their chastity, widows through their patient

---

[43] On the 'virgin, continent, married' model, and its complexities, see Cordelia Beattie, 'Meanings of Singleness: The Single Woman in Late Medieval England', D.Phil. thesis, University of York (2001), pp. 45–55; Pierre J. Payer, *The Bridling of Desire: Views of Sex in the Later Middle Ages* (Toronto, 1993), pp. 160–2.

[44] Bateson, ed., *Borough Customs*, I, pp. 222–8 and II, pp. 102–29, 130–7. The 'daughter, wife, widow' model is often employed by social historians: e.g., Mavis E. Mate, *Daughters, Wives and Widows after the Black Death: Women in Sussex, 1350–1535* (Woodbridge, 1998).

[45] 'By reason of two and poore of one', in Richard Leighton Greene, ed., *The Early English Carols*, 2nd edn (Oxford, 1977), no. 95.

endurance of suffering, and wives through maternity. The Virgin Mary, in encompassing the three states, was a complete woman. The motif is often found in secular literature: 'A man moot nedes love, maugree [despite] his heed; / He may nat fleen it, thogh he shold be deed, / Al be she mayde, or wydwe, or elles wyf'.[46] 'Loue comseþ wiþ kare and hendeþ [strikes] wiþ tene [grief], / Mid lauedi [lady], mid wiue, mid maide, mid quene'.[47] Some authors use this ordering of women as a simple trope when they want to emphasise the inclusiveness of their message, as Walter Hilton mentions the possibility of living a holy life for men and women of any estate, whether 'Prest, clerk, or lewede man, wydue, wyf, or mayden', and Chaucer's Wife of Bath speaks of the wives, maids and widows of the court who sit in judgement on the rapist knight.[48] In many other instances the orders of women are reduced to two – maidens and wives – but the principle of dividing women by sexual and marital status, with underlying implications of age, remains.[49]

Some late medieval lives of holy women made use of this scheme; my focus here is limited to those thought to have had an influence upon Margery or her scribe in the production of the *Book*. In certain redactions, Bridget of Sweden's *Vita* is structured around the periods of maidenhood, wifehood and widowhood, as is that of Elizabeth of Hungary.[50] Bridget's influence on Margery is well-attested, and while Alexandra Barratt has shown that the Elizabeth of Hungary who authored the *Revelations* which had a strong effect on Margery's text was not the same woman as the Elizabeth of Hungary whose life appeared in *The Golden Legend*, *The Gilte Legende* and Osbern Bokenham's *Legendys of Hooly Wummen*, the two were often conflated in the minds of medieval readers.[51] Jacques de Vitry's life of Marie d'Oignies speaks of the different ways of living a holy life modelled by virgins, widows and married women, although he does not go on to employ this structure explicitly in relation to Marie herself.[52]

Culturally, the maiden, the wife and the widow, in their life-cycle aspect, were subject to strongly differing representations and degrees of idealisation or condemnation. I have argued elsewhere that maidenhood represented the perfect age of woman's life in a wide range of textual and visual genres. Lives of the virgin-martyr saints, visual depictions of the Virgin Mary at her death,

---

46 Geoffrey Chaucer, 'The Knight's Tale', in *The Canterbury Tales*, ed. Larry D. Benson et al., *The Riverside Chaucer*, 3rd edn (Oxford, 1987), lines 1169–71.

47 'Loue is soffte, loue is swet, loue is goed sware', in Carleton Brown, ed., *English Lyrics of the XIIIth Century* (Oxford, 1932), no. 53, lines 27–8.

48 Walter Hilton, *The Scale of Perfection*, ed. Thomas H. Bestul (Kalamazoo, 2000), bk. 1, ch. 60; Chaucer, 'The Wife of Bath's Tale', lines 1026–7, 1043–4.

49 For example, 'a glorious legende / Of goode wymmen, maydenes and wyves', Chaucer, *The Legend of Good Women*, F. lines 483–4; see also lines 437–8.

50 Birger Gregersson and Thomas Gascoigne, *The Life of Saint Birgitta*, trans. Julia Bolton Holloway (Toronto, 1991); Osbern Bokenham, *Legendys of Hooly Wummen*, ed. Mary Serjeantson, EETS original series 206 (London, 1938). Cf. the vita bound with the *Liber Celestis* in BL MS Claudius B I, which like Margery's book omits mention of the first phase of her life: 'A Life of St Bridget' in Roger Ellis, ed., *The Liber Celestis of St Bridget of Sweden*, EETS original series 291 (Oxford, 1987), vol. 1.

51 Alexandra Barratt, '*The Revelations of Saint Elizabeth of Hungary*: Problems of Attribution', *The Library*, 6th series 14 (1992): 1–11.

52 Jacques de Vitry, *The Life of Marie d'Oignies*, trans. Margot H. King (Toronto, 1993), pp. 37–8.

assumption and coronation, the late fourteenth-century poem *Pearl*, and certain funerary monuments depict the idealised woman in the physical state she would achieve in the afterlife, and that ideal took the form of a conventionally beautiful young woman on the cusp of adulthood.[53] Jessica Cooke makes a similar point about young women in Ricardian poetry, examining the contrasting representations of young and old women in works by the Gawain-Poet and Chaucer. She directs our attention to the telling detail that the hideous old woman of the *Romaunt of the Rose* is said to have probably been attractive when 'in hir rightful age' (line 405). 'Likening the woman's youth to her *correct* or *proper* age implicitly designates all her other ages to the realm of incorrectness and impropriety, providing explicit proof for the belief that the only appropriate age for women was youth'.[54] Some medical writers advised old men at night to keep 'in constant embrace a girl who is close to menarche', as her youthful heat would cure his indigestion and insomnia.[55] This emphasis on youth or maidenhood as the most prized age of woman in a range of both religious and secular texts makes its excision from Margery's account of her life all the more noticeable.

Other depictions of maidens, on the other hand, emphasise their sexual availability, as foolish innocents who are easily won over and take pleasure in the experience. The guileless yokel maidens made pregnant on their holidays, as depicted in songs or lyrics, fall into this category, as does Chaucer's Malyne, daughter of a socially aspiring miller, in 'The Reeve's Tale'. In a slightly different category are the foolish virgins of sermon or homiletic literature who imprudently wander away from home only to be raped and who mourn the loss of their virginities.[56]

More potentially relevant to Margery were the portrayals of holy women's childhood and youth. Of the women thought to have had an influence on her *Book*, most fall into the category of the *puella senex*; that is, a girl who shows wisdom and maturity befitting a much later stage of life.[57] Marie d'Oignies would not play or show interest in frivolous things like other girls, but rather admired those who had adopted an ascetic life and rejected the adornments and fine clothes her parents tried to dress her in. Bridget of Sweden was precocious in speech, active in good works and prayer, and had visions of the Virgin and the Devil. Catherine of Siena said constant prayers at five, had a vision of Christ as bridegroom at six, and while still in childhood gave up games and took up her lifelong habits of bodily scourging and fasting. Learning of the deeds of the Desert Fathers she attempted a temporary imitation of them by finding herself a solitary space under a crag, and at seven she made her vow of virginity.

---

[53] Phillips, 'Maidenhood as the Perfect Age'.

[54] Jessica Cooke, 'Nice Young Girls and Wicked Old Witches: The "Rightful Age" of Women in Middle English Verse', in Evelyn Mullally and John Thompson, eds, *The Court and Cultural Diversity: Selected Papers from the Eighth Triennial Congress of the International Courtly Literature Society* (Cambridge, 1997), pp. 219–28 (p. 227).

[55] Luke Demaitre, 'The Care and Extension of Old Age in Medieval Medicine', in Sheehan, ed., *Aging and the Aged*, pp. 5–22 (p. 16).

[56] G. R. Owst, *Literature and Pulpit in Medieval England* (Oxford, 1966), p. 119.

[57] Burrow deals with the *puella senex* alongside the *puer senex* in *Ages of Man*, ch. 3.

Elizabeth of Hungary preferred praying in church to playing with other children, scorned fancy clothing and tried to persuade her friends to be as disciplined and devout as she. Dorothea of Montau very early took up her habits of
sleep-deprivation, fasting and extreme self-mutilation.[58] As Rosalynn Voaden
and Stephanie Volf have shown through their comparison of twenty-seven
female and thirteen male visionary accounts of their childhoods, such emphasis
on spiritual precocity was a marked feature of female *vitae*. Accounts of male
visionaries' childhood and youth were much more likely to feature misspent
youths, spiritual crises and conversions.[59]

What is meant by Margery and her scribes' evasion of the subject of her
youth? It could not be said that nothing of spiritual significance occurred during
that time, as at some point in her youth Margery had committed the sin which
would so trouble her later in life. If Charity Scott Stokes is correct in suggesting
that the error may have been some form of Lollard sympathising, then it makes
sense that the authors would have wished to skate over the subject.[60] Neither the
idealisations nor critiques of feminine youth held appeal either. The model of the
maiden as a woman in her perfect, or 'rightful' age had limited real-life use, apart
from the display of high-status maidens at court and parishes' emphasis on
maidens during May and Whitsun festivities.[61] The foolish-virgin motif was not
attractive to Margery in her self-presentation either, perhaps partly because of its
association with lower and lower-middle-status women, but largely because it
belonged to the wrong genres. The lack of emphasis on holy childhood and
youth is more remarkable, given the appeal of the *puella senex* to many authors
of holy women's biographies.

Representations of the 'wife', or married woman (for 'wife' could refer to
women in general) have not been subjected to extensive examination, but we
may note some common themes in late medieval texts. Some types include the
young, lascivious and faithless wife (for example, Chaucer's Alison of 'The
Miller's Tale' and Mai of his 'The Merchant's Tale'), contrasting with loyal and
self-sacrificing examples (including his Dorigen and Lucrece). Middle-aged
wives tend to be voluble, sometimes lecherous, and usually talk back to their
husbands (the Wife of Bath is the paradigm of this type, but Noah's gossiping
and disobedient wife of the York plays also fits in part). The favoured type of conduct books, on the other hand, was the goodwife. As Felicity Riddy has written,
' "Goodwife" is a term of respect; it is the counterpart of "goodman," which
means not only the male head of a household but a burgess or freeman. The
"goodwife" is both a virtuous woman and a citizen's wife; the bourgeois ethos

---

58 Jacques de Vitry, *Marie d'Oignies*, pp. 46–47; Gregersson and Gascoigne, *Saint Birgitta*,
   pp. 14–15; Raymond of Capua, *The Life of St Catherine of Siena*, trans. George Lamb (London,
   1960), pp. 24–35; Bokenham, 'Lyf of St Elyzabeth' in *Legendys*, lines 9553–9600; Johannes von
   Marienwerder, *The Life of Dorothea von Montau, a Fourteenth-Century Recluse*, trans. Ute
   Stargardt (Lewiston, 1997), pp. 37–57.
59 Rosalynn Voaden and Stephanie Volf, 'Visions of My Youth: Representations of the
   Childhood of Medieval Visionaries', *Gender and History* 12 (2000): 665–684. Cf. Donald
   Weinstein and Rudolph M. Bell, *Saints and Society: The Two Worlds of Western Christendom,
   1000–1700* (Chicago, 1982), chs 1 and 2.
60 Stokes, 'Margery Kempe', p. 25.
61 Phillips, *Medieval Maidens*, pp. 115–16, 188–90.

seeks to conflate those two meanings'.[62] 'Goodness' in a wife encompassed more than piety or sexual virtue, therefore: it also required that she be a capable householder. Charles Phythian-Adams notes that early sixteenth-century Coventry cappers' accounts use the term to refer to a woman who carries on a husband's business before or after his death.[63] The goodwife, given its associations with burgesses' wives, is of strong relevance for Margery. The detail that following the end of her first illness John Kempe told the servants to trust her with the keys to the buttery fits with this paradigm (1: 8). However, Margery fails to fit the model in a number of important respects, from her thwarted business interests, to her international wanderings, to making a spectacle of herself in public. Particular anxiety is expressed about her leading other men's wives astray (48: 116; 54: 133), and men of the district of Beverley attempt to force her back to conventional wifely duties: ' "Damsel, forsake þis lyfe þat þu hast, & go spynne & carde as oþer women don" ' (53: 129).

Wives as holy women do not conform to any individual pattern. Where Catherine of Siena successfully resisted her family's attempts to enforce marriage upon her, several of the women mystics whose work influenced Margery succumbed to familial pressures. Bridget, from an aristocratic background, obeyed her parents in marrying a young prince at the age of twelve. Ulf seems not to have hindered her vocation, however: at marriage, aged eighteen, he was still a virgin, and agreed to wait two years before consummating the wedding; he joined with Bridget in prayers to protect them from lust; and cheerfully agreed to Bridget's request that they adopt chastity after the birth of their eighth child, after which they went on pilgrimage together before each entering religious life. Unlike certain other holy women such as Angela of Foligno, Bridget is not shown to have struggled against her role as mother; rather, she focused on raising her children in the faith and some, including her daughter Catherine, followed her into religious life. Soon after her marriage at fourteen Marie d'Oignies persuaded her husband to adopt a chaste life, with the result that she avoided motherhood. Elizabeth of Hungary's husband supported his wife in her holy activities without demur, and although he did not imitate her he agreed to her request that he go on Crusade – only to die in the Holy Land. Dorothea of Montau's marital life was more difficult. Married at seventeen she and her husband had nine children over a period of sixteen and a half years, but sex and maternity were always a great trial for Dorothea. Finally Adalbert agreed to a vow of chastity. However, he was often puzzled and infuriated by her trances and neglect of housewifely duties, and subjected her to savage beatings.[64] 'Goodness' for Dorothea and Margery, as for Angela of Foligno, took an entirely different form for married holy women than for lay bourgeois wives, and Margery's book records the incompatibility of these ideals.

---

[62] Riddy, 'Mother Knows Best', p. 68; Tauno F. Mustanoja, ed., *The Good Wife Taught Her Daughter, The Good Wyfe Wold a Pylgremage, The Thewis of Gud Women* (Helsinki, 1948).

[63] Charles Phythian-Adams, *Desolation of a City: Coventry and the Urban Crisis of the Late Middle Ages* (Cambridge, 1979), pp. 91–2.

[64] Gregerrson and Gascoigne, *St Birgitta*, pp. 15–20; 'Life of St Bridget' in Ellis, ed., *Liber Celestis*, lines 31–2; Jacques de Vitry, *Marie d'Oignies*. pp. 48–9; Bokenham, *Legendys*, lines 10065–136; Johannes von Marienwerder, *Dorothea of Montau*, pp. 57–66, 93, 100–1.

Widowhood, for those who had not managed to avoid marriage, was the stage when holy women were able to come into their own. Having shucked off their husbands and with their children grown or dead, Dorothea of Montau and Angela of Foligno were released to follow the mystic path.[65] Bridget of Sweden performed influential public roles and travelled widely.[66] Marie d'Oignies, on the other hand, was freed not by widowhood but by her husband's agreement to live chastely,[67] and this bears greater resemblance to Margery's experience.

Another standard stereotype of the widow emphasised her financial vulnerability. Elizabeth of Hungary found herself landed in a condition of virtuous adversity, deprived of her property and scorned by her neighbours. Her poverty and ill treatment at the hands of her vicious confessor are taken as tokens of grace by her hagiographers.[68] A range of prescriptive texts in English condemned those who would deprive the widow of her 'mite', and similar concerns with poverty and defencelessness influenced official protection of widows under London laws.[69] As Hanawalt's study of 299 cases before the London Husting Courts shows, however, many of the widows suing to receive their full dower were far from indigent or friendless, and some attempted to claim property on fraudulent grounds. Canon law, influenced by scriptural tradition, also tended to emphasise the disadvantages of widowhood and the widow's need for assistance.

These types contrast with the fickle, unfaithful and sexually voracious widow. Widows and older women were often portrayed in Middle English literature as possessing alarming sexual appetites, while old men were derided for their loss of carnal vigour.[70] Margery's powerful sexual desires, however, were more apparent during the first twenty years of her marriage and again briefly in her late forties (4: 13; 59: 145). It was during the latter period that she was frequently subjected to sexual insults – as occurred during her interrogation for heresy in Leicester – and accusations of hypocrisy in her claims to chastity and wearing white clothes (for example, 44: 103–5; 47: 113).

Far more important than the schemes of the ages of man, the maid, wife, widow structure had a deep influence of women's lives. English law differentiated between the rights, responsibilities and abilities of women according to their marital status as wife or widow, where as male rights did not differ with marital status. But in thinking about medieval conceptions of life cycle it is ultimately not enough only to identify and describe the common patterns or representation. One must also ask, why does any culture establish a clear life-cycle framework such as the ages of man, or the maid, wife, widow model? What 'cultural work' do such schemes do? Women were granted a life structure in medieval representations,

---

65 Johannes von Marienwerder, *Dorothea of Montau*, 110–211; Angela of Foligno, *Memorial*, pp. 27ff.

66 Gregerrson and Gascoigne, *St Birgitta*, pp. 2–31.

67 Jacques de Vitry, *Marie d'Oignies*, pp. 48–9.

68 Bokenham, *Legendys*, lines 10137–360.

69 Barbara A. Hanawalt, 'The Widow's Mite: Provisions for Medieval London Widows', in Louise Mirrer, ed., *Upon My Husband's Death: Widows in the Literature and Histories of Medieval Europe* (Ann Arbor, 1992), pp. 21–46 (p. 21).

70 Alicia K. Nitecki, 'Figures of Old Age in Fourteenth-Century English Literature', in Sheehan, ed., *Aging and the Aged*, pp. 107–116 esp. pp. 111–12.

but it was conceived in entirely relative terms. Masculine life stages are autonomous, defined only by the age of the individual male's body and level of mental maturity. A male *puer*, *adolescens* or *senex* is defined by nothing other than his own age in body and mind. Female life stages, on the other hand, have meaning only in relation to men. Age is an implied, but secondary component of this structure. One finds occasional references to old 'maids', or women who term themselves 'puellae' or refer to their virginity.[71] Conversely, some women were made widows at an age when others were still living through the 'maidenhood' phase of their lives. The cultural work of the ages of man and the ages of woman was to reinforce models of gender which asserted the right of the male to an independent identity, one which mutated with the years but was always his own. A woman's identity was always contingent, secondary and relative to a man's, even when reaching an ideal of femininity.

Conclusions

This splitting-up of cultural- and social-historical approaches to life cycles may have the unfortunate effect of implying that such approaches should be kept separate. My belief is quite the reverse: it is more challenging, intriguing and revealing to attempt to combine the approaches. In any historical context, experience and representation intertwine and influence each other. 'All practices, whether economic or cultural, depend on the representations individuals use to make sense of their world'.[72] In late medieval England, construction of female life cycle around the maid (or daughter), wife, widow model rather than the ages of man was utterly bound up with women's actual experiences of growing up, their adult roles and their position under the law. The division of approaches may also have the effect of suggesting that cultural historians should stick to examining artistic artefacts (works of literature, of the visual arts, saints' lives and the like) while social historians should remain loyal to supposedly pragmatic documents which are more likely to reflect life as it really was. The division is here more a reflection of dominant existing practices than a recommendation.

My prescribed task, however, was primarily to reflect on medieval women's life cycles as they relate to *The Book of Margery Kempe*. The chief finding of this exercise has been that established notions of the stages of a woman's life, whether they derive from medieval or modern authors, do not fit Margery well. In part this is due to matters of genre, yet it has been shown that the portrayal of Margery's life is in many respects different from those lives of holy women most relevant to her.[73] Margery is an object lesson in the importance of taking account

---

71 For old maids, see Peter Idley, *Instructions to His Son*, ed. Charlotte d'Evelyn (London, 1935), line 2063: 'And cheryssh oolde maidones, for they be deynte'. For *puellae* or 'maids' leaving wills see my 'Four Virgins' Tales: Sex and Power in Medieval Law', in Anke Bernau, Ruth Evans and Sarah Salih, eds, *Medieval Virginities* (Cardiff, 2003), pp. 80–101 (pp. 93–5).

72 Lynn Hunt, 'Introduction: History, Culture, and Text', in Lynn Hunt, ed., *The New Cultural History* (Berkeley, 1989), p. 19.

73 This is a point also made by Sarah Salih in relation to Margery's bodily practices below, pp. 175–6.

of individual variation. The three main stages on the mystic way, of purgation, illumination and union, are also only partly applicable as an analytical framework for the *Book*. Margery certainly experiences purgation, and some illumination, but it is a stretch to suggest she attains full union.[74] Moreover, the *Book* is a far richer account of a woman's life than the narrative of the mystic path would allow for, and one only has to read the *Book* alongside the *Life* of Marie d'Oignies or *Memorial* of Angela of Foligno to see that. Sidonie Smith writes that the '*Book*'s very legibility . . . derived from its resonances with biographical and hagio-graphical representations of female mystics',[75] yet a more convincing argument would be that when set beside established forms of medieval life writing *The Book of Margery Kempe* is distinctly *illegible*. The first draft of the work was literally unreadable to Margery's second scribe but, with effort and Margery's aid, he was able to decipher it (Proem: 4). In a similar way modern readers have gradually overcome the incomprehension, and even distaste, expressed by many in early reactions to the work, and learned techniques for reading it.[76] We have come to appreciate the *Book* as a unique manuscript in more ways than one.

---

[74] Atkinson, *Mystic and Pilgrim*, pp. 39–51.
[75] Sidonie Smith, *A Poetics of Women's Autobiography: Marginality and the Fictions of Self-Representation* (Bloomington, 1987), p. 66.
[76] Atkinson, *Mystic and Pilgrim*, ch. 7.

2

Men and Margery: Negotiating Medieval Patriarchy[1]

ISABEL DAVIS

Oure fadres olde & modres lyued wel,
And taghte hir children as hem self taght were
Of holy chirche & asked nat a del
'Why stant this word here?' and 'why this word there?'
'Why spake god thus and seith thus elles where?'
'Why dide he this wyse and mighte han do thus?'
Our fadres medled no thyng of swich gere:
Þat oghte been a good mirour to vs.

If land to thee be falle of heritage,
Which þat thy fadir heeld in reste & pees,
With title iust & trewe in al his age,
And his fadir before him brygelees
And his and his & so foorth doutelees
I am ful seur who so wolde it thee reue,
Thow woldest thee deffende & putte in prees;
Thy right thow woldest nat, thy thankes, leue.

(Lines 153–68)[2]

These two stanzas come from one of the most overt discussions of late medieval social order and its underwritten gender assumptions.[3] They are the words of Thomas Hoccleve, a poet and bureaucrat of the early fifteenth century, and one of Margery Kempe's exact contemporaries. He comes from a similar cultural milieu

---

[1] I would like to thank the editors of this volume and Richard Rowland for suggesting numerous improvements to this article.

[2] [Our fathers and mothers lived well and they taught their children as they themselves were taught / about Holy Church and did not ask / 'why stands this word here?' and 'why this word there?' / 'Why did God say this and then say that elsewhere?' / 'Why did he do this when he might have done that?' / Our fathers didn't interfere in such things / they ought to be a model for us. // If land were to be bequeathed to you / which your father held in rest and peace / by just and true title for all his life / and his father before him without break / and his and his and so on indubitably / I am sure that regardless of whoever wished to rob you of it / you would defend yourself and press your own advantage / You would not want to relinquish your right voluntarily.] From 'The Ballade to Sir John Oldcastle', in Thomas Hoccleve, *Hoccleve's Works: The Minor Poems*, ed. F. J. Furnivall and I. Gollancz, rev. J. Mitchell and A. I. Doyle, EETS extra series 61and 73 (Oxford, 1970), pp. 8–24.

[3] For a slightly different gendered account of this poem, see Ruth Nisse, '"Oure Fadres Olde and Modres": Gender, Heresy, and Hoccleve's Literary Politics', *Studies in the Age of Chaucer* 21 (1999): 275–99.

to Kempe: part of the nascent bourgeoisie in the urban centres of late medieval England. I want to use Hoccleve's poem to demonstrate the kind of gendered ideologies with which *The Book of Margery Kempe* is in dialogue. In this way I hope to get at the ways in which these ideologies affected not just women, like Margery, but also men; just as Margery is pressured to conform to gender-specific ideals, men's responses to her are conditioned by social expectations.[4]

In the quotation above Hoccleve addresses the infamous Lollard agitator, Sir John Oldcastle, exhorting him to abandon his religious sedition. The first stanza here concentrates on the Lollard challenge to church doctrine; the list of trivial and impudent questions portrays the heretic as an unruly child, taxing his parents with inquiries about indubitable scriptural and divine authority. Hoccleve argues that the proper and obedient thing to do is to respect the limits of 'oure' fathers' imaginations (lines 173–4), to venerate tradition and desist from religious challenge. The repetition of 'oure' and the word 'vs' seeks to build solidarity between those who would benefit from an ordered and obeisant society, encouraging them to restrain their own behaviours in order to achieve that aim. The second stanza is much more explicit about who benefits from a deferential community. In this stanza Hoccleve uses a metaphor about land; land was the main repository of medieval wealth and the majority of it was owned by men of privilege.[5] The metaphor of land transference describes the authority of the church as part of an agnatic inheritance handed down from father to son without break. The repetition of 'his' reiterates the appropriate gendered pattern of ownership: in medieval England, with a system of primogeniture, it was normal for the eldest son alone to inherit most of his father's property and for younger sons and daughters to be provided for by other means. The hierarchy of age thus differentiated brother from brother as much as brother from sister. The metaphor, then, equates the authority of the church with the economic advantage of first-born, aristocratic men over women and other men of lower status; its traditions are thus described as being as incontestable and socially foundational as inheritance strategies. The church, Hoccleve states, ought to be defended as the property of the privileged male.

Hoccleve reads Oldcastle's offence as multi-faceted, as an attack not just on the Lancastrian regime and the church, with its monopoly over knowledge, but also upon family values, patrilineal property transfer and the class and gender hierarchies they produce. He appeals to him as a man and a knight, urging him to accept, obey and champion the social order as his masculine and aristocratic right, passed like property from father to son. Critics look at this poem in terms of what it has to say about social and religious conformity and that conformity is clearly considered in this poem to be contingent upon a supposedly 'natural'

---

4   I shall follow Lynn Staley in making a distinction between the author, Kempe, and the protagonist, Margery. Staley, *Dissenting Fictions*, p. 3.

5   This, of course, is a generalization: there were female landowners in medieval England. Widows in particular were often in sole possession of land. Hoccleve, however, is discussing an ideal of male property ownership. For a detailed account of women's rights in respect of land see Christopher Cannon, 'The Rights of Medieval English Women: Crime and the Issue of Representation', in David Wallace and Barbara Hanawalt, eds, *Medieval Crime and Social Control* (Minneapolis, 1999), pp. 156–83 (pp. 162–8).

gender imbalance.[6] Margery's challenge may seem most obviously religious but she, like Sir John, generates jumbled reactions from those she meets and interacts with; their shocked invectives so often attack her for stepping out of what was perceived as normative or ideal for her sex, perceptions which were clearly inextricably intertwined with religious ideologies. At one point in the *Book*, one of Margery's detractors describes her as Oldcastle's daughter (54: 132), an attack that is inspired not by unconventional religious beliefs – Margery is examined and acquitted on that score – but because her religious practices defy what was considered suitable in gender terms, as I shall discuss in more detail below. First we need to consider the significance of the discourses of gender and patriarchy underpinning Hoccleve's comments.

While a lot has been said about women in the Middle Ages, it is only recently in medieval studies, as in many other fields, that scholars of gender have begun to look at the question of men and their relationships to gendered ideologies.[7] Women have been more consistently and violently discriminated against in legal, economic, social and educational terms and thus the cultural boundaries which govern women's lives are more obvious. However, men's lives are also constrained by conventions of gender and those strictures, being less visible, are often more insidious. Where they were promoted, patriarchal ideals – about obedience to traditional forms of masculine authority – were as much part of men's socialization as women's and, as Hoccleve claims, taught by both fathers and mothers to their sons as much as their daughters. Rather than thinking of patriarchy only in terms of the limitations it places on women's lives – which often has the effect of describing men as an unproblematic standard against which women are measured – gender scholars who work on men and masculinity have tried to look at the mechanics of, and the gradations within, patriarchy in order to assess them more effectively. Jeff Hearn has seen patriarchy not as a system where powerful men subjugate powerless women but as a complex network of relationships between men that are arranged to best exploit women and particularly their labour.[8] R. W. Connell has described a tripartite configuration of masculine society. First there are a small, ascendant group of 'hegemonic' men who set the cultural and ethical agenda and control the central social and political institutions. Secondly there are also male minorities who are marginalized on the grounds of class, race, sexuality or age and who are disadvantaged by hegemonic institutions and agenda. Then there is the majority of the male community, who benefit from the 'patriarchal dividend' but do not themselves formulate ideology or dominate strategic societal positions.[9] Part of Hoccleve's outrage in 'The Ballade to

---

[6] See, for example, David Aers, *Community, Gender, and Individual Identity: English Writing 1360–1430* (London, 1988), p. 97.

[7] See the discussion of the transition from women's to gender studies in Thelma Fenster's 'Preface', in C. A. Lees, ed., *Medieval Masculinities: Regarding Men in the Middle Ages* (Minneapolis, 1994), pp. ix–xiii (p. xi). For a more recent account see Jacqueline Murray's introduction to *eadem*, ed., *Conflicted Identities and Multiple Masculinities: Men in the Medieval West* (New York, 1999). Other essays on medieval masculinity can be found in: J. J. Cohen and B. Wheeler, eds, *Becoming Male in the Middle Ages* (New York, 1997) and D. M. Hadley, ed., *Masculinity in Medieval Europe* (London, 1999).

[8] Jeff Hearn, *The Gender of Oppression: Men, Masculinity and the Critique of Marxism* (Brighton, 1987), esp. pp. 95–8.

[9] R. W. Connell, *Masculinities* (Cambridge, 1995), pp. 76–81.

Sir John Oldcastle' is that a man born into this hegemony will neither defend it nor assert it to the detriment of other potential beneficiaries – like, perhaps, the poet himself. So, as well as thinking about the bargains that women make with men, we must also consider the ways in which men negotiate their positions both in relation to women and other men.

The term 'patriarchy' is much contested and not currently particularly fashionable in gender scholarship for two main reasons. First, because it can be used very broadly and uncritically to describe almost any culture or society scholars turn their attention to, homogenizing the experiences of both sexes in different times and places to one simple observation about gender discrimination.[10] Second, using the term often has the effect of apportioning blame to men for an asymmetrical gender configuration when, in fact, women must have conspired in their own marginalization.[11] The question, of course, is why and the answer requires us to think less in abstract and general terms and more about specific cultural scenarios, to think about the way in which people develop strategies in order to negotiate the rules which govern their lives. Just as the most enduring and pervasive ideologies are those which are interiorized through socialization, so their most effective challenges often deploy the same language and attempt a restructuring from the inside. Investing and sharing in societal convictions gives reformers the authority they need to constitute an intelligible and persuasive countervailing force. Deniz Kandiyoti, in a seminal anthropological article on patriarchy, has written about a 'patriarchal bargain', a term which indicates

> the existence of a set of rules and scripts regulating gender relations, to which *both genders* accommodate and acquiesce, yet which may nonetheless be contested, redefined, and renegotiated.[12]

She proposes that, rather than using the term 'patriarchy' to refer to a monolithic concept of male dominance, we investigate the 'intimate workings of culturally and historically distinct arrangements between the genders'.[13] Medieval historians, such as Judith M. Bennett, although committed to the term, argue that patriarchy is not static, that it constitutes itself differently at different moments and in different places and that studying its permutations and workings can help us both to celebrate the ingenuity of people who evaded its supervision and also plot the ways in which women can challenge the discrimination which they encounter today.[14]

---

10 See, for an attack on this use of the term, Deniz Kandiyoti, 'Bargaining with Patriarchy', *Gender and Society* 2 (1988): 274–90 (275).
11 Gerda Lerner, *The Creation of Patriarchy* (Oxford, 1986), p. 5, argues that women helped to shape patriarchy as much as men and the discussion of why this should be is central to the argument of the book.
12 Kandiyoti, 'Bargaining with Patriarchy', p. 286, n. 1. My italics. I shall be using Kandiyoti's ideas throughout this article to discuss the bargains which people make with patriarchy. Of course, in many ways the classically patriarchal societies that she discusses are different from late medieval patriarchy, most crucially in terms of household formation, but there are still useful similarities to be discussed.
13 Kandiyoti, 'Bargaining with Patriarchy', p. 275.
14 Judith M. Bennett, 'Women's History: A Study in Continuity and Change', *Women's History Review* 2 (1993): 173–84 (178).

'Patriarchy' was not a term that was used in the medieval period in the way it is now. In the late Middle Ages the word was a technical religious term with only a tangential relationship to the word as we now use it. The term has Latin and Greek roots and literally means 'rule of the fathers'. It came to be used by political theorists in the seventeenth century to describe the relationship between a monarch and his people as that of a father and his children.[15] Its meaning has, over time, changed and broadened, to refer not just to fathers but to men more generally, and been popularized, in the recent past, by feminist historians keen to excavate the main themes in the lives of women in history. Although medieval people did not use the word 'patriarchy' as we do, it was orthodox to think of male superordination as natural and to consider this integral to the proper ordering, not just of individual private households and families, but also the larger institutions of church and state. The paternalism of kings was not an idea that was invented by early modern writers: they inherited it from the Middle Ages and, at a time when the nature of kingship was being fiercely debated, gave it an explicit vocabulary.[16] In the earlier period, of the late fourteenth and early fifteenth century, it is probably *because* the idea of male and fatherly ascendancy was so normative and dominant, so uncontested, that there was no associated, applicable lexicon. Certainly Hoccleve's poem repeats the word 'father' regularly, pestering Oldcastle to accept patrilineally transmitted traditions and assumptions. We might compare the way in which Margery's sense of her elite identity comes from her father's social standing and office-holding, a sense which – as Kate Parker points out in this volume – was shared by other influential people in her community.

Hoccleve expresses conservative ideals in the face of social challenge; his poem is a testament to the difficulty of installing and maintaining a perfectly ordered society of any kind. Hoccleve uses the word obedience and its various synonyms obsessively in his 'Ballade'. The anxiety of his tone is evidence that medieval people were not universally obedient and respectful, indeed that many, like Sir John Oldcastle and Margery Kempe – in their very different ways – profoundly challenged the prevailing social, religious, political and gendered orthodoxies. *The Book of Margery Kempe* is complexly related to those orthodoxies, variously appropriating, manipulating and reinforcing them for its own ends. Using the *Book* I want to investigate patriarchy not simply as a deplorable inequality between the sexes but as a complex set of compromises between women and men, and also between men and other men.

Obeying and Marrying the Father

Hoccleve's 'Ballade' is not very well thought of by literary critics and the virtue of obedience is not now considered a very poetical theme. What Hoccleve

---

[15] For a discussion of the seventeenth-century fortunes of patriarchalism see Gordon J. Schochet, *Patriarchalism in Political Thought: The Authoritarian Family and Political Speculation and Attitudes Especially in Seventeenth-Century England* (Oxford, 1975), esp. p. 19.

[16] See, for example, the discussion of the influence of Thomas Aquinas in ibid., pp. 26–8.

tries to do, though, is to glamorize deference and to describe it as empowering. This may seem very alien to modern readers but is key to understanding the central tenets of medieval Christian ethics.

> Ryse vp, a manly knyght, out of the slow
> Of heresie o lurker as a wrecche
> Wher as thow erred haast correcte it now!
> By humblesse thow mayst to mercy strecche. (Lines 105–8)[17]

Hoccleve here insists that it is humility that will make Oldcastle a 'manly knyght'. The Middle English word 'manly' carries both its modern sense of virility but could also mean noble.[18] The word comes up a number of times in Hoccleve's poem. Elite masculinity, Hoccleve claims, is signalled through religious submission. In the quotation with which I began this essay, that submission is dramatized as a confrontation with robbers; defending the status quo is not a passive but an active, martial activity, an assertive and heroic kind of virility. In the first quotation, as we saw, men's right to ascendancy was considered to derive from an unbroken patrilineage; Hoccleve is obsessed by fatherly authority, equating it with the authority both of the church and the aristocracy.

Fathers and ideas of fatherhood were central to medieval systems of authority. Fathers were expected to command their households and dependants rather as a head governs the subordinate body. It was a traditional motif in social and political philosophy – handed down from Aristotle and interpreted for the medievals by St Thomas Aquinas – that this household configuration mirrored the relationship between the pope as the father and head of the church, the monarch as father and head of the state and ultimately God as father and head of the universe.[19] Further, these three bodies were not discrete but intimately linked. Biological metaphors – about corporations, fatherhood and agnatic heritage – had the effect of naturalizing contemporary ideologies, making them difficult to contest. The supreme father, of course, was God himself. The universal belief in a father God legitimated masculine ascendancy at various levels. *The Book of Margery Kempe* makes clever use of the image of a father God and presents a glamorized portrait of its protagonist's obedience in order to borrow authority from the first person of the Trinity: God the father.

Margery is, understandably, nervous about her marriage to the Godhead which the *Book* records as taking place during her visit to Rome in around 1413. Despite being a woman of nearly forty and a wife for almost twenty years, Margery is portrayed as a coy young bride who takes no part in the marriage negotiations. She is tearful and silent, behaviour which Christ asks God to make allowances for: ' "Fadyr, haue hir excused, for sche is ȝet but ȝong & not fully lernyd how sche xulde answeryn." ' (35: 87). Although Margery is keen to be married to Christ

---

17 [Rise up, a noble / virile knight, out of the slough / of heresy, O skulker and wretch, / where you have sinned, make amends / Through humbleness you may try to find mercy.]
18 See H. Kurath et al., eds, *Middle English Dictionary* (Ann Arbour, 1956–2001) *manli*: '4a Noble, righteous, worthy; courteous, refined, humane: (a) of men'.
19 See, for example, St Thomas Aquinas, *Summa Theologiæ*, ed. and trans. Thomas Gilby, 60 vols (Blackfriars, 1964), 28, Ia2æ, 90, 3, 3.

himself – the more approachable second person of the Trinity, with whom she is already intimate and the more usual mystical spouse for medieval religious women – she is instead pushed into a union with God the father. This alliance is, of course, more prestigious, hence Margery's apprehension; a reader is, presumably, intended both to sympathize with the heroine's trepidation but also approve of such an estimable match. Indeed, the reader is incorporated into a community with Christ, a community which knows better than Margery herself what is most advantageous for her.

The vision imagines Margery as a young woman pressed by her invested community (including the text's readers) into a financially or dynastically expedient marriage with a powerful, paternal husband. This is a 'metaphor' which accords neither with the ethics nor with the practice of late-medieval marriage in the urban, bourgeois communities of the kind to which Kempe belonged.[20] Indeed, the marriage of young women to older men was a minority social practice in England and confined to society's upper echelons.[21] Kempe's is an extreme representation of female submission calculated to respond to the formidable nature of a father-God. It is also, however, an ideal and aestheticized portrait which figures Margery as a beautiful, young and perhaps also aristocratic bride, tragically separated from a handsome lover (Christ) (35: 86–7) and married to an unknown and powerful suitor, who turns out, after all, to be her heart's desire, a motif borrowed from popular romance narratives.

The vision of the spiritual marriage uses tropes of age and gender in order to emphasize the idea of obedience. This imagery, and the collusion that it expects from the reader in quasi-erotic paternalist discourses, may make us a little uncomfortable until we remember that there was nothing intrinsically feminine about submission to divine authority. Men as well as women were sometimes represented undergoing mystical marriages with God or Christ, and this did not necessarily entail the adoption of a feminine subject position for the male 'bride'.[22] As we have seen, Hoccleve presents masculine obedience to Sir John Oldcastle as part of an attractive masculine commission. Portraying gender role models in appealing ways encourages those wishing to be valued community members to internalize those models in a process that R. W. Connell has termed 'cognitive purification'.[23] Obedience was a unisex virtue which was regularly glamorized in moral and religious texts such as sermons. Indeed, it was encapsulated in the central paradox of the Christian faith – of the strength to be found

[20] For a discussion of the late and companionate marriage regime in late medieval English towns see P. J. P. Goldberg, *Women, Work and Life Cycle in a Medieval Economy: Women in York and Yorkshire, c. 1300–1520* (Oxford, 1992), pp. 212, 227 and 231.

[21] Aristocratic marriages are more likely than others to be formed for political, economic and dynastic reasons. See, for example, Jacqueline Murray, 'Individualism and Consensual Marriage: Some Evidence from Medieval England', in C. M. Rousseau and J. T. Rosenthal, eds, *Women, Marriage and Family in Medieval Criticism: Essays in Memory of Michael M. Sheehan* (Kalamazoo, 1998), pp. 121–51 (pp. 126–7).

[22] See, for example, Carolyn Diskant Muir, 'Bride or Bridegroom? Masculine Identity in Mystical Marriages', in Patricia H. Cullum and Katherine J. Lewis, eds, *Holiness and Masculinity in Medieval Europe* (forthcoming, Cardiff, 2004).

[23] R. W. Connell, *Gender and Power: Society, the Person and Sexual Politics* (Cambridge, 1987), p. 246.

in suffering – which was so perfectly demonstrated by Christ at crucifixion. However, women's deference was expected to be more extensive than men's; it was considered normal and natural that women were subordinate to men, to their fathers, husbands and religious advisors. The Christian paradox in the Kempe passage is made more stark by Margery's particularly *feminine* meekness. The effect of this extravagant abasement, though, is to make her eventual spiritual elevation more impressive by contrast; Margery's acquiescence delivers extraordinary dividends.

God promises her significant spiritual benefits from this union: ' "for I schal schewyn þe my preuyteys & my cownselys, for þu xalt wonyn wyth me wythowtyn ende" ' (35: 86). This offer is presented in the terms of a marriage proposal. God makes Margery his conspirator, offering her intimate, exclusive access to his secret places and plans – tellingly the word 'prevyteys' could also carry the sense of sexual intimacy – and his final promise figures paradise as a conjugal household. The marriage vow itself goes even further:

> "I take þe, Margery, for my weddyd wyfe, for fayrar, for fowelar, for richar, for powerar, so þat þu be buxom & bonyr to do what I byd þe do. For, dowtyr, þer was neuyr childe so buxom to þe modyr as I xal be to þe boþe in wel & in wo, – to help þe and comfort þe. And þerto I make þe suyrte" (35: 87).

While the speech begins with the standard words of present consent which were used to contract matrimony in this period, God departs from this script, calling her, affectionately, 'dowtyr' and pledging filial obedience to her.[24] This statement, and others like it in her *Book*, makes Margery simultaneously mother, daughter and wife of God, proliferating the significant roles that she plays within the Trinity and the Holy Family and increasing her spiritual authority.[25]

These are astonishing and assertive claims. Kempe represents her protagonist as shy and reluctant in order that her unique access to God is shown to be a gift rather than something acquisitively sought and greedily taken. Margery is initially infantilized only to be restored to female adulthood, first as spousal match and then as mother to God himself. Moving sequentially from bride, to wife to mother, Margery attains greater authority by progression through a figurative spiritual life cycle which mirrors that which most secular medieval women would have experienced.[26] The text is anxious to represent Margery not as a consumer but as a protected dependant who is given privileged positions as of right and by the consent of others. Margery's figurative sexual maturation and assumption of the authoritative roles which accompany social adulthood, are achieved through her spiritual union in the way that the social marriage of a young heiress could coincide with her reaching the age of majority. Kempe

---

24 See, for a discussion of medieval marriage vows, R. H. Helmholz, *Marriage Litigation in Medieval England* (Cambridge, 1974), p. 36.

25 For a discussion of Margery's familial roles in the holy story see, for example, Catherine S. Akel, 'Familial Structure in the Religious Relationships and Visionary Experiences of Margery Kempe', *Studia Mystica* 16 (1995): 116–32 (esp. 124).

26 Kim Phillips's essay in the present volume considers the relationship between the *Book* and both representations and experiences of female life cycle in greater depth.

resorts to what was, by then, the old-fashioned ideal of the young-teen bride in order to make Margery's mystical boldness decorous and permissible. In this way Kempe, unlike her protagonist Margery, *is* a consumer, using patriarchal fantasies of feminine powerlessness for her own ambitious and challenging ends.

Class and Gender

> Right so where as our goode fadres olde
> Possessid were, & hadden the seisyne
> Peisible of Crystes feith, & no man wolde
> Impugne hir right; it sit vs to enclyne
> Ther-to let us no ferthere ymagyne
> But as þat they dide! Occupie our right;
> And in oure hertes fully determyne
> Our title good & keepe it with our might. (Lines 169–76)[27]

In this quotation from his 'Ballade' Hoccleve continues his metaphors about land and ownership. Hoccleve says that because social power usually accompanies economic power and ownership, it follows that the organized church, which relies upon and reinforces secular hegemony is of itself a kind of property which needs defending. Indeed, defending the church was considered to be one of the duties of the so-called second estate in the popular vision of society as tripartite. This ideal model schematized society into three *ordo*: those who prayed, those who fought and those who worked. This, of course, was a utopian notion which overlooked women and carved up social responsibility to correspond to male occupation and status groups. Women were sometimes placed in an awkward and destabilizing fourth estate or were sporadically classified in the other three by marital status or age.[28] More often than not they were simply excluded and thought, presumably, to be represented by their husbands, fathers or other male kin. This, without explicitly acknowledging it, placed men's relationships to women, to their wives and daughters, at the heart of the class structure which governed the relationships between men. Women's exclusion from, or partial inclusion in, this and other holistic ideals of corporate community – such as the Christian political body discussed earlier – shows the way in which men's relationships to each other were thought to constitute the social fabric. Male competition and collaboration were thought to determine the health or otherwise of medieval society. Subordinate and dominant masculinities were crucial to the way in which contemporaries conceptualized their society. Patriarchy was not, then, evenly experienced by late medieval men, very few of whom found themselves in possession of controlling influence.

---

[27] [Just as our good fathers of old / were possessed of and had a freehold, / peacefully in Christ's faith, and no man wished / to oppose that right; it is appropriate for us to want for the same. / Let us not imagine more / than they did! Keep possession of what is our right / and determine our good title in our hearts / and keep it with all our might.]

[28] See Phillips above, pp. 27–8.

In the *Book*, Margery is seen exploiting the cracks between men in order to secure her own position and enlarge her potential agency. In this way she plays minor clerics off against their superiors and continually enlists God and Christ as surrogate male kin to defend her against ordinary men. Most tellingly though, as I shall discuss in more detail below, Margery reminds her husband that she has married beneath herself, that her father is of a higher social status than he is, and thus tries to insist on continuity between her pre- and post-marital status, to try to avoid her own economic and social identity being subsumed by that of her husband. In fact, it was considered normal for women's legal, economic and social status to be thus subsumed in the practice of *couverture*, where a woman's property became her husband's on marriage and her legal identity was 'covered' by his.[29] However, Margery does manage to keep her finances separate from her husband's, an extraordinary fact that we learn when John asks his wife to pay his debts before he will give his permission to her going on pilgrimage. This has puzzled commentators who remark that this was not standard practice. But it is evidence for the way in which people may have negotiated alternative arrangements to those set out in law; there was no doubt a discrepancy between legal theory and practice, and Kate Parker suggests in this volume that there may have been particular local reasons for Margery's financial autonomy.[30] This kind of independence gives Margery a strong position – and a position which may not necessarily have been peculiar for medieval women – from which to try to live her life on her own terms.

Kandiyoti tells us that the compacts that women make with patriarchy are redrawn according to social and economic status. In particular, women often experience more independence when they are able to undertake paid work outside the household – where they, like Margery, have control of their own money – and where they agree to give up this independence, accepting various forms of social and economic seclusion and exclusion, they do so in exchange for protection from their husbands and a correspondingly enhanced social status.[31] It is also a sign of status for men in classically patriarchal societies that their wives do not have to leave the home to work, saying something about their success in the workplace but also indicating the economic leverage and command that they enjoy within their marriages. In the *Book*, these kinds of economic negotiations are central to the relationship which Margery has with her husband, John.

In the second chapter of the *Book*, Kempe describes Margery's reluctance to give up her business activities which she undertakes in an effort to preserve the standard of living that she enjoyed in her natal home. After marrying, despite her husband's disapproval, Margery sets herself up in two businesses: first brewing and, when that miscarries, milling. Margery wavers in her respect for her husband's wishes on this matter: after her first business venture fails, seeing this failure as a sign of her wrong-headedness, she asks forgiveness of her

29 For an account and history of the medieval legal practice of 'coverture' see Cannon, 'The Rights of Medieval English Women', pp. 157–9.
30 See Parker, pp. 67–8.
31 Kandiyoti, 'Bargaining with Patriarchy', p. 280.

husband; she then changes her mind, starting up the second business. The narration itself is disapproving of Margery's youthful 'sins':

> sche askyd hir husbond mercy for sche wold not folwyn hys cownsel a-for-tyme, and sche seyd þat hir pride and synne was cause of alle her punschyng and sche wold amend þat sche had trespasyd wyth good wyl. But ȝet sche left not þe world al hol, for now sche be-thowt hir of a newe huswyfre. Sche had an horsmille (2: 10).

One of the main reasons for Margery wanting this economic independence in her young married life, and the aspect of good living which she is most keen on maintaining, is her wardrobe of fine clothes and headdresses. The way in which women dress has been shown, by gender scholars, to be a site where patriarchal values are contested.[32] Worthiness and respectability in particular, signs of good status and protection from fathers or husbands, both of which are crucial to securing women's economic capitulation, are signed through clothing.[33] What is more, worthiness and respectability were much more important qualities in medieval urban societies – like Margery's King's Lynn – where, without the surety of modern legal contracts, credit networks ran on trust.[34]

John is as unhappy about his wife's immodest dress and what it might signal about her virtue, as he is about the entrepreneurial activities she undertakes to finance her extravagant tastes:

> Neuyr-þe-lesse, sche wold not leeuyn hir pride ne hir pompows aray þat sche had vsyd be-for-tym, neiþyr for hyr husbond ne for noon oþer mannys cownsel. And ȝet sche wyst [knew] ful wel þat men seyden hir ful mech velany, for sche weryd gold pypys on hir hevyd [head] & hir hodys wyth þe typettys were daggyd [her hoods were cut with decorative tippets]. Hir clokys also wer daggyd & leyd wyth dyuers colowrs be-twen þe daggys þat it schuld be þe mor staryng [stirring] to mennys sygth and hir-self þe mor ben worshepd. And, whan hir husbond wold speke to hir for to leuyn hir pride, sche answeryd schrewydly [sharply] & schortly & seyd þat sche was comyn of worthy kenred [kindred] – hym semyd neuyr for to a weddyd hir, for hir fadyr was sum-tyme meyr of þe town N. and sythyn he was alderman of þe hey Gylde of the Trinyte in N. And þerfor sche wold sauyn [preserve] þe worschyp of hir kynred what-so-euyr ony man seyd (2: 9).

For the misguided Margery, her ostentatious outfits are symbols of the respectability and good status which, she feels, are conferred on her by virtue of her father's office-holding. However, the passage condemns Margery's flashy clothing as a symptom of her pride, one of the seven deadly sins against which mercantile families, like Margery's, were instructed by contemporary sermons,

---

[32] For a complex discussion of the ideologies surrounding the dress of medieval women including Margery Kempe see Dyan Elliott, 'Dress as Mediator Between Inner and Outer Self: The Pious Matron of the High and Later Middle Ages', *Mediaeval Studies* 53 (1991): 279–308 (esp. 294–6 and 305).

[33] See, for example, Kandiyoti, 'Bargaining with Patriarchy', p. 280.

[34] For a discussion of credit networks in towns and the importance of trust see Gervase Rosser, 'Crafts, Guilds and the Negotiation of Work in the Medieval Town', *Past and Present* 154 (1997): 3–31 (9).

conduct literature and other moral texts to be constantly on their guard.[35] There was a fine balance to be gained between respectability and hedonism; enterprise had to be tempered by the virtue of self-control; money and profit were off-set by donations and bequests to charities, churches and other religious houses.[36]

The text depicts Margery's clothing as an anxiety for her husband because it is an emblem of her sinful pride. However, it is also an emblem of his inability to control and discipline her and a constant reminder of his inferiority to his father-in-law. The text is scathing about the sharp tone that Margery adopts to remind her husband of his social place. Her impudence is closely associated with her showy dress sense: both are indications of her wilful rebellion and John's failed masculine authority. The figure of the sinful young Margery is constructed in line with the depiction of evil wives elsewhere in contemporary moral literature where women who rebel against their husbands so frequently don outrageous clothing. Women who dress extravagantly are also seen, in these ethical discourses, as deliberately and wickedly sexually alluring.[37] This is not a suggestion which is explicitly made in the passage from *The Book of Margery Kempe*, although I think it is implicitly assumed. In the Middle Ages, women's sexual reputations were crucial to their respectability and, for a man's social respect, it was vital that he was seen as capable of protecting his sexual property.[38] As Owst notes, much of the invective against women's extravagant dress stressed its danger for men.[39] Again, Margery's excessive clothing carries a cultural message about John's insufficiency.

The *Book* describes how Margery comes to see the error of her ways and abandon her ostentatious dresses. What she does instead though is interesting. Kandiyoti has described the way in which women often signal their respectability and worthiness – their special bourgeois and protected status – through the adoption of super-modest dress and various forms of veiling.[40] Margery, of course, puts on a simple white dress when she forswears bright textiles and sophisticated fashions. However, far from this modesty placating her community, it is seen as another sign of her excess: a colour with multivalent religious and

---

35 For a discussion of dress in sermons see G. W. Owst, *Literature and Pulpit in Medieval England* (Oxford, 1966), pp. 399–403. Also see, for example, the anxieties about dress in 'How the Good Wife Taught her Daughter', lines 94–7 and 106 – Tauno F. Mustanoja, *The Good Wife Taught her Daughter, The Good Wyfe wold a Pylgremage, The Thewis of Gud Women*, Annales Academiae Scientarum Fennicae B 61/2 (Helsinki, 1948), pp. 159–72 – which Felicity Riddy has argued is an expression of patriarchal expectations of bourgeois women. Felicity Riddy, 'Mother Knows Best: Reading Social Change in a Courtesy Text', *Speculum* 71 (1996): 66–86.

36 For a discussion of Kempe's complicity in and critique of her community's commercial ethics see Kathleen Ashley, 'Historicizing Margery: *The Book of Margery Kempe* as Social Text', *Journal of Medieval and Early Modern Studies* 28 (1998): 371–88 (373–4).

37 See, for example, *On the Properties of Things: John Trevisa's Translation of Bartholomaeus Anglicus De Proprietatibus Rerum: A Critical Text*, ed. M. C. Seymour, 3 vols (Oxford, 1975–88), I, p. 309. Trevisa uses the phrase 'stout and gay' to describe the wicked wife which means, according to the *MED*, 'showily dressed'. However, 'gay' is a hard-working adjective which can also mean 'lascivious'.

38 Defamation cases brought by women were much more likely, than those brought by men, to concern sexual slurs. See, for a discussion of this observation, L. Poos, 'Sex, Lies and the Church Courts of Pre-Reformation England', *Journal of Interdisciplinary History* 25 (1995): 585–607 (esp. 586 and 591–6).

39 Owst, *Literature and Pulpit*, pp. 402–3.

40 Kandiyoti, 'Bargaining with Patriarchy', p. 280.

sexual significances which she puts on in order to get herself noticed (44: 103–4).[41]
This is extravagant, ascetic, religious dress which is on a continuum with the elaborate dagged sleeves and gold-trimmed headdresses, and overdoes what was
normal for a secular women. Margery thus presents a curious paradox, being
exuberantly and ostentatiously pious and modest; this confusion incites many
to shout at her their hope that she resort to more conventional expressions of
modesty and devotion. Christ consoles Margery about the abuse that she suffers,
tellingly using a metaphor about clothing as an expression of marital devotion:

> &, dowtyr, þe mor schame, despite, & reprefe þat þu sufferyst for my lofe, þe
> bettyr I lofe þe, for I far liche a man þat louyth wel hys wyfe, þe mor enuye þat
> men han to hir þe bettyr he wyl arayn hir in despite of hir enmys (32: 81).

Christ figures his relationship with Margery as an ideal of marriage in which out-
rageousness is a sign of exclusivity and intimacy, a love-token that he gives to her.
This fantasy of conjugal confederacy runs counter to Margery's experience of
earthly marriage: her husband does not collude in dressing her finely in order to
snub their community. However, when Margery gives up her fine dresses, takes to
wearing white and turns fully to God, John is represented as more supportive, often
rescuing her from potentially dangerous confrontations with others. He never
demonstrates the same unqualified approval that Christ does but the text often represents Margery and her husband in an alliance against her detractors which resembles that which Christ describes in the above quotation. The permissions she
receives for her travels and actions from both Christ and her husband authorize her
in the face of the opposition she encounters in her community. Indeed the respect
she shows each of them, and the support she receives in return, shows her con-
forming to social expectations about wifeliness and pious devotion in order to legitimate more eccentric, socially and religiously suspect kinds of behaviour.

Women as Preachers; Women and Preachers

One of the central strands of the Lollard challenge, the one that most shocks
Hoccleve and the one that implicates Margery, leading to her 1417 examination at
York and her denunciation as 'Combomis [Sir John Oldcastle's] dowtyr' (54: 132),
is the insistence that women should not be barred from preaching, despite Paul's
injunction at I Timothy 2: 12.[42] In response to this heresy Hoccleve produces a
misogynist outburst which is standard for the period but rare for his verse:

> Some wommen eeke, thogh hir wit be thynne,
> Wele argumentes make in holy writ!

---

[41] For a discussion of the possible meanings of Margery's white clothes see, for example,
S. Salih, *Versions of Virginity in Late Medieval England* (Cambridge, 2001), pp. 217–24.
[42] For a discussion of Margery in relation to Lollardy and women's preaching see Lochrie,
Translations, pp. 107–14. Also see, for a discussion of Margery's complex relationship to religious orthodoxy, Ruth Shklar, 'Cobham's Daughter: *The Book of Margery Kempe* and the
Power of Heterodox Thinking', *Modern Language Quarterly* 56 (1995): 277–304 (esp. 278). See
also John Arnold below.

Lewde calates! Sittith down and spynne,
And kakele of sumwhat elles, for your wit
Is al to feeble to despute of it!
To Clerkes grete apparteneth þat aart
The knowleche of þat, God hath fro yow shit;
Stynte and leue of for right sclendre is your paart. (Lines 145–52)[43]

This is typical of the kind of language which was used to discredit women and to bar them from roles in central institutions like the church. Men's privileged positions were reinforced by legal, medical and ethical discourses which described women as deficient, inferior and dangerous.[44] The last line, and especially the euphemistic word 'paart', is telling in its ambiguity: women's share or role is dismissed as insignificant with a *double entendre* which relates it directly to the 'defective' female anatomy. The word 'calates' carries the suggestion of sexual promiscuity, again drawing attention to the female body and displaying anxiety about the possibility of women taking on public religious roles. There are two references here to the common idea, from Aristotelian philosophy and medicine, that women were naturally less intelligent and weaker than men.[45] The word 'lewde' complains about women's lack of learning, which makes them unsuitable for particular vocations but does not question – although granted it was not normal to question – the social system which reserved access to training and education for men.

Instead, Hoccleve, in a direct and derogatory address, tells women to go and spin and card; small-scale textile production, which was usually undertaken within the household, was considered to be much more suitable work for women. This tirade sounds a lot like that which Margery encounters in Yorkshire from a group of men and women who accuse her of being a Lollard. They call for her to be burnt. The women threaten her with their distaffs – a major tool and iconic emblem for the process of spinning and, therefore, for women. Both men and women shout at her:

"Damsel, forsake þis lyfe þat þu hast, & go spynne and carde as oþer women don, & suffyr not so meche schame & so meche wo. We wolde not suffir so meche for no good in erthe" (53: 129).

The *Book* depicts not just men but also women, inculcated to accept particular roles in particular spaces, outraged by Margery's gendered offence, seeing Margery's resistance to fulfilling the domestic expectations of women as an affront to their own decisions to conform to those expectations. The suggestion that Margery is

---

43 [Some women as well, although they are not clever, / will discuss matters of religious doctrine / Uneducated strumpets! Sit down and spin, / And cackle about something else, for your intelligence / Is far too weak to contest such things! / That skill is reserved for great clerics / That kind of knowledge is shut off from you by God / Stop and leave off because your part is weak / scanty / underdeveloped.] David Aers has also discussed this stanza in relation to Margery Kempe in *Community, Gender, and Individual Identity*, p. 97.

44 For a discussion of medieval misogynist traditions see R. H. Bloch, *Medieval Misogyny and the Invention of Western Romantic Love* (Chicago, 1991), esp. the introduction.

45 Joan Cadden, *The Meanings of Sex Difference in the Middle Ages: Medicine, Science and Culture* (Cambridge, 1993), p. 23.

preaching, and thus demonstrating Lollard affiliations, is expressed in terms of the sexual division of labour. She offends not just against religious sensibilities but also against social form and gender normativity.

Margery defends herself at York against the charge that she has been preaching, arguing that she has never been in a pulpit and that she teaches, rather than preaches (52: 126). These are narrow but successful distinctions. She is presented in the text, not as a male mimic but rather as St Katherine, the great female orator who converted people to Christianity through intellectual argument, cogently expressed. Margery is equivocal enough on the issue of preaching, and orthodox enough when questioned on other articles of faith, that she is cleared of heresy by the archbishop of York. Men like Sir John Oldcastle, of course, could not resort to ambiguous performances in this way. The challenges that they made to the male exclusivity of the patriarchal priesthood had to be explicitly voiced objections that were more easily read and dismissed as heretical. Margery's challenges to the church and its personnel are matched and balanced by her deference to their authority. Continually seeking support from religious men – confessors, priests, bishops, archbishops and clerkly scribes – Margery shows herself willing to be led by them.[46] At the same time she acts in what were perceived to be unfeminine ways, in ways which encroach on male, clerical prerogative, and she is often less than deferential, denouncing clerics when she thinks they are sinful or misguided.

The nature of Margery's interaction with churchmen has divided critics: does she challenge them or defer to them? On the one hand her male amanuensis can be read as a fiction devised by the female author, Kempe, to legitimate her text, to present it as an unthreatening narrative, which was not just passed but also advanced by someone with a partisan interest in preserving old orthodoxies.[47] On the other hand Margery herself has been read as a clerical fiction devised by those in the higher echelons of the church to restore order amongst the ranks of lesser clergy.[48] Both arguments have been well made and are entirely plausible; that The Book of Margery Kempe can be read in these contrastive and incompatible ways is testament to the subtlety and complexity with which its protagonist is positioned in relation to male clerics.

Although the Book has sometimes been thought of as unsophisticated, its careful and equivocal manoeuvring around complex doctrinal issues, issues which were costing some contemporaries their lives, shows an impressive control. This can be seen, for example, in the following episode where Kempe manages and manipulates, to Margery's advantage, the seemingly indubitable authority of St Paul himself whose prohibition on female preaching so circumscribes her religious activities. In this episode Christ comes to Margery and reminds her of a

[46] For example, see the discussion of Kempe's amanuensis in Ian Johnson, 'Auctricitas: Holy Women and their Middle English Texts', in Rosalynn Voaden, ed., Prophets Abroad: the Reception of Continental Holy Women in Late-Medieval England (Cambridge, 1996), pp. 177–97 (p. 187).

[47] Staley, Dissenting Fictions, pp. 31–8, esp. p. 33.

[48] Sarah Rees Jones, '"A Peler of Holy Cherch": Margery Kempe and the Bishops', in Jocelyn Wogan-Browne et al., eds, Medieval Women: Texts and Contexts in Late Medieval Britain. Essays for Felicity Riddy (Turnhout, 2000), pp. 377–91.

previous visitation she has had from Paul, a vision that is not recounted elsewhere in the *Book*:

> "Dowtyr, I sent onys Seynt Powyl vn-to þe for to strengthyn þe & comfortyn
> þe þat þu schuldist boldly spekyn in my name fro þat day forward. And Seynt
> Powle seyd vn-to þe þat þu haddyst suffyrd mech tribulacyon for cawse of hys
> wrytyng, & he behyte þe þat þu xuldist han as meche grace þer-a-ȝens for hys
> lofe as euyr þu haddist schame er reprefe for hys lofe. He telde þe also of many
> joys of Heuyn and of þe gret lofe þat I had to þe" (65: 160).

Crucially St Paul does not retract his ban on women preachers; if Kempe were
to write such a retraction it would be commensurate with denouncing her
heroine as a preacher. Paul acknowledges the trouble that his pronouncement
has caused Margery and this disadvantage is neatly cancelled out by a promise of grace and a special place in heaven, a privilege from which women were
not automatically excluded. It is significant that Christ describes this
encounter: Paul comes to her at the command of Christ and it is with Christ's
permission and authority – an authority which surpasses Paul's – that Margery
can speak boldly. This is a carefully crafted episode: instead of setting herself
against the authorities whose writings justified patriarchal forms of power,
Margery undermines them through collaboration, performing a nifty, destabilizing trick.

Male Anxiety and Defence

> Who so hath right and nat wole it deffende;
> It is no manhode it is cowardyse. (Lines 177–8)

The word 'deffende' crops up frequently in Hoccleve's poem and squares
with what the scholars of masculinity tell us about patriarchy: that it is necessarily defensive.[49] Although the over-arching structure and the men in positions
of great authority may have been secure, the day-to-day arrangements of a
marriage or a family, which were arrived at through numerous compromises
dependent on personality and happenstance, must have offered opportunities for
women to negotiate more favourable relationships within which they were more
influential.

In a society without a police force medieval men were given legal authority
over, and responsibility for, their wives, children and servants. In the later fourteenth century that authority was being strengthened into an arm of urban
government.[50] Municipal authorities and guild ordinance writers developed an
ideal of a householder who was able to manage the complex and often youthful

---

[49] See, for example, Mark Breitenberg, *Anxious Masculinity in Early Modern England*
(Cambridge, 1996), p. 3.
[50] See Sarah Rees Jones, 'Household, Work and the Problem of Mobile Labour: The Regulation
of Labour in Medieval English Towns', in James Bothwell, P. J. P. Goldberg and W. M.
Ormrod, eds, *The Problem of Labour in Fourteenth-Century England* (York, 2000), pp. 133–53
(p. 151).

household population which would otherwise present a threat both to the city's social and economic stability and the interests of the incumbent authorities.[51] However, this was an ideal which was notoriously hard to live up to; the expectations upon men to reign over their households in this way must have been daunting.[52] This inevitable gap between theory and practice produces anxiety; indeed, it is often said by historians and sociologists that masculinity is inherently 'anxious', although that anxiety is historically and culturally variable, manifesting itself in socially specific ways.[53] *The Book of Margery Kempe* documents the paranoia that Margery arouses in some of the men that she meets: that she will tempt other wives away from their homes and lead them, Pied Piper-like, into rebellion against their husbands and their settled married lives.[54] The mayor of Leicester reads this power of female leadership into her white clothing – again clothing draws out the patriarchal anxieties about women who refuse to live by convention (48: 116). Her pious practice of charitable giving is thought by her servants to be a threat to the domestic economy and it may be the fear that she will incite such immoderate generosity in other household manageresses that alienates and worries some of her male detractors. Her community is deeply suspicious of her own rejection of her conjugal life, and of what David Aers has described as her 'energetic struggle against the nuclear family; its bonds, its defences in the lay community, and its legitimating ideologies'.[55]

However, Margery is also seen working within the boundaries of a normal marriage. Her abstinent and pious practices are granted to her as concessions by her husband; in turn those practices are bargaining counters with which she can negotiate a domestic arrangement which is amenable to her. I showed above the intricacy of the text's discussion of clothing and the way in which it structures the conversion narrative of its protagonist around the moral sub-texts about women's dress. More centrally the *Book* dramatizes the couple's sexual relationship as the battleground where the pair contest the terms of their marriage. In particular Margery is depicted as keen to obtain her chastity from her husband although he is unwilling to give up his right to sexual access – canon law and contemporary sermons taught that both husbands and wives owed their spouse a marital debt which they were obliged to pay.[56] On the road from York one day John asks Margery what she would do if a man threatened to kill him unless they had sex again; Margery replies that she would rather see John

---

[51] Heather Swanson, 'The Illusion of Economic Structure: Craft Guilds in Late Medieval English Towns', *Past and Present* 121 (1988): 29–48 (29).

[52] P. J. P. Goldberg, 'Household and the Organisation of Labour in Late Medieval Towns: Some English Evidence', in Myriam Carier and Tim Soens, eds, *The Household in Late Medieval Cities: Italy and Northwestern Europe Compared* (Leuven, 2001), pp. 59–70 (pp. 69–70), notes the ideal of the male householder was probably not often seen in practice.

[53] Breitenberg, *Anxious Masculinity*, p. 3.

[54] See Aers for a discussion of the masculine paranoia in this charge: *Community, Gender and Individual Identity*, p. 100.

[55] Ibid., p. 99.

[56] See, for a discussion of the marriage debt in canon law James Brundage, *Law, Sex and Christian Society in Medieval Europe* (Chicago, 1990), pp. 241–2. For a description of how it was incorporated into marriage sermons see D. D'Avray and M. Tausche, 'Marriage Sermons in *Ad Status* Collections of the Central Middle Ages', *Archives d'Histoire Doctrinale et Literaire du Moyen Age* 47 (1981): 71–119 (96).

killed than give up her chastity. John responds, with the force of canon law behind him, telling her that she is ' "no good wife" ' (11: 23). He then agrees to allow her to live chaste if she agrees to other terms. In particular he wants her to share a bed with him, to pay his debts before heading off to Jerusalem, and to give up her practice of fasting on Fridays and eat with him. His deal is set out in the language of compromise: ' "Margery grawnt me my desyr, & I schal grawnt ȝow ȝowr desyr" ' (11: 24). Nothing more is said about the first of these; the second Margery agrees to, showing the kind of autonomy Margery can buy with her independent finances; the third she says she will not compromise on, creating an impasse in their negotiations.

Although the text usually presents John as tolerant and supportive of Margery, when his bargain breaks down and he meets an outright refusal over the Friday fast he becomes angry. His anger spills beyond the verbal disagreement that might be considered a part of a normal conjugal argument and he threatens to rape her. A medieval man would not have been prosecuted for raping his wife; indeed marital rape was not recognized as an infringement of medieval law.[57] Of course, patriarchy is finally enforced by violence against women but resort to it also hints at its vulnerability and its inability to reproduce itself without coercion. The *Book* not only exposes this vulnerability but celebrates Margery's ability to counter and circumvent John's threats through her special alliance with Christ. Ultimately – and shockingly for one of the annotators of the manuscript who saw fit to moderate this section of the text – Christ tells Margery that he will kill John if he continues to refuse her a chaste marriage (9: 21, and n. 2); Christ never allows Margery to be a defenceless victim of patriarchal power.[58]

The *Book* shows that Margery's desire for chastity is sanctioned by Christ. Although wives, like husbands, were obliged by canon law to pay the matrimonial debt if asked, there were precedents for married couples agreeing to forswear sexual relations in recognition of the medieval moral preference for chastity over, even married, sex.[59] Indeed the text may be presenting Margery's dilemma as akin to some of the married female saints – like Bridget of Sweden, Cecilia, Dorothea of Montau, Mary of Oignies and Catherine of Sweden – who persuade their husbands to let them live chaste or fend off other sexual aggressors to maintain their chastity. These are narratives that were culturally sanctioned and yet gave women, like the heroine of *The Book of Margery Kempe*, a means of evading the ecclesiastical laws which governed their sexual lives. Like them, faced with the threat of sexual violence, Margery turns to Christ, who

---

57 James Brundage, 'Rape and Seduction in the Medieval Canon Law', in V. Bullough and J. Brundage, eds, *Sexual Practices and the Medieval Church* (New York, 1982), pp. 141–8 (p. 144).

58 Indeed, a fruitful line of inquiry would be to look at the masculine readers of Kempe's book and in particular the four annotators who were probably monks in Mount Grace priory. Lynn Staley, for example, has discussed the way in which they sanitized it for a new male readership in the fifteenth and sixteenth centuries. Lynn Staley, 'Introduction' to Margery Kempe, *The Book of Margery Kempe*, ed. L. Staley (Kalamazoo, MI, 1996), pp. 1–10 (esp. pp. 4–8).

59 See, for a discussion of these options, Jo Ann McNamara, 'Chaste Marriage and Clerical Celibacy', in Bullough and Brundage, *Sexual Practices*, pp. 22–33 (*passim*).

makes her safe by allowing her to give in over her Friday fast in order to achieve sexual abstinence. Indeed, he tells her that he only asked her to fast on Fridays so that she could later abandon the habit in order to gain that more significant prize. Her response to her husband echoes the terms of the bargain as he originally set them out:

> "Sere, yf it lyke ʒow, ʒe schal grawnt me my desyr, & ʒe schal have ʒowr desyr. Grawntyth me þat ʒe schal not komyn in my bed, & I grawnt ʒow to qwyte ʒowr dettys er I go to Ierusalem. & makyth my body fre to God so þat ʒe neuyr make no chalengyng in me to askyn no dett of matrimony aftyr þis day whyl ʒe leuyn, & I schal etyn & drynkyn on þe Fryday at ʒowr byddyng" (11: 25).

The text is keen to show Margery not capitulating under exceptional duress but inventing a tactical asceticism with which she can trade to achieve the things she most desires. Although this episode can be read as evidence for the deeply depressing fact of violence in the lives of medieval wives, the text itself chooses to turn it to its female protagonist's personal advantage, showing her in an intimate, exclusive coalition with Christ. *The Book of Margery Kempe* produces an ingenious manoeuvre and thus champions a woman who overcomes her unequal position in law.

Conclusions and Continuations

Finally, men must have traded in and softened their insistence on their strict legal rights in order to win the assistance and affection of their wives and families. Certainly John Kempe is represented as remarkably tolerant of his wife's eccentricities. The pilgrims that Margery travels with advise her that 'þei wold not suffren hir as hir husbond dede whan sche was at hom & in Inglond' (26: 61). While John sometimes pretends not to know his wife, Kempe represents this in a sympathetic way which pities him as weak rather than condemning him as uncooperative:

> he was euyr a good man & an esy man to hir. Þow þat he sumtyme for veyn dred lete hir a-lone for a tyme, ʒet he resortyd euyr-mor a-geyn to hir, & had compassyon of hir, & spak for hir as he durst for dred of þe pepyl (15: 32).

This should not be viewed, of course, as evidence of actual practice; John is as fictional as Margery and is so often a foil designed to show the *Book*'s protagonist in the best light, as she is at once tested and supported by her marriage partner and the patriarchal values he might be said to represent. However, in the representation of their marriage, the potential flaws in a seemingly indubitable system of masculine authority are exposed. Individual men were not necessarily part of an aggressive and oppressive hegemony; they were also men in need of their wives' support and affection. Felicity Riddy has argued that Margery's nursing of her husband during his final illness, through his incontinence and senility, empowers her with the knowledge that 'dying dethrones the patriarch'; the body with its attendant needs, needs which are so

often provided by female household manageresses, disallows absolute male
authority and self-sufficiency.[60]

A fruitful line for further research might investigate the representation of
men's bodies in Kempe's text. Margery learns how to care for her mentally and
physically incapacitated husband by imagining him as a version of Christ.
Indeed, Christ and John Kempe have much in common and a study which compared – or even contrasted – them, reading John's body in terms of the very emotional and physical responses that Margery has to the body of Christ would, I
think, produce some very suggestive parallels. While much has been said about
the feminine body in Margery's particular brand of devotion, Margery sees
Christ in the men around her. Often this is a result of a physical similarity: infant
boys, good-looking men and men with authority or charisma all remind Margery
of Jesus in his various guises (for example, chapter 35). She also explicitly con-
trasts her visions of the body of Christ with the demonic apparitions she sees
during her periods of mental illness of priests who reveal their genitals to her
(59). How might Kempe's representations relate to the understandings of the
male body to be found more widely in her culture? Many, like Thomas Hoccleve,
believed that the body, and in particular the male body, was a microcosm both of
society and of the universe, and so held that if the body of the individual was
disordered, this chaos would be replicated in the larger corporations of Christian
belonging. Kempe also has interesting things to say about the male body both in
and out of control. Much has been made of the bodily nature of women in the
Middle Ages but the history of men's bodies also needs to be written and represents a scholarly gap which could be creatively closed by the scholar of medieval
masculinities.[61]

[60] Felicity Riddy, 'Looking Closely: Authority and Intimacy in the Late Medieval Urban Home',
    Gendering the Master Narrative: Women and Power in the Middle Ages, ed. M. C. Erler and
    M. Kowaleski (Ithaca, NY, 2003), pp. 212–28 (p. 223).
[61] See, for a discussion of how we ought to rethink the subject of the body and gender in this
    way, I. Davis, 'Consuming the Body of the Working Man', in T. Walters and L. Herbert
    McAvoy, eds, *Consuming Narratives: Gender and Monstrous Appetite in the Middle Ages and the
    Renaissance* (Cardiff, 2002), pp. 42–53.

3

Lynn and the Making of a Mystic[1]

KATE PARKER

> Late medieval England contained, and had done for many
> years before Margery Kempe, many communities gov-
> erned by men whose wealth came from trade . . . Their
> elite was driven by the desire for economic success and
> security, for political power and social recognition.
> Perceptions, desires, and discourses were shaped by a web
> of economic and social relationships . . .[2]

In 1417 Margery Kempe left Lynn to travel to the shrine of St James at
Compostella (44: 106). Her retelling of subsequent events on her journey points
to Margery's social standing as a member of a mercantile elite as does no other
episode in her *Book*. Weather conditions had prevented her from taking ship from
Bristol for six weeks, and during that time she aroused local antipathy and suspicion. Margery was often mistaken for a Lollard and must have been well aware
of the dangers: William Sawtre, priest of Lynn, had been the first man sentenced
to be burned for this in 1401; he had made a public recantation in 1399 in the
churchyard of St James's, and on the following day took an oath to relinquish his
errors at the church of St John's Hospital on the main east–west thoroughfare in
Lynn.[3] At length she was summoned by Bishop Peverell of Worcester, an experienced Lollard investigator, to appear before him in his nearby hall.[4] She had the
presence of mind to ask a local worthy to accompany her. At first Peverell kept
them waiting, perhaps to intimidate her, and she seems to have been unsettled
by his sumptuously attired staff for she roundly condemned them for their inap-
propriate appearance. She then decided to quit the bishop's hall and stalked off
into the nearby church, like a seasoned general picking the ground for the ensuing encounter. Eventually the bishop came out to meet her and at this juncture
seems to have realised who she was and, in acknowledging this, made the most

[1] My sincere thanks are due to Professor Christopher Harper-Bill, for his helpful comments
and suggestions; to Professor Tony Goodman for his copy of the indictment for the 1405 riot;
and to John Arnold who first inspired me to pursue postgraduate research. This article forms
part of the context for my 'Lordship, Liberty and the Pursuit of Politics in Lynn, 1370–1420',
Ph.D. thesis, University of East Anglia (forthcoming).
[2] D. Aers, *Community, Gender and Individual Identity* (London, 1988), p. 75.
[3] John Foxe, *Acts and Monuments*, ed. J. Pratt, 8 vols, 4th edn (London, 1877), 3, p. 225.
[4] John Badby, burned for heresy in 1410, was condemned in Peverell's diocesan court. See
A. B. Emden, *A Biographical Register of the University of Oxford to A.D. 1500* (Oxford, 1957),
pp. 1472–3.

extraordinary remark of the whole encounter. Speaking to her almost as an equal, notwithstanding that she was a woman, a lay person, and a stranger, he said: ' "I pray þe be not wroth, but far fayr wyth me, & I xal far fayr wyth the, for þu xalt etyn wyth me þis day" ' (45: 109). He went further, inviting her companion to dine with him as well. Afterwards 'sche a-bood wyth hym tyl God sent wynde þat sche myth seylen, & had gret cher of hym & of hys meny also'.

One is struck by the complete change in the atmosphere before and after their encounter. At a stroke she had apparently changed from an unknown, troublesome lay woman of dubious religious orthodoxy into a welcome guest. It is noticeable, however, that he did not, like the archbishop of Canterbury, invite her into his garden to share her experiences till the stars shone in the sky (16: 37); nor did he invite her to talk to him for hours of the love of God, as Richard Caister had done (17: 38). Instead, Peverell invited her to dinner. Perhaps the contemporary description of him as 'of evil life and unseemly conversation who spent his life in the company of lords and ladies' explains his attitude.[5] His immediate comment at that initial encounter reveals his primary interest in her was the fact that she was 'Iohn of Burnamys dowtyr of Lynne' (45: 109), and *that* in Peverell's view was Margery's chief attribute.[6] Peverell knew Lynn: in 1377 he had been living in the Carmelite friary there.[7] Significantly, 1377 was the year when John Brunham was mayor of Lynn for his second tenure and when one of the more dramatic events of Lynn's history occurred, when the town attacked its lord, the bishop of Norwich. This may provide a clue to Peverell's apparent volte-face.

We learn elsewhere in the *Book* that John Brunham was mayor and alderman of the Trinity Guild in Lynn. Margery also could not forbear to explain, although she tells it against herself, that her poor husband, Kempe, should in her opinion never have married into her exalted family (2: 9). Significantly, she sees their marriage in terms of his marrying into her family, rather than the other way round. It is not easy now for the terms 'mayor' and 'alderman' to convey anything like the honour and respect, the 'worship', that was afforded these offices in the medieval period. Margery was born into the family of one of the most powerful and influential men in a powerful and influential town. (One indication of disposable wealth in Lynn is the fact that there were nine goldsmiths recorded there between 1408 and 1417, serving an estimated population of perhaps 5,500 people.)[8] Other rich and prestigious families, the oligarchy of Lynn, were her usual society. As a merchant and vintner, mayor, commissioner of the peace, collector, coroner and alderman of the pre-eminent merchant guild, John Brunham and his household would have been involved in international trade, local politics, royal service and merchant banking, all aspects of which were run

---

5   B. Windeatt, ed., *The Book of Margery Kempe* (Harlow, 2000), p. 224, n. 3592 in which he quotes Bodleian Library MS Arch. Seld. B. 23, fol. 114.
6   For a different view of this encounter see Goodman, *World*, p. 130.
7   A. Little and E. Stone, 'Corrodies at the Carmelite Friary of Lynn', *Journal of Ecclesiastical History* 9 (1958): 8–29 (20 where his name appears among the witnesses to a corrody).
8   K(ing's) L(ynn) / C(ouncil) 10/2 (*William Asshebourne's Book*) fols 15v, 16, 19v, 27v, 40, 41v, 42, 91v, 101v, 102, 125 and KL/C39/48 (borough account series). H. Clarke and A. Carter, *Excavations in King's Lynn 1963–1970*, Society for Medieval Archaeology Monograph Series 7 (London, 1977), p. 429.

from his home in Lynn.[9] He had widespread and influential connections: he was, for example, a fellow witness with the celebrated Richard Wittington, mayor of London, to a property transaction.[10] As we shall see, his astute leadership, and without doubt his willingness to place his personal wealth at the town's disposal, saved Lynn from financial and political ruin at a time of crisis, and set the seal on what was to prove nearly twenty-five years of unity and prosperity within his community.[11]

Margery's asperity towards Bishop Peverell (and in her other encounters) was doubtless bolstered by her firm conviction that she was beloved of God. But there was more to her self-confidence than that alone. It was the accident of her birth, her position as John Brunham's daughter, which gave her all the faculties she needed to become the Margery of the *Book*. She was an innovative and skilful manipulator of the English language. At different times she was an inveterate and wide-ranging traveller; and she was a socially confident participant at many a gathering, as at ease with clerics and bishops, as with aristocratic ladies. This chapter will describe the activities of Margery's social milieu in the late fourteenth and early fifteenth centuries, and show how the events which overtook her family and their town would shape the emerging mystic and author. The governing class of Lynn, of which Margery was part, had become masters at manipulating a complex structure of balance and counterbalance between powerful external interests. In Margery's lifetime these relationships were at first brilliantly manipulated to the town's advantage, not least by her own father. Later, national events were to exert insupportable stresses which caused seismic shifts in the erstwhile certainties of Lynn society. Margery was the product, at least in part, of these contexts.

Lynn's Geographical Position and Economic Background

Lynn stands at the south-east corner of the Wash, at the mouths of the river Ouse and of two smaller rivers: the Nar and the Gaywood.[12] In 1086 the site of the future town was an outlying area of saltmarsh, sand dunes and creeks (or fleets) of the manor of Gaywood, which then belonged to the bishop of Thetford (the bishopric was relocated to Norwich in 1091). To the south and west stretched the fens, a richly productive area crossed by several river systems which drained the inland upland areas. Until the late thirteenth century only the Little Ouse, Nar and Gaywood rivers flowed out through Lynn. Then the Great Ouse, which formerly ran to Wisbech, turned east, moving its course to exit at Lynn, opening a vast hinterland to the port. Thereafter water transport was possible as far as Bedfordshire and Warwickshire. Lynn had already provided access to the international Stourbridge Fair, near Cambridge. The town appears on Matthew Paris's map of

---

[9]   Evidence for John Brunham's career is reproduced in *BMK*, Appendix iii, pp. 359–62.
[10] *Calendar of Close Rolls 1396–9*, p. 224.
[11] See below, pp. 61–3.
[12] See D. M. Owen, 'King's Lynn: the making of a new town', *Anglo-Norman Studies* 2 (1979): 141–53, *passim*, and D. M. Owen, ed., *The Making of King's Lynn* (Gloucester, 1984), pp. 1–64.

c.1250 and, significantly for its international trading relevance, it also appears on an Italian navigation chart (c.1325).[13] To the west, along the southern edge of the Wash, were the towns of the silt fen, such as Terrington St Clement, Long Sutton, Gedney and Holbeach, which occupied, then as now, the most productive agricultural zone in East Anglia. East of Lynn was the highly populated area of west Norfolk, in which thirty religious houses were founded by 1300, testament to the wealth of the population and the productivity of the land which supported them.[14] Thus Lynn's broad hinterland was richly productive agricultural land which needed a regular outlet for its surpluses, and its wealthy inhabitants provided a market for a wide range of goods: luxuries, bulk raw materials such as timber, iron, coal, and building stone, and staples such as dried, smoked and salted fish and, crucially in times of dearth, grain from the north German plain.

Herbert de Losinga (first bishop of Norwich 1091–1119), who founded Norwich cathedral and the Benedictine priory of All Saints which served it, established a settlement at Lynn in his distant manor of Gaywood at the end of the eleventh century. At the request of 'his sons around the Lynn' he had started to build a church there and gave this to the Benedictines of Norwich, who created a dependent cell whose prior was to manage a Saturday market and a fair, and to provide a priest for St Margaret's church.[15] Within fifty years the town was booming, with an area of rapidly developing suburb to the north where Bishop Turbe (1147–74) founded his 'newelonde', effectively a second town (fig. 1). The bishop kept this second foundation for himself, in competition with the prior. By the turn of the century these expanding settlements were joined together by Bishop John de Gray (1200–14), under his own jurisdiction, as Bishop's Lynn, and acquired a royal charter from King John in 1204. In the charter the king confirmed the town's right to have its merchant guild (the same Trinity Guild which John Brunham was to head two centuries later, and which admitted Margery Kempe in 1438, in her old age). By 1216 Lynn also had a mayor.

Thus, the town into which Margery was born around 1373 was an episcopal town. Its spectacularly flourishing trade, particularly in wool in the thirteenth and early fourteenth centuries, had made it a prime source of royal revenue in export and import taxes and subsidies.[16] This gave the crown a keen interest in the town's prosperity, and its burgesses (those freemen who had been awarded the freedom of the borough as heirs of burgesses or their apprentices, or who had purchased that right for forty shillings) were royal officials who competed for influence with the bishop's bailiffs. In 1337 the d'Albini family's share of Lynn's tolls reverted to the crown, thus increasing royal interest in its fortunes.[17]

[13] British Library Cotton MS Julius D.vii, fols 50v–53; British Library. Add. MS 27376, fols 180v–181.
[14] D. Knowles and R. N. Hadcock, *Medieval Religious Houses: England and Wales* (London, 1953), *passim*.
[15] Owen, *Making of King's Lynn*, p. 68.
[16] As early as 1203–5 the customs records show that after London and Southampton, Boston and Lynn were the wealthiest ports of England. The post-plague subsidy of 1377 placed Lynn seventh among provincial towns and it remained in the top ten into the sixteenth century. N. S. B. Gras, *The Early English Customs System* (Cambridge, MA, 1918), pp. 221–2; M. McKisack, *Parliamentary Representation of English Boroughs during the Middle Ages* (Oxford, 1932), p. 143.
[17] *Calendar of Close Rolls 1402–1405*, pp. 30–1.

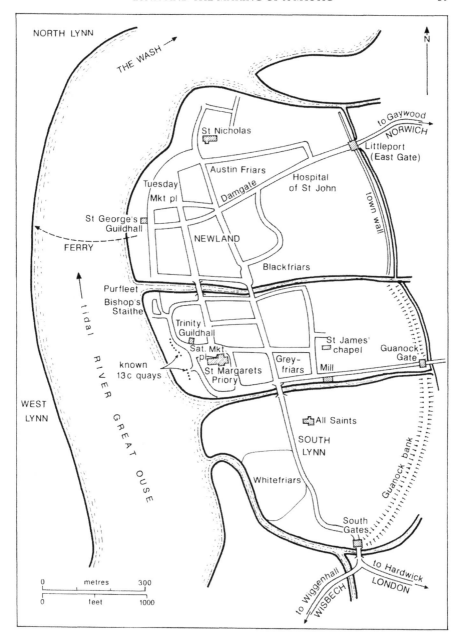

Figure 1. Lynn in the fourteenth century.

The Trinity Guild developed into the leading lay institution in the town. It provided spiritual benefits and capital for its membership and, since the mayor and council were in the normal course of events members of the guild, it also supplied financial backing for borough government as well. When John Brunham became alderman of the guild he was effectively elected to be simultaneously chairman of the merchant bank, leader of the senior lay religious organisation in the town, and pre-eminent personality in its social life as well. In this dynamic and entrepreneurial environment it is not surprising that the Lynn elite, in continual pursuit of greater autonomy and a freer hand in control of their affairs, was perfectly capable and even accustomed to play the bishop and the king against one another.

Not that the town progressed without occasional difficulties. During the thirteenth century the trade in the town was overwhelmingly concerned with wool exports to Flanders, much of which was managed by Hanseatic merchants; in the early fourteenth century Lynn men made a concerted effort to take over the shipping interests themselves, coming into direct conflict with the powerful *Hanse*. In 1302 the Hanseatic League initiated a boycott of Lynn which fomented enormous stresses and strains within the community. Internal quarrels arose which caused Bishop John Salmon (1299–1325) to impose in 1309 a 'Composition' or agreement on the town.[18] Among many other clauses, it stated that internal taxes should not be imposed by the rich on the poor of the town, but agreed by the whole community. Those disputes with the *Hanse* were settled in 1310, but similar problems arose exactly a century later which were equally disruptive and which directly concerned Margery's social stratum, the so-called *potentiores*, the powerful men in town. Then Bishop Salmon's 'Composition' came once again to play a prominent role.

After the Black Death the trade pattern changed completely. Records show that when John Brunham was a young man the wool business went into decline, and never recovered its pre-plague dimensions. Lynn merchants, including the Kempe family, moved their commercial interests further east into the Baltic.[19] They shipped cargoes, predominantly of cloth, to Danzig (modern-day Gdansk) and set up a trading colony there.[20] By the 1380s they had taken over 80–90 per cent of Anglo–Prussian trade. It was a time of spectacular opportunities for Lynn, despite the antagonisms engendered among the Prussians, who at one time said that the English merchants were becoming so powerful that they would soon ruin the country with their merchandise: in 1438 Danzig warned that the English would soon make Prussia a colony, like Gascony.[21]

When Prussia flexed its muscles and arrested English shipping in 1385, the crown entrusted John Brunham with the collection of money from all the merchants outside London who had connections with Prussia, to pay for a diplomatic embassy over there.[22] It must be assumed that the crown's choice of

---

[18] KL/C10/6.

[19] Owen, *Making of King's Lynn*, p. 331–3, no. 395.

[20] Ibid., pp. 278–80, no. 348.

[21] S. Jenks, 'King's Lynn and the Hanse: Trade and Relations in the Middle Ages', in K. Friedland, ed., *Proceedings of the Hanseatic History Union; Lynn, 1998* (forthcoming); *idem, England, die Hanse und Preussen: Handel und Diplomatie, 1377–1474*, Quellen und Darstellungen zur Hansischen Geschichte NS 38, 3 vols (Cologne/Vienna, 1992), 1, pp. 444–50; and *idem*, 'Die preussischen Hansestädte und England', in Z. H. Nowak and J. Tanxeci, eds, *Die preussischen Stadte und ihre Stellung im Nord – und Ostssraum des Mittelalters*, Ordines Militares – Colloquia Torunensia Historica 8 (1998), pp. 111–29; T. H. Lloyd, *England and the German Hanse 1157–1611* (Cambridge, 1991), esp. chs 2 and 3; K. Koppmann, ed., *Die Recesse und andere Akten der Hansetage von 1256–1430*, 8 vols (Leipzig, 1870–97), 2.2.221§ p. 178 (May 1438).

[22] *Calendar of Close Rolls 1385*, pp. 572, 578. Lynn's claim for damages against the Prussians totalled £1,913 3s 4d. Lloyd, p. 91. Cf. York's claim for £1,636: see L. Attreed, *The King's Towns* (New York, 2001), pp. 231–2.

Brunham for this task was dictated by the widespread respect in which he was held in those other ports. On that occasion there are records of him dealing with Beverley and York; Margery later visited both. She made several journeys to York and the friendly hospitality she received there may indicate some previous personal contacts between their families. Archaeological evidence from Lynn has revealed Yorkshire pottery as the most frequently found non-local ware throughout the period, witness to the close trading links which existed between the counties at this time.[23]

There were other, less concrete, links with Yorkshire: in common with the burgeoning eremitical movement in the diocese of York, Lynn supported several anchorites, and Norfolk is the only county which approaches the numbers of recluses in Yorkshire. Margery was familiar with John of Bridlington and William Sleightholme, whom she used as a confessor, as she did the Dominican recluse of Lynn. She advised members of the Yorkshire Neville family of Raby. She knew some of the works of Richard Rolle and Walter Hilton, both northern writers.[24] These contacts imply wide Yorkshire interests in the town, and the presence of a *potentior* named John Thoresby in Lynn then perhaps adds a further dimension: Thoresby is a village in Nottinghamshire, in York diocese, but a John Thoresby was archbishop of York (1352–73), and other Thoresby relatives held important ecclesiastical and secular appointments in the area. The John Thoresby in Lynn appears frequently in the civic records, and was ancestor to several mayors and other dignitaries, one of whom notably founded Thoresby College to house the thirteen chantry clerks employed by the Trinity Guild.

Politics at Home and Abroad

At all times the elite of Lynn were jealous of their rights, on the lookout for any opportunity to extend them, and ready to sacrifice a great deal in their defence. In April 1377 Lynn men felt, as they often had in the past, that their liberties were being usurped by their own bishop. A group of inhabitants (including a *potentior* and the town clerk) physically attacked Henry Despenser (bishop of Norwich, 1370–1406). It was doubtless due to Brunham's skill that Lynn was able to minimise repercussions to a mere fine. There can be few local fracas which have such a wealth of surviving incidental record, testament to the stir it caused far and wide at the time. Evidence for the attack survives from all interested parties: the bishop, the king, the town government, the local Franciscan friary and the chronicler of St Albans abbey. The *oyer et terminer* proceedings initiated by the bishop name twenty-three individuals who, with others, had assaulted him, chased him into the priory and besieged him there, and meanwhile killed twenty of his household's horses, and fought with his men and servants. A letter close from the king (or, more likely, from John of Gaunt since it is dated four days

---

[23] Clarke and Carter, *Excavations in King's Lynn*, p. 212.
[24] J. Hughes, *Pastors and Visionaries: Religion and Secular Life in Late Medieval Yorkshire* (Woodbridge, 1988), pp. 65, 68, 305. N. P. Tanner, *The Church in Late Medieval Norwich* (Toronto, 1984), pp. 57–66.

before the coronation and five days before the appointment of Richard's first Council) to the sheriff of Norfolk assumes there was fault on both sides of the quarrel, a stance which may be seen as an early example of Lancastrian bias in favour of the town. The community minute book records the award of two pensions of £50 each over five years to two Lynn merchants, as damages for injuries sustained in the mêlée with the bishop's household (later entries show these payments being made); the borough accounts itemise the expenses of men riding poste-haste throughout the county, calling in favours and drumming up support, even from so powerful an advocate as Joan, Princess of Wales. In the Greyfriars' chronicle the writer was of the opinion that the trouble was initiated by a few stupid people (*fatuos*) but noted that the town was put under interdict for two months.[25]

The fullest explanation comes from the chronicler of St Albans.[26] He described how the young and arrogant bishop, against the advice of the mayor and elders of the town, insisted that the mace, customarily borne before the mayor, on this occasion should be carried before himself. The bishop had conceded the undisputed right to free election of their own mayor as recently as 1352. For the townsmen the mace, the staff of office, was the symbol of their mayor's undisputed authority in the town. Such symbols, in a world permeated with symbolism, were imbued with immense power in themselves, and thus it might just as well have been the mayoralty itself which Despenser was usurping. One must not suppose, either, that the bishop was not fully cognisant of how his actions would be seen. There is no doubt that he was trying to put the men of Lynn in their place, and remind them that he was their lord, and all accoutrements of hierarchy and power in the town rightfully resided in him. The attack on the bishop in 1377 must be regarded as the result of several years of rising resentment. Despenser was never the archetypical churchman: he had been fighting in Italy in the *condottieri* for Pope Urban V when in 1370 the latter appointed him to the see of Norwich at the age of twenty-eight. Since then relations between the town and its lord had become increasingly strained. In 1373 he had already closed the grammar school being held in the church.[27] Such a move would have blocked the aspirations of local men for their sons' advancement. Throughout his thirty-six-year incumbency the town viewed him with guarded suspicion and, from time to time, even less favourably. The relationship was not helped by his decision to quarrel with the prior at Norwich cathedral.[28] Every move made by the bishop was staunchly countered by Alexander Tottington (prior 1382–1406). Any resentment fostered within the cathedral would inevitably have been transmitted to the leading burgesses in Lynn through the prior at St Margaret's. Furthermore, on two occasions the crown removed Lynn, together with his other temporalities,

---

25 *Calendar of Patent Rolls 1374–1377*, p. 502; *Calendar of Close Rolls 1377–1381*, p. 85; H. Ingleby, *The Red Register of Lynn*, 2 vols (King's Lynn, 1919–22), 2, pp. 134–5, fols 160d and 161; KL/C39/36; A. Gransden, 'A Fourteenth-Century Chronicle from the Grey Friars at Lynn', *English Historical Review* 72 (1957): 270–8.

26 V. H. Galbraith, ed., *The St Albans Chronicle 1406–1420* (Manchester, 1927), pp. 139–40.

27 Owen, *Making of King's Lynn*, p. 134, no. 125.

28 For details of this see I. Atherton et al., eds, *Norwich cathedral: Church, City and Diocese 1096–1996* (London, 1996), pp. 297–8.

from the bishop's control: after the abortive crusade to Flanders in 1384 and after the rebellion of the *Ducetti* in January 1400, in which Despenser was implicated through his nephew, who was one of the conspirators. It is no surprise that Margery viewed bishops without awe; she would respect those whom she considered good and spiritual men, but others, like Bishop Bowet, she could judge harshly. Lynn was never overawed by Despenser, and Margery followed the example set at home.

Once the 1377 attack had occurred Brunham rallied all available support and by dint of enormous expenditure the town was able to withstand this threat to its independence and prestige. The borough account for the year amounted to over £800 (£300 was more usual). It is difficult to make monetary comparisons with today's values, but one multiplier brings that account to a modern figure of more than £2,266,666.[29] The town could not have afforded the luxury of its principled stand without loans from the Trinity Guild.[30] In 1378 the guild loan account amounted in all to a massive £1,272 15s 7d. Following 1377 not one of the rioters was disciplined by the town: those who had suffered in support of its liberties were awarded pensions; all possible well-disposed nobility, gentry and lawyers were brought on-side, and the town was confirmed in its solidarity and common cause against the bishop. When, in 1381, there is evidence for attacks against the elite of other towns in the region, such as at Peterborough, St Albans, Bury St Edmunds, Cambridge and Norwich, there is no record of similar disturbances in Lynn. A popular stand had been made, and every man persuaded that he had common cause with the rest, rich and poor alike. John Brunham must be credited to a very large extent with establishing this cohesion and singularity of purpose. It was to last, in the main, for the next twenty-five years. It is, therefore, little wonder that the young Peverell should have been so impressed by John Brunham, and hence later by his daughter.

Lynn's Intellectual, Religious and Educational Environment

Michael Clanchy has noted that between 1100 and 1300 'an acquaintance with Latin became increasingly widespread. . . . Merchant dynasties . . . took on the social colouring of the landed gentry . . . [and] knightly merchants were as educated as other knights.'[31] A record made in 1738 details many Lynn merchants' marks then surviving in the churches, witness to the prestigious religious patronage of their owners.[32] Placed centrally on shields, mimicking the heraldic devices of the aristocracy, they appeared on misericords, on bosses, on memorials and on brasses. On the two surviving larger-than-life-size Flemish brasses of mayors

---

[29] I have used as a multiplier a priest's stipend averaging £17,000 p.a. in 2003 (I am grateful to Reverend Jan McFarlane, chaplain to the bishop of Norwich, for this information), assuming it to average £6 p.a. c.1400: *English Historical Documents 1327–1485*, ed. A. R. Myers (London, 1969), p. 729.

[30] KL/C39/36.

[31] Michael Clanchy, *From Memory to Written Record*, 2nd edn (London, 1979), pp. 187–8.

[32] B. Mackerell, *The History and Antiquities of the Flourishing Corporation of King's Lynn in the County of Norfolk* (London, 1738).

Adam de Walsoken (d.1349) and Robert Braunche (d.1364) and their wives, the figures are framed in elaborate architectural details, with angels, weepers and narrative scenes.[33] To the right of each man is a shield displaying the royal arms of England mirrored, on the left, with the owner's merchant mark (Walsoken) or coat of arms (Braunche) incised into a shield of the exact same size.[34] The use of the royal arms not only reminded their fellow townspeople of their close connection with the monarch, but tells us how these men saw themselves: members of an urban nobility. For them social status would have demanded a knightly education.

According to Clanchy, lesser merchants only needed to be able to read and write once they ceased to travel and directed business from their offices.[35] It is very likely that this was occurring in Lynn by the end of the fourteenth century. If the English merchant houses followed the same customs as the Hanseatic merchants, then the foreign business would have been managed for the merchants by junior members.[36] Margery's *Book* offers useful additional insights. Someone, possibly Margery's son, acted as her amanuensis, writing down everything she dictated in the short time before he died (Proem: 4). The story that Margery relates of her son's life (II, 1: 222) contains striking parallels. It seems probable that Margery's son was sent out to the Lynn community at Danzig, whither Margery later travelled with her daughter-in-law.[37] Late in the fourteenth century statutes for the Lynn merchant community in Danzig were drawn up because lack of order had proved 'to gret undoynge of menne yong men', one item being of interest:

Item if ther be ony of the cumpanye that ys prentys or servant and he be mysgovernd it is to seyve in disinge or pleyinge at the qwek or ony other disonest gamonis or kepyng dishaunttyngely to ony onnonest woman he schall be warnid and but yif he amendit with the wernyng . . . the cumpanye to wryte to hys mayster of hese mys gouernance.[38]

The remedy recommended was to write home to the culprit's master. There is no evidence of clerks being employed by the Danzig community. It is possible, therefore, that all the apprentices and merchants serving abroad needed to be able to read and write.[39]

After the death of Margery's amanuensis, we are told Friar Aleyn had recourse to his business associate for help in reading the manuscript because, as he says in the preface, the writing appeared 'neiþer good Englysch ne Dewch', being oddly

---

33 H. K. Cameron, 'The Fourteenth-Century Flemish Brasses at King's Lynn', *Archaeological Journal* 136 (1980): 151–72.

34 Edward III was indebted to both mayors for large loans. *Calendar of Patent Rolls 1334–1338*, p. 319; *1350–1354*, p. 145; *1354–1358*, p. 427.

35 Clanchy, *From Memory to Written Record*, pp. 187–8.

36 I. Origo, *The Merchant of Prato* (London, 1963), pp. 114ff gives further evidence that merchant houses throughout Europe employed youngsters to run foreign *Kontors* and depots.

37 *BMK*, pp. 225ff.

38 Owen, *Making of King's Lynn*, pp. 278–9; KL/C10/2 fols 6v–8.

39 Sylvia Thrupp considered that by the fourteenth century 40 per cent of English tradesmen could read Latin and more than 50 per cent could read English, *The Merchant Class of Medieval London 1300–1500* (Ann Arbor, 1962), p.158.

shaped and formed (Proem: 4). So the *Book* mentions two merchants in Lynn, her amanuensis and his associate, accustomed to corresponding personally, and in English. One could dismiss the literary efforts of Margery's amanuensis as evidence for rudimentary schooling, compounded by lack of practice. Or, alternatively, one could suggest that his willingness to write Margery's autobiography indicates someone accustomed to write easily and fluently and confident in his own ability to take down whatever Margery might dictate. The initial difficulties that the friar had in deciphering the original manuscript disappeared the second time he tried, when perhaps he had simply 'got his eye in', as palaeographers would say.

The question remains, however, where these merchants acquired their boyhood schooling. There is oblique evidence for the existence of schools in the town from the middle of the fourteenth century onwards, including two wills in which merchants left money for their sons' education.[40] Nicholas Orme detected a school 'by 1383'.[41] There must have been one earlier, however, because by 1361 a school was maintained in the parish church, the members of which had formed the Guild of Young Clerks of Lynn, meeting in St John's chapel there.[42] Moreover, as noted above, in 1373 Bishop Despenser made a point of forbidding the continuation of a school.[43] By 1389 the Trinity Guild stated in their reply to the crown's guild inquisition that they awarded regular sums 'to poor clerks keeping school'.[44]

There is no doubt that there were schools in the Lynn friaries: these provided the chief regional scholastic centres for the various orders. The provincial theological school in the Augustinians' Cambridge limit was located at Lynn, and also their *studium generalium*.[45] The Dominicans had a philosophy school in Lynn in 1397.[46] In addition, the cartulary of the Carmelites contains various corrodies which are signed by all friars present at the time. By this means we can see that the change in personnel was very frequent. As several friars were doctors of divinity and described as lectors, one of whom may have gone on to teach in Paris, it is probable that the Carmelites, too, were offering a course of study which friars would come to the Lynn house to attend for a fixed but limited time.[47] Such a course may explain the presence of Peverell there in 1377. The Lynn friaries produced nationally renowned writers, including John Capgrave (1393–1464), Friar Aleyn of Lynn (d.1428), William Welles, senior (d.1422) and William Welles, junior

---

[40] J. Beauroy, 'Family Patterns and Relations in Bishop's Lynn Will-makers in the Fourteenth Century', in L. Bonfield, R. M. Smith and K. Wrightson, eds, *The World We Have Gained* (Oxford, 1986), pp. 23–42, at p. 39, n. 43.

[41] N. Orme, *English Schools in the Middle Ages* (London, 1973), p. 306.

[42] Owen, *Making of King's Lynn*, p. 149: (PRO C47/43, no. 253). N. Orme, *Education and Society in Medieval and Renaissance England* (London, 1989), p. 30, for usage of the term 'clerks' for schoolboys.

[43] Owen, *Making of King's Lynn*, p. 133.

[44] See Trinity Guild rules in W. Richards, *History of Lynn*, 2 vols (Lynn, 1812), 2, pp. 454–67.

[45] W. J. Courtenay, *Schools and Scholars in Fourteenth Century England* (Princeton, 1987), p. 74, and Orme, *English Schools*, p. 231.

[46] H. J. Hillen, *The History of the Borough of King's Lynn*, 2 vols (Wakefield, 1978), 2, p. 708, and Orme, *English Schools*, p. 97, n. 2.

[47] See Little and Stone, 'Corrodies', pp. 9, 15–17.

(d.1440).[48] The mother-house of the Benedictine priory based at St Margaret's had a celebrated cathedral school to which continental scholars journeyed. Consequently, learning and books were part and parcel of religious life within the town.

Margery herself mentions the books which she knew well and says that a particular priest read to her for seven years. It is hard to believe that she was the only lay person who could have received such a service. One can perhaps imagine a number of people for whom mystical literature and the lives of continental exemplars, such as St Bridget, St Elizabeth of Hungary, and Mary d'Oignies were the staple fare, and the subject of much earnest conversation.[49] The influence of these and many others has long ago been discovered in Margery's own work. All of this goes to indicate that Margery was surrounded by a society accustomed to reading, writing, and books, and that she had access locally to better informed mentors and a more varied religious literature than might be supposed.

One of the many idiosyncrasies of the *Book* is that it is the earliest surviving English-language 'autobiography', and it is perhaps worth considering why this might be. It is true that Margery was not capable of composing in Latin herself: she states categorically in the *Book* that she did not know the language (47: 112–13). However, her amanuensis, the Carmelite Friar Aleyn, would have been able to translate her words if that had been her wish, so that in itself is not the reason. Julian of Norwich, an author using both Latin and the vernacular, was a contemporary whom she visited on a number of occasions. It is pertinent, perhaps, that Friar Aleyn was a member of an order committed to evangelising the unschooled of society. A book in English would be accessible to other unlettered folk, and was probably behind her decision to use the vernacular. The *Book* describes crowds of people thronging eagerly to hear visiting preachers, and they used vernacular exemplars. However, there were other instances in the political life of Lynn in the early fifteenth century when important Latin documents were translated into English for common consumption, and to inform and persuade a wider audience. The 1309 'Composition' was one notable example she would have known.[50] It is at least possible that the experiences of her own family, against whom that English translation was used as a weapon (see below) may have brought home to her the potential strengths of English work.

Margery and the Wider World

Margery would have enjoyed another advantage as the daughter of a wealthy merchant in that she would not have had to leave home at an early age, as so many young girls did as part of their domestic education, but would have stayed

---

48 P. J. Lucas, 'A Bequest to the Austin Friars in the Will of John Spycer 1439–40: John Capgrave O.S.A. (1393–1464), William Wellys O.S.A. (fl. 1434–40) and Augustinian Learning at Lynn in the Fifteenth Century', *Norfolk Archaeology* 41 (1993): 482–9.

49 For further discussion of such reading groups see Jacqueline Jenkins's below, pp. 116–8.

50 KL/C10/6.

there until she married.[51] It has already been pointed out that her father's house was the centre of his very varied business and political ventures. Whilst there she would have come into contact with the many foreign merchants whom borough custom and later English law required to be lodged with denizen merchants while they were staying in the port. To this, perhaps, one can attribute her ease with and even some fondness for Germans. Her son went off to Danzig, married there and had a daughter, which met with her full satisfaction (II, 1: 223). When she and her husband visited Canterbury, they stayed with a German merchant (13: 29). When Margery was in Rome she struck up a friendship with a German priest, who became her confessor (33: 82–3). When she nearly fell off her donkey in the approach to Jerusalem, two 'duchemen' rushed forward to help her (28: 67). Unfortunately there is absolutely no evidence for any personal contacts between any German merchants and Margery Brunham, although there must have been interest in her potential for prestigious family connection through marriage.

The frequent visits of foreigners to the town and to her own home, and the everyday comings and goings of seafaring men and merchants must have made distant travel second nature to the inhabitants of Lynn. The dangers were no less than they had ever been (and Margery disliked sea travel [II, 4: 233]), but what fears there might have been connected with travelling were countered by its very routine occurrence. Margery would have grown up seeing, and who knows, perhaps envying, the frequent departures of apprentices, brothers and cousins to distant places, and enjoyed on their return their travellers' tales. The responses of her travelling companions are usually reactions to her unexpected clothing, ostentatious crying, and narrow discourse rather than surprise that she should be travelling far from home, so perhaps her intrepid journeying was viewed as relatively unremarkable.

The Role of Women in the Urban Community

Margery's ill-fated attempts at brewing and milling have received some attention, particularly in an attempt to discover how much financial independence she might have had. Brewing was an ordinary female occupation, but a horse mill would have required a good deal more capital investment. She might well have been tempted into both because of the steady requirement for their products in ships' supplies. Anthony Goodman has noted that Margery's name does not appear in the Leet Roll brewers' listings, but that John Kempe's does.[52] This would suggest that there was nothing unusual in Margery's status, and that like many women she pursued such activities only by right of her husband. Nevertheless, Margery states that she did such things against her husband's advice, thus indicating that she had some control over resources which she could

---

[51] The life cycle experiences of a woman of Margery's status are explored in more depth by Kim Phillips above.

[52] Goodman, *World*, p. 70.

spend at her own whim (2: 10). Other evidence, although scant, from Lynn at this period suggests that some women, at least, were able to act on their own behalf, not only locally but in international affairs. A contemporary of Margery's, Margaret or Margery Wyth, who came from a similarly wealthy merchant background and inherited several properties in Lynn, had been married to a London merchant and grocer called John Lawnay. In 1414 William Asshebourne, the town clerk, made a note that Wyth had returned to Lynn to forward some business on her own account. She asked the mayor to counter-seal with his mayoral seal a bond she was making in favour of Bartholomew Chyolde, a Lombardy merchant, in the 'duchyssh' language, because her own seal was not known.[53] Asshebourne made other notes about one Margaret Galyon, wife of Roger Galyon who was mayor and alderman of the Trinity Guild in 1411–13. Her first husband, John Drewe, had been a member of a rich and well-connected Lynn family. When John Drewe died Margaret refused to manage her deceased husband's business, but some years later there were questions about this which Asshebourne recorded.[54] In the meantime she married Roger Galyon, and as his wife (not his widow) she appears in the Trinity Guild loan account of 1409 as a debtor in the sum of five pounds.[55] This would seem to indicate that, despite Margery's own inability to run a small business, other women could do so, and managed concerns of their own even when married. This might suggest that for a certain class of woman there was acceptance of independence and a certain autonomy. In the borough account of 1401–2, there is a note of rent received from an independent 'duchewoman' living in one of the properties owned by the town.[56] The fact that she was considered a suitable tenant for their property also indicates a confidence in her ability to manage her own affairs. She was possibly the widow of a Lynn merchant, although there is no indication that this was the case or any further explanation as to why a German woman should have become a tenant on her own account.

There is one more enigmatic inclusion from among Asshebourne's memoranda: a copy of a letter from a priest to an unnamed 'very reverend lady'. The writer thanks the lady for her efforts in suggesting a suitable marriage for his sister, which would not only be beneficial for her, but also, she has told him, have great advantage for himself. The priest excuses himself from coming to discuss this as he is ill in bed with all sorts of complaints. This intriguing scrap of correspondence presents many questions, and answers very few. What is particularly interesting is that the letter, between a priest and a nun or abbess, appears in Asshebourne's records of borough affairs. It does present, even without this puzzling dimension, a glimpse of the managing role that women could play in the social aspirations of a community. Women may have been sidelined by common and canon law: in reality, personality and status could obtain for women in Lynn an independence of action that documentary evidence elsewhere often fails to disclose.

53 KL/C10/2 fol. 22.
54 KL/C10/2 fol. 96v.
55 Printed in *Historical Manuscripts Commission Report xi*, Appendix III, pp. 228–9.
56 KL/C39/43.

The Fall of John Brunham and His Associates

In 1399 Henry IV usurped the throne. As the eldest son of John of Gaunt he inherited a Lancastrian antipathy to the Despenser family which dated back to the reign of Edward II.[57] When, in 1400, the king removed Despenser's temporalities, including Lynn, to royal control for more than a year, he installed his own man, Henry of Nottingham, as community clerk to the borough. Lynn already had close contacts with the Lancastrian affinity in the county: the town's retained counsel, Edmund Gurney, was the duchy's lawyer too. The reaction of John of Gaunt to the 1377 riot has already been noted. The influence of such powerful royal contacts at the hub of borough affairs must have been significant in the ensuing policy adopted by the oligarchy: between 1399 and 1406 (when Despenser died) Brunham and the five mayors in office embarked on an expensive anti-Despenser campaign. This cannot have been unwelcome, in view of the previous truculent attitudes of the oligarchy vis-à-vis the bishop.

Unfortunately, their financial security was about to be dangerously threatened. There was one major problem with the lucrative Prussian market: the town was so inextricably linked to Prussia for its commercial success that when anything interrupted this Lynn was bound to suffer.[58] A period of political instability in the early years of the fifteenth century, both at home and in Prussia, was to prove extremely damaging to this mainstay of Lynn's prosperity. Moreover, the bishop was not prepared to capitulate without a fight, and the policy soon led to heavy expenditure in bribes, legal costs and fines at a time when trade income was becoming increasingly curtailed, and when national taxation was rising steeply. The Trinity Guild, that financial bastion of town government for as long as men could remember, failed. The guild loan account for 1409 amounted to £1213 18s 7d, and it is not surprising if, in the harsh economic climate, guild members were pressing for further loans to support them.[59] However, on this occasion the income to balance the outgoings was simply not there.

The earliest indications of dissatisfaction occurred in 1405. By then the town had good cause to have become increasingly jaundiced by Henry's rule. Foreign and fiscal policy was causing disastrous interruptions to trade with increased imposts on foreign merchants, sudden closure of all ports, summary requisition of shipping and the removal of the wool staple from Lynn to Yarmouth. In June 1405 a northern rebellion was crushed at York and Archbishop Scrope and Thomas Mowbray, the Earl Marshall, were executed without trial. Both were subsequently regarded as martyrs, and Richard Scrope became the object of a widely popular cult.[60] This revolt had west Norfolk support too: Lynn's neighbouring magnate, Thomas Bardolf, had been one of the leaders, and was forced to

---

[57] Henry IV's maternal grandfather had been instrumental in the downfall and death of the two Despensers in 1326.

[58] Lloyd, *England and the German Hanse*, p. 94.

[59] *Historical Manuscripts Commission Report xi*, pp. 228–9.

[60] Hughes, *Pastors and Visionaries*, pp. 305ff esp. p. 308. On the cults of such political martyr-saints see also Katherine Lewis below, pp. 206–7.

flee to Scotland.[61] There was widespread horror and revulsion at Scrope's execution, and this reaction appeared to be given added justification by the king's sudden illness immediately after. Already by September 1405 practical measures had been instituted at York to curb the crowds of pilgrims to Scrope's allegedly miraculous tomb.[62] The close connections between York and Lynn have already been discussed. In October discontent with Lynn's anti-Despenser/pro-Lancastrian town management manifested itself, apparently in a food riot. However, as the matter was later the subject of judicial enquiry and an appeal to Parliament there is every reason to suppose that this was regarded as something more than a local crisis in food supply.[63] Cheaper grain was only part of the rioters' demands. They also wanted to depose the mayor and hold an election to elect another, and showed scant respect for royal authority.[64] The apparent loss of control in town governance played into the hands of the ageing Bishop Despenser who in 1406, only a matter of days before his death, was able to persuade Henry IV personally to endorse a reissue of the Composition of 1309. This gave strength and comfort to the 'mene and poure' of the town against the 'grete', those men, including John Brunham, who had so relentlessly countered his lordship since 1399.[65]

The largest debtor on the Trinity Guild account was the borough, which owed a total of £453 9s 2d. This sum is remarkably close to the debt of £457 19s 7d claimed back by the community from the five mayors under whom it was authorised. Individual expenditures amounting to this were *retrospectively* disallowed on the borough accounts made between 1399 and 1405 (the 1406 account has not survived). Achieving the reimbursement was not to be an easy task as the five mayors and their adherents had no intention of paying it back. They counterclaimed that they were owed £380 which they had spent on behalf of the town. Moreover, they insisted that, as mayors, they were indemnified against such financial liabilities because all decisions had been made in their official capacity. Their opponents, however, were well prepared and had devised a means of denying this argument once and for all. They took as precedent the decisions of Richard II's judges at Nottingham which had been used in the Parliament of 1397 to accuse the appellants of treason.[66] Richard had had a similar problem then as the anti-mayoral faction had in Lynn later: he had wanted to accuse men of treason when he had already given them full pardons – in other words to override a previously enacted indemnity. The ruse devised by his legal team was to accuse

---

61 Bardolf died in battle against Henry in 1408. His corpse was quartered and one quarter sent to Lynn to be hung in a metal contraption above the South Gates for several months. It cost the council 7s 6½ d in making the metal framework, taking it down and cleaning it, and in sums to the king's esquire who rode in with two other quarters to collect Lynn's on his way to reunite the bits for his widow to bury. KL/C39/46 and *Calendar of Patent Rolls 1405–1408*, pp. 317, 323.

62 See Hughes, *Pastors and Visionaries*, p. 305ff; *Cronica Monasterii St Albani*, ed. H. T. Riley (Rolls Series 1886), p. 410.

63 *Rotuli Parliamentorum* IV, p. 583.

64 PRO KB 27/580. The rioters told the mayor they would make him eat the wax seals of any royal writs procured against them.

65 KL/C10/2 fol. 13; and KL/C10/6 for the fifteenth-century English translation of the royal exemplification for the preservation of the bishop's liberties in the town.

66 KL/C10/2 fol. 13; M. McKisack, *The Fourteenth Century 1307–1399* (Oxford, 1959), pp. 448–9 and 484–7.

the appellants of 'an accroachment of power' and actions 'done without authority and against the will and liberty of the King and the right of his Crown'. So this was the same argument rehearsed in Lynn, and virtually the same wording was used to disallow the expenditures in the borough accounts. William Asshebourne made a copy of the judgments of Nottingham in his record book, and added his own opinion: 'whence it appears the misery arose'. The copy appears directly following a copy of the 1309 Composition which, it has been noted, states that financial decisions should be taken by the whole community. The Composition gave the anti-mayoral faction the leverage they needed to bring all and sundry to the Guild Hall to force the mayors and their adherents to agree to accept the decision of an arbitration panel of eighteen men, comprising some of each of 'the grete, the mene and the poure'.[67] So that people could be sure of what the Latin-language Composition said, an English-language version was made.[68] There can be no doubt that this was made entirely for the purposes of political advantage, and Margery cannot have been unaware of this since the action was taken against her own father and his fellows.

At sometime between 1411 and 1413 an auditor was brought in to check over the previous twelve years' accounts, and it is most likely that the amendments were written on the rolls then: they specifically name John Brunham and the five mayors as having 'dishonestly, unjustly, inordinately and wantonly' conspired 'against Henry Despenser, the late Bishop of Norwich and Lord of the same town . . . without and against the consent and agreement of the burgesses and non-burgesses of the assembly'.[69] The dispute at length descended to riot and affray between the factions, an eventuality which must have added to the bitterness of those who formerly had regarded themselves as the pinnacle of town society.[70] It was possibly the unimpeachable legal precedent behind this case that led to nearly a decade of wrangling between the parties, drawing in three successive bishops of Norwich, the chancellor of England, the archbishop of Canterbury, Thomas Beaufort, and finally both Henry IV and Henry V, all of whom tried to arbitrate between the disputing factions. Because no one, with commendable discretion, would explain to these noble and exalted persons exactly how the quarrel arose – and I would argue that this was partly disaffection with Henry IV – they were consequently hampered in their efforts to effect a successful compromise.[71] Henry V, at least, seems to have had an inkling that there was much more

---

[67] John Cressyngham, skynner, who had been named first among the rioters in 1405 was named as one of the eighteen arbitrators. The English translation of the 1309 Composition describes the 'grete, the mene and the poure', but in the Latin language documents they are described as *potentiores, mediocres, et inferiores non burgenses*. Cressyngham was included in the latter description. Some individuals who were also named among the *inferiores non burgenses* would seem to have been better described simply as non burgesses, rather than 'poure', although William Asshebourne seems to have lumped all these individuals together, whether 'poure' or not. Asshebourne recorded very large attendances in the Guild Hall – on occasion as many as four hundred people 'by estimation'. KL/C6/3.

[68] KL/C10/6.

[69] KL/C39/45.

[70] KL/C10/2 fols 105v–109.

[71] There is further evidence for a swing in affiliation towards Prince Henry's faction away from that of the king after 1409 which is discussed in Kate Parker, 'Lordship, Liberty and the Pursuit of Politics in Lynn, 1370–1420' Ph.D. thesis, University of East Anglia (forthcoming).

to these disputes than mere settlement of debts.[72] By 1420 most of the old guard, the former mayors, the tainted King Henry IV – and Margery's own father – had died and Bishop Wakeryng (1415–25) was able to effect a compromise which endured until Henry VIII acquired the town, thereafter to be known as King's Lynn.

Conclusion

In the early fifteenth century national events caused a shift in the political climate in Lynn which brought down Margery's social group and must have been personally distressing to her. She had been brought up as the daughter of a wealthy, successful and honoured man. Her whole upbringing would have persuaded her that she was to be respected and deferred to. The long years of political harmony which existed in the town must have led her to assume that the status quo was unassailable and secure. After 1399 the political and commercial difficulties which overwhelmed the town were to overthrow those social certainties which had been the bedrock of her existence. Her husband's business was ruined and she had to use her own inheritance to pay his debts. The most constant of the experiences recounted in the *Book* is that of the shame, humiliation and isolation meted out to her by her fellow townsmen and women, and indeed by people everywhere: 'sche sufferyd meche despyte & meche schame in many dyvers cuntreys, cyteys, & townys, thankyd be God of alle' (44: 104). She felt that these experiences were the mainstay of her conversion: as she described it, 'Lord Cryst Jhesu . . . turnyd helth in-to sekenesse, prosperyte in-to adversyte, worshep in-to repref, and love in-to hatered' and 'þan was pompe & pryde cast down & leyd on syde' (Proem: 1).

One cannot but be struck by the parallels of endurance suffered by those closest to her, who at a stroke, and one can argue through no fault of their own, were subjected to the reproof and even physical attack of their fellow townsmen. Her beloved father and his colleagues had governed in good faith and yet were derided and vilified as having acted not merely in derogation of good governance, but 'dishonestly, unjustly, inordinately and wantonly'. They were accused of failing to honour the lordship of the bishop implying the opposite of good governance, the promulgation of rebellion against a rightful lord. Their reverses were all the more striking because the town had hitherto been so united and consensual in its relationships. Margery's descriptions of the town's disparagement of her own spiritual manifestations mirror that endured by her friends and family. The constant reassurance by Jesus that this suffering was pleasing to him must have given comfort and justification both for herself and her family. It could have offered an explanation of these upsetting events, for her as for them, to regard this total reversal of public opinion as God's testing of the righteous, honing

---

72 *Calendar of Inquisitions Miscellaneous 1399–1422*, no. 517 pp. 289–91 – 'concerning divers dissensions, discords and debates which have continued for no small time and still do so daily between the mayor and certain of the burgesses of King's Lynn and certain other burgesses and the commonalty of the town, since the king . . . has so far been unable to induce the parties to compromise, negotiate and make a final agreement . . . or to obtain true knowledge of the cause'.

them for heaven – as Dame Julian explained it to her, like the smith burnishing his chosen metal with the rasp (18: 44).

This chapter has described the turbulent social, political and financial *boule-versements* which Margery's immediate family suffered at the period she was later to recall as pivotal to her own spiritual experience. It provides a fuller local context to the *Book* than has hitherto been available and has sought to show how local politics may have provided the emerging mystic with both reason and justification for her career and authorship. She herself felt assured of her place in heaven, but her strenuous piety was performed not only for Christ but for the benefit of those she knew. As she was to advise about charitable giving: 'it was mor almes to helpyn hem þat þei knewyn wel for wel dysposyd folke & hir owyn neybowrys þan oþer strawngerys whech þei knew not' (24: 56).

4

Margery's Trials: Heresy, Lollardy and Dissent[1]

JOHN H. ARNOLD

Introduction: Are you, or have you ever been, a Lollard?

> Than sche went owt of þe monastery, þei folwyng & cry-
> ing vp-on hir, "Þow xalt be brent [burnt], fals lollare. Her
> is a cartful of thornys redy for þe & a tonne [barrel] to bren
> þe wyth." And þe creatur stod wythowtyn þe ӡatys [out-
> side the gates] at Cawntyrbery, for it was in þe euening,
> mech pepyl wonderyng on hir. Þan seyd þe pepyl, "Tak &
> bren hir." . . . And a-non, aftyr sche had mad hir prayerys
> in hir hert to owyr Lord, þer komyn tweyn fayr ӡong men
> [two fair young men] & seyd to hir, "Damsel, art þow non
> eretke [heretic] ne no loller [Lollard]?" And sche seyd,
> "No, serys, I am neyþyr eretyke ne loller" (13: 28–29).

To ask, in chorus with the two handsome young men, whether or not Margery is a heretic is a more complex question than may first appear. Historiographical opinion has usually dismissed the charges on Margery's behalf, suggesting that she is clearly not 'guilty', not 'one of those'.[2] But this response perhaps fails to recognise (and hence becomes complicit with) the manipulative call of the question: to draw doctrinal lines, placing Margery on one side and 'Lollards' on the other. Not only is heresy in the eye of the beholder, but the *charge* of heresy is always linked to a particular historical moment, and depends upon the historical context (the shape of theology, the strictures of practice, the relationship between church and secular power) for its sustainability or otherwise. And it is a charge always open to revision: the French mystic Marguerite Porete was burnt in 1310, but her *Mirror of Simple Souls* lived on as an orthodox devotional text; Joan of Arc was executed, then later rehabilitated (and eventually, in the twentieth century, sanctified); in 1382 John Wyclif retired to Lutterworth but some years after his death was dug up and burnt. So to ask whether Margery was a heretic we might

---

[1] For discussion, references, comments and the reading of drafts, I am most grateful to Andrew Finch, Shannon McSheffrey, Peter Biller, Katherine Lewis, Simon Middleton and Victoria Howell.
[2] For example, R. N. Swanson, *Church and Society in Late Medieval England* (Oxford, 1989), p. 337. Note however the suggestion by Charity Scott Stokes that Kempe may have had Lollard sympathies in her younger days: 'Margery Kempe: Her Life and the Early History of Her Book', *Mystics Quarterly* 25 (1999): 9–67 (25).

fairly answer 'no', since her several encounters with legal processes failed to convict her; but we might also answer 'nearly', since (the *Book* tells us) many people *wanted* her to be a heretic, and attempted to make that ascription stick.

If we widen the field from heresy to dissent, the issue grows yet more complicated. Various modern authors have celebrated Kempe as a dissenter, challenging the repressive forces of her time.[3] But what is the nature of dissent, and what is the nature of the orthodoxy – social, political or religious – from which it demurs? In the particular case of Kempe, are we talking about the figure (whether 'real' or a textual character) of Margery herself, interacting with people such as the crowd at Canterbury; or are we discussing the *Book* and its position as a piece of late medieval writing, in relationship to potential readerships and perceived censors? My working assumption, for the purposes of this essay, is that there was a real, living woman from Lynn and that she was active in the creation of the *Book*; but that the *Book* is, indubitably, a text. No simple relationship can be assumed between what is written and historical reality; we might, for example, wonder whether the Canterbury crowd really did have a 'cartful of thorns' and a barrel standing ready. As for all historical sources, there are questions of representation and production. This does not, however, prevent us from attempting to examine the emphases and elusions within the *Book* in relation to their historical contexts. This chapter focuses particularly on the historical events, as represented in the *Book*, with a few further thoughts on the composition of the text. It will: (1) explore the context of heresy in England; (2) examine in some detail the arrests and trials Margery experienced; and (3) consider the relationship between heresy, dissent, and Kempe's faith. Throughout I am interested not only in trying to understand better what happened to Margery and why, but also what her experiences tell us about orthodoxy and heresy in England at this time. And my project, whilst sympathetic to the aims of those who position Margery as a heroic dissenter, is to place such readings under question.

'Are you neither a heretic nor a Lollard?' Was there, in this question, some meaningful distinction drawn between a heretic and a Lollard? To concentrate first upon the former label, the meaning depends upon the context, in several ways. 'Heretic' was a label to be thrown at one's enemies to see if it would stick. Legally – where perhaps it mattered most – a heretic was someone who held a view contrary to the opinion of the church, and *stubbornly defended it*. The stubbornness mattered: it was the refusal to accept ecclesiastical correction that placed one in the legal category of 'heretic'. But the figure of the heretic also had an existence in polemic, extending beyond this more specific usage. As one kind of 'Other' against which the orthodox centre could construct itself, a number of tropes were associated with heresy: that it was madness, devilish, a poison, and frequently hid behind a veil of false piety. Thus, when Margery Kempe was berated as a 'false ypocryte' (15: 33), 'false lollare' (13: 28) and 'fals deceyuer of þe pepyl' (46: 112), one way of reading such calumnies is through a tradition of anti-heretical language stretching back over many centuries. Similarly, the priest who accosted her in York minster saying, ' "Þu wolf,

---

3   For example Staley, *Dissenting Fictions*; Ruth Shklar [Nissé], 'Cobham's Daughter: *The Book of Margery Kempe* and the Power of Heterodox Thinking', *Modern Language Quarterly* 56 (1995): 277–304; Lochrie, *Translations*.

what is þis cloth þat þu hast on?"' (50: 120) was perhaps drawing upon the familiar trope of the heretic as a wolf in sheep's clothing.[4] On the various occasions when
people accuse Kempe of having a 'devil' inside her, this may be read as more than
a figure of speech: devils did inspire people to speak cunning words of evil, heresy
dressed up as piety.[5]

What, then, was a Lollard? Let us answer firstly from the viewpoint of
medieval orthodox commentators. In the 1370s, at Oxford, the theologian John
Wyclif had developed a number of controversial positions: an emphasis upon the
'literal sense' of scripture and the desirability of making it accessible to the laity
through vernacular translation; calls for the disendowment of the church; criticism of the cult of saints and the mechanisms of salvation; and, worst of all,
doubt that the Eucharist truly involved the sacramental transformation of bread
and wine into the body and blood of Christ. Despite the ecclesiastical condemnation of these ideas the theology had apparently spread, first to other Oxford
scholars, and then more widely. After Wyclif's death, it was believed that a 'sect'
adhered to his beliefs, and these people were known as Lollards. They were
heretics, schismatics and seditious – a threat not only to the church but also to
the secular power. They met in secret conventicles, and spread their beliefs
through preaching and through books; they were, to orthodox medieval eyes, a
pestilence. However, we must supplement this picture with modern historians'
views. These, of course, have varied. On the one hand, there are those who see
Lollards as a small-scale, ultimately irrelevant popular response to Wyclif's
teachings – a disparate bunch whose appearance as a 'movement' or sect
depends more upon the paranoia of medieval bishops and the enthusiasm of
modern historians than any innate coherence or strength.[6] On the other, there are
those who have depicted a well-informed network whose thoughts continued to
rest upon a Wycliffite tradition of theology, posing a coherent reform movement
that foreshadowed sixteenth-century changes.[7] In between one finds a variety of
positions, varying in the degree of stability, importance, size, coherence, and
connection to Wyclif they ascribe to Lollardy.[8]

To understand what connected Margery with Lollardy in the minds of
(amongst others) the Canterbury citizens we need to chart a little more of what

---

[4] As Barry Windeatt notes, Richard II had, in 1399, forbidden entry into England of a 'new
sect . . . dressed in white clothes and pretending a great holiness', who may have been the
Flagellant Albi or Bianchi connected to the papal jubilee (*Rotuli Parliamentorum* III, p. 428).
However, some fifteen years lay between this unrepeated legislation and Kempe's experiences. A different possible context for reactions to the white clothing is presented by its use
by certain indigenous religious orders such as the Cistercians and the Bridgettines; see Sarah
Salih, *Versions of Virginity in Late Medieval England* (Cambridge, 2001), pp. 217–24.

[5] On speech, devils and authority see Sarah Beckwith, 'Problems of Authority in Late
Medieval English Mysticism: Language, Agency and Authority in *The Book of Margery
Kempe*', *Exemplaria* 4 (1992): 171–99 (192).

[6] See, to differing degrees, K. B. MacFarlane, *John Wycliffe and the Beginnings of English Non-
conformity* (London, 1952); Swanson, *Church and Society*; E. Duffy, *The Stripping of the Altars:
Traditional Religion in England 1400–1580* (New Haven, 1992).

[7] Pre-eminently the highly influential Anne Hudson, *The Premature Reformation: Wycliffite Texts
and Lollard History* (Oxford, 1988).

[8] For a recent summary (though from a more conservative and MacFarlane-esque position
than it proclaims) see Richard Rex, *The Lollards* (Houndmills, 2002).

had happened – or what, at any rate, people thought or had been told had happened – in England during the previous thirty years. Detailed analyses of Wycliffite activity, ecclesiastical reaction and parliamentary legislation are available elsewhere.[9] For the purposes of this essay, let us just speed quickly through some key moments. The uprising of 1381 led some legislators and chroniclers to connect Wycliffite theology to rebellion, and began the initial push for laws against heretical and seditious preaching.[10] After 1382 a number of academics and clergy at Oxford (including Philip Repingdon, later to meet Margery Kempe) were prosecuted for their Wycliffite beliefs; they largely backed down and 'corrected' themselves. In 1395, twelve 'conclusions' of Lollard belief were posted up at Westminster, apparently as a kind of petition to Parliament. This probably formed the first public sense of what 'Lollardy' stood for, and was long (if not always accurately) remembered. A handful of prosecutions and subsequent abjurations, often of clergymen, were conducted in the last decade of the fourteenth century. The death sentence for Lollardy was introduced in 1401. In that year Archbishop Thomas Arundel – another person to later encounter Kempe – had the first person burnt for heresy: William Sawtre, a priest from Lynn, Margery's home town. Arundel drew up 'Constitutions' in 1407 that aimed to police religious discourse, specifically banning the publication of Wycliffite works, and vetting vernacular religious writings. In 1410 John Badby, a layman with arguably Wycliffite (but somewhat individual) views, was burnt at Smithfield.

Perhaps most importantly, regarding Kempe's experiences, in January 1414 an attempted revolt supposedly led by the Lollard knight Sir John Oldcastle was put down swiftly and efficiently. Although Oldcastle himself was not captured until 1417, the majority of the rebels were arrested and tried in 1414 and 1415. A parliamentary commission had ordered a report from twenty-two shires on the presence or otherwise of Lollards and seditionaries. Around 250 people were arrested (considerably fewer than the supposed '20,000 men' feverishly imagined by the chroniclers), of whom about 50 were tried for Lollardy and rebellion, another 100 for rebellion alone, and the remainder simply for Lollardy. Thirty-eight were executed in the immediate aftermath of the revolt (on 13 January 1414) and another seven in the later investigations.[11] Whatever the truth behind the 'rebellion' – Paul Strohm has recently argued that it was at least stage-managed, and perhaps entirely invented, by the authorities – the investigatory commissions ensured that both secular and ecclesiastical authorities were keyed up for the presence of dangerous, seditionary heretics.[12] It was immediately following this fraught period, with Oldcastle still on the loose, that Kempe found herself before a variety of tribunals.

---

9   H. G. Richardson, 'Heresy and the Lay Power under Richard II', *English Historical Review* 51 (1936): 1–28; Peter McNiven, *Heresy and Politics in the Reign of Henry IV: The Burning of John Badby* (Woodbridge, 1987); M. Aston, 'Bishops and Heresy: The Defence of the Faith', in *eadem, Faith and Fire: Popular and Unpopular Religion, 1350–1600* (London, 1993), pp. 73–93.
10 *Rot. Parl.* III, pp. 124–5.
11 Edward Powell, *Kingship, Law and Society: Criminal Justice in the Reign of Henry V* (Oxford, 1989), pp. 141–167.
12 Paul Strohm, *England's Empty Throne: Usurpation and the Language of Legitimation 1399–1422* (New Haven, 1998), pp. 63–100.

Understanding the contemporary suspicions of Margery Kempe can therefore lead us both to consider very broad contexts – medieval ideas and fears about holiness, authenticity and dissent – and also some very specific ones. Understanding her experiences depends in part upon deciding where the contextual balance should go. A broad view might note, for example, that for several centuries before Kempe's time ecclesiastical writers had depicted women as having a particular predilection for heresy. We might therefore suspect that this misogynist trope affected Margery's experiences; except that in the particular context of early fifteenth-century England, contemporaries do *not* seem to have strongly associated women with Lollardy in this period.[13] Even by 1420 only thirty or so women had found themselves questioned by bishops about heresy.[14] It is difficult even to decide how much of fifteenth-century English experiences of heresy can contextualise the *Book*: if we consider events up to the final composition of the text, one might legitimately discuss it in connection with the Norwich heresy trials of 1428–31. However, if we focus upon the events the *Book* depicts (problems with precise dating notwithstanding), those cases lay a decade in the future. In 1417, the year in which Margery encountered her most serious legal problems, an English bishop would not have experienced these kinds of inquiries. Such a bishop – Philip Repingdon, for example – would have had a different mixture of earlier precedents, orders and images in mind when encountering Margery. There were, for example, countrywide mandates against unlicensed preachers stretching back several decades, and Repingdon had particular worries in 1417 about Lincoln citizens hearing unlicensed sermons (apparently by Franciscans) preached in the vernacular. Perhaps more acutely, in November 1413 he, with other English bishops, had received a mandate for Oldcastle to be denounced in all churches, and a copy of Oldcastle's trial.[15] In February 1414 Repingdon cited his clergy to attend a chapterhouse meeting as part of an episcopal enquiry into heresy that he believed was widespread within Lincoln. There was also (presumably later in 1414, though the entry is undated) a commission for a regular investigation into heresy: three or four representatives from each parish were to appear under oath before the bishop's commissaries, to report on whether any heresy was known or suspected in their locality.[16] These, then, were the immediate contexts for a

---

[13] Shannon McSheffrey, *Gender and Heresy: Women and Men in Lollard Communities 1420–1530* (Philadelphia, 1995), p. 11. For different views – but largely discussing later evidence – see Claire Cross, ' "Great Reasoners in Scripture": The Activities of Women Lollards, 1380–1530', in D. Baker, ed., *Medieval Women*, Studies in Church History subsidia 1 (Oxford, 1978), pp. 359–80; and Margaret Aston, 'Lollard Women Priests?', *Journal of Ecclesiastical History* 31 (1980): 441–63. Goodman's comment (*Margery Kempe*, p. 143) that 'Lollard women . . . had long been denounced for expounding scripture' is a rather chronologically loose reading of Aston's article.

[14] Shannon McSheffrey, 'Women in Lollardy, 1420–1530: Gender and Class in Heretical Communities', Ph.D. thesis, University of Toronto (1992), pp. 30–5. I am very grateful to the author for this source, and for discussion and advice on the topic.

[15] *Register of Bishop Philip Repingdon, 1405–1419*, ed. Margaret Archer, 3 vols, Lincoln Record Society 57 (1963), 58 (1964), 74 (1982), I, pp. 7–8; III, p. 180; III, pp. 10–13. For the full text circulated regarding Oldcastle, see *Register of Nicholas Bubwith, bishop of Bath and Wells 1407–1424*, ed. T. S. Holmes, 2 vols, Somerset Record Society 29 and 30 (1914): I, pp. 154–64.

[16] *Reg. Repingdon*, II, pp. 379–80; III, pp. 193–94, this following the 1414 Convocation.

bishop encountering doubtful orthodoxy. It is difficult to know what legal actions specific bishops took against heretics, because trial records only infrequently enter the episcopal registers. We do, however, catch sight of Repingdon ordering proceedings against some Oxfordshire Lollards, public penance in Lincoln cathedral for people suspected of Lollardy and the protection of Lollards, the examination of books belonging to a suspected vicar (and subsequently against the vicar himself) and, in 1417, against followers of Oldcastle.[17] Perhaps most interestingly, given Kempe's experiences, in June 1417 we also see one John Smith of Weston caught up by the bishop's commissaries – but for necromancy, sorcery and fortune-telling, rather than heresy.[18] Thus the pursuit of Lollardy was bringing other people into the church's legal processes. Margery had picked a perilous time to be wandering the country, dressed for effect, whilst spreading the word.

In fact, when Repingdon met Kempe (at some point between June 1413 and Arundel's death in February 1414) he treated her kindly; he suggested, indeed, that she should put her experiences into writing, although she was not to do so for another twenty years (15: 34). His initial enthusiasm was, however, tempered by his counsellors: ' "my cownsel wyl not 3yf me to professe 3ow in so synguler a clothyng wythowtyn bettyr avysement" ', and he suggested that she take herself to Jerusalem first, in order to demonstrate her faith and be ' "bettyr preuyd & knowyn" ' (15: 35). Their meeting occurred prior to the alarms following the 1414 rebellion, but a degree of anti-heresy context nonetheless clearly racked up the demands of orthodoxy: if an aversion to saints and pilgrimage, amongst other things, led to a suspicion of Lollardy, in Margery's case a clear demonstration of commitment to these practices was necessary to divert suspicion. In other words, what was previously an optional practice had, in this very particular case, become a necessity. Margery's very public and theatrical piety played a part, of course, in prompting this demand for reassurance: her attempts at holiness 'up the stakes' and are more liable to be read as heterodox. In this, she is not alone but part of a long line of medieval folk teetering on the border between holiness and heresy.

Repingdon's admission that he had been 'advised' not to approve formally Margery's dress reminds us that the policing of religious orthodoxy happened not simply according to the whims and wishes of individual bishops, but via a legislative framework (pretty much in place by 1414) and a professional class of ecclesiastical officials. In thinking about the influence of contemporary perceptions of heresy upon the actual business of prosecuting dissent, it is this group who can most squarely be placed in the frame: the people who were most likely to be aware of parliamentary mandates, ecclesiastical citations, the circulation of documents like Oldcastle's trial, and *perhaps* also the more polemical anti-Wycliffite literature being produced. But although Margery experienced their attentions first hand she also records what are presented as 'popular' reactions against her. At Canterbury, in the vignette with which we started, it is apparently 'the people' who call for her to be burnt. In London, waiting to see Archbishop

---

17 *Reg. Repingdon*, III, pp. 73–4, 69–70, 118–19, 185–6.
18 *Reg. Repingdon*, III, pp. 194–6.

Arundel at Lambeth in 1413, a well-dressed woman 'al for-schod [reviled] þis creatur, bannyd [cursed] hir, & seyd ful cursydly to hir in þis maner, "I wold þu wer in Smythfeld, & I wold beryn a fagot to bren þe wyth; it is pety xat þow leuyst [it is a pity that you continue to live]" ' (16: 36). When visiting Hull (in per-haps 1417 or 1418) 'as þei went in processyon, a gret woman al-to-despysed [utterly despised] hir . . . Many oþer folke seyd þat sche xulde be sett in preson [prison] & madyn gret thretyng [made great threats]' (53: 129). And shortly after, at Hessle, having been arrested by the duke of Bedford's men, 'þer men callyd hir loller, & women cam rennyng owt of her howsys wth her rokkys [distaffs], crying to þe pepil, "Brennyth þis fals heretyk." ' (53: 129). These are the most pointed moments, though there are other points at which the text notes a general feeling of disapprobation for her lifestyle and piety.

Does this mean that the ordinary English laity, by the second decade of the fifteenth century, were firmly 'anti-Lollard'? It is a difficult question to answer, for several reasons. First, there is a paucity of evidence: the surviving trial mater-ial (prior to the late 1420s) is sparse, and questions of how people came to be tried – for example, whether they were 'ill-famed' of heresy in their commu-nities – are unclear from what exists. Chronicle material on the period is so clearly ideological on the topic that it cannot be used very precisely. The *Book* is itself a key source. But, second, the *Book* has its own agenda, and was written after the events depicted. By the time of its composition in the 1430s, there had been fairly substantial heresy trials in Norwich and elsewhere, and more anti-Lollard literature produced. Furthermore, it is clear that Kempe regards these calumnies against her faith as a necessary form of Christ-like suffering or quasi-martyrdom: she *needs* 'the people' to be against her, to show that her way of life was a struggle and a sacrifice (for example, 14: 29–30).

If we admit to an element of truth behind Kempe's depiction of popular reac-tions (and remember that on other occasions, such as her trial and imprisonment at Beverley, the laity are depicted as supporting her [54]) it is important to note that the fear to which they attest had been *taught* to them, and perhaps taught relatively recently. England had not experienced the spectre of large-scale heresy before Lollardy, and there was no earlier tradition, beyond a few chronicles dis-cussing southern France, of 'the heretic' as bogeyman. Whatever popular under-standings of Lollardy were abroad in the period 1413–17, they were highly dependent for their information upon recent ecclesiastical preaching and royal propaganda. Given that the focus of governmental worry had been, right up until Badby's execution in 1410, heresy amongst the clergy and particularly from Oxford, it is not clear that any great campaign to inform the general populace had begun until after the 'rebellion' of January 1414. Thus it is difficult to see the reactions depicted by the *Book* as evidence of a deep-seated and long-held antip-athy to Lollardy; whatever reaction occurred was connected very much to recent events. And indeed the fact that Kempe was the target of hostility strongly sug-gests a large degree of haziness about popular understandings of what a 'Lollard' was: from other evidence, they were not usually famed for wearing white, being highly emotional about the Eucharist, and crying a lot. By the end of the fifteenth century, people were certainly using 'Lollard' as a term of abuse (though still, therefore, with a very broad sense of what it denoted) as a couple of defamation cases in the Norwich consistory court attest.[19] But this attitude had been learnt, and in Kempe's time of activity the lesson had just begun.

The Trials of Margery

Þe Styward . . . spak Latyn vn-to hir . . . Sche seyd to þe Stywarde, "Spekyth Englysch, yf 30w lyketh, for I vndyrstonde not what 3e sey." Þe Styward seyd vn-to hir, "Þu lyest falsly in pleyn Englysch." Þan seyd sche vn-to hym a-3en, "Syr, askyth what qwestyon 3e wil in Englysch, & thorw þe grace of my Lord Ihesu Cryst I xal answeryn 30w resonabely þerto". And þan askyd he many qwestyonys, to þe whech sche answeryd redily & resonabely þat he cowde getyn no cawse [legal case] a-geyn hir (47: 112–13).

Margery Kempe was cited or arrested seven times: at Norwich, probably in 1413; at Bristol in 1417; at Leicester, around August of that year; the following month, twice, in York (latterly brought to Beverley for the trial); and then later that year arrested but quickly released having crossed the Humber, and arrested and released outside Ely. Four of these occasions led to formal interrogations. What do we make of these experiences? Were bourgeois female pilgrims and self-promoting mystics particularly prone to arbitrary arrest and questioning? To bring the events into a clearer light, it is necessary to examine them quite closely and to engage in a degree of re-narration, for which I beg the reader's indulgence.

We cannot say very much about her first experience of episcopal interrogation. All the *Book* tells us is that 'whan sche was on a tyme moneschyd [ordered] to aper be-for certeyn offycerys of þe Bysshop [of Norwich] to answer to certeyn artyculys whech xuld be put a-geyn hir be [by] þe steryng of envyows pepyl, þe good Vykary [vicar, Richard Caister], preferryng þe lofe [love] of God be-for any schame of þe world, went wyth hir to her [hear] hir examynacyon & delyueryd hir fro þe malys [malice] of hyr enmys' (17: 40). It is worth noting that unlike the later, post-Oldcastle trials, it would appear that this did not involve arrest but citation, and was the result of accusation rather than an *ex officio* inquisition. Nor is it entirely certain that Kempe was being questioned as a suspected heretic: although a hostile Dominican witness at her 1417 trial at Beverley said that she should have been burnt at Lynn, which might be a reference to this occasion, the allegation is terribly vague (54: 132). And there were other reasons why one might be cited to appear before a bishop or his officials. In 1394, for example, an episcopal visitation in Dorset noted that John Gyrle and Ellen Gyrle were no longer living as man and wife but were domiciled in separate villages, and thus they were cited to appear before the episcopal court. The same bishop had found, in 1391, that one Agnes Wormes had abandoned her blind husband and refused him conjugal rights; again she was cited.[20] Given later disapproval of the marital arrangements between Margery and her husband, one might wonder whether

---

19 E. D. Stone and B. Cozens-Hardy, eds, *Norwich Consistory Court Depositions* (Norwich Record Society 10, 1938), p. 4.

20 *Register of John Waltham, Bishop of Salisbury 1388–1395*, ed. T. C. B. Timmins (Canterbury & York Society, 1994), No. 1009, p. 143; No. 929, p. 117.

earlier calumnies of this nature had been visited upon her – though this can only be supposition. It is impossible to specify the nature of 'certain charges' laid against Margery in Norwich. They might indeed have been of a heretical nature; but if so, it is curious that she does not discuss the issue in any detail, choosing not to develop it as a demonstration of her suffering and ultimate orthodoxy, as she does with her later experiences.

The first clear accusation of heresy comes, then, in Leicester in 1417 (chapters 46–49).[21] She was first questioned and then arrested by the mayor (probably John Arnesby), and subsequently by the steward of Leicester. The context must surely be the recent memory of royal commissions ordered after the 1414 revolt, and Oldcastle's continued flight. The mayor conducted an initial interrogation, asking where she came from and her family background. As Katherine Lewis has noted elsewhere, the *Book* uses the opportunity to position Kempe in imitation of St Katherine of Alexandria, first facing down the emperor Maxentius.[22] The mayor makes the link explicit, but says ' "& ȝet ar ȝe not lyche [you are not alike], for þu art a fals strumpet, a fals loller, & a fals deceyuer of þe pepyl" ' (46: 111–12). Linking sexual dishonour with heresy was part of a very long tradition, and Thomas Marchale and another unnamed companion, arrested along with Kempe, were later asked to attest not only to her orthodox faith but also whether she was 'continent & clene of hir body, er not' (47: 114). However, these accusations of strumpetry might alternatively suggest that in arresting Kempe it was not just 'heresy' but other possible transgressions that sprang to mind: perhaps that she (like the Somerset women mentioned above) had abandoned her husband; or possibly that she was a runaway nun; or simply that she was a woman 'out of place'. It is simply not clear what brought Margery to the mayor's attention: the only event she records in Leicester prior to her arrest is that she wept at a crucifix such 'þat many a man and woman wondryd on hir', and then refused to tell an unnamed man why she was crying (46: 111). Perhaps this display of affective piety was sufficient to arouse suspicion, in which case we again see how vague the idea of 'Lollard' was at this moment. But it may be, following the mayor's mention of St Katherine, that Margery had been doing more than weeping: engaging in what she would doubtless have called 'spreading the word' but that others might consider preaching. This was forbidden to women (though perhaps suspected of Lollards);[23] but, as we saw when considering Repingdon above, fears about unlicensed preaching were not limited simply to the spectre of Wycliffism. All unlicensed preaching was of concern.

The mayor's role was essentially to arrest and insult Kempe; it was the steward who first questioned her properly.[24] The occasion was formal, and there

---

[21] It seems likely that her earlier encounter with Bishop Peverell at Bristol – on which see Parker in this volume – was a citation to appear before him, but no formal trial is conducted nor is she explicitly accused (such that the *Book* records) of heresy.

[22] Katherine J. Lewis, *The Cult of St Katherine of Alexandria in Late Medieval England* (Woodbridge, 2000), pp. 251–2.

[23] See Aston, 'Lollard Women Priests?', but note also comments above regarding women and Lollardy.

[24] The steward was the officer of the duke of Lancaster and might therefore, through his connection to higher government, have been considered better equipped to handle detailed

were priests and others present. Why did he begin in Latin? It has been suggested this was to tempt a Wycliffite autodidact into revealing her learning.[25] But it is not clear that a woman possessing Latin would automatically be considered a Lollard; again, she might rather be thought a runaway nun.[26] It may, however, have been nothing more than Kempe's reaction to standard legal procedure since Latin was commonly a feature in the formal opening to trials.[27] At any rate, after asking a number of unspecified questions, the steward led her to his private chamber and, the *Book* suggests, attempted to rape her; or, at any rate, gave her the impression that he would rape her, and threatened her with prison, which prompted her to confess that 'sche had hyr speche & hir dalyawns [conversing] of þe Holy Gost & not of hir owyn cunnyng' (47: 113). 'Her speech' may indicate here her responses to the earlier interrogation; or it might again suggest that she had been spreading the word at Leicester, and that this is what had prompted her arrest.

After the steward's attentions, she was once more imprisoned, albeit comfortably, at the house of the gaoler. One can read the steward's interrogations as exploring whether a case was there to be answered, and, finding that it was, passing the matter on to the ecclesiastical authorities. All of this was in accord with the 1414 parliamentary statute on heresy.[28] Thus, on the following Wednesday the trial proper began. Facing the abbot of Leicester, the dean of Leicester, various canons, the mayor, and other lay people – so many, in fact, that 'þei stodyn vp-on stolys [stools] for to beheldyn hir & wonderyn vp-on hir' (48: 114) – Margery was put formally under oath for the first time, and asked about the articles of faith, beginning with the Eucharist. The pattern here was as with the trials of Oldcastle, Badby, Sawtre and others: initial questions on the key issue of the presence or otherwise of Christ's body in the host. The answer recorded by the *Book* is exemplary in its orthodoxy – one might even say strenuously exemplary – and certainly informed by a knowledge of what one should *not* say and where no doubt should be left. In Oldcastle's 1413 trial, for example, he presented an initial statement of faith which provided what appeared to be an orthodox belief on the host, by fudging the details; his refusal to accept transubstantiation was only revealed under questioning. This would have been known to the bishop and the dean, from the circulated copy of Oldcastle's trial transcript. It was apparently also known to Margery – whether at the time or in the later composition of the *Book* – in that she avoided any shred of uncertainty in her answer. Having passed the theological test, the trial ended; but the mayor, doubtful of whether she meant what she said, was unwilling to let her go. He questioned once again her sexual honour, her mode of dress, and feared that

interrogation. Goodman has identified William Babthorpe (deputy steward, brother of the steward himself) as Kempe's probable interrogator (Goodman, *World*, p. 144).

25 Goodman, *World*, p. 8.

26 Bishops were enjoined in this period to order enquiries for apostate monks and nuns (see, for an example from 1413, *Reg. Repingdon*, II, p. 371) and to ask secular aid in so doing. See Christopher Harper-Bill, 'Monastic Apostasy in late Medieval England', *Journal of Ecclesiastical History* 32 (1981): 1–18.

27 A. Musson, *Medieval Law in Context* (Manchester, 2001), p. 20.

28 *Statutes of the Realm*, II, pp. 181–4.

' "þow art comyn hedyr to han [lure] a-wey owr wyuys [wives] fro us & ledyn hem wythe þe" ' (48: 116).[29] The *Book* depicts the mayor as Kempe's 'dedly enmy', and many modern writers have seen a distinction being drawn (either rhetorically or in reality) between an ignorantly repressive secular authority and more enlightened clerics.[30] The fact is, however, that from the 1414 legislation, the secular authorities had a key responsibility for combating heresy, and had to take an oath to that effect. Thus, given his doubts over the truthfulness of her answers, Arnesby's demand was that Kempe go to the bishop of Lincoln, who was the higher ecclesiastical authority for the area, to secure his approval so ' "þat I [Arnesby] may be dischargyd of þe [freed from responsibility for you]" ' (48: 116). This Margery proceeded to do.

The origins of the case at York in the following month are again unclear. Kempe initially went to see an anchoress that she knew there, but was refused an audience due to the bad things that the anchoress had heard about her. Subsequently, in York minster, she told a cleric who asked how long she planned to stay that she would remain for two weeks (50: 119). It is only after breaking this deadline for departure that legal problems began, and she was not arrested but cited to appear at the chapterhouse (attached to the minster) on a specific day. Two things thus suggest themselves: that Kempe had a reputation in York which had acquired a negative slant for some people (the precise grounds of which are unclear); and that she was not initially suspected as a Wycliffite or Oldcastle supporter – for why allow such a person two weeks unhindered? The labels of 'Lollard' and 'heretic' would be raised shortly, but her initial notoriety may have been more broadly based on accusations of hypocrisy; and given the close trading links between the two towns, any negative gossip about Margery from Lynn could well have been passed on to York.[31] We do not know who it was that cited and subsequently questioned Kempe, as she simply describes him as a 'worthy doctor'. It is possible that, given the location of the trial, this was the dean, as the court of dean and chapter enjoyed a peculiar jurisdiction. Like the mayor of Leicester, her anonymous interrogator conducted an initial interrogation, establishing what she was doing in York (making a pilgrimage to St William's shrine, she replied), and whether she had permission from her husband and could prove it by letter (which again raises the spectre of women who have abandoned their marriages). She was then examined on the articles of faith and 'many oþer poynts . . . to þe whech sche answeryd wel & trewly þat þei myth haue non occasyon in hir wordys for to disesyn [harm] hir' (51: 122).[32] Nonetheless she was cited to appear on a subsequent day before the archbishop of York (which, if the initial trial was before the dean, probably complied with the rules for passing on particular cases to the episcopacy). The threat of imprisonment until that day loomed, but 'þe secler [secular] pepil answeryd fro hir & seyde sche xulde

29 On the clothing see note 3 above.
30 See, for example, Janet Wilson, 'Communities of Dissent: The Secular and Ecclesiastical Communities of Margery Kempe's *Book*', in Diane Watt, ed., *Medieval Women in Their Communities* (Cardiff, 1997), pp. 155–85 (156).
31 On links between Lynn and York see in this volume Parker, pp. 61.
32 One might consider translating 'to disesyn her' as 'to take her belongings', given the earlier confiscation of her luggage at Leicester prior to her trial.

not comyn in preson' – that is, they would stand pledge for her, more likely indicating the presence of particular contacts of good social standing in York, rather than, as the text represents it, a general groundswell of lay support for her.

Kempe's second interrogation, before Henry Bowet, archbishop of York, happened at Cawood. Before the actual trial began, accusations of heresy and the threat of burning were flung about, Bowet asked whether she wore white as a claim to virginity, and some people apparently wondered if she might be a Jew (52: 124). Then, in fetters and trembling from fear, she was brought before the archbishop's audience court. Again the questioning focused upon the articles of faith, which she answered 'wel & trewly & redily wythowtyn any gret stody [great reflection] so þat he myth not blamyn hir' (52: 125). Thus the trial ground to a halt, with the archbishop appealing to his counsellors ' "What xal I don wyth hir?" ' (52: 125). After (the text claims) a brief turning of the tables by Margery, wherein she reprimanded Bowet for being a wicked man, Kempe was granted permission briefly to go back into York, so long as she swore not to teach the people. This she refused to do, saying ' "me thynkyth þat þe Gospel ʒeuyth me leue to spekyn of God" ', which prompts the famous argument about whether or not she was preaching (52: 126). The situation is resolved after Margery recounted a lengthy tale about a bear who eats pear blossoms then shits them out, which symbolised the ill-considered living of an unworthy priest. The *Book* here presents a surface conformity – that Margery, as a woman, does not preach but uses 'good words' – whilst rather suggesting the opposite: like a preacher she provides an apposite exemplum in the tale of the bear. Interestingly the bishop goes along with this: treating her much like an unlicensed preacher, he asks her not to disrupt the city.

However, shortly after, Margery found herself back before Bowet once again, this time at the chapterhouse in Beverley. She had been arrested by two yeomen of the duke of Bedford (who was at that point governing England whilst Henry V was in France). The clear accusation, according to the yeomen, was Lollardy. In contrast to previous occasions witnesses were heard immediately: a cleric who had previously examined her and found her to be 'a parfyte [perfect] woman & a good woman' (54: 131); and a Dominican who said that she 'disprauyd [disparaged] alle men of Holy Chirche', mentioned earlier problems at Lynn (discussed above), and said that she claimed ' "sche may wepyn & han contricyon [contrition] whan sche wil" ' (54: 132) – which could suggest the Lollard position of rejecting the need for sacramental confession. Finally the two who arrested her alleged that she was 'Cobham's daughter' – that is, connected to John Oldcastle, Lord of Cobham – 'sent to beryn [carry] lettrys abowtyn þe cuntre' (a recognised method for spreading sedition), and had never been on pilgrimage to Jerusalem as she claimed. The enmity of Bedford was amplified, after a break in the trial and a short period of imprisonment for Margery, into a charge that she had advised Lady Greystoke (Bedford's cousin) to leave her husband.[33] Interestingly, 'preaching' was not raised as an issue.

---

33 On the implications of this charge, and the complex political and semiotic contexts which Kempe had disrupted see the excellent analysis in Nancy Bradley Warren, *Spiritual Economies: Female Monasticism in Later Medieval England* (Philadelphia, 2001), pp. 164–72.

In these encounters with Bowet the *Book* resembles in some ways the trial narratives written by the Wycliffites Richard Wyche and William Thorpe after their interrogations in 1403 and 1407 respectively. All are preceded by scriptural archetypes: the Acts of the Apostles, Pauline epistles, and Christ before Pilate.[34] Thorpe depicts Arundel becoming enraged by his passive resistance to inquisitorial authority; similarly Kempe, at the Cawood interrogation, has Bowet enraged by her veiled accusations against him (' "Why, þow wrecche, what sey men of me?" ' [52: 125]). Both Kempe and Wyche indicate, through the voices of onlookers, that the threat of burning hangs over them. But there are important differences, not simply in what each defendant does, according to their faith (Kempe has no problem swearing an oath to tell the truth, nor with affirming the nature of the Eucharist), but in what the texts choose to *represent* from the trial scene. The *Book* cleverly gives the impression of a forthright and independent Margery, who stands up to her inquisitors. But there is an element of misdirection here, for when Kempe argues with Bowet, it is *after* the conclusion to the trials: at Cawood, she has clearly already been exculpated when launching into the argument over whether or not she would preach in York and telling the exemplum of the bear. More importantly, and very much unlike the Wycliffite trial narratives, the *Book* avoids elements of detail. It is perhaps unsurprising that there is no theological debate as such, but the performance of the orthodox articles of faith is left shrouded, and the nature of some charges against her remain unclear ('And so he multiplyed many schrewyd [sharp] wordys befor þe Erchebishop – it is not expedient to rehersyn hem [repeat them]' [54: 133]).[35]

In fact, when in greatest danger after her arrest by Bedford's men, Kempe is notably (and understandably) submissive: brought from her brief imprisonment she bows before Bowet and thanks him for 'hys gracyows lordschip þat he had schewyd to hir be-for-tyme', and responds carefully to interrogation about her dealings with Lady Greystoke, offering to go to her to gain a testimonial letter. She is threatened with further imprisonment to loosen her tongue (a standard inquisitorial tactic). This, however, does not transpire: asked what she had said to Lady Westmorland (Lady Greystoke's mother, and Bedford's aunt), once again Kempe tells Bowet a story that pleases him. The details are very brief: 'a lady þat was dampmyd [damned] for sche wolde not louyn [love] hir enmijs [enemies] & of

---

[34] For a detailed analysis of these texts, see Rita Copeland, *Pedagogy, Intellectuals and Dissent in the Later Middle Ages: Lollardy and Ideas of Learning* (Cambridge, 2001), pp. 141–219. On some comparisons between Kempe's representation of episcopal encounters (principally her non-judicial interview with Archbishop Arundel) and Thorpe's narrative see Staley, *Dissenting Fictions*, pp. 138–50. As noted above, the model of St Katherine was also available to Kempe.

[35] See similarly the debate between Kempe and the mayor of Leicester, the steward of Leicester, and at the York chapterhouse: 'þe clerkys examynde hir in þe Articles of þe Feyth & *in many oþer poyntys as hem likyde*' (51: 122). The lack of detail over her early citation in Norwich is discussed above. It might be argued, in each case, that the *Book* edits out accusations in order to avoid any inadvertent spreading of heretical ideas; but it also therefore edits out any detailed defence of orthodox doctrine (with the exception of Margery's brief gloss on the nature of the Eucharist). One suspects two things at work: (1) the shifting nature of orthodox discourse, such that the writer in the 1430s was wary of committing to text any detailed statements in case the ground moved once again; and (2) a desire to mould the trials into narratives of suffering, legitimation and spiritual autonomy, editing out anything that presented Kempe in a different light.

a baly [bailiff] þat was savyd for he louyd hys enmys & forȝaf þat þei had tres-
pasyd a-ȝen hym, & ȝet he was heldyn an euyl man' (54: 134). This was apparently
sufficient to acquit her, and secure a testimonial of her orthodoxy from Bowet
himself. While the final comment on the bailiff could obviously be read as standing for Kempe herself, the text here is clearly obscuring other negotiations. Since
she seems to have been escorted outside the county and the bishop's letter then
withdrawn, it would appear that Bowet (like Arnesby before him) simply wanted
her out of his jurisdiction so that she became somebody else's problem. And in
fact it is later revealed that Bowet had 'ȝeue[n] no credens to my wordys' and told
her to get a letter from Henry Chichele, archbishop of Canterbury (55: 136).
Essentially, the trial ended therefore by another transferral of jurisdiction, this
time between York and Canterbury. She was, as it transpired, rearrested immediately after crossing the Humber, but freed by the intervention of someone who
had seen the York trial; and further arrested then freed outside Ely, having gained
letters from Canterbury.

So where does our re-narration of events lead us? I would suggest that three
things become apparent. The first is that the *Book* works to present the reader with
a certain image of repression, the primary purpose of which is to frame Kempe's
experiences as akin to the mocking and scourging of Christ.[36] These hardships are
patiently borne, emphasizing her orthodox authority and holiness. Secondly,
however, it is possible to read 'behind' the text, not to a hard and fast historical
reality, but nonetheless to catch glimpses, through the impressions they have
made upon the *Book*, of the prosaic workings of legal mechanisms and proce-
dures. This may provide a different sense of the motivations of, and pressures
upon, Margery's inquisitors. Moreover, we may wonder whether every calumny
thrown against Kempe was necessarily 'heresy' – or whether this picture is partly
an assumption made by modern critics, trained to seek out the Lollard, and partly
a deliberate effort by the *Book* to emphasise a charge (heresy) more easily rejected
by the time of its composition (because of the bona fides Kempe had by then
gained) in order to attract attention away from other possible concerns. Thirdly,
considering the confusion of charges, the repeated passing on of jurisdictional
authority, and Kempe's varied experiences of secular and ecclesiastical authority,
we should note that whatever pretensions fifteenth-century England had to being
a 'police state', the practice fell far short.[37] Whilst recognising that Kempe
undoubtedly was prosecuted and was in some danger, we should not over-
emphasise the efficiency of repression in practice; and we should particularly note
the difference that *class* could make, even given the marginalising disadvantages
of gender, in negotiating those repressive mechanisms that did exist.[38]

---

36 See similarly Goodman, *World*, p. 131.
37 Thus, for example, Jeffrey Cohen's recent comments that Kempe's ability to obtain episcopal
    letters was 'an astonishing achievement' and that she suffered 'unabated persecutions' seem
    to me to accord repression a greater degree of power and control than it actually possessed
    in this context; and, more simply, fails to recognise the legal mechanisms half-reflected in the
    text. See J. J. Cohen, 'The Becoming Liquid of Margery Kempe', in *idem, Medievel Identity
    Machines* (Minneapolis, 2003), pp. 154–87 (160).
38 See also Kate Parker's analysis, in this volume, of Kempe's encounter with Peverell. For a very
    interesting account of how class, among other factors, could complicate later prosecutions see

Conclusion: What is Dissent?

Upon the xxviii daye of apryll [1495] was an old cankyrd heretyke that dotid
ffor age namyd Johanne Bowgthon . . . [b]rent In Smythffeeld . . . She was
a dyscypyll of Wyclyff whom she accomptid ffor a Seynt, and held soo ffast
& ffermly VIII of his XII oppynyons that alle the doctors of london cowde not
turn hyr ffrom oon of theym, and when It was told to hir that she shuld be brent
ffor hyr obstynacy & ffals byleve, She set nowgth at theyr wordis but deffyed
theym, ffor she said she was soo belovid wt God & his holy angelys That all the
ffyre In London shuld not hurt hyr, But upon the morw a quarteron of ffagot
wyth a ffewe Rede consyumyd hir in a lytill while, and whyle she mygth Crye
she spak offtyn of God & owir lady, But noo man cowde cause hyr to name
JHESUS, and soo she dyed. (*The Great Chronicle of London*)[39]

This was the end fantasised for Margery by various of her enemies: death by
fire at Smithfield. By Bowgthon's time there were a good number of precedents,
but much less so during the period of Kempe's troubles. Seven people were
hanged and then burnt in the aftermath of the 1414 rebellion, but at St Giles
Fields. Only two – William Sawtre in 1401 and John Badby in 1410 – had been
killed by the fire itself, and these at Smithfield. But fire had an imaginary presence prior to the 1401 statute *De heretico comburendo* that formalised execution for
heresy, both in the minds of those fighting Lollardy and in the self-dramatisa-
tions of Wycliffite writings.[40] We may therefore read the *Book* as employing a
highly resonant image of hostility towards heresy. This might perhaps have more
accurately reflected contemporary reactions and associations (the image of
Smithfield, in particular) from the period of composition – when more executions
had occurred – than the time of the depicted events. In any case, the threat was
deployed on Kempe's behalf as a further spectre of martyrdom.

To return to an earlier question: why was Margery arrested and interrogated
so frequently? Was it something specific about *her* (as the duke of Bedford business would suggest) or the wider context of the times? Did the interrogation of
middle-aged bourgeois mystics serve any larger purpose within the Lancastrian
polity? There are, as we have seen, several contexts: the aftermath of the supposed
1414 rebellion, Henry V's absence in France, fears about Scottish rebellion, and
Bedford's specific anger with Kempe's apparent meddling in dynastic politics.
Kempe had particular problems because she made herself extremely visible
through her affective piety, and because she was a woman travelling away from
home (though, as we have seen, this was balanced at points by the support
she received in York). Among other things, this removed the possibility of her
clearing her name at any trial through the use of compurgators, as such character

---

Shannon McSheffrey, 'Heresy, Orthodoxy and English Vernacular Religion, 1480–1525', *Past
& Present* (forthcoming).

[39] A. H. Thomas and I. D. Thornley, eds, *The Great Chronicle of London* (1938; repr., Gloucester,
1983), p. 252.

[40] Paul Strohm, 'Walking Fire: Symbolization, Action, and Lollard Burning', in *idem, Theory and
the Premodern Text* (Minneapolis, 2000), pp. 20–32.

witnesses had to be neighbours of the accused.[41] It is not clear to what extent any travellers – pilgrims, merchants, officers of the crown – needed letters attesting to their bona fides in the climate of early fifteenth-century England.[42] As argued above, it may be that the initial cause of Kempe's arrest in York was not heresy, but a more general suspicion of a woman publicly out of place – which we might therefore posit as applying more widely.

In a different sense, however, what got Kempe into trouble was hermeneutics: the problems that people had, in the context of religious fears, of deciding on how to 'read' the interior person from the exterior shell. Repingdon raised the matter early on, by suggesting that Margery carry out her pilgrimage plans as a kind of external proof of her orthodoxy. The *Book* emphasises this as a legitimating device – except that, at Beverley, people questioned whether she had actually ever gone to Jerusalem. The problem had long haunted her: in Norfolk, recording the general tenor of slander against her, the *Book* notes that 'Oþer [other people] which had no knowlach of hir maner of gouernawns, saue only by sygth owtforth [outward appearance] er ellys be jangelyng [gossip] of oþer personys' spoke evil of her (18: 43). During the Leicester trial, the Mayor alleged that ' "sche menyth not with hir hert as sche seyth with hir mowthe" ' (48: 115), a distinction and phraseology frequently applied to heretics. This problem of legibility lay at the heart of all heresy prosecutions and drove forward the inquisitorial mechanism. And it may have been particularly prominent in the minds of fifteenth-century bishops, who had dutifully copied the trial of John Oldcastle into their registers: Oldcastle had first proffered to his judges what purported to be an orthodox statement of faith, but which then demanded further interrogation and interpretation – leading to the discovery of his heresy – by the inquisitors. Thus the spectre of heresy was framed as feigned piety; hence 'false Lollard', 'false heretic' and so forth, all insults hurled at Kempe and others. ' "Eyþur [Either] þu art a ryth good woman er ellys a ryth wikked woman" ', said the steward of Leicester (47: 113) – the essential problem for all those fearful of heresy.

But unlike poor Johanna Bowgthon, Margery escaped the fire, and it is worth reflecting upon that fact. There has been a strong historiographical desire to see Kempe as having, or being perceived as having, 'a Lollard style'.[43] That is, the *Book*, its character and its author have been read as challenging social, cultural and political norms of various kinds: gender roles, normative piety, legal jurisdiction, even 'the ways in which the lines had been blurred between the institutions and laws of church and state'.[44] Such readings need to be situated within wider contexts of dissent and conformity within the period. Thus Ruth Shklar's attempt to

41 Richard Helmholz, 'Crime, Compurgation and the Courts of the Medieval Church', *Law and History Review* 1 (1986): 1–26 (17).
42 Certainly in the late fourteenth-century, pilgrims who depended upon charity – which, to some extent, includes Kempe – were under statutory order to carry letters attesting their bona fides and specifying the date of their return home. See Diana Webb, *Medieval European Pilgrimage* (Houndmills, 2002), p. 73.
43 Nancy F. Partner, 'Reading *The Book of Margery Kempe*', *Exemplaria* 3 (1991): 29–66 (33).
44 Staley, *Dissenting Fictions*, p. 128; such a reading seems more situated in regard to the ideals of Jeffersonian democracy than the fifteenth-century English polity.

read Kempe's encounter with the Canterbury monks as appropriating 'the force of Wycliffite critique' over church ownership of property – a reading apparently resting upon the *Book*'s comment that an elder monk had been the queen's treasurer before entering the monastery – should be placed relative to the rather more forceful criticisms of church wealth and power expressed in both Wycliffite literature and by those tried as Lollards.[45] Margery's berating of those who swear oaths *could* be read as 'Lollard' – as, in *The Canterbury Tales*, the host suggests the Parson might be Lollard when the latter reprimands his swearing – but criticism of unnecessary oaths (that is, 'swearing', closer to our modern sense of foul language) was also commonplace in orthodox discourse, as various preaching materials recount.[46] Weeping for heretics and including them in her prayers (57: 141, and II, prayers: 250–2) may have suggested to some critics a certain sympathy for Lollardy. In fact these are entirely orthodox gestures: bishops enjoined such prayers in their diocesan parishes.[47] And to suggest that Kempe's frequent use of the qualifier 'good' before 'man', 'woman' and 'priest' is in some way similar to what Anne Hudson has identified as a 'Lollard sect vocabulary' would surely be to indict the compilers of every civic archive and most medieval literature, so ubiquitous are those terms.[48]

The strongest claim for Kempe's 'dissent' is her apparent desire to preach, which various commentators have linked with Lollardy. But the text makes quite clear that, in its terms, Kempe does *not* preach: she uses 'good words' and is legitimate in so doing.[49] And, as Edwin Craun has recently shown, her criticisms of various bishops, clerks and monks were based in a very traditional discourse of spiritual correction, explicitly and canonically available to someone like Kempe (particularly given her social background).[50] Her reprimands, even to Henry Bowet, are not 'talking back to power': unlike Bowgthon she did not 'set nowgth at theyr wordis but deffyed theym'.[51] Instead, regarding the realm of religious thought and behaviour, Kempe talked *within* power, within the accepted strategies power permits for the regulation of its subjects' positions and responsibilities. There is very little challenge to orthodox *structures* in the *Book*: Kempe's strategy is constantly to seek approval for her actions within existing patterns of

---

45 Shklar, 'Cobham's Daughter', pp. 288–9.
46 Staley, *Dissenting Fictions*, pp. 5, 147. See, for example, *Fasciculus Morum*, ed. S. Wenzel (Philadelphia, 1989) pp. 166–9, and examples from John Bromyard in Edwin D. Craun, '*Fama* and Pastoral Constraints on Rebuking Sinners: *The Book of Margery Kempe*', in T. Fenster and D. L. Smail, eds, *Fama: The Politics of Talk and Reputation in Medieval Europe* (Ithaca, NY, 2003), pp. 187–209.
47 For example *Reg. Waltham*, p. 15.
48 Staley, *Dissenting Fictions*, p. 10. See Anne Hudson, 'A Lollard Sect Vocabulary?', in eadem *Lollards and Their Books* (London, 1985), pp. 166–73. On the degree to which her bodily piety, and particularly her crying, were perceived as rebellious, see comments by Salih in this volume, pp. 173–5.
49 Although wishing to preserve an element of 'Lollard' resonance, Karma Lochrie notes that the distinction Kempe draws is shared with contemporary orthodox literature: *Translations*, p. 111.
50 Craun, '*Fama*', p. 189 and *passim*.
51 For a contrary view see C. Dinshaw, 'Margery Kempe Answers Back', in *eadem, Getting Medieval: Sexualities and Communities, Pre- and Postmodern* (Durham, 1999), pp. 143–182, and most recently Cohen, 'Becoming Liquid', p. 158.

power and authority.[52] She does not seek to defend women's preaching, but calls upon a pre-existing discourse of legitimation. Kempe may be 'yearning for autonomy' (as Nancy Partner puts it),[53] but her route to that autonomy is via clerical sanction and is directed solely towards herself: there is no pro-feminist element to the text, only pro-Margery. Indeed, in examining Kempe's encounters with authority over questions of orthodoxy, what becomes clear is the large degree to which she is interpellated into the discourse of doctrinal policing. She repeatedly asks for written authorisation from bishops, as protection against further accusation. This was doubtless a sensible tactic – Bowet's letter may have contributed to saving her when she was rearrested after crossing the Humber, and Chichele's letter certainly saved her when arrested outside Ely – but it makes it hard to see Kempe (unlike, say, Johanna Bowghton) as *dissenting* against these power structures in any very strong sense of the word. Similarly, the wider cultural discourse that fretted over the relationship between outer appearance and inner reality – an essential element of the discourse on heresy that lay behind many of Kempe's brushes with authority – was also spoken by Kempe herself. She advised a Lynn burgess not to help out a young man being championed by her priestly amanuensis, on the grounds that there were local poor to whom one should give rather than to a stranger, 'for many spekyn & schewyn ful fayr owtward to þe sygth of þe pepyl, God knowyth what þei arn in her sowlys' (24: 56).[54] As the target herself of many charges of hypocrisy, this strikes as a little ungenerous; but, more importantly, illustrates again the extent to which Kempe stands *inside* the discourses of her time.

There were differing viewpoints on Margery's faith in the fifteenth century, and there are differing viewpoints in modern scholarship. It is undoubtedly true that Margery's travels and the creation of the *Book* do represent something of a triumph over medieval attitudes towards women's roles and female voices. Whether this social dissent – itself surely aided by her fairly elite social standing – necessarily informed a challenge to religious or ecclesiastical orthodoxies is another matter. Anthony Goodman has recently suggested that Kempe's affective piety presented contemporary bishops with a reassuring orthodox alternative to Lollardy,[55] whilst various other writers take the opposite view, linking Kempe to dissent and her experiences to a repressive ecclesiastical and secular hierarchy. However, the extremes of both interpretive poles may assume too firm, clear and fixed a religious landscape in early fifteenth-century England. Orthodoxy and heresy were not clearly defined and were certainly not self-evident even to learned commentators.[56] Consider, for example, the chronicler's remarks on Johanna Bowgthon, confusingly recorded as believing 'eight of the twelve opinions of Wyclif' (that is, presumably, of the twelve 'Lollard Conclusions' of 1395) and holding Wyclif

---

52 See similarly Davis in this volume, pp. 00–00.
53 Partner, 'Reading *The Book of Margery Kempe*', pp. 32–3.
54 For further discussion of this episode and the argument that it demonstrates Margery's parochial attitude to charity see P. H. Cullum below, pp. 49–50.
55 Goodman, *World*, p. 132.
56 This was arguably still the case even in the early sixteenth century: see McSheffrey, 'Heresy, Orthodoxy and English Vernacular Religion'.

'saint'. Even by the end of the fifteenth century, ideas about what Lollards thought and believed were not only pretty vague (Wycliffites were not keen on the idea of saints), but also confused about how one ascribed belief and adherence to heresy (why, for example, only eight of the twelve 'conclusions'? What distinction did the chronicler understand to be drawn between calling out to God and Mary but not to Christ?). One of the consequent effects of the growing fear of heresy at the beginning of the fifteenth century was an increased concern about what constituted orthodox practice and belief, and to what extent such 'normality' had to be *demonstrated* rather than assumed. Things previously seen as quite orthodox (such as the possession of vernacular religious literature) or merely a minor moral lapse (such as failure to attend mass) could, in particular circumstances, become recoded as highly suspicious. What might in an earlier age have been labelled 'doubt' – such as uncertainty about Christ's presence in the host – could be seen as heresy. Thus it is true that on occasion, and in particular religio-political contexts, Margery's public, mystical and affective piety came under question; but as one element within a much larger spectrum of piety that had come under question. Thus it is also difficult to see her as conducting a self-conscious revolt against orthodox norms. Where those norms existed, and particularly where they took the form of mechanisms of authority, Kempe stayed well within the boundaries.

A final thought: if we wish to locate 'dissent' in *The Book of Margery Kempe*, we might consider looking beyond its main character. The slanderous tale told about Margery Kempe by various people – 'A, þu fals flesch, þu xalt no good mete etyn' as she helped herself to a nice bit of pike (II, 9: 243) – is itself part of a wider discourse: the criticism of hypocritical asceticism.[57] This could be seen as 'Wycliffite', but even that may circumscribe a wider dislike of the way in which the symbolically poor displaced the real poor.[58] As we consider the 'penances' that Margery Kempe, daughter of the mayor of Lynn, underwent in an effort to achieve piety – the disavowals, strictures and liminal practices that could mark one out as holy, but which depended for their symbolic reversals upon a fairly 'high' social starting point – there is a reminder that not everyone was necessarily impressed by such performances. They, too, could dissent.

---

[57] This tale is perhaps referred to earlier, in chapter 18 (possibly), and chapter 44 (more probably). One can also note other accusations of hypocrisy against her: that she had had a child whilst abroad (chapter 43), and that her bodily piety was due to illness (chapters 17, 44, 61).

[58] M. Aston, 'Caim's Castles: Poverty, Politics and Disendowment', in *Faith and Fire*, pp. 95–131.

5

A Shorte Treatyse of Contemplacyon: The Book of Margery Kempe *in its Early Print Contexts*

ALLYSON FOSTER

While *The Book of Margery Kempe* has been the subject of a wide range of scholarly inquiry since the recovery of the Salthouse manuscript in 1934, significantly less attention has been paid to Margery Kempe's place in early print culture. In 1501 the early English printer Wynkyn de Worde published a very short selection from *The Book of Margery Kempe* with the colophon, 'Here begynneth a shorte treatyse of contemplacyon taught by our lorde Ihesu cryste, or taken out of the boke of Margerie kempe of lynn.'[1] This redaction appeared again in 1521 when printer Henry Pepwell included it in a small collection of devotional works. That this redaction was printed twice within a span of twenty years indicates not only that early modern readers were familiar with Kempe and her *Book*, but also that the treatise was popular and deemed valuable in some way for those interested in seeking instruction in the practice of contemplation. Given the important place of *The Book of Margery Kempe* in late medieval scholarship, and given that for centuries *A Shorte Treatyse of Contemplacyon* was the only surviving evidence of the *Book*'s existence, it is rather surprising that the treatise has received only a smattering of critical attention. Its date of publication may have something to do with this lack of attention; falling within the 'gap' between the late medieval and early modern periods, it lies just outside the traditional, chronologically determined parameters of scholarly inquiry – slightly too late for late medievalists, but too early for early modernists. However, in light of the significance of *The Book of Margery Kempe* to studies of late medieval mysticism, lay piety, and literary culture, this explanation is inadequate in itself to explain the oversight. Rather, the neglect of the treatise appears to have far less to do with when it circulated than with its reputation as being merely a reductive product of censorship that does not merit careful scrutiny.

Although the treatise is comprised of a number of short passages taken from *The Book of Margery Kempe*, it bears very little resemblance to the *Book* at all. While the life of Margery Kempe was steeped in controversy, any trace of the outspoken, boisterous, independent Margery that is presented in her *Book* has been removed, and replaced by a rather passive figure who, for the most part, listens

---

[1] From this point on I will refer to this redaction of *The Book of Margery Kempe* as *A Shorte Treatyse of Contemplacyon*.

rather than speaks. In addition, the details of her life and spiritual journey which make her *Book* such a rich source of information about female lay piety (and other matters) in the later Middle Ages are all but completely absent. As such, the responses to *A Shorte Treatyse of Contemplacyon* have generally been negative, ranging from categorizing the *Book* as simply boring or anodyne to the far more damning ahistorical and reductive.[2] However, we should remember that the initial enthusiasm which heralded the discovery of the Salthouse manuscript itself soon gave way to a grave sense of disappointment when it failed to live up to preconceived expectations, and it was many years before new modes of inquiry revealed its value to late medieval literary and cultural studies.[3] *A Shorte Treatyse of Contemplacyon* deserves re-examination not only because it can help us speculate further on who may have read Kempe's work, but because considering how *The Book of Margery Kempe* was reshaped, and to what purpose, can contribute to a more specific understanding of Kempe's place in early modern piety, reading practices, and literary culture.[4]

A Shorte Treatyse of Contemplacyon was first printed in 1521 as a quarto pamphlet only four leaves long, or approximately one eighteenth the size of the Salthouse manuscript.[5] It consists of twenty-eight short passages that have been culled from *The Book of Margery Kempe* in what initially seems rather a haphazard fashion. The extracted passages, ranging in length from two to seventeen lines, are taken from twenty-four of the eighty-nine chapters that comprise Book I of *The Book of Margery Kempe*, but the order in which they appear in the redacted version does not correspond to their original sequence. As such, a passage from chapter 85 is followed by a passage from chapter 28, which is followed by a passage from chapter 72, and so on. However, the composition of this version is, in reality, anything but random; the extractor has clearly gone to a great deal of trouble to select particular passages and rearrange them to form a coherent text. Indeed, the manner in which the passages have been arranged gives no indication that they have been drawn from such different contexts. Thus, while the incipit indicates that the piece is 'taken out of the boke of Margerie kempe of lynn', it would be a mistake to understand it as simply an abridged version of Kempe's *Book*.

A Shorte Treatyse of Contemplacyon is, in essence, an exchange between Margery and Christ in which Margery seeks to know 'þe ryght way to heuen' and Christ

---

2   See, for example, Anthony Goodman, 'The Piety of John Brunham's Daughter of Lynn', in Derek Baker, ed., *Medieval Women* (Oxford, 1978), pp. 347–58 (p. 357); Sue Ellen Holbrook, 'Margery Kempe and Wynkyn de Worde', in Marion Glasscoe, ed., *The Medieval Mystical Tradition in England: Exeter Symposium IV* (Cambridge, 1987), pp. 27–46 (p. 35).

3   See Barry Windeatt's essay in the present volume.

4   The most important recent study to reconsider *A Short Treatyse of Contemplacyon* is Jennifer Summit's *Lost Property: The Woman Writer and English Literary History, 1380–1589* (Chicago, 2000), pp. 126–38.

5   De Worde's print has the Short Title Catalogue number 14924, and copies exist in the Cambridge University Library and the Huntington Library. A modernised transcription of the print exists in *BMK*, pp. 353–7. A normalised transcription exists in Barry Windeatt's edition of the Salthouse manuscript (London, 2000), pp. 429–34. Quotations from *A Shorte Treatyse of Contemplacyon* will be from *BMK* and page numbers will be cited in the text.

instructs her on various means of achieving spiritual perfection. As Sue Ellen Holbrook explains in her very thorough consideration of the de Worde quarto pamphlet, the twenty-eight passages have been arranged into five clusters, each with a 'focal motif': group one, passages 1–10, emphasises that, rather than wearing hair shirts, excessive fasting, incessant prayer, and giving alms (all of which are familiar conventions of hagiography), the best way for Margery to please God and demonstrate her love is to think continually on Christ, let him speak in her soul, and weep tears of compunction. Group two, passages 11–15, further addresses tears of compassion and explains that weeping is a sign of her intensified love and knowledge of Christ. In group three, passages 16–19, Margery is assured that she will have as great a reward in heaven for her good will and desires as she would for her bodily acts. Group four, passages 20–1, deals with the pardon God has granted her for her sins. And lastly, group five, passages 22–8, emphasises that in order to perfectly love God, one must suffer shame and tribulations patiently, and for that reason Margery has received God's grace while it has been withheld from some religious men and priests.[6]

Immediately, the most striking thing about this redaction to any reader familiar with *The Book of Margery Kempe* is the virtual absence of Kempe's own voice. Of the twenty-eight passages that comprise the treatise, her voice is heard directly in only five (one of which is shared with Christ's voice), while Christ speaks in twenty. A third-person narrative voice that describes Margery's actions and occasionally leads into the speech in other passages accounts for the remaining three. The discrepancy between voices is even more startling when the comparative length of the passages is taken into account: the passages in which Kempe speaks are only one to five lines long, while some of Christ's directives run as long as nineteen lines. Furthermore, passage 23 which reads, 'Pacyence is more worthe than myracles doyng' (357) is seemingly attributed to Christ, while in *The Book of Margery Kempe* it is spoken by Margery in response to an interrogation by a clerk (51: 121).

However, it is not merely the length or frequency of the passages that render Margery's voice subordinate, but the way in which her voice functions within the text. While at times the structure of the piece is reminiscent of a dialogue, it is by no means an equal exchange. When Margery does speak, she doesn't deliver any spiritual guidance or recount any of her experiences as she does in the *Book*. Her input consists of praying that she might always have mourning and weeping for God's love (354) and that God will have mercy on her wickedness (354); proclaiming that she will undergo public humiliation for God's love (356); and asking God to have mercy on her 'lytell payne' (357) and show his grace to religious men and priests rather than to herself (357). Furthermore, her voice is not heard until nearly a third of the way into the treatise, and, unlike her *Book*, it is Christ who quite literally does have the last word, telling her that he will not privilege religious men and priests over her because 'he that dredeth þe shames of this worlde may not parfyghtly loue god' (357). Margery's voice seems to function primarily as a means of occasioning Christ's doctrines, as the points at which

---

[6] Holbrook, 'Margery Kempe and Wynkyn de Worde', pp. 28–9.

she speaks roughly coincide with the shifts in focal motif that were discussed above. Rather than voicing her own understanding of spiritual matters, as she so often does in her *Book*, the Margery Kempe of the redacted version seems a rather passive receptacle of the knowledge Christ imparts to her. Moreover, the characteristic conversational and intimate exchanges in which 'þe Fadyr of Hevyn dalyd to hir sowle as pleynly and as veryly as o frend spekyth to a-noþer be bodyly spech' (17: 39) have been replaced by a more didactic type of colloquy in which Christ instructs, guides and corrects her when she is engaged in the 'wrong' types of devotion, and she, for the most part, accepts without comment.

If Kempe's voice has largely been expunged from *A Shorte Treatyse of Contemplacyon*, the same can also be said for her corporeality. The bodily expressions that were so characteristic of and crucial to Kempe's piety, and which made her such a vital and controversial figure (the copious weeping and roaring, the wearing of hair shirts and dressing in white clothing, the fasting, the chaste marriage she negotiated with her husband, the sexual temptations, shame, and fears which she struggled with so intensely), have been almost entirely omitted. While she is encouraged to weep tears of compunction because 'thynkynge, wepynge, & hye contemplacyon is þe best lyf in erthe' (354), the fact that weeping is mentioned alongside such introspective activities as thinking and contemplation suggests that it is also meant to be a private form of devotion. Unlike the loud and public displays of weeping that Margery makes in her *Book*, tears of compunction should be wept privately and without drawing attention to oneself. In a similar fashion, while a short section of the treatise recounts one of her visions of the Passion, it lacks the vivid detail of the visions and her physical responses to them, such as writhing and convulsions, that are described in the *Book*, stating simply that 'Our mercyfull lorde Ihesu cryste drewe this creture vnto his loue, & to the mynde of his passyon, that myght not endure to beholde a lepre, or an other seke man, specyally yf he had ony woundes apperynge on hym. Soo she wepte as yf she had seen our lorde Ihesu with his woundes bledynge' (355).

As noted above, *A Shorte Treatyse of Contemplacyon* is also almost completely free of the very details of Margery Kempe's life and experiences that make her *Book* so compelling. Gone are any references to her family and the people she knew, the places she travelled, the conversations she had, the books she was familiar with, or her numerous confrontations with family members, townspeople, fellow pilgrims and ecclesiastical authorities.[7] Other than the relatively vague reference to her meditation on the Passion, the details of her mystical experiences are also conspicuously absent. We hear nothing of her presence at Christ's birth and crucifixion; her conversations and encounters with the Virgin Mary and the saints; the 'tokens' she receives from God; and, perhaps most obviously, her mystical marriage to the Godhead. These omissions are even more conspicuous given that several of the passages that are included in the redaction are taken from the very chapters of *The Book of Margery Kempe* in which these mystical phenomena are recounted in great detail. One particularly striking example

---

[7] Two notable exceptions are the references to the priests in Lynn (16) and the pardon she received at 'Rafnys' (21).

of this process of selection and omission occurs in chapter 35 of the *Book*. This chapter is arguably one of the most important in the entire book in terms of representations of female spirituality and mysticism: not only is this the chapter in which Margery is wedded to the Godhead in a ceremony witnessed by Christ, the Holy Ghost, the Virgin Mary, the twelve apostles and a host of angels and saints, but this chapter is also distinguished by the rich detail it provides about the physical tokens she receives throughout her life such as the sweet smells, beautiful melodies, the sight of angels flying about her 'in a maner as motys in the sunne', and the flame of fire that burns for sixteen years. And yet, the only portion of this chapter that is included in *A Shorte Treatyse of Contemplacyon* are the final lines in which God tells her, 'dowtyr, þis lyfe [of contemplation] plesyth me mor þan weryng of þe haburion or of þe hayr or fastyng of bred & watyr, for, 3yf þu seydest euery day a thowsand Pater Noster, þu xuldist not plesyn me so wel as þu dost whan þu art in silens & sufferyst me to speke in thy sowle' (35: 89; 353 for its appearance in the *Shorte Treatyse*). Why, out of all the abundant material in chapter 35 to choose from, might the extractor have chosen to include only this short passage and omit all reference to Kempe's mystical experiences? What sort of text was the extractor interested in creating, and for what audience?

A Shorte Treatyse of Contemplacyon is, in essence, a brief, practical guide to the process of spiritual perfection, whereby Christ instructs Margery on approved, orthodox modes of devotion. And, it must be noted, the approved modes of devotion, while drawing on the mystical tradition, are singularly private modes: prayer, contemplation, weeping tears of compunction, and the patient suffering of tribulation. As the passage just quoted indicates, silence is indeed golden – a message that is strongly reiterated in the very next passage when Christ tells Margery that, 'thou shalt haue more meryte in heuen for one yere thynkynge in thy mynde than for an hondred yere of prayeng wyth thy mouth' (354). A heavy emphasis is also placed on the idea that contemplation and prayer alone can win heavenly reward. Christ assures her that, 'thou shalt haue mede & rewarde in heuen for the good wylles & good desyres, as yf thou haddest done them in dede' (355), and this message is immediately reiterated in the next passage: 'Doughter þu shalte haue as grete mede & as grete rewarde with me in heuen for thy good seruyce & thy good dedes that thou haste do in thy mynde as yf thou haddest do þe same with thy bodely wyttes without forth' (355–6). This is in keeping with the treatise's discouragement of ascetic practices: one need not actually martyr oneself or submit the body to physical pain as an expression of love for God; it is enough simply to be willing to do so. While in one sense this is a very comforting message for laywomen who are unwilling or unable to put their bodies through physical trials or devote the majority of their time to the act of prayer, in this context it has the simultaneous effect of once again absenting Kempe's body from the text.[8]

Thus, it would seem that *A Shorte Treatyse of Contemplacyon* is characterised by nothing so much as lack: lack of Margery's voice, her body, her life, and the most

---

[8] For Karma Lochrie's reading of *A Shorte Treatyse of Contemplacyon* as a 'disembodied text' see her *Translations*, esp. pp. 220–35.

expressive forms of her spirituality. In light of what seems a very heavy-handed process of omission, it is not surprising that the treatise is often characterised as reductive and anodyne. However, while this perception of the text is understandable, especially when viewed in the context of the Church's growing anxieties about lay devotional practices and ecclesiastical attempts to regulate those practices, it is also limiting because it precludes further investigation of the ways in which *The Book of Margery Kempe*, albeit in a much altered form, continued to function in the context of later medieval and early modern piety. And so, rather than focusing exclusively on what the text fails to do, it is also important to consider what it does do, and to what ends.

Precisely who was responsible for compiling *A Shorte Treatyse of Contemplacyon*, and when it was done is unclear, but it does seem fairly unlikely that Wynkyn de Worde selected the passages for printing himself. Perhaps the most convincing argument is offered by Holbrook, who suggests that the treatise may have been composed, or at least sponsored by, Margery Kempe's parish priest and principal confessor, Master Robert Springold. She observes that the slant of the treatise, with its emphasis on private modes of devotion, is very much that of Springold, as indicated by a passage from *The Book of Margery Kempe* in which God admonishes Margery to heed her confessor because he recommends the same modes of devotion that God himself does: '[. . .] I am hyly plesyd wyth hym, for he biddith þe þat þu xuldist sittyn stille & ȝeuyn thyn hert to meditacyon & thynkyn swech holy thowtys as God wyl puttyn in þi mende' (88: 217–18).[9] As the parish priest of Lynn, Robert Springold would have been all too privy to the controversy surrounding Margery Kempe and her enthusiastic practices and, indeed, at times seemed to have ambivalent feelings about her visionary claims and practices himself (e.g. 18: 44, 69: 168). However, he was for the most part very supportive of Kempe, and would have been just as aware of the positive influence she could wield. While *The Book of Margery Kempe* contains numerous examples of negative reactions to Margery and her particular expressions of piety, it also recounts that she found supporters among rather a diverse group of people, both lay and religious. Springold may have felt that in spite of its enthusiastic themes and controversial mystical elements, Kempe's *Book* also contained a message that would be beneficial to lay people, perhaps in particular to laywomen, and sought to offer a less controversial version of her text. Whether or not Springold is responsible for *A Shorte Treatyse of Contemplacyon* is largely a matter of speculation; however, pointed reference to the priests of Lynn (355) suggests that it was likely created not long after *The Book of Margery Kempe* was completed in 1436–38, if not by Springold, then by another contemporary of Kempe's.

In any event, *A Shorte Treatyse of Contemplacyon* would certainly have found a ready market when de Worde printed it as a quarto pamphlet in 1501. Quarto pamphlets were relatively inexpensive to buy compared with manuscripts, making them accessible to a wider audience than the prohibitive cost of manuscripts allowed. More importantly, by the time of the treatise's printing, vernacular

---

[9]   Holbrook, 'Margery Kempe and Wynkyn de Worde', pp. 38–40.

books about the contemplative life were in high demand among clerical and lay audiences alike. The years between 1350 and 1450 saw a proliferation of vernacular devotional and religious works, and works of popular piety were far more numerous than even lyrics, narrative poetry and dream visions. In terms of early printed books, devotional works made up the largest subject category during the last quarter of the fifteenth century.[10] Whereas lay piety had formerly been characterised largely by rote recitation of prayer, and passive attendance at service, by the fifteenth century reading and contemplation were increasingly encouraged, resulting in the ideal of devout literacy.[11] Furthermore, the number of laywomen who owned books increased quite significantly in the fourteenth and fifteenth centuries, and Anne Clark Bartlett has noted that 'records of book ownership, bequest, and patronage show that a progressively more literate and sophisticated English female audience wanted guidance in an affective, even ecstatic, piety, a type of devotion that had formerly been available only to a demographically narrower group of readers'.[12]

While the majority of the religious works published by de Worde fell into the category of devotional rather than mystical literature, the first decade of his press saw the publication of several mystical treatises. During the course of the 1490s he printed the *Chastysing of Goddes chyldren* (c.1492); *Tretyse of loue* (1493); the *Lyf of Saynt Katherin of senis* with *the reuelacions of saynt Elysabeth the kynges doughter of hungarye* (1493); and Walter Hilton's *Scala perfecconis* and *Vita mixta* (1494). The early sixteenth century saw the publication of Richard Rolle's *Deuoute Medytacyons* (1503, 1505, 1517); *Contemplacyons of the dread and love of God* (1506, 1525); *Remedy ayenst temptacyons* (1508, 1517, 1519) and *The VII Shedyngs of the Blode of Jhesu Chryst* (1509); Bonaventure's *Incendium amoris* (1511); and Catherine of Siena's *Orcherd of Syon* (1519), which was commissioned for the nuns of Syon Abbey by the steward of Syon, Master Richard Sutton.

We can see from this list that not only was de Worde responding to a demand for readings on mysticism in general, but that he was responding to an interest in the type of mysticism associated in particular with two monastic orders: the Bridgettines and the Carthusians. The role these orders played in both the production and dissemination of vernacular devotional and mystical literature in fifteenth- and sixteenth-century England cannot be underestimated, and any consideration of the potential audience of *A Shorte Treatyse of Contemplacyon* must locate it within this context. Founded in 1415 by Henry V, the Carthusian monastery at Sheen and its sister-house across the Thames, the Bridgettine Syon Abbey (also originally at Sheen), were responsible for, among many other texts, the transmission of the *Revelations* of St Bridget of Sweden and Julian of Norwich, and

---

[10] Mary C. Erler, *Women, Reading, and Piety in Late Medieval England* (Cambridge, 2002), p. 4.

[11] Hilary M. Carey, 'Devout Literate Laypeople and the Pursuit of the Mixed Life in Later Medieval England.' *Journal of Religious History* 14 (1987): 361–81 (372).

[12] Anne Clark Bartlett, *Male Authors, Female Readers: Representation and Subjectivity in Middle English Devotional Literature* (Ithaca, NY and London, 1995), p. 118. For a more detailed account of the stages in the development of female literacy and women's relationship to devotional texts see pp. 6–17 especially. For further information on late medieval women's literary culture see Jacqueline Jenkins's essay below.

The Cloud of Unknowing. The connections between Syon, Sheen, and the Carthusian London charterhouse were strong, and evidence suggests that manuscripts circulated among the three houses.[13] However, the influence of the Bridgettines and Carthusians extended beyond the copying and translation of manuscripts, as they also had a significant impact on early print culture. As the above list of publications illustrates, the Bridgettine house of Syon had a considerable influence on de Worde's press, especially during the second and third decades of the sixteenth century. While it is impossible to say precisely how or when Syon's influence on the press began, it may actually have originated with de Worde's predecessor, William Caxton. In 1491 Lady Margaret Beaufort, who was the mother of Henry VII and renowned for her literary patronage and love of learning, commissioned a copy of the *Fifteen Oes*, a prayer often attributed to St Bridget.[14] After Caxton's death, de Worde strove to maintain the connection with Lady Margaret, eventually fashioning himself 'Prynter vnto the moost excellent Pryncesse my lady the Kynges mother.'[15] Furthermore, in about 1499 he printed a life of St Jerome that was originally written for Lady Margaret's grandmother by a member of the monastery at Syon.

Considering *A Shorte Treatyse of Contemplacyon* within the complex network that existed between Syon Abbey, royal patronage, and de Worde's printing press may allow us to speculate on the potential reception of the text. While there was certainly a keen audience for works of a devotional and mystical nature, how might this particular work have fared? Might people encountering this redaction in 1501 have been encountering it as an entirely new text? Or might they even already have been familiar with Margery Kempe or her *Book*? Although it is impossible to know for certain, George R. Keiser suggests that even in 1501 Kempe's name would have had a certain 'cachet' among the laity and that the redaction was an ideal means both of cashing in on her name and catering to the preference among late medieval English readers for the compendious compilation: texts with highly concentrated, often proverbial, statements that were able to stand free from their larger context.[16] Holbrook agrees that the reputation of *The Book of Margery Kempe* would have 'pricked interest' in the treatise because, even though more than sixty years had passed since Kempe's visit to Syon Abbey in 1434, the inhabitants and friends of Syon would almost certainly have been familiar with her and her *Book*. Several circumstantial details bear out this assertion, such as the references to St Bridget, the founding saint of Syon in *The Book of Margery Kempe*; Bridget's influence on Kempe's devotional practices; Kempe's familiarity with mystics like Rolle and Bonaventure, whose works were favoured by Bridgettines and Carthusians; the presence of the Salthouse manuscript in the Carthusian charterhouse of Mount Grace; and of course, the fact that Kempe herself visited Syon.[17]

---

13 Michael Sargent, 'Walter Hilton's *Scale of Perfection*: The London Manuscript Group Reconsidered', *Medium Aevum* 52 (1983): 189–216.
14 George R. Keiser, 'The Mystics and the Early English Printers: The Economics of Devotionalism', in Marion Glasscoe, ed., *The Medieval Mystical Tradition in England: Exeter Symposium IV* (Cambridge, 1987), pp. 9–26 (p. 12).
15 Short Title Catalogue numbers 18566, 19305.
16 Keiser, 'The Mystics and the Early English Printers', p. 16.
17 Holbrook, 'Margery Kempe and Wynkyn de Worde', p. 42.

Syon Abbey was a very high-profile religious house, with an excellent reputation for learning and for the devoutness of its sisters. Many vernacular devotional treatises were produced for the use of the nuns of Syon, two of the most well-known being the *Myroure of Oure Ladye*, and the *Orcherd of Syon*, a translation of St Catherine of Siena's *Dialogo*. These devotional works portrayed the Syon nuns as exemplars of the religious life, and while they were written specifically for the sisters, there may have been an understanding that the works would also be read by the public.[18] Lay people were urged to model their behaviour and reading practices upon that of the nuns, and it is possible that if the nuns of Syon were familiar with Kempe and her *Book*, the lay people in the surrounding community may also have heard about Kempe. And so, while it seems that *A Short Treatyse of Contemplacyon* was originally intended for a lay audience, and a female lay audience in particular, as will be seen, it may have been read and appreciated by a monastic audience as well. While it may seem unusual that texts circulated among such seemingly diverse audiences, more recent investigations into late medieval manuscript and print culture have shown that the boundaries between the laity and enclosed religious were far more fluid than previously assumed. Even devotional texts originally intended for religious recluses or those in enclosed orders often found their way into the hands of devout lay people through networks of manuscript and print transmission, and the opposite is also true, as texts intended for the laity sometimes made their way inside the convent walls. Furthermore, given that the cultural and spiritual ideals offered to laywomen and female religious were very similar, it would not be unusual for them to have shared a common interest in certain texts.[19]

The contention that the edition of extracts from Kempe's *Book* was of interest to lay people, and that the instruction it offered was deemed valuable, is borne out by the fact that it appeared again in print when English printer Henry Pepwell included it in a small collection of devotional works in 1521.[20] The seven short pieces included in Pepwell's quarto volume, in order, are Richard of St Victor's *Benjamin Minor or On the Preparation of the Soul for Contemplation; Dyuers Doctrynes*

[18] C. Annette Grisé, ' "In the Blessid Vynezrd Oure Holy Saueour": Female Religious Readers and Textual Reception in the *Myroure of Oure Ladye* and the *Orcherd of Syon*', in Marion Glasscoe, ed., *The Medieval Mystical Tradition in England, Ireland and Wales: Exeter Symposium VI* (Cambridge, 1999), pp. 193–211 (pp. 195–6). For information about the contents of the sisters' library at Syon Abbey see Ann M. Hutchison, 'What the Nuns Read: Literary Evidence from the English Bridgettine House, Syon Abbey', *Mediaeval Studies* 57 (1995): 205–22.

[19] See Ann M. Hutchison, 'Devotional Reading in the Monastery and in the Late Medieval Household', in Michael G. Sargent, ed., *De Cella in Seculum: Religious and Secular Life and Devotion in Late Medieval England* (Cambridge, 1989), pp. 215–27. This point is also discussed by Jenkins, pp. 120–1.

[20] Pepwell's print has the Short Title Catalogue number 20972, and a copy is housed in the British Library. For a modernised version see *The Cell of Self-Knowledge: Seven Early English Mystical Treatises Printed by Henry Pepwell in 1521*, ed., Edmund G. Gardner (orig. pub. 1910; this edition New York, 1966). Gardner has collated Pepwell's texts with various extant manuscript or other printed versions, using de Worde's edition for *A Shorte Treatyse of Contemplacyon*. He acknowledges that in most cases the readings of the manuscripts have been adopted in preference to Pepwell's print; however, for the most part the variances are minimal. John Griffiths has also edited a modernised transcription of *The Cell of Self-Knowledge* for the *Spiritual Classics* series (New York, 1981). Parts of Pepwell's book also appear in *Richard of St Victor's Treatise of the Study of Wisdom that Men Call Benjamin*, trans. and ed. Dick Barnes (New York, 1990).

Deuoute & Fruytfull, taken out of the lyfe of that gloryous vyrgyne & spouse of our lorde Saynt Katheryn of Seenes; A Shorte Treatyse of Contemplacyon taught by our lorde Jhesu cryst, or taken out of the boke of Margery kempe deuoute ancres of Lynn; Walter Hilton's *Song of Angels;* and three short works associated with the author of *The Cloud of Unknowing: The Epistle of Prayer, The Epistle of Discretion in Stirrings of the Soul* and *A Devout Treatise on the Discerning of Spirits.* When Edmund G. Gardner edited Pepwell's untitled collection in 1910, he christened it *The Cell of Self-Knowledge,* a reference to Catherine of Siena's assertion that, 'My cell is not to be made of stone or wood; instead it will be the cell of self-knowledge.'[21] Each of the pieces in *The Cell of Self-Knowledge* gives instruction on the process of contemplation, placing a common emphasis on the necessity of knowledge of self and purity of heart to ascend to the highest levels of contemplation and achieve the ultimate goal of one-ness with God. *The Song of Angels* and the three epistles by the *Cloud* author are more specifically concerned with helping the reader distinguish between good and evil inclinations of the soul, and showing the soul how to discern false feel-ings and sensations from those which arise from the true fire of love and light of knowing. As Gardner describes them, the pieces by the *Cloud* author 'show us mysticism brought down [. . .] from the clouds for the practical guidance of the beginner along this difficult way', and indeed, this description can apply to all of the works in the collection. Pepwell seems to have intended *The Cell of Self-Knowledge* for the use of lay people interested in living the 'mixed life', as the col-lection offers practical guidance on how one might live actively in the secular world while at the same time seeking to know God through the process of con-templation.

The *Benjamin Minor,* the pieces by the *Cloud* author, and *The Song of Angels* frequently circulated together in various combinations in fifteenth- to seventeenth-century English manuscripts, and as such, it may not seem terribly unusual that they were eventually compiled in a printed edition.[22] What is remarkable, however, is the inclusion of Margery Kempe's *A Shorte Treatyse of Contemplacyon* and Catherine of Siena's *Divers Doctrines Devout and Fruitful.* These pieces are similar in that they both have holy women at the centre; were deemed suitable reading for the laity; present a particular kind of holy woman as a model; and were composed of excerpts from a larger text. In a similar fashion to *A Shorte Treatyse of Contemplacyon,* the *Divers Doctrines Devout and Fruitful* consists of thirteen passages of varying lengths that have been extracted from various sections of the *Lyf of Saint Katherin of Senis.* Much like the Kempe piece, the *Divers Doctrines* is composed of passages (identified as 'doctrynes') spoken by Catherine and God. However, in this case the passages have not been extracted in quite so scattered a fashion: the vast majority are taken from Book II (the 'conversations' between Catherine and God), and in particular from chapters 10 and 11, and for the most part are arranged in the order in which they appear in the *Lyf.* Furthermore, Catherine's voice is dominant: of the thirteen

---

[21] Gardner, *The Cell of Self-Knowledge,* p. xxv. I will adopt Gardner's title throughout this paper.
[22] For a list of manuscripts and their contents see *Deonise Hid Diuinite, and Other Treatises on Contemplative Prayer Related to The Cloud of Unknowing,* ed. Phyllis Hodgson, EETS original series 231 (1955), pp. i–xix.

extracted passages, her voice accounts for ten while God's voice is heard in only three. And, whereas God speaks the final passage of *A Shorte Treatyse of Contemplacyon*, in the *Divers Doctrines Devout and Fruitful* it is Catherine who delivers the final address to her disciples; indeed, God delivers his three doctrines at the very beginning of the piece and is not heard again thereafter. However, if Catherine has a more authoritative voice than Margery in *A Shorte Treatyse of Contemplacyon*, the more radical and potentially controversial elements of Catherine's life are similarly absent. There are some marked similarities in the experiences of Catherine and Margery. Like Margery, Catherine was also a very public figure who travelled extensively, visiting anchorites and conversing with ecclesiastical authorities. Catherine was also a divisive figure who met with some opposition from clerics and who had a mystical marriage. And, like Margery Kempe, Catherine of Siena occupied a liminal space in that she was not an institutionalized nun, but not quite a laywoman either. She was a Dominician *sorror de poenitentia* ('sister of penance'), or what was referred to in 14th-century Italy as a *mantellata*. While she wore the black and white colours of the Order of St Dominic, she had not taken orders and was not enclosed in a religious community as a nun would have been. While she was committed to the spiritual life, she was also known for her charitable and political activities, and for acting as a spiritual director to both lay and religious alike. Like Margery Kempe, she was free to travel about and speak publicly, and indeed, Karen Scott has asserted that '[i]t was her lay status in the church that made Catherine's career possible'.[23]

The Lyf of Saint Katherin of Senis the blessed virgin, from which the *Divers Doctrines Devout and Fruitful* was taken, is a redaction of a Middle English translation of the Latin *Legenda Major*, a spiritual biography of St Catherine that was written after her death, between 1383 and 1395, largely by her confessor and biographer Raymond of Capua.[24] The *Lyf* was translated into Middle English after her canonisation in 1461, was eventually edited by William Caxton, and then published by Wynkyn de Worde in 1493. Interestingly, Wynkyn was the first printer outside of Italy to print a Catherine of Siena text, and was also one of a very few to print a second work, going on to print Catherine's major work, the *Orcherd of Syon*, in 1519. That Wynkyn published these works indicates that he was responding to an interest in works by and about Catherine. Translations of the lives and writings of continental saints had become increasingly popular since the late fourteenth century. In her study of Catherine's cultural and literary reception in late medieval and early modern Britain, Jane Chance has shown that her influence did indeed extend to England, and that it was amplified by factors such as the advent

---

23 See David Wallace, 'Mystics and Followers in Siena and East Anglia: A Study in Taxonomy, Class and Cultural Mediation', in Marion Glasscoe, ed., *The Medieval Mystical Tradition in England: Exeter Symposium III* (Cambridge, 1984), pp. 169–91 (p. 171). For an illuminating discussion of how Catherine of Siena's holiness was related to her lay status, see Scott, 'Catherine of Siena and Lay Sanctity in Fourteenth-Century Italy', in Ann W. Astell, ed., *Lay Sanctity, Medieval and Modern: A Search for Models* (Notre Dame, IN, 2000), pp. 77–90 (p. 79).

24 The *Divers Doctrines Devout and Fruitful* was not, as is often assumed, taken from the *Orcherd of Syon* (also known as the *Dialogo*).

of printing and the increase in female readership, and the use of Catherine's writings to foster the spiritual lives of the sisters of the Bridgettine order at Syon.[25]

While the precise origin of the *Divers Doctrines Devout and Fruitful* is uncertain, we may be able to speculate to some degree on what its audience might
have been. While St Catherine had followers among men and women alike, she
was apparently particularly popular among laywomen; indeed, from the fourteenth to the sixteenth century her writings captured the attention of an aristocratic audience composed mainly of women in England and Scotland.[26] An
almost verbally identical selection of passages from Catherine's life to that found
in *The Cell of Self-Knowledge* is found in a manuscript dating from the fifteenth
century, BL MS Royal 17 D.v., where it follows *The Cloud of Unknowing*. The Royal
collection consists of manuscripts collected by English sovereigns from Edward
IV onwards, and we know that Edward's mother, Cecily Neville, was distinguished for her piety and her collection of devotional writings, so this manuscript may possibly have belonged to her. Cecily certainly had an interest in St
Catherine and other texts associated with Bridgettine devotion, and upon her
death in 1495 she bequeathed, among other texts, a manuscript copy of the life
of St Catherine to her granddaughter Bridget who was in the Dominican convent
at Dartford.[27] While there is no direct evidence to suggest that the *Divers
Doctrines Devout and Fruitful* was composed specifically for Cecily, it seems likely
that it was a work with which she was familiar, and that it also found an audience among other laywomen.

Women certainly formed part of the initial readership of both *A Shorte Treatyse
of Contemplacyon* and the *Divers Doctrines Devout and Fruitful*, and in light of this,
I would now like to consider why Henry Pepwell might have chosen to include
them in *The Cell of Self-Knowledge* in 1521. As women formed an increasingly
significant group of readers and owners of vernacular books, Pepwell would have
had a vested financial interest in addressing the needs of this growing audience,
if nothing else. *A Shorte Treatyse of Contemplacyon* and the *Divers Doctrines
Devout and Fruitful* are thematically very similar to the other selections in *The Cell
of Self-Knowledge*, as, in one way or another, all of the pieces offer practical guidance
to lay people with an interest in contemplation and mysticism. But I would argue
that the Margery Kempe and Catherine of Siena texts function in a slightly
different way. While all of the selections are meant as guides to inward devotion,
Margery and Catherine also serve as exemplars, very concrete examples of women
engaging in certain types of devotional practices and ways of religious living. This
is not to say that they did not also speak to a male readership; however, one can
imagine that women might have identified with these figures in a far more personal
way, using them as very specific models for their own devotional practices.

---

[25] Jane Chance, 'St Catherine of Siena in Late Medieval Britain: Feminizing Literary Reception
Through Gender and Class', *Annali d'Italianistica: Women Mystic Writers* 13 (1995): 163–203
(166). For further information on St Catherine's reception in Britain see Diane Watt, 'The
Prophet at Home: Elizabeth Barton and the Influence of Bridget of Sweden and Catherine of
Siena', in Rosalynn Voaden, ed., *Prophets Abroad: The Reception of Continental Holy Women in
Late-Medieval England* (Cambridge, 1996), pp. 161–76.

[26] Chance, 'St Catherine of Siena', p. 166.

[27] Keiser, 'The Mystics and the Early English Printers', p. 23.

Certainly hagiography, and in particular hagiography of female saints, was one of the most popular forms of literature among late medieval laywomen, and women were expressly encouraged to model their behaviour and devotional practices on those of the remarkable holy women of whom they heard and read. [28]

A Shorte Treatyse of Contemplacyon and the *Divers Doctrines Devout and Fruitful* portray a fairly particular type of holy woman and offer similar lessons to their readers: the value of contemplation and prayer as modes of devotion, and the desirability of these modes over strict ascetic practices; the validation of tears of compunction and thinking on the Passion as legitimate expressions of piety; and the importance of learning to suffer trials patiently and pray for the salvation of others. That Henry Pepwell amended the colophon of de Worde's pamphlet to identify Kempe as 'ancresse of Lynne', strengthens the connection between Catherine and Margery even further, as they are both presented as dedicated and insitutionalised holy women. If Margery Kempe was to be offered as a spiritual role model for laywomen, any trace of the controversy that marked her life must be erased. Pepwell's removal of her to the anchorhold seems a further attempt to complete the process of moulding her into a more orthodox figure that was begun with the initial composition of *A Shorte Treatyse of Contemplacyon*.[29] Pepwell's designation of Margery as an anchoress recalls the incident from the *The Book of Margery Kempe* in which an old monk in Canterbury, threatened by Margery's knowledge of scripture and freedom of mobility tells her that, 'I wold þow wer closyd in an hows of ston þat þer schuld no man speke with þe' (13: 27). Casting Margery as an anchoress further validates the message of *A Shorte Treatyse of Contemplacyon*, as the figure of the anchoress is associated with respectability, containment, and quiet devotion – the very values that the treatise espouses for its women readers.

In being placed side by side in the collection, the Margery Kempe and Catherine of Siena pieces play off each other in a highly effective manner, each reinforcing the spiritual lessons and model of female piety presented in the other. Both *A Shorte Treatyse of Contemplacyon* and the *Divers Doctrines Devout and Fruitful* advocate what we might consider rather general Christian values.[30] In a very

---

[28] For further discussion of how medieval women were encouraged to model themselves on female saints see Katherine J. Lewis, 'Virgin Martyrs and the Training of Young Medieval Women', in Katherine J. Lewis, Noël James Menuge and Kim M. Phillips, eds, *Young Medieval Women* (New York, 1999), pp. 25–46; Karen A. Winstead, *Virgin Martyrs: Legends of Sainthood in Late Medieval England* (Ithaca, NY, 1997); Jocelyn Wogan-Browne, *Saints' Lives and Women's Literary Culture c. 1150–1300* (Oxford, 2001).

[29] Goodman argues that, 'Henry Pepwell . . . transposed Margery to where the secular world always wants to put spiritual dissidents – out of it': 'The Piety of John Brunham's Daughter of Lynn', pp. 357–8. However, while this implies that putting Margery in an anchorhold removes her entirely from the world, Summit makes the important point that this is not necessarily the case. Drawing a parallel with Nicholas Watson's study of the anchoress Julian of Norwich, she notes that: 'Though physically isolated, medieval anchoresses were not isolated from religious and political controversies of late medieval England', *Lost Property*, p. 127. See also Nicholas Watson, 'The Composition of Julian of Norwich's *Revelation of Love*', *Speculum* 68 (1993): 637–83.

[30] When quoting from Pepwell's version of *A Shorte Treatyse of Contemplacyon* and *Divers Doctrines Devout and Fruitful*, I have silently expanded abbreviations and contractions, and have represented ampersands as *and*. I consulted an unpaginated microform of Pepwell's collection so the numbers in brackets within the text following quotations from both signify

lengthy passage, God praises Margery for the charity she has shown to all people: 'I thanke the for the charyte that thou haste to al lecherous men and women, for thou prayest for them and wepest for them many a tere desyrynge that I sholde delyuer them out of synne and be as gracyous to them as I was to Mary Magdaleyne' (18).[31] Likewise, Catherine advises that, 'for to gete and pourchace purete of soule, it were ryght necessary that a man kepte hymselfe from all manere of jugementes of his neyghboure's dedes, for in euery creature we sholde behold onely the wyll of God. [. . .] [I]n no wyse men sholde deme creatures; that is nother dyspyse them by theyr dome nor condempne them all be it that they se them do open synne before them, but rather they sholde haue compassyon on them & pray for them [. . .]' (13). Both pieces also remind readers of the virtue of patience: God tells Margery that 'pacyence is more worthe than myracles doynge' (23),[32] and instructs Catherine, 'for My loue, doughter, suffre pacyently bytter thynges' (5). However, the two pieces also address and endorse particular expressions of piety that are more historically and culturally specific, especially in regards to female devotional practices. By the thirteenth century, a recognisable 'female piety' had emerged that was largely associated with mysticism and ecstasy.[33] It focused primarily on three aspects of Christ's humanity: Christ as infant, as bridegroom, and his death. The later Middle Ages saw an increased emphasis on affective forms of piety that focused on Christ's humanity and encouraged people to identify with Christ in a very personal manner as a fellow human being. Meditating on Christ's Passion was one of the primary expressions of affective piety, an expression that is clearly endorsed in the *Divers Doctrines Devout and Fruitful*, as God tells Catherine that, '[the] Crosse shall be to you a grete refresshynge in all your temptacyons, yf ye haue mynde of the paynes that I suffred theron and temptacyons. And certaynly the paynes of the Crosse may well be called refresshynge of temptacyons, for the more payne ye suffre for My loue, the more lyke ye be to Me' (5). Likewise, in *A Shorte Treatyse of Contemplacyon*, Margery is so affected by contemplating the pain Christ suffered for the sake of humanity's salvation 'that she myght not endure to beholde a lepre, or another seke man, specyally yf he had ony woundes apperynge on hym' (15).[34] One physical manifestation of Margery's being overcome by the sight of anyone or anything that reminds her of Christ's suffering is her weeping of tears of compunction, as the same passage continues: 'So she wepte as yf she had sene our Lorde Jhesu, with his woundes bledynge; and so she dyde in the syght of the soule; for thrughe the beholdynge of the seke man, her mynde was all ravysshed

---

passage number. In the case of quotations from Pepwell's version of *A Shorte Treatyse of Contemplacyon* the footnote in each case gives the page number of *BMK* containing the equivalent passage of the de Worde version. Pepwell's print of *A Shorte Treatyse of Contemplacyon* varies very slightly from that of de Worde. The textual and spelling variants can be found in both Meech and Allen's, and Windeatt's transcriptions of *A Shorte Treatyse of Contemplacyon*.

31 356.

32 357.

33 Caroline Walker Bynum's works *Jesus as Mother: Studies in the Spirituality of the High Middle Ages* (Berkeley and Los Angeles, 1982) and *Holy Feast and Holy Fast: The Religious Significance of Food to Medieval Women* (Berkeley and Los Angeles, 1987) are the classic accounts of this brand of piety.

34 355.

in to our Lorde Jhesu.' While in *The Book of Margery Kempe* Margery's tears are sometimes met with disapproval and suspicion, her weeping on Christ's Passion was certainly not without precedent. The scribe of the *Book* mentions that reading the life of Marie d'Oignies, helped convince him that Margery's weeping was divinely inspired, for Marie was a holy woman renowned for weeping tears of compunction (62: 191, also 68: 205). Although one had to be cautious about indulging in tears too much and growing to love God on their account rather than for God himself, in moderation, tears of compunction were held to be a genuine expression of piety; indeed, for Walter Hilton they were a necessary first stage in the process of contemplation.[35]

As mentioned previously, one of most important lessons to be learned from *A Shorte Treatyse of Contemplacyon* is that of keeping God in the mind and meditating on his love. Margery is repeatedly reminded that 'thou mayst no better please God than to thynke contynually in his love,' (3) and that 'yf thou wylte be hyghe with me in heuen, kepe me alwaye in thy mynde as moche as thou mayst' (8).[36] In a similar fashion, Catherine is instructed to, 'Thynke on me and I shall thynke on the' (2). Both selections ground their devotional practices in prayer and contemplation, and Catherine explains in one of her doctrines that 'to suche a state of perfeccyon, in the whiche al the herte is gyuen to God, a soule maye not come perfytely without medyacyon of deuoute prayer' (13). She then proceeds to outline two specific modes of prayer, vocal and mental: 'Vocall prayers [. . .] sholde be kepte certayne houres in the nyght and in the daye ordeyned by holy Chyrche; but mentall prayer sholde euer be had, in acte or in habyte of the soule' (13). We see here that while vocal prayer is something that should be made a part of one's daily spiritual routine, keeping God ever in one's mind is even more imperative. A similar ideal is presented in *A Shorte Treatyse of Contemplacyon*, as Christ tells Margery that, 'thynkynge, wepynge, and hyghe contemplacyon is the best lyfe in erthe, and thou shalte haue more meryte in heuen for one yere thynkynge in thy mynde than for an hondred yere of prayenge with thy mouthe; and yet thou wylte not byleue me, for thou wylte bydde many beedes' (6).[37]

This last passage is particularly interesting, not simply for the type of direction it gives, as this instruction is fairly typical of both of the selections, but because of what it implies about Margery's reaction to these approved modes of devotion. Christ's admonishment, 'yet thou wylte not byleue me' indicates that Margery is having doubts about whether or not these private forms of devotion really are sufficient to express her love, and it is in this light that I would like to further consider the interplay between *A Shorte Treatyse of Contemplacyon* and the *Divers Doctrines Devout and Fruitful*. In being placed side by side these works not only engage in a process of reinforcement, in which each reflects the values espoused in the other, but also in a process of affirmation whereby through the

---

[35] Sandra J. McEntire, *The Doctrine of Compunction in Medieval Literature: Holy Tears* (Lewiston, NY, 1990), p. 141.

[36] 353; 354.

[37] 354. For a discussion of the privileging of 'mental' activities such as contemplating inwardly and hearing texts read, over 'vocal' activities such as reading and praying aloud in *The Book of Margery Kempe*, see Jenkins in this volume.

example of Margery Kempe, any similar doubts that the reader may have about the prescribed modes of devotion which they contain are quelled. The tone of Margery's and Catherine's voices, and the way the women interact with God are quite noticeably different. Catherine speaks with conviction and authority in the *Divers Doctrines Devout and Fruitful*: she has received these doctrines of religious living directly from God, and imparts them to her disciples without reservation. In contrast, Margery Kempe is at times uncertain: she has a great desire to please and demonstrate her love for God, but needs reassurance that she is demonstrating that love sufficiently. This is a familiar pattern in her *Book*, especially in relation to her concern that her married state would be a hindrance to her spiritual perfection, and that wives could not obtain the same divine favour as virgins (e.g. 21: 48–9; 22: 50). Although *A Shorte Treatyse of Contemplacyon* presents Margery in an entirely different context and she is characterised as an 'anchoress', she occasionally continues to express many of the concerns, doubts, and anxieties that other laywomen might have had about their ability to live the life of the sprit while at the same time living in the secular world and fulfilling their earthly obligations. In a sense, *A Shorte Treatyse of Contemplacyon* addresses the very questions that a laywoman might have upon reading the *Divers Doctrines Devout and Fruitful*. However, this very act of questioning, rather than negating the validity of Catherine's words, actually serves to reinforce the lessons that she is imparting. One can imagine that laywomen would identify with Margery's insecurities, and in seeing her being reassured by Christ, would also be reassured themselves. Paradoxically, it is when Margery is the least secular – when she is transformed into an anchoress, a figure that is farthest away on the spectrum of the contemplative life – that she is enabled to 'speak' most directly to laywomen.

The Cell of Self-Knowledge as a whole is geared towards those who are seeking direction on how best to live the mixed life, and the Catherine of Siena and Margery Kempe pieces work together quite effectively, not only to instruct readers in the process of perfecting the spirit, but in subduing any doubts or anxieties that readers might have about their ability to do so. This dynamic, which we first saw above in relation to thinking and praying, occurs most obviously in relation to the merit of engaging in strict ascetic practices. It is important to note the rather striking point that, although Catherine of Siena was well known for her extreme asceticism, absolutely no mention of it is made in the *Divers Doctrines Devout and Fruitful*. What would laywomen reading this text, who were familiar with the story of Catherine's life, have made of this omission? Certainly it might be very comforting in the sense that it would provide them with a more realistic saintly model to imitate – although, granted, Catherine never advocated that other people follow her example to the same extreme, as it was part of her own personal calling. At the same time, might readers not have wondered about the exclusion of this acetic element, and question whether choosing what might be perceived as an easier path might prevent them from achieving a perfect union with God? Margery Kempe certainly seems to ask such questions, and, interestingly enough, the very first section in *A Shorte Treatyse of Contemplacyon* is the one in which Kempe proclaims that she has desired many times to have her head smitten with an axe for the love of Jesus. Clearly, she is positioning herself within the hagiographic tradition of martyrdom with which late medieval laywomen were very familiar.[38] While it could be argued that, when taken out of the larger context of *The Book of Margery Kempe*, this declaration gives the impression that she is bravely and willingly prepared to martyr herself – erasing the fact that she is, in reality, frightened by the prospect of death and is looking for the most quick and painless means to attain martyrdom – I would contend that her anxieties are still very much present. Indeed, her anxieties actually serve the important function of allowing God to assure her that martyrdom – or even, for that matter, strict bodily penance – is not necessary to win his love: 'I thanke the, doughter, that thou woldest dye for My loue; for as often as thou thynkest so, thou shalte haue the same mede in heuen, as yf thou suffredest the same dethe, and yet there shall no man slee the' (1).[39]

The idea that physical suffering is unnecessary is reiterated shortly afterwards. In response to her query of how she might best love him, God tells Margery that, 'yf thou ware the habergyon or the heere, fastynge brede and water, and yf thou saydest euery day a thousande Pater Nosters, thou shalte not please me so well as thou doest whan thou arte in sylence, and suffrest Me to speke in thy soule' (5).[40] And still, this assurance is not enough, and Margery continues to make declarations of the extreme lengths she will go to in order to prove her love and devotion: '[G]ood Lorde, I wolde be layde naked upon an hurdell for thy loue, all men to wonder on me and to caste fylth and dyrt on me, and be drawen fro towne to towne euery daye my lyfe tyme, yf thu were pleased therby, and no mannes soule hyndred' (19).[41] In response, God acknowledges her anxieties and tells her in no uncertain terms that, 'Doughter, it is more pleasure to me that thou suffre despytes, scornes, shames, repreues, wronges, and dyseases, than yf thyn hede were stryken of thre tymes a daye euery day in seuen yere' (24).[42] By the end of the treatise, Margery comes to accept what God has advised her is the best way to love him, and urges that, 'these graces thou sholdest showe to relygyous men and to prestes' (27).[43] This recommendation of Margery's that men should share her experiences suggests a way in which her exemplary conduct could therefore have been seen as relevant to male readers, as well as female.

While there is no doubt that *A Shorte Treatyse of Contemplacyon* is problematic because it removes the more radical and subversive elements from Kempe's text and recommends a far more traditional ideal of pious femininity, we can see that the treatise nevertheless offered something very beneficial to the devotional reader, both female and male. Along with the other pieces in *The Cell of Self-Knowledge*, Kempe's treatise showed lay people how to construct their own inner cell through the process of meditation – a cell which, rather than being restrictive, could be

---

[38] Although Margery is not seen to engage in extreme ascetical self-injury either within the *Book*.
[39] 353.
[40] 353.
[41] 356.
[42] 357.
[43] 357.

a place of retreat from the worries and obligations of everyday life, a place to nourish the spirit. When *A Shorte Treatyse of Contemplacyon* is viewed in the context of its position next to the *Divers Doctrines Devout and Fruitful*, to some small degree Margery regains the voice that was removed in the original process of creating the redaction. Engaging in a 'dialogue' with the Catherine of Siena piece allows her to speak, as it were, quite directly to devotional readers' doubts, uncertainties, and desire to love God perfectly. While we cannot overlook the fact that this was achieved at great expense to the figure of Margery Kempe that is presented in the *Book*, the expunging of controversial elements that makes the treatise so problematic to modern scholarship is also what preserved at least a semblance of Margery's message in a time of religious debate and transition. Indeed, it is possible that the *Treatyse* actually engaged with some of this debate, for Jennifer Summit argues that Pepwell used Margery Kempe as a tool against the spread of Lutheran Protestantism, because the treatise's legitimisation of the doctrine and practice of indulgence engaged directly with contemporary debates over the matter.[44] Moreover, the textual history of *A Shorte Treatyse of Contemplacyon* shows that, although *The Book of Margery Kempe* itself survives in only a single manuscript, parts of it were much more widely known and obviously valued enough to be circulated in print almost a century after the *Book* was written. It also demonstrates that, far from being unknown, Margery Kempe in this period was recognised as a holy woman whose writings could appropriately be set alongside those of a canonised saint such as Catherine of Siena.

---

[44] Summit, *Lost Property*, pp. 126–38.

6

Reading and The Book of Margery Kempe[1]

JACQUELINE JENKINS

At first glance, it may seem curious to devote an entire chapter to questions of reading and literacy in *The Book of Margery Kempe*, given the *Book*'s own apparent ambiguity about the literary abilities of its protagonist, Margery.[2] After all, many readers have seemed willing to accept Kempe's disavowal of literate practices in her narrative: for example Edmund Colledge, whose early belief that 'without a doubt, she could neither read nor write' caused him to interpret all possible references to Margery's literacy in ways consistent with this acknowledged bias.[3] That Kempe was influenced by contemporary devotional literature in a variety of genres, both in terms of narrative event and style, is now widely acknowledged. That Kempe may have had significantly more control over and authority in the composition of her narrative than was frequently assumed by earlier scholars has been effectively argued.[4] But that Kempe might have been more practically literate (in terms of reading) than she chooses to describe is seldom admitted by modern readers. This essay, therefore, will consider the cultural practices of literacy in Kempe's England, the evidence in the *Book* for Kempe's awareness of and participation in these practices, and the role of reading in the lives of late medieval laywomen. It is my contention here that not only is it probable that Margery Kempe was able to read English, but that her presentation of herself as the illiterate (non-reading) 'Margery' is a deliberate self-construction. Further, I shall argue that Kempe's deployment of this trope of illiteracy comprises a part of the carefully scripted performance of late medieval devotion the *Book* consciously enacts.

[1] I would like to thank the editors of this volume for their insightful comments on an early draft of this essay, as well as Nicholas Watson who read and commented on the paper, and the members of the Department of English at the University of Geneva, and in particular Denis Renevey, who offered several very helpful and constructive comments after hearing a version of this paper in November 2003. I am grateful to the Social Sciences and Humanities Research Council of Canada for support for this research.
[2] In this essay, I maintain a distinction between 'Margery Kempe', or 'Kempe', the historical woman and author of *The Book*, and 'Margery', the *Book*'s protagonist and constructed subject. This is by now a familiar convention in Kempe studies, developing out of Staley's argument in *Dissenting Fictions*.
[3] Edmund Colledge, 'Margery Kempe', in J. Walsh, ed., *Pre-Reformation English Spirituality* (Bronx, NY, 1965), pp. 210–23 (p. 217).
[4] See Nicholas Watson, 'The Making of the Book of Margery Kempe', *Voices in Dialogue* ed. Kathryn Kerby-Fulton and Linda Olson (South Bend, IN, forthcoming 2004); Staley, *Dissenting Fictions*; Josephine Tarvers, 'The Alleged Illiteracy of Margery Kempe', *Medieval Perspectives* 11 (1996): 113–24. This essay will not take up the issue of Margery Kempe's ability to write, and the related question of her compositional authority over the book; rather, it will focus on the implications of Kempe's self-construction as a particular kind of reader.

Margery Kempe and Late Medieval Literacy

On the one hand, many of the references to reading in the *Book* do seem to suggest that Margery was unable either to read, or to write. For instance, she searches for a 'lystere' (a reader) to read to her the devotional books she longs to study (especially chapter 58); she asks the angelic child in her vision to point out where her name is written in the Book of Life, rather than identifying it herself, a sign many readers have taken to mean that she could not read her name on her own (85: 206–7); and, she denies knowledge of Latin during one of her many trials for Lollardy (47: 113). Moreover, as the Proem so dramatically describes, she expends much energy finding a scribe both willing and able to write down her spiritual experiences. On the other hand, however, these descriptions conflict with the *Book*'s more general picture of Margery's thirst for text-based knowledge, a thirst she describes in prayer as an insatiable hunger:

> On a tyme, as þe forseyd creatur was in hir contemplacyon, sche hungryd ryth sor aftyr Goddys word & seyd, "Alas, Lord, as many clerkys as þu hast in þis world, þat þu ne woldyst sendyn me on of hem þat myth fulfillyn my sowle wyth þi word & wyth redyng of Holy Scriptur, for alle þe clerkys þat prechyn may not fulfillyn, for me thynkyth þat my sowle is euyr a-lych hungry" (58: 142).

Furthermore, as the *Book* makes clear, Margery's literary tastes were refined and specific, with obvious favourites, as discussed in more detail below. Indeed, the miracle of the falling stone and beam in St Margaret's church incidently demonstrates that she had in her personal possession at least one book: 'Sche knelyd up-on hir kneys, heldyng down hir hed and hir boke in hir hand' (9: 21). This book may have been a book of hours, as it was commonplace for laywomen of a certain social status to take these to church and use them during services. But could Margery have read it? Why would she own it, and carry it to church with her, if she couldn't use it? And what might the possession and, more to the point, display of that book have been intended to signal to the audience around her, or to the audience of her narrative?

Part of the difficulty in attempting to answer these questions concerns the very terms for discussion: until relatively recently, literary historians have shared medieval attitudes about what constituted 'literacy' in the Middle Ages, defining the term, and the range of abilities it denotes, in ways which exclude large categories of text-based activities. 'Literacy', to the medieval academies, meant specifically Latin literacy: the *litterati* were educated in Latin, the *illiterati* were not (in Middle English, the 'lered and laued'). To be able to read one's vernacular language, to be able, even, to write one's vernacular language (though the two did not necessarily go hand in hand), and not to be able to read or write Latin, meant that in these terms one was illiterate. In other words, even if Margery could read the English in the book in her hand, she would have been understood to be 'illiterate' (both by herself and by the clerical authorities). More to the point, given her sex and her class, she would have been expected to be 'illiterate', as women were unlikely to receive any education in Latin outside the convent. These narrowly defined terms continued to be in use throughout the Middle Ages, even though the distinction became increasingly more problematic to maintain in the face of increasing lay ability to read the vernacular languages of England after the twelfth century, a fact amply demonstrated by the survival of vernacular manuscripts.[5] Moreover, the officially supported distinction between the categories of literate and illiterate was always invested with forms of social power, as the example of Margery repeatedly demonstrates. Women, especially laywomen, who challenged these distinctions very quickly found themselves on the wrong side of the ecclesiastical authorities, or, on the un-side of orthodoxy. Thus, definitions of literacy could be and were employed in the struggle to preserve social hierarchy or class status quo (as we will see below), and not just by medieval commentators.[6]

Certainly, for most of the Middle Ages, formal education and Latin literacy was a mark of sex and status privilege, excluding all but men in the highest classes, and the religious of both sexes (though even then, religious women in general seem to have had considerably less access to formal Latin education than their male counterparts).[7] As Franz Bäuml has noted, the problem with the traditional way of understanding 'literacy' lies in the important contradiction inherent in medieval society: that despite the fact that 'At all levels of society, the majority of the population of Europe between the fourth and fifteenth centuries was, in some sense, illiterate', nevertheless, 'medieval civilization was a literate civilization'. He continues that, for this reason, defining literacy in the medieval period exclusively as Latin literacy cannot assist the literary historian when her or his 'intention is to describe, implicitly or explicitly, the *function* of literacy in medieval society'.[8] Modern critics following Bäuml have continued to demonstrate the ways in which a restrictive notion of 'literacy' does not serve the social history of medieval English society, and though their analyses have seldom extended to Kempe's *Book*, their conclusions provide essential contexts for understanding the picture of Margery's textual activity the narrative suggests.

For instance, Joyce Coleman, in her discussion of late medieval English court literature offers a lucid and important defence of late medieval aurality (the reading of texts aloud to one or more people). In her view, the notion of 'literacy' historians apply to the Middle Ages must stretch to accommodate the wide practice of public reading and reading-through-hearing which remained in place throughout the medieval period, and, she insists, even into the English Renaissance. She argues that, in opposition to the scholarly assumption that 'learning to read instantly converts people into private readers', and thus that

---

5   See M. B. Parkes, 'The Literacy of the Laity', in D. Daiches and A. Thorlby, eds, *The Medieval World* (London, 1973), pp. 555–77; Franz H. Bäuml, 'Varieties and Consequences of Medieval Literacy and Illiteracy', *Speculum* 55 (1980): 237–65.
6   On this topic see the introductions in Jocelyn Wogan-Browne, Nicholas Watson, Andrew Taylor and Ruth Evans, eds, *The Idea of the Vernacular: An Anthology of Middle English Literary Theory 1280–1520* (University Park, PA, 1999).
7   See, for instance, Eileen Power, *Medieval English Nunneries, c.1275 to 1535* (New York, 1964).
8   Bäuml, 'Varieties and Consequences of Medieval Literacy and Illiteracy', pp. 237, 239.

'rising literacy' equates to 'the increased habit of private reading', medieval literature frequently posits public reading as one of various possibilities for engagement with the text, and presents listening-readers as exercising their preference for such activity.[9] Coleman insists that far from being synonymous with the rowdiness associated with the early medieval meadhall, or with the passivity modern critics associate with hearing, those who participated through listening in the transmission of texts in the late medieval period, were 'literate, sophisticated people who participated actively both with their attention and their response'.[10] Similarly, Rebecca Krug, in her recent discussion of the role of family-based networks in the education of medieval women and the transmission of medieval texts between them, argues that 'literacy' is too static a term for attempting to describe the variety of ways women engaged with texts in the English Middle Ages. Her suggested alternative, 'literate practices', allows her 'to resist the notion that the individual either is or is not literate, and to avoid a related idea, that individuals' literate investments never change'.[11]

Coleman's and Krug's approaches, along with other recent discussions, encourage the modern historian of literacy to comprehend the shapes and textures of medieval literacy beyond the static definition of individual ability: literacy thus can include a range of practices related to texts and the transmission of text-based knowledge. 'Reading' can imply both the ability to read words on a page (in the vernacular languages as well as in Latin) and the interaction of an intellect with a text (even when the encounter is aural). Thus, adopting the idea of 'literate practices' enables a modern reader to make more sense of the *Book*'s depiction of Margery's 'reading'. In the first place, the debate over whether or not Margery is literate in the strictest sense recedes from a position of central importance: she can 'read' without having to be able to actually read the words on the page. Further, these approaches encourage the modern reader to discount the notion of 'passivity' long associated with Margery's text-based activities. That is, she *may* require a 'lystere' in chapter 58 because she is unable to do the reading herself, though as we will see below, she might choose to engage a 'lystere' despite being able to read. Nevertheless the relationship is not configured in the predictably hierarchical way: he does not simply read to her according to his version of her spiritual needs. Rather, as the *Book* emphatically insists, theirs is a mutual, even reciprocal, relationship. She provides much of the shape the reading takes, actively participating in the selection of material, and we can only assume from the description, in the interpretation of its meanings. Kempe describes their experiences:

> And aftyrwardys þe same preyste louyd hir & trustyd hir ful meche & blissed þe tyme þat euyr he knew hir, for he fond gret gostly comfort in hir & [she] cawsyd hym to lokyn meche good scriptur & many a good doctowr whech he wolde not a lokyd at þat tyme had sche ne be [if not for her] . . . Þe forseyd preste red hir bokys þe most part of vij ʒer er viij ʒer [7 or 8 years] to gret encres

9   Joyce Coleman, *Public Reading and the Reading Public in Late Medieval England and France* (Cambridge, 1996), p. 40; see also p. xiv.
10 Ibid., p. xiv.
11 Rebecca Krug, *Reading Families: Women's Literate Practice in Late Medieval England* (Ithaca, NY, 2002), p. 7.

of hys cunnyng [understanding] & of hys meryte, and he suffryd many an euyl worde for hyr lofe in-as-meche as he red hir so many bokys & supportyd hir in hir wepyng & hir crying. Aftyrwardys he wex benefysyd [was beneficed] & had gret cur of sowle [spiritual charge of souls], & þan lykyd hym ful wel þat he had redde so meche be-forn (58: 143–4).

The priest, at Margery's urging, seeks out works he would not otherwise have encountered, and which she must have known by reputation or earlier experience. Over the course of their reading together, she therefore helps to increase both his intellect ('hys cynnyng') and his religious standing ('hys meryte'), before he finally receives the material reward of a large benefice. Her participation in his spiritual and material improvement is equal, in this description, to his participation in her spiritual improvement. More to the point, 'being read to' by a spiritual adviser does not necessarily mean 'being led by', an important distinction often lost in the modern prejudicial association of full literacy with intelligence.[12]

That reading-through-hearing (passively receiving the texts) is by no means an intellectually passive act is made manifestly clear in a later, often perplexing, passage of Christ's speech to Margery. At the end of Book I, Margery records her anxiety that the work of composing her *Book* is preventing her regular and attentive attendance to her routine spiritual observances such as going to mass and saying her beads. Christ assures her that he credits her with what she means to do, rather than what she has done (' "for as many bedys as þu woldist seyin I accepte hem as þow þu seydist hem" ' [88: 216]), much like his earlier credit of her desire to be chaste, even when it is not possible for her as a married woman (21). In a long passage of praise for her, Christ tells her that he is most pleased when she sits in stillness and opens her heart and mind to God:

> And also, dowtyr, I am hyly plesyd wyth hym [her confessor, Master Robert], for he biddith þe þat þu xuldist sittyn stille & ȝeuyn thyn hert to meditacyon & thynkyn swech holy thowtys as God wyl puttyn in þi mende. And I haue oftyn-tymys bodyn þe so my-self, yet þu wilt not don þeraftyr but wyth meche grutchyng [complaining]. & ȝet am I not displesyd wyth þe, for, dowtyr, I haue oftyn seyd on-to þe þat wheþyr þu preyist wyth þi mowth er thynkist wyth thyn hert, wheþyr þu redist er herist redyng, I wil be plesyd wyth þe (88: 217–18).

This reference to reading or hearing texts read (' "wheþyr þu redist or herist redyng" ') is important, though seldom fully understood. The language here may echo, as Colledge suggested, the formula 'often found in indulgences attached to prayers and books', one 'deriving from the opening phrase, *Omnibus visuris vel audituris*, of the medieval writ'.[13] However, the choice between reading and hearing texts read is part of a carefully constructed range of activities Christ

---

[12] For a discussion of the reciprocal relationships between female patrons and their male writers see Anne Clark Bartlett, *Male Authors, Female Readers: Representation and Subjectivity in Middle English Devotional Literature* (Ithaca, NY, 1995).

[13] Colledge, 'Margery Kempe', p. 217.

places before Margery: reading or hearing texts read are paired with praying aloud (' "wyth þi mowth" ') and contemplating inwardly. In fact, the structure of the passage suggests a correspondence between praying aloud and reading on one's own as well as between contemplating inwardly and hearing texts read. This suggests that hearing a text read, by virtue of the activity's very stillness and outward passivity, is closer to the stillness of inward contemplation. By this logic, then, praying aloud and reading on one's own (perhaps reading the words aloud to oneself, a regular part of medieval reading) are less the actions of the inward-turning mystic. In fact, Christ seems to confirm this. Though he assures Margery that whatever her choice, he will be pleased with her, he finally admits that his preference is for stillness and inward thought: he concludes, ' "& ȝet, dowtyr, I telle þe, yf þu woldist leuyn me, þat thynkyng is þe best for þe & most xal incresyn thy lofe to me" ' (88: 218). Thus this passage, far from merely mimicking a familiar opening to texts Kempe might have consciously or unconsciously pulled from her memory, indicates the possible significances and cultural meanings the two possibilities (reading and hearing texts read) might have held for late medieval readers. If, as this passage seems to suggest, hearing texts read was a more contemplative act, then Kempe's depiction of her desire to have spiritual works read to her is at least in part the result of her consistent self-construction of herself as a contemplative – and her awareness of the devotional status the description might create – and not simply a sign of an inability to read.

More to the point, however: how likely is it that Margery Kempe would not have had some ability to read English? The *Book* is as silent on Margery's early education as it is on the rest of her life before her first visionary experiences, but as the daughter of John Brunham, five times mayor of Lynn, frequent Member of Parliament and alderman of the Trinity Guild for many years, we might expect that she would have had the same educational opportunities enjoyed by other urban women in her class.[14] Late medieval women learned to read in a variety of ways, though they probably only rarely learned to write, since as Alexandra Barratt has argued, reading and writing were very separate skills and writing, in the Middle Ages, required 'a specialised set of tools, a suitable working space, and access to expensive raw materials such as parchment'. Besides, she continues, clerks who would write for pay were readily available, at least for the short jobs of letter writing and document copying.[15] Most women in late medieval England who received any education would have learned to read in their home, as children, in groups of girls and preschool-age boys, taught perhaps by their own mothers, or by the family's priest, or by their brothers' tutors, or by their brothers or fathers.[16] Some women in late medieval London and thus perhaps in other urban centres, may even have had attended informal English schools, as Caroline Barron has

14 For extracts from documents related to John Brunham see *BMK*, Appendix II, 359–62; see also chapter 46 in the *Book*. For further discussion of Margery Kempe's social status and family background see Kate Parker's chapter in the present volume.
15 Alexandra Barratt, ed., *Women's Writing in Middle English* (London, 1992), p. 4.
16 Michael Van Cleave Alexander, *The Growth of English Education 1348–1648* (University Park, PA, 1990), p. 40.

argued. These schools, later known as 'dame' schools, left few records since they were neither regulated by or even of interest to ecclesiastical or civic authorities, nor were the proprietors or teachers, who in at least some cases were women, members of a specific craft guild.[17] That some girls must have attended schools is witnessed to in a parliamentary statute from 1406, which guaranteed the right of 'every man or woman, of whatever estate or condition he be, to set their son or daughter to take learning at any manner of school that pleaseth them'.[18]

Margery Kempe's family would have been both sufficiently affluent and socially ambitious to have provided her with an opportunity to acquire some basic education, including the ability to read. Indeed, it seems likely it was so unremarkable as to require no comment. Michael Alexander has, perhaps optimistically, proposed that 'by the eve of the Reformation, some 25 to 30 percent of England's adults could read'.[19] He further argued that despite their reduced opportunities, 'determined and resourceful women almost always learned how to read, while females of high social position often acquired fluency in one or more foreign languages'.[20] And as a businesswoman, certainly 'determined and resourceful', Margery is even more likely to have needed to acquire at least basic reading, if not writing skills, as we know both men and women involved in the urban trades did. As Barbara Hanawalt has argued, given that late medieval women (as widows, for instance, but as wives also in some cases) needed to be able to carry on business on their own in the large urban centres, 'parents had to prepare their daughters for this eventuality'. She continues that, in the higher classes, 'One can imagine that an educated young woman would be more desirable as a marriage partner'.[21] In fact, the omission of Margery's early education in the *Book*'s description of her preparation for the visionary experiences of her adult life almost certainly has more to do with the generic demands of the text than with the facts of actual childhood experiences. While the depictions of her failed businesses, which coincidentally imply her literate abilities, are motivated by the narrative of the text (as demonstrating her initial, sinful, resistance to God's call to her as a visionary), descriptions of her childhood, and any education or training she might have received as a girl, are less essential to the narrative of her life as a mystic.[22]

---

[17] Caroline Barron, 'The Education and Training of Girls in Fifteenth-Century London', in Diana E. S. Dunn, ed., *Courts, Counties and the Capital in the Later Middle Ages* (New York, 1996), pp. 139–53 (p. 147). See also Barron, 'The Expansion of Education in Fifteenth-Century London', in John Blair and Brian Golding, eds, *The Cloister and the World: Essays in Honour of Barbara Harvey* (Oxford, 1996), pp. 219–45; and Barbara Hanawalt, *Growing Up in Medieval London: The Experience of Childhood in History* (New York, 1993).

[18] 7 Henry IV c. XVII, *Statutes of the Realm* II, pp. 157–8. Given and discussed in Alexander, *Growth of English Education*, p. 37, and Barron, 'Education and Training', p. 139.

[19] Alexander, *Growth of English Education*, p. 36. Slyvia Thrupp has speculated that an even higher per cent (40) of English tradesmen in London could read some Latin, while fully 50 per cent could read English. *The Merchant Class of Medieval London, 1300–1500* (Ann Arbor, 1962), p. 158.

[20] Alexander, *Growth of English Education*, p. 40.

[21] Hanawalt, *Growing Up in Medieval London*, p. 83.

[22] The excision of any reference to Margery's childhood is also discussed by Kim Phillips above.

Margery Kempe and Vernacular Books of Devotion

If Margery Kempe's will had survived to us, it might have revealed any number of books she owned that she wished to be presented to the people who survived her after her death. Bequests of vernacular devotional books, as well as other devotional books such as primers or books of hours, from women and often to women, became a common and expected way of displaying one's religiosity at a time when it counted the most, and wills have become an important means of reconstructing late medieval book ownership. For example Agnes Stapilton made reference to several books in her will dated 1448, leaving copies of the Middle English devotional texts *Prick of Conscience* and the *Book of Vices and Virtues* to two convents in the West Riding of Yorkshire. Another house of nuns was left a copy of the *Meditations on the Life of Christ*, and a collection of saints' lives in French was left to her granddaughter. A psalter and other prayer books are also mentioned in her will.[23] Though wills only provide one part of the picture, by virtue of their social role as items intrinsically linked with the preparation for death and the testator's desire to represent her or himself as devoutly as possible, what they tell us is late medieval laywomen of Margery's class and higher commonly owned devotional manuscripts in English, and sometimes in other languages too, even when they could not read them themselves. Devout laywomen were increasingly drawn to religious literature at the end of the fourteenth and beginning of the fifteenth centuries; in fact, as Carol Meale has argued, 'religion was by far the dominant reading interest of medieval women; they owned a variety of texts in addition to their service books, ranging from lives of the saints, to didactic works . . . to various of the treatises of the fourteenth-century mystics'.[24]

But late medieval laywomen of the upper classes did not just own books; their participation in medieval book culture, both as patrons and as the means for the transmission of books between family groups and even geographical locations, 'substantially influenced the development of lay piety and vernacular literature in the Middle Ages'.[25] Women readers (who read both privately and by hearing texts read) knew what they wanted to read much as Margery did. Their demands helped shape the production and availability of texts, so much so that recent scholarship has confidently concluded that late medieval

---

23 For the full text of Agnes Stapilton's will see J. W. Clay, ed., *North Country Wills*, Surtees Society 2 (Durham, 1825), pp. 48–9. For further discussion of it and other comparable examples of female reading and lending networks see Anne Dutton, 'Women's Use of Religious Literature in Late Medieval England', D.Phil. thesis, University of York (1995), esp. pp. 46–87.

24 Carol M. Meale, ' "alle the bokes that I haue of latyn, englisch, and frensch": Laywomen and Their Books in Late Medieval England', in *eadem*, ed., *Women and Literature in Britain, 1150–1500* (Cambridge, 1993), pp. 128–58 (p. 137); see also, in the same volume, Felicity Riddy's ' "Women Talking About the Things of God": A Late Medieval Sub-culture', pp. 104–27; Mary C. Erler, *Women, Reading and Piety in Late Medieval England* (Cambridge, 2002); and Ann M. Hutchison, 'Devotional Reading in the Monastery and in the Late Medieval Household', in Michael G. Sargent, ed., *De Cella in Seculum: Religious and Secular Life and Devotion in Late Medieval England* (Cambridge, 1989), pp. 215–27. See also Allyson Foster above.

25 Susan Groag Bell, 'Medieval Women Book Owners: Arbiters of Lay Piety and Ambassadors of Culture', *Signs* 7.4 (1982): 742–68 (743).

laywomen may be called 'the "first generation" of English female readers'.[26] Far from being the passive recipients of literary trends, medieval women inspired, solicited and funded new translations and versions of devotional works. As Felicity Riddy has provocatively suggested, 'In the relation between the male clerks and their women readers it must often have been difficult to tell who followed and who led.'[27]

This is precisely the picture the *Book* suggests in the passage cited above: Margery 'cawsyd' her reader to become familiar with previously unfamiliar devotional works. In other words, she led, he followed. And, although the *Book* offers no direct evidence, there is no reason to think that Margery did not purchase at least some of the books she wanted to hear her reader read. Indeed, a related incident suggests some informed familiarity with regard to the late medieval book trade. As a means of testing her 'felyngys', her priest-scribe admits to asking 'hir qwestyons & demawndys of thyngys þat wer for to komyn, vn-sekyr & vncerteyn as þat tyme to any creatur what xuld be þe ende' (24: 55). Margery, through her prayers and communications with God, is to provide him with the answers to these questions and her ability to know the outcome is to be proved, he confesses, 'ellys wold he not gladlych a wretyn þe boke' (24: 55). One of the tests he gives her concerns the offer of a book for sale, made to him by a 'fals schrewe', an old man who claims to have 'a portose [portable breviary], a good lytyl boke' from a nearby priest for whom he is an executor (24: 57). Though her priest is tempted by the offer and the man's story, Margery counsels against his consideration of the deal:

> Þe preste went to þe forseyd creatur, preyng hir to preye for hym & wetyn whedyr God wolde he xulde by [should buy] þe boke er not . . . "Syr", sche seyth, "byith no boke of hym, for he is not to be trustyn vp-on, & þat xal ȝe wel knowyn ȝyf ȝe medyl wyth hym" (24: 57).

According to God, as revealed through Margery's revelations, this is not a trustworthy means of acquiring a book, and true to her word, the old man disappears without ever presenting the object he claimed to have had for sale. Though incidental to the real purpose of the anecdotal history recounted here (that Margery's 'felyngys' are to be trusted, and that they come from God) this story demonstrates the movement of books between owners, and that this movement had both acceptable and less acceptable means of exchange. Most importantly, it demonstrates Margery's authority in, perhaps even her experience with, the economies of the book trade in highly literary East Anglia. More specifically, the point of this passage seems to be not that the book trade was inherently suspect or unfamiliar (or the priest would not have considered making the purchase),

---

26 The description is taken from Bartlett's *Male Authors, Female Readers*, p. 7. For an introduction to recent work on medieval women and books see the essays in *Women and Literature in Britain, 1150–1500*; Bell, 'Medieval Women Book Owners'; Krug, *Reading Families*; Mary C. Erler, *Women, Reading, and Piety*; and Jocelyn Wogan-Browne, *Saints' Lives and Women's Literary Culture: Virginity and its Authorizations* (Oxford, 2001).

27 Riddy 'Women Talking About the Things of God', p. 107.

but that the prospective seller was false, even though he appeared trustworthy, and Margery's gift is her ability to see through his guise with God's help.

Margery need not have actually bought the books her readers read to her; for instance, she may have had the books she enjoyed on loan from others within her network of spiritual friends, some of whom at least are mentioned by name in the *Book*. Manuscripts were traded between social networks, often moving between religious and laywomen, and in both directions, and medieval writers recognized that they must yield control over access to their work once it entered circulation.[28] As the prologue to *The Cloud of Unknowing* makes evident, the most a writer could do was hope his well-intentioned and wide-ranging cautions were heeded:

> I charge þee & I beseche þee, wiþ as moche power & vertewe as þe bonde of charite is sufficient to suffre, whatsoeuer þou be þat þis book schalt haue in pos-session, ouþer by propirte, ouþer by keping, by bering as messenger or elles bi borrowing, þat in as moche as in þee is by wille & auisement, neiþer þou rede it, ne write it, ne speke it, ne ȝit suffre it be red, wretyn, or spokyn, of any or to any, bot ȝif it be of soche one or to soche one þat haþ (bi þi supposing) in a trewe will & by an hole entent, purposed him to be a parfite folower of Criste, not only in actyue leuyng, bot in þe souereinnest pointe of contemplatife leuing [. . .] For elles it acordeþ noþing to him.[29]

The *Cloud*'s author provides a carefully detailed (and anxious) account of the ways books could fall into the hands of medieval readers: through outright own-ership, through a loan from a monastic library to a member of the order ('keping'), or through a shared network of readers. Its potential audience, and his inability to restrict it to those whose internal state qualify them for the message of the work, is a matter of great concern for the writer, though he can do nothing to prevent the ill-prepared or unworthy from reading it, except to discourage them heartily: as he writes, 'myn entent was neuer to write soche þing unto hem' (p. 2, 11.3–4).

Like *The Cloud of Unknowing*, the works Kempe names in her *Book* were con-templative texts whose audiences had expanded considerably beyond the origi-nal ones initially imagined by the writers. In chapters 17 and 58, Kempe lists the books which, in addition to the 'many a good boke of hy contemplacyon & oþer bokys, as þe Bybyl wyth doctowrys þer-up-on' (that is, a glossed Bible, pre-sumably in Latin), she heard read, and knew well: 'Seynt Brydys boke, Hyltons boke, Bone-ventur, Stimulus Amoris, Incendium Amoris' (58: 143). That this list is twice given ('Hyltons boke, ne Bridis boke, ne Stimulus Amoris, ne Incendium Amoris' [17: 39]) indicates the importance of these books for Kempe as she constructs an account of her spiritual education and her active religios-ity.[30] More precisely, as we will see, it is very possible this list also functioned as

---

28 See Erler, *Women, Reading, and Piety*, and Krug, *Reading Families*.

29 *The Cloud of Unknowing and Related Treatises on Contemplative Prayer*, ed. Phyllis Hodgson (Salzburg, 1982), p. 1, 11.8–21.

30 Many modern critics have discussed the list of books Kempe provides; for a recent and com-prehensive description see Barry Windeatt's Introducton to his edition of *The Book of Margery Kempe* (Harlow, 2000), pp. 9–18. The brief account provided here is heavily indebted to Windeatt's summary.

a convenient means of signalling a devout identity to her audience, a kind of shorthand that we perhaps no longer fully comprehend, but can attempt to reconstruct.

Though in some ways remarkably specific with this repeated list as compared to the vague description 'good boke of hy contemplacyon', Kempe obviously assumed her readers would be able to recognize the works from the brief summary she offered; and in fact, based on extant manuscripts as well as the frequent and often direct allusions to specific works within the *Book*, modern readers have been able to fill in the few details Kempe omitted. Thus, 'Hyltons boke' seems likely to be either *The Scale of Perfection* or *The Epistle on the Mixed Life*, by the fourteenth-century English mystic Walter Hilton (d.1396). It may even have been a combination of both, since by the end of the Middle Ages they were regularly copied together.[31] Hilton, an Augustinian canon, composed *The Scale* initially for an anchoress, but by the time he wrote its second book he had acknowledged that his actual readership included those among the laity who sought to incorporate elements of the interior life of contemplation into their own devotional practices.[32] Hilton further universalized the contemplative life in his *Epistle on the Mixed Life*, advocating a theology which sought to harmonize the active life of the laity with the life of interior devotion of the contemplatives; both texts would have held obvious appeal and interest for Margery in her experience of her own worldly mysticism, and both texts had a wide circulation among the laity, even forming the contents of one surviving example of a late medieval 'common-profit' book (Lambeth Palace Library MS 472).

By 'Bone-ventur, Stimulus Amoris' in chapter 58, Kempe may mean to indicate that she assumes that *Stimulus Amoris*, a series of meditations on the Passion and a treatise on the contemplative life, was written by St Bonaventura, a common misattribution through the Middle Ages (though the scribe's ommision of the genitive abbreviation for 'Bonaventur's' in the extant manuscript confuses this somewhat). Certainly, in chapter 62, Kempe's reference to the Middle English translation of the *Stimulus Amoris*, that is, *The Prykke of Lofe*, attributed to Walter Hilton, confirms that she shared the assumption about the original's authorship. Here she explicitly states that in 'Þe Prykke of Lofe . . . Bone-auentur wrot of hym-selfe þes wordys' (62: 154). The reference to *The Prykke of Lofe* here further indicates that Kempe knew the text in its English translation (though she may also have heard her reader translate the Latin too, at other times). Kempe also makes considerable use of another important contemplative text attributed to St Bonaventura: the *Meditationes Vitae Christi*, adapted (by 1410) into Middle English by Nicholas Love as *The Mirrour of the Blessed Lyf of Jesus Christ*. Though she does not name this text directly, it could be implied in the reference to the name 'Bonaventur'. Regardless, these two texts (either separately, or as

---

[31] Michael G. Sargent, 'Walter Hilton's *Scale of Perfection*: The London Manuscript Group Reconsidered', *Medium Aevum* 52 (1983): 189–216 (206).

[32] See Nicholas Watson, 'The Middle English Mystics', in David Wallace, ed., *The Cambridge History of Medieval English Literature* (Cambridge, 1999), pp. 539–65; J. P. H. Clark and R. Dorward, ed. and trans., *The Scale of Perfection* (Mahwah, NJ, 1991); B. A. Windeatt, *English Mystics of the Middle Ages* (Cambridge, 1994); Michael G. Sargent, 'Walter Hilton's *Scale of Perfection*'.

received through Love's *Mirrour*) were vastly influential on Kempe's construction
of her devotional life and her expression of her mysticism, and the allusions to
the works frequent her account of her visionary experiences, most evidently in
the compassion Margery has with the sufferings of Mary, and in her conversations and intimate relationship with the Virgin.[33]

Equally important to the *Book* in terms of influence, however, is the model of
affective devotion and contemplation offered by the first and most widely read
of the English mystics, Richard Rolle, in his *Incendium Amoris* (*The Fire of Love*).
Though Rolle (d.1349) wrote in both Latin and English (and his English texts
were written for women religious), the *Incendium Amoris*, in Latin, was intended
for an audience of 'rudibus et indoctis' (the 'simple and untaught'), with, as
Nicholas Watson has noted, a 'fine disregard for the restrictions imposed by the
complicated Latin in which it is written'.[34] Popular with readers, religious and
lay, Rolle's works were copied, adapted, anthologized and translated throughout the fifteenth century, and Margery may have encountered and adapted his
description of the sensual characteristics of spiritual love (*fervor, dulcor* and
canor) either from the Latin directly, as paraphrased by a reader, or from
a Middle English translation like the one made in 1435 by the Carmelite Richard
Misyn.[35]

'Seynt Brydys boke', the Middle English translation of St Bridget of Sweden's
Revelations, was wildly popular in the fifteenth century with religious women
and laywomen alike.[36] Her popularity with high-status women must have in
large part derived from the fact that Bridget was 'a very modern saint'.[37] High
status herself, married and a mother of eight (though she and her husband lived
chastely for a time), adviser to rulers both secular and ecclesiastical, a pilgrim
and a mystic, Bridget was also the founder of the order of Bridgettines, to whose
English house, Syon abbey, Margery is described as making a pilgrimage in
Book II (10). More importantly for late medieval laywomen, as Barratt states,
Bridget 'exemplified the "mixed life" that combined the pursuit of contemplation with active virtue and political involvement, even though the nuns of her
own religious order were strictly enclosed'.[38] Much has been made of Margery
Kempe's particular devotion to the cult of St Bridget, and her awareness of the
role which that devotion could play in her own saintly self-construction in the

33 See Windeatt, *Book of Margery Kempe*, pp. 11–12; Gail McMurray Gibson, *The Theater of Devotion: East Anglian Drama and Society in the Late Middle Ages* (Chicago, 1989), pp. 47–51; Denis Renevey, 'Margery's Performing Body: The Translation of Late Medieval Discursive Religious Practices', in Denis Renevey and Christiania Whitehead, eds, *Writing Religious Women: Female Spiritual and Textual Practices in Late Medieval England* (Toronto, 2000), pp. 197–216; David Lawton, 'Voice, Authority and Blasphemy'.
34 Watson, 'Middle English Mystics', p. 548.
35 See Nicholas Watson, *Richard Rolle and the Invention of Authority* (Cambridge, 1991); see also Windeatt, *English Mystics of the Middle Ages*.
36 Roger Ellis, ' "Flores ad Fabricandum . . . Coronam": An Investigation into the Uses of the Revelations of St Bridget of Sweden in Fifteenth-Century England', *Medium Ævum* 51 (1982): 163–86.
37 Alexandra Barratt, 'Continental Women Mystics and English Readers', in Carolyn Dinshaw and David Wallace, eds, *The Cambridge Companion to Medieval Women's Writing* (Cambridge, 2003), pp. 240–55 (p. 248).
38 Ibid.

Book.[39] Indeed, as Barry Windeatt and others have noted, Bridget provides a 'particularly powerful' model for Margery to emulate, one whose narrative, familiar as it would have been to English readers, 'could lend endorsement to Margery Kempe's own experience'.[40] But the use Kempe made of the model of 'saintly heroine' offered by the legend of St Bridget (and by the legends of other saints Margery knew and alludes to, notably St Katherine of Alexandria) was more complicated than simply providing a handy formula for the life of a holy woman, though Kempe clearly does use the life of St Bridget in this way. This complicated relationship is nowhere as apparent in the *Book* as it is in one of Margery's visions early in Book I. During mass, she saw the sacrament 'schok and flekeryd to & fro as a dowe flekeryth wyth hir wengys', and the chalice containing the sacrament 'mevyd to & fro as it xuld a fallyn owt of hys [the priest's] handys' (20: 47). As she strains to see it happen again, Christ appears to her and tells her that she will not, but she should give thanks for having seen it once, since, as he says, ' "My dowtyr, Bryde, say [saw] me neuyr in þis wyse" ' (20: 47). He further reveals that the sign is a token of a coming earthquake, and she is to tell it to the people. This gift of prophecy has a double purpose: besides protecting the people who live in the vicinity, Christ will use it to add to the honour accorded Margery as even more precious to him than Bridget was (she sees things Bridget was not privileged to see), and will cause the particulars of her life (Margery's) to contribute to the respect shown Bridget. He tells her, ' "rygth as I spak to Seynt Bryde ryte so I speke to þe, dowtyr, & I telle þe trewly it is trewe euery word þat is wretyn in Brides boke, & be þe it xal be knowyn for very trewth" ' (20: 47).

Kempe uses the example of St Bridget in this incident much as she uses the other holy women and saints who make appearances in her narrative and visions. They are presumably familiar to her readers in a way that Margery may not be, but hopes to be; and the reader, through allusions and parallels with these women in Margery's narrative, begins to attribute their characteristics (holy, spiritually gifted, chosen by God) to Margery. As Rebecca Krug has recently noted, 'Margery alternately held up for admiration and competitively set aside Bridget's mystical experiences as she constructed her own visionary authority.'[41] A large part of the spiritual authority Kempe sought to realize came directly from the associations readers were encouraged to draw from her relationship to the devotional books she names and employs as models in the *Book*. Thus the group of texts the *Book* gives as central to Margery's reading performs two important functions. First, they provide a context for interpreting the events of Margery's life, as with, for instance, the parallels drawn with the life of St Bridget. The events of Bridget's biography provide more than just a template for the autohagiography of the *Book*; they provide an essential authority-invoking familiarity, as we

---

[39] See, for instance, Carolyn Dinshaw, 'Margery Kempe', in Dinshaw and Wallace, eds, *The Cambridge Companion to Medieval Women's Writing*, pp. 222–39 (p. 230); Clarissa Atkinson, *Mystic and Pilgrim: The Book and the World of Margery Kempe* (Ithaca, NY, 1983), pp. 168–79.

[40] Windeatt, *Book of Margery Kempe*, p. 13.

[41] Krug, *Reading Families*, pp. 158–60, on Margery as an extreme example of the devotion to St Bridget and her competition with her. See also Dinshaw's discussion of this incident, 'Margery Kempe', p. 230.

have seen above. This authority is more explicitly addressed in the *Book* itself, however, in an unusually rare moment of scribal interference in the text.[42] In chapter 62, the priest-scribe confesses to a period of doubt concerning Margery's manifestations and her 'felyngys', a doubt brought on by the preaching against her tears made by a visiting friar in Lynn. But, he continues, he was eventually returned to a greater love for her and trust in 'hir wepyng & hir crying þan euyr he dede be-forn' (62: 152), not through the consistency of her actions, or by the truth of her prophecies, but solely through the example provided to him in the contemplative texts he consults: namely, *The Prykke of Lofe* (the Middle English *Stimulus Amoris*), Rolle's *Incendium Amoris*, and the legends of Marie d'Oignies and Elizabeth of Hungary. All of these works treat the matter of the gift of tears, and it is through knowing them that the veracity of Margery's mystical gifts is confirmed within the world of the narrative, and, by extension from this example, in the minds and hearts of her potentially sceptical readers.[43] Thus the contemplative material contained in the books Kempe offers for comparison to her own *Book* backs the specific identity of a mystic and holy woman she is so careful to construct.

The second function the group of texts performs is quite closely related to this first: concomitant with the depiction of Margery as being read to, this grouping of books becomes a means of signalling a devout identity, a means of interpellating a particular reading subject through the texts.[44] This particular group of texts becomes, in other words, a means of fashioning the reader it describes: she is who she is by virtue of what she reads, or more to the point, by what she is depicted reading. The books Kempe names were popular with women, not perhaps exclusively, but certainly notably so, and, more to the point, would have been recognizably inoffensive reading material for late medieval women.[45] Some recent work on late medieval women readers has focused on the ways writers interpellate a reader's identity through the address of the text, an identity characterized by its gendered experience of the text and the reader's submission to the version of femininity the text assigns.[46] However, what I am describing here is not the way the writer calls the reader into being, but the way

---

[42] See Watson, 'Making of *The Book of Margery Kempe*'. Watson argues that part of this chapter is an actual scribal addition to the first text of the *Book*, and further argues that it is a very rare occurrence in the text.

[43] Almost precisely the same thing happens again in chapter 68: another friar defends her weeping during the sermon as a result of his recognizing that the 'holy woman' of whom he had read (Marie d'Oignies, presumably) had the same gift and it had been confirmed (68: 165).

[44] For a discussion of the value of Louis Althusser's use of the term 'interpellation' for medieval literary studies see Wogan-Browne et al., *The Idea of the Vernacular*, pp. 110–11.

[45] This phrase consciously echoes Bell's argument that women readers, discouraged from participating in the patriarchal ecclesiastical institutions of late medieval England, began to substitute private devotional reading for the more public expressions of the religious life, and thus devotional reading of religious literature in the home, undertaken by women not in orders or in other ways upsetting the social status quo, was considered 'inoffensive because of its privacy'. 'Medieval Women Book Owners', p. 752.

[46] See for instance, C. Annette Grisé, 'Women's Devotional Reading in Late-Medieval England and the Gendered Reader', *Medium Ævum* 71 (2002): 209–25. Grisé argues that the 'portrait of the ideal reader' produced by the women's devotional texts she discusses 'acts to enforce regulatory measures of proper behaviour of the audience as to their devotional activities and readerly responses', p. 219.

the reader can manipulate her or his identity through claiming a relationship with specific texts. Thus, in this case, the identity is created through being known or seen to read, and the reading participates in the performance of the self, much like the contemporary reader shapes her or his identity through the selective placement of books on publicly visible shelves. For Kempe, reading thus becomes part of the system of self-fashioning she embraces throughout the *Book*, contiguous with the visible manifestations of spiritual grace she describes (weeping, crying), and the public demonstrations of her status she narrates (wearing white, undertaking pilgrimages).

Moreover, the books Margery hears read provide a powerful counterbalance to the Lollard panic running through the *Book*. The Lollard heresy, and the fear which it occasioned in the late medieval imagination, surfaces repeatedly in the *Book*, perhaps not surprisingly, as Norwich was a centre of Lollard activity in the fifteenth century.[47] Margery is accused of the heresy on several occasions in the *Book*, and though her form of devotion is unconventional enough to arouse suspicion in her audience, her religious beliefs are repeatedly found to be orthodox. Nevertheless, Margery's determination to prove her orthodoxy takes priority through much of the narrative, and nowhere as obviously as when her knowledge of the Bible and other holy works is questioned. As Margaret Aston has shown, reading women were already always suspect in light of the heresy's reliance on the written word, and women who used their learning to teach others as Margery did were increasingly more the target of the accusers' energy.[48] To be a reading woman, especially in the fifteenth century, was to court criticism; thus, Kempe, composing her account at a remove of many years, employs her description of her reading practices to deflect accusation and censure.[49] Many of those accused of Lollardy succeeded in avoiding the charges by denying the ability to read the books they were accused of possessing or reading.[50] Kempe, however, deliberately fashions her literary practices to conform to orthodoxy. She does this in two ways. First, the *Book*'s depiction of Margery's dependence on a 'lystere' is an important means of deflecting criticism, by portraying the woman reader as subject to clerical authority. As we have seen, however, the reality of the relationship, as revealed in the *Book*, is not so straightforward, though on the surface the appearance of spiritual guidance and clerical control is sustained, and the fear of the reading woman is contained by the portrait of women's reading the *Book* describes. Second, she mentions only works which are clerically sanctioned, and considered orthodox, thus foregrounding a

---

47 For a discussion of Margery Kempe and Lollardy, and a slightly different reading of the accusations of heresy within the context of early fifteenth-century England, see John Arnold's essay in the present volume.

48 Margaret Aston, 'Lollard Women Priests?' in *eadem*, ed., *Lollards and Reformers: Images and Literacy in Late Medieval Religion* (London, 1984), pp. 49–70; see also, Claire Cross, ' "Great Reasoners in Scripture": the activities of women Lollards, 1380–1530', in Derek Baker, ed., *Medieval Women*, Studies in Church History subsidia 1 (Oxford, 1978), pp. 359–80.

49 In 'The Alleged Illiteracy of Margery Kempe', Josephine Tarvers argues that Kempe's description of herself as illiterate (in this case, specifically not writing), and dependent on her male scribes, is also a response to the Lollard threat.

50 See Aston, 'William White's Lollard Followers', and 'Devotional Literacy', in *eadem*, ed., *Lollards and Reformers*, pp. 71–100 and pp. 101–33.

programme of reading that complies with the 'environment of self-censorship' Nicholas Watson has identified as the result of Thomas Arundel's attempt to limit heretical writing and the transmission of vernacular translations of the Bible.[51] Margery and her 'lystere' apparently read together for seven or eight years (58), but whatever other books they shared have become obscured now in the deliberately vague 'many a good boke of hy contemplacyon & oþer bokys'.

Conclusion

Though *The Book of Margery Kempe* is silent on the topic of Margery's youth and early education, it seems almost inevitable that an urban woman of Margery's class would have learned to read at least some English at the end of the four-teenth century. Nevertheless, the *Book* is careful to construct a portrait of Margery's dependence on spiritual advisers for her access to contemporary reli-gious material, and to construct as well a carefully delineated range of vernacu-lar devotional books Margery claims to have known. Kempe takes great pains to nurture this characterization, obscuring some information in her account (what else she might have read, what books she might have owned, how she might have found them) and emphasizing others (the list of orthodox books). Besides deflecting the Lollard panic which haunts the *Book* even centuries after its com-position, the model of reading Kempe creates, and the trope of illiteracy that model depends on, are a fundamental part of the identity of the devout woman the *Book* is so determined to protect.

---

[51] Nicholas Watson, 'Censorship and Cultural Change in Late-Medieval England: Vernacular Theology, the Oxford Translation Debate, and Arundel's Constitutions of 1409', *Speculum* 70 (1995): 822–64 (831).

7

Drama and Piety: Margery Kempe

CLAIRE SPONSLER

It happened one Friday in 1413, in very hot weather on Midsummer's Eve, so we are told at the start of the eleventh chapter of *The Book of Margery Kempe*. Margery and her husband were walking home from York, she with a bottle of beer in her hand and he with a cake tucked inside his shirt, when John suddenly asked his wife if she would make love with him if that were the only way to prevent his having his head struck off. In the ensuing scene, husband and wife quarrel over the competing demands of Margery's newly adopted spirituality and their still-shared domestic life. At what seems an insoluble impasse, their argument is resolved by Jesus, who speaks to Margery 'wyth gret swetnesse' (24: 34–5) commanding her to ask her husband one last time to agree to her desire to have a chaste marriage, whose granting Jesus helps assure by absolving her of her vow to fast on Fridays, a practice that her husband had begged her to give up. Apparently won over by this divine intervention, Margery's husband cedes his conjugal rights, saying ' "As fre mot ȝowr body ben to God as it hath ben to me" ' (25: 12–13). The reconciled couple then kneel before a cross in the fields, say three paternosters in thanks for 'þe gret grace' (25: 16) that had been granted to them, and cheerfully sit down to eat and drink together.

While no reader is likely to skip over this episode given its gripping depiction of intimate marital relations, it is particularly compelling for anyone interested in the intersection between drama and piety, given the references to York and to Midsummer's Eve, both of which raise the distinct possibility that this marital spat and its happy resolution were in some way inspired by religious theatre. The evening in question was almost certainly 23 June 1413, since 1413 was the only year between 1405 and 1414 – dates in Margery's life that provide beginning and end points for negotiations over her vow of chastity – in which Midsummer's Eve fell on a Friday. While Margery often associates important events in her life with Fridays even when they may not have occurred on that day, the explicitness of the statement of time here – mentioned at the beginning and again at the end of this chapter of the *Book* – suggests that it is correct both as to the day of the week and the ritual holiday.[1]

This dating is important since the preceding day – 22 June 1413 – was Corpus Christi Day, the occasion for the annual performance of the great York biblical

---

[1] For the dating of this episode to 23 June 1413 see *BMK*, p. 269. Goodman, *World*, p. 69, sets the date as 'probably' 26 June 1413.

plays. Although we cannot be certain, it seems highly likely that Margery and her husband encountered the York plays during their visit to that city.[2] If that was indeed the case, their marital dispute would have been preceded by a day spent watching the story of Jesus' life and death as it was staged by guildsmen on lavishly decorated pageant wagons that were pulled through the streets, stopping to perform at specified locations throughout York. Along with other spectators, Margery and her husband could have seen the portrayal of Jesus' conception and birth, watched his near escape from Herod, and followed along as he was betrayed, tortured, and condemned to death. Not only would they have observed these events from distant biblical history being brought to life in contemporary York, but they would also have been constantly reminded of the relevance for their own lives. After the resurrection scenes, for instance, Margery and her husband might have heard the actor playing Jesus in the Saddlers' *Harrowing of Hell* promise to protect the faithful from their foes, and might have listened as the Jesus of the Mercers' *Last Judgment* reminded onlookers of what he had suffered for them and why. They might also have seen Noah and his wife quarrel over whether or not she would board the Ark, and observed Joseph's apologies to Mary for questioning her chastity in the Pewterers and Founders' *Joseph's Troubles About Mary*. In short, they would have seen vividly played out before them the most essential features of what Gail McMurray Gibson has described as the 'incarnational aesthetic' that characterized late medieval popular piety, an aesthetic in which abstract religious ideas were given a concrete and material form the better to have meaning for people in their ordinary daily lives.[3] These plays represented sacred doctrine as public, immediate, and fully present to contemporary individuals. If Margery and her husband did indeed witness the York cycle in June of 1413, then their marital spat on the way home suggests that in order to understand Margery's piety we should look more closely at the theatrical discourses of religion available to a lay person in early fifteenth-century England, not least because Margery's own spiritual expression – as described in the *Book* – is emphatically theatrical.

Indeed, as any reader immediately notices, Margery's piety is remarkably demonstrative and histrionic. Margery is an obvious expert in the arts of the theatre, adept at the use of evocative gestures (weeping, falling to the ground, throwing her arms out as if crucified, kissing lepers), symbolic costuming (wearing white garments), strategic impersonation (delivering spontaneous homilies in the style of clerical discourse with pitch-perfect accuracy, imitating holy women), and carefully managed scene-stealing (disrupting church services, one-upping obstructionist authorities). Even her private contemplations take a theatrical form, either as dialogues (with Christ or less frequently the Virgin Mary, God, and other holy figures) or as visions in which key scenes from biblical history are re-enacted right before her eyes, in vivid detail, and with Margery's participation. In these

---

2   Barry Windeatt believes that Margery and her husband probably witnessed the York plays in 1413; see *The Book of Margery Kempe*, trans. B. A. Windeatt (Harmondsworth, 1985), p. 305, ch 11, n 1.
3   Gail McMurray Gibson, *The Theatre of Devotion: East Anglian Drama and Society in the Late Middle Ages* (Chicago, 1989).

visions, Margery replays the events of the New Testament Gospels and popular non-biblical elaborations on those events: the Virgin's birth; her marriage to Joseph; her visit to Elizabeth; the birth of Jesus and his presentation in the temple; the flight to Egypt; Jesus' parting from his mother, the apostles, and Mary Magdalene; his betrayal by Judas; his buffeting by the Jews, crucifixion, deposition, and burial; the laments of Mary, John, and Peter; and Jesus' appearances to Mary and Mary Magdalene after the resurrection.[4] The scenic quality of these visions suggests that Margery was especially influenced by visual imagery, perhaps of the kind found in panel painting, carvings, and statuary, as Anthony Goodman notes.[5] But given how active and participatory her visions are, it is hard not to imagine that they were inspired not just by pictorial images but also by religious plays.

This source of inspiration should not be surprising, since late medieval religious plays formed part of a broad culture of vernacular lay spirituality, the same culture into which Margery's *Book* was itself embedded. Like the sermons preached by itinerant preachers that the *Book* describes people flocking to, or like the visionary and mystical literature that Margery was fond of having read to her, drama was a key aspect of a non-Latinate religious culture that, while the consequence of clerical efforts to meet the needs of lay people, had by Margery's day moved well beyond the control of the church. Corpus Christi processions and plays offer a case in point. The church's promotion of the feast of Corpus Christi, which derived in large part from a desire to satisfy lay demand for increased participation in religious life, took a clerical ritual (the procession) and passed it to the laity – although in slightly changed terms since the Corpus Christi procession's focus on the body of Christ rather than on the mass underscored the difference between clerical and lay celebration, and protected the privilege of the former. When around 1375 some towns began presenting plays along with these processions, it was in places where the laity had established strong secular governments organized around the trade guilds. Although the dramatization of biblical history was in theory congruent with the church's interest, especially since Lateran IV (1215), in educating the laity, the biblical plays produced in towns like York seem to have been beyond the purview of ecclesiastical authorities, who ceded control over the moral instruction provided by urban religious dramas to civic authorities.[6]

Religious drama may have been envisioned by the church and by civic sponsors as being useful for instructing the laity, but it was also an unusually polysemous and open cultural form that provided plenty of space for oppositional, adversarial, or simply digressive positions vis-à-vis authority. Its structures of performance ensured this, since it was locally controlled and produced, used amateur lay actors speaking in English, and took place in ideologically indeterminate performance spaces such as city streets or fields. Not surprisingly, members of the urban bourgeoisie, from which Margery herself came, found drama a potent vehicle for the

[4] See *BMK*, p. 270, n. 27, 30–1, for these references.
[5] Goodman, *Margery Kempe*, p. 105.
[6] Lawrence M. Clopper, *Drama, Play, and Game: English Festive Culture in the Medieval and Early Modern Period* (Chicago, 2001), pp. 140–2.

expression of a distinctively urban and bourgeois spirituality that perhaps inevitably entailed a critique of monastic and clerical structures of authority.

While Margery obviously performs her piety in a highly public way and with a keen eye for the effects of her actions on her varied audiences, it is perhaps more significant that Margery's construction of herself as a figure of spiritual significance seems to have been shaped in part by the example of drama (indeed one critic has seen her as a kind of 'performance artist', whose *Book* follows her from 'neophyte improvisationalist' to master thespian).[7] Recent performance theory has pointed to the ways in which even such seemingly unique and highly individualized performances as Margery's are shaped by social contexts and by prior performances. Margery's 'performance' of herself – that is, her acts of deliberate and public self-presentation – while deriving from the whole range of her social and cultural experiences as well as the material and economic circumstances of her life and the symbolic and expressive possibilities open to her, seems in particular to have been indebted to religious dramas, which perhaps suggested to her both a way of reshaping church rituals to her own ends and a method for articulating her own oppositional spirituality.

Even if Margery did not see the York cycle on that June day in 1413, she would have had plenty of opportunities to witness both liturgical and popular performances in and around King's Lynn. Indeed, surviving texts suggest that East Anglia had one of the most vibrant performance traditions of medieval England in the fifteenth century. It was home to the N-Town plays, which were performed in the mid-fifteenth century and which, as their name suggests, were designed for touring production but have been variously associated with Lincoln, Thetford, and Bury St Edmunds.[8] Also from the region are the *Castle of Perseverance* (1400–25); *Dux Moraud* (c.1425–50), a player's part for a moral play about incest; the Croxton *Play of the Sacrament* (c.1461), based on the story of the torture of the eucharistic wafer by Jews; *Wisdom* (c.1470–77); *Mankind* (1474–79), which John Marshall has argued was originally performed for the St Edmund's Guild in Lynn;[9] the play of *Mary Magdalene*, a long play from the end of the fifteenth century that combines morality, biblical history, and saint's life; the Brome *Abraham and Isaac* (late fifteenth century); *The Killing of the Children* (c.1512), a farcical *Slaughter of the Innocents*; *The Conversion of Saint Paul* (1500–25), a saint play; and the Norwich *Grocers' Play* (two versions dated 1533 and 1565).[10]

---

7   See Nanda Topenwasser, 'A Performance Artist and her Performance Text: Margery Kempe on Tour', in Mary A. Sudyan and Joann E. Ziegler, eds, *Performance and Transformation: New Approaches to Late Medieval Spirituality* (Houndmills, 1999), pp. 97–131 (p. 99).

8   Hardin Craig's earlier suggestion that N-Town plays were performed in Lincoln has been displaced in recent years by arguments for Thetford and Bury St Edmunds; touring is implied in the *Proclamation*'s use of 'N' (that is *nomen*, indicating that the name of a town was to be filled in, l. 527), see Craig, *English Religious Drama of the Middle Ages* (Oxford 1955), pp. 265–80. Alan J. Fletcher, 'The N-Town Plays', in Richard Beadle, ed., *The Cambridge Companion to Middle English Theatre* (Cambridge, 1994), pp. 163–88 (pp. 164–7), argues for Thetford; and Gibson, *Theatre of Devotion*, pp. 124–7, makes the case for Bury St Edmunds.

9   John Marshall, ' "O ȝe Souerens þat Sytt and ȝe Brothern þat stoned right wppe": Addressing the Audience of *Mankind*', *European Medieval Drama* 1 (1997): 189–202.

10 For a discussion of the southern plays, see John C. Coldewey, 'The Non-cycle Plays and the East Anglian Tradition', in Beadle, *Cambridge Companion*, pp. 189–210.

In addition to this list of plays testifying to a flourishing local theatre, there is also evidence of drama being sponsored by a wide range of groups in East Anglia. Local noble families, and especially the duke of Norfolk, apparently patronized drama: the duke's players visited Lynn in 1416–17, on what was perhaps an annual holiday performance.[11] Guilds also seem to have had plays, as is suggested by a record from Ipswich in 1445, when John Causton was admitted as a burgess on the condition that he care for the 'ornaments of the pageants of the guild of Corpus Christi and provide and supervise the repair of the stage and furnish the stage for the players'.[12] In 1494 John Benale left a long black gown and a short gown of damask 'to the gylde of Seynt john Baptyst in Bury and also for the revell on Seynt Edmund's nyght', implying that the guild participated in a revel in the monastery's refectory on the eve of the feast that commemorated the translation of Edmund's relics to Bury.[13] Documents also suggest that there were professional or semi-professional producers of drama or artisans working in the region, such as one Parnell of Ipswich (identified as 'a great man of subtleties, plays, and pageants') who in 1469 was called upon to help with Queen Elizabeth Woodeville's entry.[14]

Records enumerate many East Anglian playing places, indoors and out: fields, a circular outdoor theatre at Walsham-le-Willows in Suffolk that apparently held a thousand spectators, place-and-scaffold stages, a 'game house' at Yarmouth, guildhalls, country houses, churches, and priory halls.[15] East Anglian drama was also produced and sponsored by local parishes, as Victor Scherb observes, with small towns contributing towards a performance in a major centre, usually a market town; this method of collaborative production was made easier by the dense network of towns and villages in East Anglia linked by trade routes – rivers, canals, and the remains of the old Roman road system. Banns criers (many of the surviving East Anglia plays have banns) would have advertised the play in surrounding towns' records; most of them from the sixteenth century suggest an active parish theatre aimed at fundraising for such things as church repairs.[16] The church, too, sponsored drama in the form of liturgical plays and processions on holy days that transformed the city into a sacred stage.

While not all of these plays and records of performance date to within Margery's life, they point to the vibrant theatrical traditions of the region and to the kinds of drama to which Margery had access. Indeed, the surviving evidence suggests that Margery could hardly have encountered a richer theatrical tradition in any other part of England. Nonetheless, because Margery travelled

---

[11] See Suzanne Westfall, *Patrons and Performance: Early Tudor Household Revels* (Oxford, 1990), p. 47; and Victor I. Scherb, *Staging Faith: East Anglian Drama in the Later Middle Ages* (Cranbury, NJ, 2001), p. 30.

[12] Alan H. Nelson, *The Medieval English Stage* (Chicago, 1974), pp. 197–8.

[13] Gibson, *Theatre of Devotion*, p. 115.

[14] Robert Wright, 'Medieval Theatre in East Anglia: A Study of Drama and the Community in Essex, Suffolk, and Norfolk, 1200–1580, with Special Reference to Game, Interlude and Play in the Late 15th and Early 16th Century', Ph.D. thesis, University of Bristol (1972), 108; cited in Scherb, *Staging Faith*, p. 35.

[15] Scherb, *Staging Faith*, p. 35.

[16] Ibid., pp. 30–2.

widely, she might also have come into contact with both liturgical and lay performances elsewhere – particularly in London, Bristol, York, Leicester, Canterbury, and Beverley.

Unfortunately, we do not know which, if any, of these dramas Margery might have seen on her travels or at home – did she, for example, see the *Interludium* of St Thomas the Martyr that was performed at King's Lynn in 1385? – yet her book offers both direct and indirect evidence that she was indeed influenced by performances. Direct evidence comes in the form of references to solemn public processions on feast days and to the performance of the liturgies (14: 31, 28: 68). On one day when she was in St Margaret's churchyard for the Palm Sunday procession, she had a vision of Christ inspired by the occasion (78: 184–5); on another day, during a Corpus Christi procession in Bristol (probably 10 June 1417), she experienced an uncontrollable outburst (44: 107); on many other occasions, Palm Sunday processions and the rituals of Holy Week made her imagine that she was witnessing the original events represented in those rituals (78). In one example that shows the impact of performances on Margery as well as her creative appropriation of them to further the ends of her own spiritual self-definition, Margery mentions watching a liturgical drama at Lynn on Good Friday, when priests knelt before the sepulchre 'representyng' the death of Jesus and the Virgin Mary's lamentations. Margery tells us that her mind was drawn wholly into the Passion, which she saw with her 'gostly eye' as clearly as if it had been her 'bodily eye'. This performance affected her so forcefully that she was moved to sob, roar, and cry aloud, spreading her arms wide and saying in a loud voice ' "I dey, I dey" ' (57: 139–40), which not surprisingly caused the other worshippers to wonder what was wrong with her.

As this episode reveals, Margery's characteristic response to drama seems to have been to incorporate it into her own religious practices, whether public or private. Gibson's notion of the 'incarnational aesthetic' that informed East Anglian religious cultures points to a late medieval tendency to give material form to abstract spiritual ideals. Drama, of course, is particularly well suited to transform the abstract into the concrete, since it operates by means of embodied action. In drama, inert ideas are turned into spoken words and live actions performed in the here and now before the eyes of spectators. This advantage of drama was not lost on commentators. Of the many discourses of religion available to late medieval lay people – including sermons, mystical treatises, visual images, music, catechisms, and prayer books – drama was the privileged vehicle for lay religious expression, because like devotional imagery it could speak to illiterate people, but in even stronger terms. In fact, as medieval dramatic theory argued, plays were considered to be more efficacious than visual images because the liveliness of performance fixed their religious messages more firmly in the mind.[17]

In Margery's case, spirituality is made material through her body, which she uses as a performative vehicle to express her piety. Scholars have called attention to the materiality of Margery's embodied piety, noting that her spirituality is a gendered one grounded in the (female) body as much as the mind.[18]

---

17 See *A Tretise of Miraclis Pleyinge*, ed. Clifford Davidson (Kalamazoo, MI, 1993), p. 98, 11:183–5.
18 See, most notably, Lochrie, *Translations*.

Her religiosity, which the *Book* tells us was inspired by bodily events (her lengthy illness after giving birth), manifests itself through physical events and bodily behaviours such as her distinctive roaring and crying. Much of her penance is bodily in nature and aims at subduing the body: she wears a hair shirt, she fasts, she abstains from sexual activity, she kisses lepers, she goes on arduous and dangerous pilgrimages. Even her visions emphasize the physical, as holy figures appear in person in her mind's eye and talk and interact with her. There is absolutely nothing abstract or immaterial about Margery's devotional practices.

That preference for an embodied piety helps explain Margery's use of theatrical tactics. Like a sponge, Margery soaked up all the workings of the culture around her and internalized it into what Pierre Bourdieu has called the '*habitus*', a term (borrowed from Marcel Mauss) he uses to describe the socially determined beliefs and habits unconsciously internalized by the members of a society, which then come to generate and organize social practices and representations.[19] The norms of the *habitus* are the result of an individual's exposure to social processes, which means that a person's habitual modes of thought and action are governed by the social. It is the internalization of external social and material structures that constitutes the *habitus* and thus guides one's thought and behaviour – including the way one moves through the world (Bourdieu argues that the structures of the *habitus* are not only incorporated into consciousness but are also inscribed on the body and therefore shape one's lived experience). Most people absorb the 'socialized subjectivity' that is the *habitus* and live it out quietly, without much awareness on their part or on the part of observers that their behavior is pre-shaped by existing social structures. What Margery, as portrayed in the *Book*, quite unusually does is externalize the *habitus* and make it visible. Part of that externalizing is no doubt a consequence of the nature of autobiography, which as a genre depends on the revealing and making public of what is usually concealed. Almost by necessity, the *Book* is obliged to show us Margery's spirituality in action, thus externalizing her innermost feelings in order to explain her behaviour, its motives, and its results. But another part of that externalizing has to do with Margery's characteristic sense that acting out or acting up, to use modern terms for her behaviour, was a suitable way of expressing her piety. And the highly theatricalized atmosphere of East Anglia might well have suggested that expressive route to her.

In Bourdieu's formulation, a key element of the nexus between the *habitus* and power is that force is successful because it derives from assumptions and beliefs that go without saying: in other words, power can work insidiously since it is the nature of the *habitus* to take in quietly and unobtrusively the social structures that shape it. Authority thus stealthily reproduces itself as existing structures and their latent power relations are incorporated over and over again into the *habitus* of successive generations of people. And because the structures that form the *habitus* tend to go unnoticed and unremarked, power relations are usually not questioned. In Margery's case, however, her acting out calls attention to the hidden structures that control laywomen's behaviour. Her externalizing of the *habitus* in

---

[19] See Pierre Bourdieu, *The Logic of Practice*, trans. Richard Nice (Cambridge, 1990).

this way constitutes a disruption of power from an unexpected source – that of a woman who seeks to live an exemplarily holy life and undertakes that task through a notably bodily form of pious behavior.

Although Margery almost certainly did not see the Digby *Mary Magdalene*, which probably dates to the end of the fifteenth century, it is worth looking at the model of outspoken female spirituality provided by that play, since it points to the possibilities for vigorous female piety available in late medieval culture as well as to anxieties over the conflict between material and spiritual values.[20] In the sprawling Digby play, Mary Magdalene moves between the worlds of the flesh and the spirit, advocating a new kind of spirituality that risks being seen as heterodox. Starting off as a fallen woman, Mary like Margery embraces a life of faith, not however as a quiet and obedient recluse but as an active and highly visible advocate for spirituality. In her wide-ranging travels and encounters with important dignitaries, Mary is clearly meant to be regarded as a spokeswoman for religious messages and she is presented as a powerful woman, one who is skilled in the manly arts of preaching and conversion.[21] The play seems to derive pleasure from showing Mary as equal to or better than various male authority figures, and her virtuous presence is highlighted by its contrast with the corruption of the play's tyrants – men like Tiberius, Herod, Pilate, and the king of Marseilles. At the same time, the Digby play stages the tension between worldliness and asceticism, a tension that, as Theresa Coletti points out, had particular resonance for the prosperous gentry and bourgeois of late medieval East Anglia who desired a way of reconciling material interests with spiritual values. For these well-off lay people, the Digby play in Coletti's words 'works to resolve contradictions between a spiritual ideology whose highest value counseled renunciation of the world and a prosperous social and economic environment whose moral fissures registered in anxieties about property, status consciousness, and promotion of charity', moral fissures that surface in the *Book* as well.[22]

Even though the Digby play of *Mary Magdalene* was almost certainly not performed during Margery's lifetime, the legend of Mary Magdalene on which the play is based was widely known in Margery's day. Indeed, as Victor Scherb suggests, Margery, who states that her amanuensis began to write on the day after Mary Magdalene's feast day, seems to have felt an affinity for Mary Magdalene and links her own spiritual journey with the saint's (she also takes pains on her pilgrimage to the Holy Land to stand in the same place where Mary Magdalene stood when Christ asked her why she wept [30: 75]).[23] In one of her visions, which occurred on Calvary during her pilgrimage to Jerusalem, Margery saw mourning figures who included Mary Magdalene (28: 68), and the *Book* contains a number of other references to this same figure, who for Margery perhaps was a particularly inspiring model of the unworthy made worthy (as Jesus says to

---

[20] For the text of the Digby play see Donald C. Baker, John L. Murphy and Louis B. Hall, Jr., eds, *The Late Medieval Religious Plays of Bodleian MSS Digby 133 and e Museo 160*, EETS original series 283 (Oxford, 1982), pp. 25–95.

[21] Scherb, *Staging Faith*, p. 180.

[22] Theresa Coletti, 'Paupertas est donum Dei: Hagiography, Lay Religion, and the Economics of Salvation in the Digby Mary Magdalene', *Speculum* 76 (2001): 337–78 (341).

[23] Scherb, *Staging Faith*, pp. 173–4.

Margery [21: 49]). At one point, Jesus tells Margery that he loves her as much as he loved Mary Magdalene (74: 176); at another, he says that he knows that Margery has called Mary Magdalene into her soul (86: 210). Mary Magdalene is also mentioned in the prayer that comes at the end of the *Book*, where Margery asks for the same mercy that God showed to Mary Magdalene (II, prayers: 253).

While we cannot assume any direct connection between the Digby play and Margery's behaviour, both are examples of a previously worldly (and sexually active) woman who becomes an exemplar of piety and a performative female spirituality acting boldly in the public sphere. Margery's references to Mary Magdalene often contain sexual overtones, as when she describes Mary as Christ's 'trewe louer' (73: 174), which suggest that Mary offers Margery a way of converting carnal desire to spiritual purposes. Margery also seems to view Mary Magdalene as an illustration of the virtues of demonstrativeness, as when the Virgin Mary reminds her that Mary Magdalene ' "was not aschamyd to cryen & wepen" ' for her son (29: 73). One of Margery's most detailed visions includes the imagined scene of Mary Magdalene's participation in the events following Jesus' crucifixion, when he is taken down from the cross, buried, and then appears to Mary Magdalene, a scene that also figures in the Digby play, as we might expect. But in the Digby play, that scene while still central is overshadowed by the attention that is paid to Mary's formerly sinful life – in which she is tempted by Lechery, Flesh, and World, and is courted by a sexually predacious gallant in a tavern (a scene that resembles the story Margery recounts in chapter 4 of the man who 'wold ly be hir & haue hys lust of hys body' [4: 14]) – as well as by the lengthy description of Mary's conversion of the king of Marseilles, which finds a counterpart in Margery's many encounters with men who initially resist but then often are persuaded by her outspoken faith.

Margery's spiritual adventures – particularly her pilgrimages and journeys that bring her into contact with worldly authorities – may only be echoed in the Digby *Mary Magdalene*, but other aspects of her piety – especially her visions – seems more directly influenced by contemporary drama. Margery's visions in fact look quite strikingly like scenes from biblical plays focused on the life of Christ and, like those plays, her typical late medieval devotional emphasis was on the humanity and sufferings of Christ, which she dwelt on in great detail. As in those plays, the *dramatis personae* of her visions include Jesus, the Virgin, God the father, and other holy figures, who re-enact scenes from biblical history while allowing Margery to watch and occasionally join in. One of the most vivid of her visions was a re-creation of the Passion that year after year came to Margery during the rituals of Palm Sunday, which were themselves a symbolic enactment of the Passion. In these recurring visions, Margery 'beheld in þe syght of hir sowle' the events leading up to the crucifixion. She saw Jesus parting from his mother before going towards his Passion, and imagined herself as part of the scene, falling at Jesus' feet weeping and vowing that she would rather die than remain in the world without him. She then envisioned Jesus comforting her by telling her to sit with the Virgin Mary and promising her that he will not leave her forever but will return. After that, Margery saw herself urging Mary to get up and follow along to watch as Jesus says prayers on the Mount of Olivet, then is betrayed by Judas, beaten and buffeted, and finally stripped naked, bound to a pillar and whipped.

These sights, which she saw 'as freschly & as verily as ȝyf it had ben don in dede in hir bodily syght' caused Margery to weep and cry (79).

In another vision, she witnesses the crucifixion, describing details that are remarkably similar to the representation of the crucifixion found in the York and Towneley plays. She imagines, for instance, the stretching of Jesus' arms to fit pre-drilled holes in the cross, the ramming and dropping of the cross into a mortise (80: 192), and Mary's offer to carry the cross (80: 191). These details are echoed in the biblical plays, in the remark in the York 'crucifixion' about the pre-drilled holes now being too far apart, since Jesus' muscles have shrunk so much from the pain ('It failis a foote and moore, / The senous [sinews] are so gone ynne'); in the same play's description of the cross being in the same manner raised and dropped into a mortise; and in the Towneley 'Scourging', where Mary also offers to carry the cross.[24] More generally, Margery's vision of the crucifixion is, like the version found in the York cycle, a vivid and detailed account that relies on gesture, recounted speech, and the strong evocation of emotion.

Whether directly inspired by drama or not, in this vision Margery begins as an observer but soon finds herself a participant, for instance imagining herself running about as if she were a mad woman, as Jesus is dying, and then falling on her knees before the Virgin Mary and telling her to cease mourning, since her son is now dead and out of his pain (80: 193). In such scenes, Margery is not just a passive witness, but rather an actor in an imagined drama that unfolds in stages that echo the Passion scenes from the cycle plays.

For Margery, as for the biblical cycle plays like York's or the N-Town play from East Anglia, the mystical body of Christ was the focus of a new non-institutional style of lay piety, one that could exist with institutionalized religion but also was to some degree at odds with it. Expressive, emotional rather than rational, prone to value individual and personal response over collective and public expectations, and inclined to take a dim view of officialdom in all its guises, this increasingly popular piety found in Margery an unusually effective avatar. For it was not only in her private devotions that Margery drew on biblical drama as an inspiration for her spirituality but also in her public activities. Contemplation of Jesus' sufferings was a frequent trigger for her uncontrollable outbursts of crying and weeping, two of the most vivid demonstrations of her spiritual feelings. The power of her contemplative acts, compared with other kinds of devotional practices – such as reading – is explicitly spelled out in the *Book* when Margery comments that no book – not even well-known religious texts like Hilton's or Bride's or the *Stimulus Amoris* or the *Incendium Amoris* – could speak to her so effectively of God's love as her contemplations in which she conversed or interacted with divine figures (17: 39). Likewise, although Margery had clearly absorbed the teachings of verbal and written religious culture, as she herself recognizes when noting that through having holy books read to her and through listening to sermons her contemplations gradually grew and deepened (59: 144), her contemplations most often came in response to visual stimuli, such as holy

---

24 See 'The Crucifixion', in *The York Plays*, ed. Richard Beadle (London, 1982), pp. 319, 11.107–8 and 321, 11.229–30, and the 'Scourging', in *The Towneley Plays*, ed. Martin Stevens and A. C. Cawley, 2 vols, EETS supplementary series 13 and 14 (Oxford, 1994), 1: 282/426–9.

dolls representing the Christ child (30: 77–8), the pietà (60: 148), or ritual enactments of the Passion. Such stimuli were what initiated Margery's bouts of weeping and crying, those seemingly uncontrollable and oh so visible manifestations of the strength of her feelings.

Margery's histrionic behaviour might strike the modern reader as comic, annoying, or even daft, but within the context of the religious cultures of late medieval England, and of East Anglia in particular, it makes perfect sense as a vehicle for the expression of the piety of a bourgeois married laywoman for whom religiosity was tied up with social aspirations. The *Book* makes clear that in religion Margery found a way of defining her own identity and of satisfying desires for independence and status – and she wasn't alone. As recent scholarship suggests, late medieval religion was the complicated and heterogeneous ideological terrain on which a variety of groups struggled for recognition and autonomy, often through the manipulation of religious symbols.[25] Religion was a particularly useful symbolic tool for marginalized groups – such as the emergent middle classes and women – who sought ways around a church that increasingly seemed an economic institution indifferent to the spiritual needs of ordinary people. Such dissatisfaction with the church as an institution has been identified with the growth in such forms of lay piety as saints' cults, confraternities, private devotional practices, and Lollardy. While not always at odds with the church, these heterodox practices – not 'heresy' as such, but varying from the orthodox norm – point to a degree of discontent with the church as an institution and an authority. As the *Book* shows, an emphasis on private affect of the sort exemplified by Margery's 'feelings' would become a means of challenging the power of the church.

Closer to home and thus perhaps even more relevant for Margery, the hallmark of East Anglian religious culture was a non-institutionalized radical new religion that nonetheless in some ways continued to mesh with church teachings in a combination of what Gibson has called 'traditional and exploratory means of reaching toward a closer relationship with the divine'.[26] The religious cultures of East Anglia were indeed rich in manifestations of both the traditional and the new. The region was home to great monasteries like Bury St Edmunds, the Benedictine cathedral priory of Norwich, as well as other official religious institutions. Yet it also sheltered hermits and religious recluses, communities of pious laywomen, confraternities, Lollard preachers, and other individuals and groups seeking an alternative to the 'official' religiosity offered by the church as an institution. East Anglia's geographic location, and the economic activities spawned by that location, had something to do with the proliferation of these exploratory spiritual practices on a scale not seen elsewhere in England. Trade with the continent provided a route for new models of lay piety imported from abroad, especially those based on the tradition of continental mysticism – Norwich, for example, was the only English city to have *beguinages*, those communities of

---

[25] See, for example, David Aers and Lynn Staley, *The Powers of the Holy: Religion, Politics, and Gender in Late Medieval English Culture* (College Park, PA, 1996), p. 16.
[26] Gibson, *Theatre of Devotion*, p. 29.

pious laywomen popular on the continent.[27] Trade also enriched and empowered the middle classes, and the piety of the region was defined by the struggles of a nascent merchant class with monastic and ecclesiastical authorities, in which, as Gordon Leff suggests, the church was viewed less as a mediator of the divine than as a human institution with a history of involvement in wielding economic and political power.[28]

Margery's piety, as characterized in the *Book*, is deeply embedded in East Anglian discourses of popular religion, nowhere more obviously than in its combination of conformity to orthodox norms with radical heterodoxy. That Margery's story was understood to be consistent with the aims of the church is demonstrated in the Proem, which presents the *Book* as a spiritual handbook useful for orthodox devotion. The Proem recounts how Margery, worried about the delusions and deceits of her spiritual enemies, consulted many 'worshipful clerkys' (Proem: 3), including archbishops, bishops, and doctors of divinity, who advised her to follow her feelings and to believe that they came from the Holy Spirit and not from an evil spirit. The Proem also positions the book as having the blessings of clerical authorities, some of whom had urged Margery to record her spiritual experiences, particularly given that, as the Proem states, those experiences can help readers 'vndyrstondyn þe hy & vnspecabyl [high and unspeakable] mercy of ower soueryn Sauyowr Cryst Ihesu' (Proem: 1). In the eyes of the scribe-clergyman who served as Margery's amanuensis, the piety illustrated by Margery's life is fully orthodox and hence acceptable to existing patterns of church authority.

At the same time, however, the *Book* is certainly aware of the nonconformist aspects of Margery's behaviour. Even while offering an official endorsement of her spirituality, the Proem points to the difficulty of fully containing Margery's devotional practices within an orthodox framework. That difficulty shows up vividly in Margery's struggles to find a scribe for her book. It is notable that her first amanuensis was a layman, not a cleric, suggesting that she turned to someone outside the church because she feared that a cleric might refuse to write down her words or would try to reshape her experiences. That suspicion might have been what triggered her refusal of the offer of her confessor – the Carmelite, Alan of Lynn – to write down her experiences.[29] Her fears seem to have been justified, given the reaction of the priest to whom she took the resulting manuscript after the death of her layman-scribe. According to the Proem, claiming he could not read the manuscript but also frightened away by the evil things that were being said about Margery and her weeping, that priest put the book aside for more than four years, before telling her that he would not put himself in peril and referring her to another layman, who only managed to copy one folio. At this point, troubled by the fact that he had promised to help her, the priest asked to see this book again; when she brought it to him, she promised to pray that he might

27 Norman Tanner, *The Church in Late Medieval Norwich, 1370–1532* (Toronto, 1984), pp. 58–66; Gibson, *Theatre of Devotion*, pp. 6, 22–3.
28 Gordon Leff, 'The Apostolic Ideal in Later Medieval Ecclesiology', *Journal of Theological Studies* NS 18 (1967): 58–82 (71).
29 *BMK*, 6: 9; 259, note 6/9.

be granted the grace to read it. Trusting to her prayers, the priest took up the book and finding the task much easier, read the text over to her aloud as he made his copy. These exchanges, which are carefully recorded in the Proem, suggest that while the priest eventually grew settled in his opinion of the orthodoxy of Margery's experiences, he was not initially convinced on that count and in fact feared the consequences – presumably including the disfavour of the church hierarchy – of proceeding with a transcription.

A similar mingling of conformist and nonconformist practices is revealed in Margery's religious experiences as recounted in her book. Many of Margery's religious activities would not have raised any official eyebrows and in fact might have been taken as exemplary manifestations of a completely acceptable lay piety. She went to mass, she sought and followed the advice of clerics, she appears to have followed church doctrine and not to have questioned established beliefs – or so the *Book* takes pains to affirm. The *Book* goes out of its way to show Margery's awareness of the value of keeping on the right side of official religion. Time and again she seeks to assuage fears that her practices might be too extreme and to counter perceptions that they approach heresy. Even during one her most perilous moments, when in Leicester she has been imprisoned as a heretic and is subsequently questioned by the abbot and dean of Leicester, she satisfactorily relates articles of faith, satisfying them of her orthodoxy (48: 114–17), as she does again at York a while later. Similarly, her belief in the Trinity is asserted and is labelled as being a true faith and a right faith (86: 211).

Margery clearly walked a fine line in deferring to official ecclesiastical hierarchies while engaging in practices that in many instances presented a strong challenge to traditional networks of power relations. If the characteristic forms of lay piety in the fifteenth century – Lollardy, confraternities, private meditations, saints' cults, pilgrimage – expressed varying degrees of discontent with the religious status quo and demonstrated the ways in which people sought their own social spaces grounded in assertions of spiritual self-determination, then we have to see Margery's piety doing just the same. For despite her orthodox practices, Margery also engaged the forms of popular piety: she was accused of being a Lollard, joined the Trinity Guild at Lynn, spent untold hours in private meditation, showed unusual devotion to the cult of Mary, and went on pilgrimage to Rome, Jerusalem, and other holy sites. And Margery carried challenges to the church even further with her wearing of white, her weeping, and her preaching, the last of which most directly impinged on clerical privilege. Margery's strongly individualistic and public piety continually brought her up against church officialdom and the *Book* recounts a number of encounters she has with those in authority who question her. Notably, even when she successfully defends her behaviour, their reaction is to get rid of her, as the archbishop of York does while giving a man five shillings to escort her away (52: 128) or the friar who is so disturbed by her crying that he refuses to preach unless she is removed from the church (61: 149). Even the man who wrote down her experiences for a time turned against her, we are told, before reading of the similar behaviour of Mary d'Oignies and other holy figures (62: 152).

Numerous episodes in the *Book* are attuned to the need to resolve the tension between orthodoxy and heterodoxy. In most of these episodes, while appearing to defer to officialdom, Margery remains firmly fixed on her own path. But the appearance of deference is crucial. On her way back from a pilgrimage to Rome, for instance, when she arrives in Norwich the first thing she does is make an offering to the Trinity with some small change that other pilgrims had given her; next she arranges a friendly chat with Richard Caister, the vicar of St Stephen's; and after that she pays a visit to an anchorite – probably the Benedictine monk Thomas Brakleye – who had turned against her after hearing evil talk about her, including that she had conceived and given birth to a child while abroad. The purpose of Margery's visit is conciliatory, as the *Book* makes clear in its emphasis on her attempts at being humble and meek (43: 103). Yet when the monk does not believe her, chides her for her decision to dress all in white, and asks her to come again and be governed by him, she cagily invokes a higher authority, saying that if it were God's will, she would do so. Are we at all surprised when God tells her that he does not wish her to be governed by the monk? As this exchange shows, in the end Margery generally does what she wishes to do, but is always careful to disguise the fact that she is doing just that.

Mindful of the possibility that Margery's behaviour can be seen as a threat to official religion, the *Book* continually arranges ways to suggest that it is not just acceptable but also admirable. In an episode near the end of the *Book*, two priests arrange a test for Margery, in order to discover whether she weeps and cries only when she has an audience; when they find out that she is just as expressive in her devotion without a crowd, they are reassured that she isn't a fraud (83: 200). The *Book* also describes how nuns would seek her out in order to gain inspiration from her, and attests that her crying benefited those who believed in her (83: 200–2). The ending chapters of the first part of the narrative offer an even stronger validation of Margery's heterodox piety, particulary in chapter 84, in which God promises her the same rewards in heaven for the good deeds she has done in her mind as she would reap if she had done such actual deeds as fund churches, endow abbeys, pay priests, and support lepers and criminals. In scenes like these, Margery's heterodox spirituality is clearly receiving the stamp of approval from the cleric wielding the pen.

One of the things drama as a model for the performance of Margery's spirituality offered was a way of integrating orthodox with non-orthodox religious practices. Drama was adept at remaining acceptable to church authorities, toeing a doctrinal line and fitting within the structures of the church as an institution, while at the same time offering a vehicle for critiquing authority and giving vent to the demands of lay piety. For the most part, plays sponsored by lay groups such as trade guilds, civic and town governments, and religious guilds, were tolerated by ecclesiastical authorities, despite an anti-ludic strain in the late medieval reformist period that tried first to control indecorous behaviour by clerics and later to regulate a wider variety of ludic activity – including summer games, church ales, wrestling in churchyards and so forth. As Clopper has shown, anti-ludic regulations, which came in the form of episcopal letters, church synods, canon law, and other instruments of clerical control, did not affect the biblical cycles and moralities because those were not understood to fall under the church's purview, since they were sponsored by lay groups.[30] Official religion also found little to object to in lay religious plays given that, as Clopper observes, urban governments sponsored plays such as the York cycle because they felt an obligation to provide for the spiritual needs of citizens.

By using the strategies of drama, Margery developed a way of remaining acceptable to traditional religion while giving vent to what is in some ways a quite radically heterodox spirituality. As Goodman observes, some of Margery's most heterodox performances are presented as arising from within the most orthodox of occasions – such as, for example, her pilgrimage to Jerusalem.[31] This was when she experienced 'þe first cry þat euyr sche cryed in any contemplacyon' and when her crying became loud and disruptive (28: 68–9). Margery was also moved to outbursts on other orthodox occasions, during Palm Sunday processions, for instance, at which, so she tells us, she for many years had visions and outbursts of weeping (78: 184–5). Whether or not orthodoxy in fact engendered such extreme heterodoxy, the *Book*'s careful staging of Margery's nonconformity as being inspired by official religion, suggests an attempt to tame its radical force. Drama's status as an officially approved yet notoriously slippery and hard-to-police form of religious activity no doubt conditioned not just Margery's own piety but official responses to it. Whatever nagging concerns authorities might have had about the appropriateness of Margery's behaviour could – like occasional doubts about the propriety of certain dissident actions within biblical drama – be assuaged by looking to the larger spiritual service it did as an example of lay piety. Drama taught Margery a lesson or two, helping her craft a piety that disguised a new and dissident religiosity under the cloak of orthodoxy.

---

[30] Clopper, *Drama, Play, and Game*, pp. 268–9, argues that there was no attempt to regulate the northern biblical cycles until fifteen years into Elizabeth's reign.

[31] Goodman, *World*, p. 105.

8

Political Prophecy in The Book of Margery Kempe[1]

DIANE WATT

Introduction

In the later Middle Ages, then, female saints and holy women had great value as sources of propaganda and intercessory power. Their cultural value, though, was not confined to these spheres. Propaganda and politically driven attempts to secure divine intercession are parts of the larger process of making visible desired identities. . . . Female saints, nuns, and holy women became sources of symbolic capital fit for kings, playing crucial roles in the process of constructing royal identities.[2]

In her study of late medieval women religious, Nancy Bradley Warren examines the ambiguous status of holy women in the Lancastrian polity. Seen as both of use to the English crown and a threat to it, their cause might be championed, as was that of St Bridget of Sweden (to whom Henry V was devoted), or they might be persecuted or condemned, as was Joan of Arc. Yet spiritual causes are not always subordinate to secular ones; they can have their own autonomy and power. By the later Middle Ages, traditions of popular and specifically female prophecy, although open to appropriation, had the potential to be political forces in their own right. In this chapter, I examine Margery Kempe's self-representation as prophet – a self-representation that was far from unique, even for a laywoman. By placing her *Book* in the wider context of the European women prophets, I explore the extent of Kempe's engagement with current religious and political affairs on a series of levels: local, international and national. In so doing, I take issue with the view put forward by critics such as Lynn Staley that *The Book of Margery Kempe* bears no necessary relationship with actual historical events.[3] I also challenge recent claims by Anthony Goodman that Kempe was politically naive.[4] I argue instead that Kempe was fully conversant with what was going on

---

[1] In the present article I revisit and revise my argument in *Secretaries of God: Women Prophets in Late Medieval and Early Modern England* (Cambridge, 1997), ch. 2 (pp. 15–50). Some paragraphs and sentences have been borrowed and adapted from that chapter. I am grateful to Boydell & Brewer for permission to reuse this material.
[2] Nancy Bradley Warren, *Spiritual Economies: Female Monasticism in Later Medieval England* (Philadelphia, 2001), pp. 114–5.
[3] Staley acknowledges that 'some version of events in the *Book* may well have happened' but she takes pains to emphasize the *fictionality* of the text: *Dissenting Fictions*, p. 174.
[4] Goodman, *World*, e.g., pp. 143, 145 and 150.

in the wider world, and did not remain silent on matters that she considered important. Nevertheless, even as she laid claim to her prophetic voice, she seems to have refused to be treated as what Warren terms 'symbolic capital', perhaps because she recognized the dangers for a holy woman of engaging with political affairs in times as volatile as her own.

Margery Kempe's Prophetic Voice

At the end of chapter 20 of the first volume of *The Book of Margery Kempe*, we hear the unmistakable voice of the vengeful God of the Old Testament, describing the punishment He inflicts on a world that will not heed His messages or acknowledge His messenger.

> "I may no mor, dowtyr, of my rytfulnesse [righteousness] do for hem þan I do. I send hem prechyng & techyng, pestylens & bataylys, hungyr & famynyng, losse of her goodys wyth gret sekenesse, & many oþer tribulacyons, & þei wyl not leuyn [believe] my wordys ne þei wyl not knowe [recognize] my vysitacyon. & þerfor I xal sey to hem þat I made my seruawntys to prey for ȝow, & ȝe despysed her werkys [deeds] & her leuyng [lives]" (20: 48).

We might compare this passage to Leviticus 26: 14–39, in which the Lord describes to Moses the chastisement that will befall those who break God's commandments. Chapter 20 as a whole is, despite its short length (only 24 lines, or just over a page of printed text), crucial to Margery Kempe's self-identification as religious prophet and inspired teacher, as one who speaks for God, who proclaims his message and interprets his word.[5]

Chapter 20 begins with Kempe's account of a eucharistic miracle which took place on one occasion when the pious laywoman was attending mass. At the moment of the elevation of the host, Kempe sees the sacrament fluttering like a dove. This vision is repeated a moment later when the priest lifts up the chalice with the sacrament within it and the chalice itself sways back and forth. Similar revelations are not uncommon in the recorded experiences of late medieval women mystics. One example can be found in *The Orcherd of Syon*, the Middle English translation of Catherine of Siena's mystical treatise *Il Libro* or *Dialogo*. This text, produced for the Bridgettine nuns of Syon abbey, describes a vision of a 'culuer' or dove which 'flikeride [fluttered] or smoot [struck] hise wyngis togydere aboute þe hoost [the consecrated bread], ofschewynge [exhibiting] ioye and gladnesse for vertu of þo wordis þat þe prest seyde in tyme of consecracioun'.[6] In such a vision, the transformation of the host into a dove, symbolizing the Holy Spirit, mirrors the process of transubstantiation, in which the whole substance of the bread and wine is converted into Christ's body and blood. As well as confirming the authority of the priest who consecrates the

---

5   *Middle English Dictionary*, eds H. Kurath et al. (Ann Arbour, 1956–2001) s.v. 'prophet(e)'. For a discussion of the meaning of prophecy in the Middle Ages see *Secretaries of God*, pp. 19–21.
6   Catherine of Siena, *The Orcherd of Syon*, ed. P. Hodgson and G. M. Liegey, EETS original series 258 (London, 1966), p. 250.

sacrament, and indeed of the church itself, it is clearly intended to indicate the blessed state of the communicant who beholds it. What *is* remarkable in Kempe's account is what follows the description of the miracle. Kempe tells us that when the consecration is over, she remains rooted to the spot, waiting to see if the marvellous occurrence will be repeated. As she lingers, she hears the voice of Jesus Christ telling her that she will not witness the miracle again, but that she should be grateful because ' "My dowtyr, Bryde, say me neuyr in þis wyse [never saw me in this way]" ' (20: 47).

The Bride or Bridget alluded to here is, of course, St Bridget of Sweden (1303–1373), an important visionary and the founder of the Bridgettine Order. St Bridget's influence on Kempe has been well documented, and, in this essay, it will be explored in relation to Kempe's prophetic role.[7] At this point in her narrative, Kempe makes the comparison between herself and St Bridget explicit. Indeed, she goes further, and records that Christ revealed to her that in one respect at least, she, Kempe, was blessed more than her foremother. The ensuing dialogue between Kempe and Christ is very telling indeed:

> Þan seyd þis creatur in hir thowt, "Lord, what betokenyth þis ?" "It betokenyth veniawnce [vengeance]". "A, good Lord, what veniawnce?" þan seyd owyr Lord a-ȝen to hir, "þer xal be an erdene [earthquake], tel it whom þow wylt in þe name of Ihesu. For I telle þe forsoþe [in truth] rygth [just] as I spak to Seynt Bryde ryte so I speke to þe, dowtyr, & I telle þe trewly it is trewe eeuery word þat is wretyn in Brides boke, & be þe [through you] it xal be knowyn for very trewth. And þow xalt faryn [fare] wel, dowtyr, in spyte of alle thyn enmys . . ." (20: 47).

The voice of Kempe's Jesus Christ, with whom she enjoys so much holy and delightful 'dalyawns' or 'conversation', blurs with that of the God of St Bridget. The warning of natural disaster as a token of divine anger is of a kind with the ensuing prognostications of disease, war and starvation. It has all the force of some of St Bridget's own divine messages, such as the revelation in which God tells her, ' "I shall plow the field with my wrath and pull up bushes and trees by their roots. Where a thousand people lived, barely a hundred will be left." '[8] While Kempe does attempt to intercede on behalf of the people, begging for mercy and praying that they might be sent contrition, she nevertheless adopts the role of prophet so much favoured by St Bridget. Kempe does this not only in an attempt to justify her own position (Christ effectively promises her that her enemies will be punished), but also to defend Bridget herself. As will become

---

[7] See, amongst others, Clarissa Atkinson, *Mystic and Pilgrim: The Book and the World of Margery Kempe* (Ithaca, NY, 1983), pp. 168–79; Gunnel Cleve, 'Margery Kempe: A Scandinavian Influence on Medieval England', in Marion Glasscoe, ed., *The Medieval Mystical Tradition in England 5* (Cambridge, 1992), pp. 163–78; Susan Dickman, 'Margery Kempe and the Continental Tradition of the Pious Woman', in Marion Glasscoe, ed., *The Medieval Mystical Tradition in England: Papers read at Dartington Hall, July 1984* (Cambridge, 1984), pp. 150–68.

[8] Quoted by R. K. Emmerson in 'The Prophetic, the Apocalyptic, and the Study of Medieval Literature', in J. Wojcik and R. J. Frontain, eds, *Poetic Prophecy in Western Literature* (London, 1984), p. 48.

evident in what follows, in so doing, Kempe involves herself in the religious debates of her own time.

Political Conflict in Lynn (1431–32)

Margery Kempe's active engagement with matters of politics on a local level is most vividly illustrated in chapter 25 of the *Book*. Here Kempe and her scribe describe the former's involvement in a dispute between clergy and laity in her home town of Lynn. The background to it is as follows.[9] When at home in Lynn, Margery Kempe usually worshipped in the parish church of St Margaret's. However, there were two other principal chapels in the town, St James's and St Nicholas's. During Kempe's lifetime, both chapels repeatedly sought full parochial rights. As early as 1378 (when Kempe would only have been around five years old), a papal bull granted the chapel of St Nicholas privileges for administering the sacraments of baptism, marriage and the purification of women. The grant was however subject to the provision that it should not have a negative impact on the parish church. It was resisted by Norwich cathedral priory; by Margery Kempe's father, John Brunham, who was in his second term of office as mayor of the town; and by other burgesses of Lynn, including one John Kempe, plausibly Margery Kempe's father-in-law. Shortly afterwards Brunham successfully opposed a bid on the part of the chapel to renew these privileges. Around 1426, the supporters of St James's and St Nicholas's revived their endeavours to increase the standing of the chapels and sent a petition to the pope requesting the privileges be reinstated. Despite the fact that public opinion had now apparently shifted in favour of the chapels, the suit was denied following an ecclesiastical inquiry. In 1428, the chapel of St James – with the backing of an important merchant of the town, one John Waterden, as well as the then mayor, John Permonter, and much of the local community – requested permission to install a font. In 1432, the chapel of St Nicholas likewise renewed its efforts, and on this occasion it too had the support of the mayor and the townspeople.

It is this last attempt by the chapel of St Nicholas that is recorded in *The Book of Margery Kempe*. Typically, at the beginning of the account, some efforts are made to hide the identities of the church and the prime movers in the dispute, and indeed, in this case, the identity of the town itself:

> It happyd in a worshepful [notable] town wher was o parysch cherch & tweyn [two] chapelys annexid, þe chapellys hauyng & mynystryng [administering] alle sacramentys, except only cristenyng & purificacyons, thorw sufferawns of þe person [as permitted by the parson] . . . (25: 58).

The *Book* gives a very partisan account of events, implicitly endorsing the position adopted in the 1370s by Kempe's father and his associates. Nevertheless, explicitly Kempe is represented as opposing rather than siding with the urban community.

---

9 See *BMK*, Appendix III, vii, pp. 372–4; and the discussion in Goodman, *World*, pp. 82–4 and notes.

The narrative takes the side of the prior of St Margaret's church, who can be identified as John Derham, and also (although he is not mentioned in this context) that
of Robert Springold, parish priest at St Margaret's and one of Kempe's main
confessors.[10] The parishioners of the two chapels, motivated by vain ambition,
bring about 'gret ple & gret heuynes [considerable litigation and a great deal of
distress]' (25: 59). The dispute over the granting of a font to the chapel of St
Nicholas is constructed as a conflict between 'mede' ('money', but with connotations of a 'gift', 'reward', 'fee' and 'bribe'), and 'trewthe' ('truth' which can denote
'faithfulness' and 'loyalty' as well as 'integrity' and 'righteousness').[11] The narrative
draws upon the *communis sententia* of proverbial wisdom: 'Gold may speed in every
need' and 'Meed may speed rather than truth'.[12] It opposes the power that comes
with material wealth, status and patronage to the authority of a poor servant of God
who relies on the support of his devout congregation. If the nameless merchants
who support the chapel are 'worschepful' or esteemed, their honour and dignity
are worldly rather than spiritual, while the prior's 'manful' opposition to the
bullying of these esteemed citizens echoes the descriptions of the tribulations
of numerous saints.

The legal system is proven to be incapable of resolving the matter, which drags
on to the dissatisfaction of all concerned. Even the intervention of the bishop of
Norwich, William Alnwick does not appear to hasten the proceedings. At this
point in the episode, it becomes apparent that it is being narrated not by Kempe
herself, but by her principal scribe, who characteristically describes himself as 'þe
preste whech [who] aftyrward wrot þis boke' (25: 59). He reports that having given
up on the official process, he turns to Kempe, as, he tells us, 'he had don be-forn
in þe tyme of ple' [in time of litigation] and asks her to look into her soul and pre-
dict the outcome. Kempe's answer is instantaneous and unambiguous, ' "Drede
ȝe not, for I vndyrstond in my sowle, þow [although/even if] þei woldyn ȝeve
[give] a buschel of nobelys, þei xuld not haue it." ' Despite Kempe's confidence
in her own revelation, and in the incorruptibility of the legal process, the narrator
admits that he is not entirely reassured; he is aware that Alnwick had started
negotiations with the merchant party. It is then all the more remarkable that
Kempe's predictions are fulfilled: the proposed compromise is rejected and the
court finds in favour of the prior. This narrative episode has an exemplary function within the larger narrative of Kempe's *Book*, as its conclusion makes clear:

> And so, blyssed mot God ben, þe parysch cherch stod stylle in her worschep &
> hyr degre [remained in its diginity and its status] as sche had don ij hundryd
> ȝer befor & mor, and þe inspiracyon of owyr Lord was be experiens preuyd for
> very sothfast [true] & sekyr [certain] in þe forseyd creatur (25: 60).

Not only are the righteous rewarded, but, more significantly, experience proves
the authenticity of the prophetic voice, the authority of God-given inspiration.

---

[10] See Goodman, *World*, p. 84.
[11] *MED*, s.v. 'mede' and 'treuth'.
[12] B. J. Whiting, ed., *Proverbs, Sentences, and Proverbial Phrases from English Writers mainly before
1500* (Cambridge, MA, 1968), G302 and M493.

While Nicholas Watson has recently dismissed the dispute over the granting of privileges to the chapels in Lynn as a mere 'squabble',[13] Goodman regards the account of these events in *The Book of Margery Kempe* as exceptional. Goodman observes: 'This issue of public policy in Lynn is the only one on which a strong opinion was expressed in the *Book*.'[14] Indeed, Goodman goes so far as to contend that on the whole the *Book* avoids political controversy, and that this tendency renders it the more remarkable. He observes that Kempe's 'prime exemplar St Bridget had made the castigation of the wrong-doings of rulers and elites an integral part of her spirituality', but goes on to argue that 'the *Book*'s silence on political matters may have a certain eloquence'.[15] For Goodman, the explanation for such reticence in the *Book* lies in Kempe's social background. Kempe was the daughter of one of the most pre-eminent and influential townsmen of Lynn. As Kate Parker's essay in this volume reveals, in the early fifteenth century, in other words during Kempe's adult life, the privileges and power of the merchant classes within this thriving urban community, including that of her own family, had been challenged and undermined. But to contend, as Goodman does, that Kempe would not have wanted to open herself up to attack by overtly associating herself with an unpopular élite, is to oversimplify a complex situation.

It is certainly true to say that throughout the *Book*, there are remarkably few occasions in which Kempe involves herself in purely secular affairs, and none on a public level either in Lynn or in the world beyond. Yet there are a number of instances recorded in the *Book* in which Kempe does become embroiled in the spiritual concerns of her home town, and specifically in matters relating to the parish church of St Margaret's. St Margaret's was, after all, an establishment that played a central role in her religious life, and thus very dear to her heart. In chapter 71, the *Book* records an occasion when a priest who 'had gret trust' or 'faith' in Kempe nonetheless decided to test her prophetic abilities (71: 170). This priest asked Kempe to tell him whether or not the prior of Lynn (identifiable as Thomas Heveningham) would be recalled to Norwich. Kempe's predictions proved accurate. The *Book* records that Kempe was not only granted further private revelations concerning Heveningham's successor (Derham), but also asked by another cleric to prophesy whether or not the new prior would take part in a mission to join Henry V in France. Again, Kempe is shown to have access to divine secrets: the king died and so, as she foretold, the priest stayed at home. The chapter ends with one final example: at a time when it was rumoured that the bishop of Winchester (Henry Beaufort) had died, Kempe knew from her 'feelings' that this was not the case. All of these events took place in the early 1420s: Heveningham and Henry V both died in 1422; the rumour concerning the bishop of Winchester may well have circulated around the same time, or a few years later. A slightly earlier episode, again relating to St Margaret's church, is recorded in chapter 67.

---

13 Nicholas Watson, 'The Making of *The Book of Margery Kempe*', in Katheryn Kerby-Fulton and Linda Olson, eds, *Voices in Dialogue* (forthcoming, South Bend Indiana, 2004). I am grateful to Professor Watson for providing me with a copy of this article prior to publication.

14 Goodman, *World*, p. 83; but cf. pp. 207–8, where he states that 'the controversy was not exactly tearing the place apart' (p. 208).

15 Ibid., p. 51.

Here we are told of a crisis in which Kempe's confessor, Robert Springold, put his faith in her prophetic abilities. Following her advice, when a fire consumed the Guildhall of the Trinity and St Margaret's was itself in danger, he carried the blessed sacrament to the flames, trusting in its supernatural power as a relic of Christ to save the church. Seemingly in response to Kempe's prayer, the fire was suddenly extinguished. Documentary evidence dates this event to 23 January 1420/1421.[16] Parker comments on the extent to which Kempe is portrayed in her *Book* as being disparaged by her own townspeople, and suggests that this reflects the fall in status of her own family.[17] However, Kempe's Lynn prophecies establish that spiritual authority in the locality was growing even as her family's social and political power was diminishing, and they may have been intended in part as an attempt to reverse that negative process.

Carolyn Dinshaw has recently proposed that episodes such as these, which serve to demonstrate Kempe's prophetic abilities, are evidence that Kempe 'exists in some sense out her world's time, in a spiritual time frame (the everlasting *now* of the divine) that is radically separate from the secular chronology governing others around her'.[18] Yet the opposite is also true. Kempe is also very much *in* her world's time, sharing the secular time-frame of her contemporaries. In other words, the timing of the local prophecies is significant. As we have seen, the events in chapters 67 and 71 all seem to date from the first half of the second decade of the fifteenth century. They were probably originally recorded by Kempe's first scribe. Kempe's prognostications confirmed her supernatural abilities, but do not in themselves seem to have been particularly controversial. The events in chapter 25, however, took place almost exactly ten years later. Although the original composition of the first draft of *The Book of Margery Kempe*, dictated in all probability to her son visiting from Germany where he had settled, has been conventionally dated to 1430–31, this view has been recently challenged.[19] Watson puts the convincing case that Kempe's son was actually working on the *Book* during an earlier and longer visit the previous year (i.e. 1429–30).[20] Following this view, it is impossible that the son could have been responsible for chapter 25, which must therefore have been added later. There can be no doubt that the second main scribe interpolated this chapter, written as it is from his point of view, when he was working on the *Book* between 1436 and 1438. In other words, the events are recorded only about five years after they occurred, at a point when they would still have been relatively fresh in the scribe's mind. Indeed the narrative opens by pointing out that the chronology is being disrupted here in order to include it. For the second scribe, as no doubt for the visionary herself, Kempe's involvement in a local – and comparatively recent – controversy was particularly noteworthy and deserving of detailed treatment.

[16] *BMK*, p. 327, n. 162, 29–31.
[17] See above, pp. 69–73.
[18] Carolyn Dinshaw, 'Margery Kempe', in Carolyn Dinshaw and David Wallace, eds, *The Cambridge Companion to Medieval Women's Writing* (Cambridge, 2003), pp. 222–39 (p. 226).
[19] For the argument that Kempe's son wrote the *Book* from dictation in the month before he died, when he was suffering from a debilitating illness, see *BMK*, p. 342, n. 225, 11.
[20] Watson, 'The Making'.

Even if it was hardly of national importance, the issue of the granting of privileges to the two chapels in Lynn was an urgent issue of real import for the town's clergy and laity alike.

International Controversy in Rome (1414–15)

Goodman claims that Kempe's knowledge of current affairs was 'gravely, even recklessly, defective'.[21] How valid is this assertion? The extent of Margery Kempe's engagement with international politics can be gauged by examining her fairly extended account in chapters 31–42 of her visit to Rome. Kempe stayed in Rome for approximately six months on the return leg of her pilgrimage to Jerusalem. It seems she arrived in Rome between August and early October 1414 and left after the following Easter. Her visit would have coincided with the Council of Constance, which finally resolved the Great Schism, debated the authenticity of the revelations of St Bridget and confirmed her canonization,[22] and tried and condemned the Bohemian religious reformer Jan Hus and another notable continental follower of John Wyclif, Jerome of Prague. Indeed, Kempe had passed through Constance in 1413 at the time when the city was preparing for the council, on her way to Venice, from whence she travelled by boat to the Holy Land. While she was in Constance, she had benefited from the patronage of an English friar and papal legate, who agreed to act as her confessor at that time (27: 63). It is, then, inconceivable that she could have been oblivious to the deliberations that were about to take place. Likewise, it is reasonable to assume, given her thirteen-week sojourn in Venice (27: 65), that she would have known about, and discussed with others, the canonization of Catherine of Siena which was under consideration there at that time (Catherine was not actually canonised until 1461). Yet, Kempe makes no direct mention of either the council, or the so-called 'Venetian Process'.

Other instances of Kempe either failing to mention, or only alluding to, major international events include her stay in Bristol en route for Santiago de Compostella, and her travels through northern Europe in 1433. On the former occasion, Kempe's sailing was delayed because all the ships 'wer arestyd & takyn up [requisitioned] for þe kyng' (44: 107). This must refer to Henry V claiming ships for his French expedition of 1417. On the latter occasion, Kempe describes how she was afraid to leave Danzig (now Gdansk) and travel by land 'for þer was werr [war] in þe cuntre þat sche xulde passyn by' (II, 4: 232). She goes on to mention further difficulties she experienced making her way home, caused by hostilities between England and the countries through which she had to journey (II, 4: 232, 233). There are indirect references to the Polish invasion of the Duchy of Pomerania, which belonged to the Teutonic Order of Prussia, and to conflicts between England and the Teutonic Order and Hanseatic cities. However, there are marked differences between the omissions in these instances, and those in Kempe's accounts of her visits to the southern German and Italian cities. Whereas Kempe remained in both Bristol and Danzig for about six weeks (not surprisingly

21 Goodman, *World*, p. 150.
22 On Jean Gerson's criticisms of St Bridget's revelations see Watt, *Secretaries of God*, pp. 35–6.

she seems to have travelled rather quickly through northern and central Germany), she stayed in Venice for more than twice that period, and resided in Rome for much longer still. Kempe would, therefore, have had plenty of time to involve herself in the controversies taking place, especially those relating to St Bridget to whom she was evidently so devoted, and it would seem remarkable if she had failed to do so. Why then does she make no mention of them?[23]

Margery Kempe structures her account of her visit to Rome in terms of familiar mystical and hagiographic themes and topoi. She describes in detail both her marriage to the Godhead and the nature of her visionary experiences in Rome (see especially 35: 86–91 and 41: 98–9), and also the life of voluntary poverty and abjection she led in the city (chapters 34–39). However, equally central to her narrative is the idea of the prophet who goes unrecognized by his – or, in this case, her – own people. According to the Gospel of Matthew, those who knew Christ's family and background disparaged Him. Christ's response, 'A prophet is not without honour, save in his own country, and in his own house' (Matthew 13: 57), resonated with Kempe during her stay in the Eternal City. Although not in her own land geographically, Kempe found herself spiritually at home with the Italian people and German residents and visitors, and rejected by her compatriots. Kempe journeys from Assisi not with her own band of pilgrims, but in the company of a wealthy Roman lady and her entourage (31: 79–80). Later, the same woman, finding Kempe living in poverty, invites her to dine with her on Sundays, and provides her with food to help her during the week (38: 93). Other lay people in Rome, women in particular, even those who are themselves struggling to survive, consider her virtuous and pious, and treat her charitably (33: 84, 38: 93–4, and 41: 98–9). The clergy also hold her in some esteem and have compassion for her. A priest at the church of Santa Caterina in Ruota welcomes her and agrees to give her communion (31: 80–1). A German priest at the church of St John Lateran's, who speaks no English, is miraculously blessed by God so that he can understand Kempe and hear her confession (33: 82–3).

In contrast, Kempe repeatedly emphasizes that 'hir owyn cuntremen wer obstynat [obdurate]' (33: 84). One of the English pilgrims from her group, a priest, has her excluded from the hospital of St Thomas of Canterbury (31: 80). Later, he tries to turn Kempe's German confessor against her, and accuses her of having a devil within her (33: 84, 34: 84–5). Her own former maidservant, who had found herself a good position in the hospice, provides her with alms but refuses to return to her service (39: 95). The exception amongst the English is another priest, whom Kempe adopts as her spiritual son (40: 96). Having heard distant rumours of Kempe's piety and travelled to Rome in search of her, he takes her in, provides for her and helps her to return home (chapters 40–43).

Towards the end of her chronicle of her stay in Rome, following a revelation concerning the sanctity of the decaying city, stricken as it is with destitution and penury, Kempe incorporates a series of recollections designed to demonstrate her spiritual affinity to St Bridget. Kempe begins by mentioning that she had agreed

---

[23] Goodman also points out that Kempe does not refer to the fact that John XXIII, responsible for the confirmation of St Bridget's canonization in 1414, was in Bologna when she passed through the city. He suggests that this may be because he was later declared anti-pope: *World*, p. 157.

to be godmother to the child of 'a gret jentyl-woman' whose family had known the Swedish saint (39: 94).[24] The child was of course given the saint's name. A little further on in the narrative, Kempe describes the pilgrimage she made on one of the saint's feast days to the church on the site of St Bridget's home. There she attended a sermon in the chapel that had been converted from the chamber in which the saint had died, and where, kneeling on a stone, the saint had received the divine knowledge that her death was imminent. Just as in Jerusalem, Kempe had been able to retrace the steps of the Holy Family, so in Rome, she was able to mirror the movements of this influential 'modern' holy woman. To introduce this episode, Kempe moves from her re-encounter with her servant who refuses to return to work for her to her meeting with a woman who had attended St Bridget. In so doing she draws an implicit contrast between the behaviour of her own intractable maid and the loyal behaviour of this elderly attendant. Through a translator, Kempe is informed that the saint 'was goodly & meke to euery crea-tur & þat sche had a lawhyng cher [laughing countenance]' (39: 95), a portrait confirmed by Kempe's landlord in Rome. As a consequence of her cheerful and sympathetic disposition, he for one had not recognized the extent of Bridget's piety. Given the extent of the hostility of her fellow English pilgrims to her own appearance and behaviour, Kempe would no doubt have felt reassured and con-soled by the knowledge that her role model's sanctity was not always self-evident.

The emphasis placed on St Bridget's demeanour, rather than on her visions and revelations, may suggest that she was principally a model of devout conduct for Kempe. Tellingly, the sermon Kempe listened to not only described Bridget's 'reuelacyonys' [revelations] but also 'hir maner of leuyng' [manner of life] (39: 95). However the ensuing passages in Kempe's narration indicate otherwise. St Bridget had lived in Rome, imposing poverty upon herself, for the last 20 or more years of her life (although she went on pilgrimage to Jerusalem shortly before her death). During that time, which coincided with the end of the so-called 'Babylonian Captivity', when the papal court was based in Avignon in France, she uttered many prophecies urging the papacy to return and condemning the city. One Middle English manuscript of St Bridget's *Revelations* describes the Virgin Mary's complaint about the ingratitude of the city in which the relic of the Holy Prepuce is preserved, ' "O Roome, o Roome, yff thou knewyst [under-stood], thou shuldest yoye ye sowthly [truly rejoice]; yf thou cowldest wepe, thow shuldest wepe evyr more, for thou hast my most dere tresour and doyst not honour and worshype [venerate] ytt." '[25] In the English translation of St Bridget's *Liber Celestis*, we find recorded Christ's own words of condemnation in response to the visionary's prayers for the city:

> Bot nowe mai I speke to Rome as þe prophet spake to Jerusalem 'þat sometime dwelled in rightwisenes [righteousness], and þe princes þareof luffed pees

---

24 The *Book* states rather ambiguously that 'they haddyn knowlach of hir [known her] in hir lyue-tyme'. Given that St Bridget had died some forty years previously, it seems likely that it is the family of the gentlewoman rather than the gentlewoman and her husband who are being referred to here.

25 Oxford, Bodleian Library, MS Rawlinson C.41; extracted and edited in Alexandra Barratt, ed., *Women's Writing in Middle English* (London, 1992), p. 90.

[loved peace].' Bot nowe is turned to rusti colure, and þe princes of it are menslaers [murderers]. Wald God [God wishes], Rome, þat þow knewe þi daies. Þan suld þou morn [mourn] and noght be glad. Sometime was Rome wele colourde with rede blode of martires, and set togidir with þe bones of saintes. Now are Rome ȝates [Rome's gates] desolate, for þe kepers are all bowed to couetise [all submit to covetousness]. Þe walles are pute done [broken down] . . . . And þe holi place . . . is nowe turned to luste and vanite of þe world.[26]

At the time of Kempe's visit, papal rule had been reinstated but Pope John XIII was absent, and Neapolitan opposition continued. As Goodman notes, Kempe was in Rome 'at a time of high political instability'.[27] Nevertheless, the prolonged period of division in the Western church was coming to an end. For Kempe, Rome is a city which is blessed rather than cursed as Christ's words to her – ' "Thys place is holy" ' (39: 94) – confirm. Nevertheless, Kempe does herself make a number of pronouncements during her residence, the most striking of them actually occurring during her visit to chapel and concerning St Bridget.

Owr Lord sent swech tempestys of wyndys & reynes & dyuers impressyons of eyrs [various atmospheric disturbances] þat þai þat wer in þe feldys & in her labowrys wyth-owtyn-forth [at their work outdoors] wer compellyd to entyr howsys in socowryng of her bodijs to enchewyn dyuers perellys [to protect themselves and to avoid various dangers]. Þorw swech tokenys þis creatur sup-posyd þat owr Lord wold [wished] hys holy Seyntys day xulde ben halwyd [hallowed] & þe Seynt had in mor worshep þan sche was at þat tyme [held in more respect than she was at that time] (39: 95).

Once again, the disorder of the external world, in this case tempestuous weather, is taken as a sign that validates the sanctity of Bridget. However, whereas it is difficult to date the comparable revelation in chapter 20 (discussed in the introduction to this essay), the year in which the events being described here actually took place is crucial.[28] The divine manifestation of God's anger coincided with the reassessment of St Bridget's own revelations in Constance. Kempe's interpretation – presumably aimed in the first place, although by no means exclusively, at those currently dwelling in Rome – actually echoes Bridget's own prayer for 'þe moste excellent cite of Rome . . . Þat more wirship be done [more respect be shown] to þi [God's] saintes and to relikes of þaime, þat þe pepill hafe more deuocion [devotion] to þaime'.[29] Indeed, it is plausible

---

[26] *The Liber Celestis of St Bridget of Sweden*, ed. Roger Ellis, EETS original series 291 (Oxford, 1987), pp. 238–9.

[27] Goodman, *World*, p. 195.

[28] We might guess that the two revelations about the authenticity of St Bridget's visionary experiences were roughly contemporaneous. Yet, there is no indication that the miracle in chapter 20 took place outside England. The preceding chapter is concerned with events that took place some time before Kempe's departure to Jerusalem. Chapter 21 also shows the influence of St Bridget on Kempe. If the events in chapter 20 *do* also date to 1413 or earlier, then this would suggest that even before she left England, Kempe was both very familiar with Bridget's life, miracles and revelations, and informed about debates surrounding the saint.

[29] *Liber Celestis*, p. 236.

that Kempe saw St Bridget's residence in Rome as the fulfilment of the saint's own prediction that, despite its current lamentable state, 'ȝit [yet] sall þere be gaderd þeder [thither] fyshes as swete as þai were before'.[30] Nevertheless, because no reference is made to the larger significance of Kempe's interpretation of the atmospheric conditions in Rome, its timeliness is easily overlooked. Indeed the narrative is structured in such a way as to deflect our attention from it. Kempe goes on to describe the tempests in greater detail, telling the reader that sometimes she had foreknowledge that they would occur. She also describes how, in response to the pleading of the Roman people, she interceded with God on their behalf and in response God abated the storms. But the point remains that at least in her revelations concerning Bridget, Kempe demonstrates her knowledge of what is taking place on the world stage and engages with current religio-political debates. As was the case in the dispute over the privileges of the chapels in Lynn, Kempe is taking a stance on an issue of importance to her.

National Crisis in England (1417)

Margery Kempe was inspired by the example of St Bridget as a saint who had married and had children but who subsequently made a vow of chastity with her husband, and lived a mixed life combining mysticism and pilgrimage. Critics have also suggested that St Bridget's concerns about her son Karl, a reformed sinner, may provide a model for Kempe's analysis of her relationship with her own son, whom Kempe discusses in the second part of her *Book* (II, 1: 221–5) and who was responsible for drafting the first part.[31] Other more minor episodes also seem to mirror some of St Bridget's experiences. What is more, clear echoes of St Bridget's revelations can be heard in the reassurances Kempe received about the status of married women in heaven (21: 49).[32] Kempe evidently knew not only of St Bridget's holy life, but also of her revelations and prophetic vocation, and the evidence suggests that she imitated both. But to what extent did Kempe, like St Bridget, try to influence the powerful and the mighty? Bridget after all reproached Pope Urban V and had damning revelations concerning the Swedish king, Magnus Erikson. Kempe certainly reprimands not only mere priests but also members of the higher clergy in England. These include Thomas Arundel, archbishop of Canterbury, whom she reproaches for keeping an unruly household (16: 37), and Henry Bowet, archbishop of York, whom she predicts will never reach heaven if he is as wicked as she has heard, unless he repents (52: 125). She also receives a revelation for Philip Repingdon, bishop of Lincoln, concerning Christ's anger at him for putting off granting Kempe the mantle and ring she seeks as confirmation of her vow of chastity (15: 35). Her strongest opprobrium is however reserved for

---

[30] Ibid., p. 256.
[31] e.g. Atkinson, *Mystic and Pilgrim*, pp. 176–8.
[32] *Liber Celestis*, p. 316.

figures of secular authority, such as John Arnesby, mayor of Leicester, whom she thinks of as her 'dedly enmy' (48: 115). According to the *Book*, Kempe was not without influence, possibly especially amongst women. We are told that the abbess of Denney and the sisters in her convent consulted her (84: 202), and her example may have swayed members of the aristocracy such as Joan Beaufort, countess of Westmorland, the aunt of Henry V, and her daughter Elizabeth Lady Greystoke (54: 133).[33] But no authoritative revelations are recorded in these contexts. Indeed most of Kempe's prophecies concerning the dying and the dead and other prognostications, relate to her clerical supporters and people in the middling ranks.[34]

Yet Kempe does not avoid national politics altogether. Kempe's spiritual vocation brought her considerable public attention, and even though she eventually received a letter from Henry Chichele, archbishop of Canterbury, legitimizing her religious practices (55: 136), at least once in 1413 and four times in 1417 she was brought before the authorities and examined concerning her beliefs and activities. Her first examination occurred at Norwich (17: 40). She was also interrogated at Leicester (chapters 46–48), and later questioned by a doctor of divinity at York, and then by the archbishop of York himself (chapters 51 and 52). Following her arrest by men in the service of the duke of Bedford, she was brought to Beverley, where she was once more taken before the archbishop of York (chapters 53 and 54). In recounting the arrests that took place following Kempe's return from Rome and Jerusalem, and especially in its rendering of the final arrest in the sequence, the *Book* engages with significant events of the time.[35] John of Lancaster, duke of Bedford, was brother to Henry V and was appointed custodian of the realm during the king's French campaign in the summer of 1417. This was a time of internal crisis: the Lollard knight, Sir John Oldcastle, had escaped from prison four years previously and was still at large, and apparently stirring up rebellion. Bedford pursued a vigorous campaign against heresy and insurrection. Oldcastle was eventually captured in November, and Bedford was present when he was executed the following month.[36] According to the *Book*, Kempe was arrested on the duke's instructions, and one of his own men alleged that Kempe was Oldcastle's daughter, entrusted with carrying letters around the country (53: 129, 54: 132). The reference to Oldcastle ('Combomis' in the text; presumably a rendering of Oldcastle's title Lord Cobham) is all the more noteworthy because Kempe does not mention any other heretic in her *Book*.[37] There is,

---

[33] For the view that Kempe's influence over the countess of Westmorland and Lady Greystoke may have been understood by her enemies as politically subversive, in that it was designed to threaten important Lancastrian alliances, see Warren, *Spiritual Economies*, pp. 166–8.

[34] For a fuller account see Watt, *Secretaries of God*, p. 28.

[35] In her stimulating analysis of the events of 1417, Warren draws extended comparisons between Kempe and Joan of Arc, arguing that both holy women were viewed as dangerous (if not equally so) by the Lancastrian regime: *Spiritual Economies*, pp. 163–82, esp. pp. 165–72.

[36] Staley, *Dissenting Fictions*, p. 163; Goodman, *World*, pp. 143–5.

[37] For the suggestion that 'Combomis' (or, alternatively, depending on how one reads the minims, 'Combonus') is a corruption of 'Cobhamis' see *BMK*, p. 316 n. 132, 12–14. 'Combomis' may also be a pun playing on the Latin verb *comburo* meaning 'to burn up, consume', alluding to the fate of many relapsed heretics. Exactly who is responsible for the wordplay (Kempe, her scribe, the duke's servant) is open to question.

for example, no mention of the Lynn priest William Sawtre, a former chaplain of St Margaret's church in Lynn who gained notoriety in 1401 as the first Lollard to be executed under the provisions of the statute *De heretico comburendo*. Goodman sees the accounts of the 1417 examinations as important. He states 'this is the one part of the *Book* that contains important evidence bearing on national affairs – on the challenges to Bedford's rule posed by the plots of opponents of the Lancastrian regime, and the reactions of secular and ecclesiastical government to them'.[38] It is then highly significant that in fashioning her self-representation (with the help of her priest-scribe) in these accounts Kempe rejects one prophetic model – that of the modern saint Bridget – for another – that of the legendary saint Katherine of Alexandria. In so doing, she abandons the role of the prophet as seer, in favour of that of the prophet as teacher.

The influence of St Katherine of Alexandria on Margery Kempe has been fully documented by Katherine Lewis.[39] The mayor of Leicester, keen to discredit her, is reported as having reproached Kempe in the following terms: ' "Seynt Kateryn telde what kynred sche cam of [of what kindred she came] & ȝet are ȝe not lyche [you are not alike]" ' (46: 111). However, when it comes to Kempe's examinations, it is St Katherine alone to whom Kempe looks for inspiration for how to conduct herself. The reason is clear: St Katherine famously debated with the emperor Maxentius and his pagan philosophers about the Christian religion; Kempe debates with the churchmen and lay officers about the legitimacy of her own form of piety. Throughout her interrogations, Kempe is depicted as self-assured and in control, while her opponents, whom she outwits St Katherine-like with her pragmatic arguments and greater understanding of scripture, are made to appear disorganized and uncertain. As Lewis explains, 'The *Book* presents Margery's experiences as analogous to a martyr's passion. Margery uses the public performance of the role of the examined and persecuted virgin-martyr to stage confrontations with male representatives of both secular and religious authority.'[40] I would argue, however, that the situation is more complex than Lewis acknowledges.

In comparing herself to St Katherine, Kempe is refuting further the claims that she is, in the words of the mayor of Leicester, ' "a fals loller [Lollard]" ' (46: 112). One principal function of the series of examination accounts, which are given prominence in the middle of Kempe's *Book*, must be to establish Kempe's orthodoxy on the points of faith and other matters.[41] But at the time when Kempe was writing, alongside the legends of saints such as Katherine, another, in some ways very similar, form of biographical or autobiographical religious writing that also centred on the examination or trial was in existence. These were texts written by or about Lollard martyrs such as William Thorpe, who was interrogated by

38 Goodman, *Margery Kempe*, p. 205. Issues of Lollardy and dissent in the *Book* are also considered by John Arnold above.
39 Katherine J. Lewis, *The Cult of St Katherine of Alexandria in Late Medieval England* (Woodbridge, 2000), pp. 242–56. Cf. also Goodman, *World*, pp. 122–3.
40 Lewis, *Cult of St Katherine*, p. 249.
41 See further, Watt, *Secretaries of God*, pp. 40–1.

Archbishop Arundel in 1407.[42] In these texts the ingenious prisoner, whose faith is rooted in his reading of the Bible, inevitably gains the upper hand, in intellectual and spiritual terms, over his narrow-minded and slow-witted clerical and secular persecutors. The same verses from the Gospel of Matthew (10.19–20) both encouraged and consoled St Katherine and Margery Kempe and provided these righteous men with their inspiration and confidence. By adopting a familiar legendary saint such as Katherine as a role model in her examinations, Kempe tries to further distance herself from the English heretics. Indeed, the examination sequences in *The Book of Margery Kempe* may even be intended as a response to and a refutation of such heretical texts as Thorpe's *Testament*. This argument is backed up by Goodman's belief that Kempe's clerical scribe and other religious supporters must have urged the composition of the *Book* because they felt that Kempe's spirituality would counter Lollard claims 'to have authoritatively rediscovered the true route to [God's] grace'.[43] That others were not so convinced of its efficacy in this context may be deduced from the *Book's* limited circulation.

Conclusion

Ultimately we cannot be sure why Kempe did not emulate more fully the prophetic aspect of St Bridget's vocation, especially in relation to national and international politics. Was it because she lacked supporters, or because her supporters did not encourage her to, or because her supporters themselves were neither politically influential or politically minded? It is feasible that the answer lies in a combination of all three factors. Kempe's engagement with political concerns certainly may have been limited by her class and by the circles in which she travelled. Ultimately, most of Kempe's followers were of more or less the same rank as herself. Although she encountered archbishops and bishops, abbots and abbesses, legates and aristocrats, and sometimes gained their support and respect, she does not seem to have influenced, or tried to influence, popes and kings, cardinals and princes. But it is important to avoid seeing female visionaries and prophets merely as pawns of more powerful Svengali-like churchmen, and to acknowledge their own agency and authority. Kempe's public role was probably constrained by a widespread fear of heresy, a fear that affected Kempe as well as

---

[42] Oxford, Bodleian Library, MS Rawlinson C.208; edited in *Two Wycliffite Texts: the Sermon of William Taylor 1406; the Testament of William Thorpe 1407*, ed. Anne Hudson, EETS original series 301 (Oxford, 1993). A section of the examination is reprinted in *Selections from English Wycliffite Writings*, ed. Anne Hudson (Cambridge, 1978), pp. 29–33. For an analysis of Thorpe's self-representation in the trail see Anne Hudson, 'William Thorpe and the Question of Authority' in G. R. Evans, ed., *Christian Authority: Essays in Honour of Henry Chadwick* (Oxford, 1988), pp. 127–37. For a comparative reading of Kempe's and Thorpe's examination accounts see Staley, *Dissenting Fictions*, pp. 138–9, 141 and 147–51. For another, later autobiographical Lollard examination account see F. D. Matthew, 'The Trial of Richard Wyche', *English Historical Review* 5 (1890): 530–44; and M. G. Snape, 'Some Evidence of Lollard Activity in the Diocese of Durham in the Early Fifteenth Century', *Archaeologia Aeliana* 4th series 39 (1961): 355–61. Wyche was executed in 1440.

[43] Goodman, *World*, p. 6.

her supporters and opponents, clerical and secular. From the analysis offered in this essay, it should be evident that Margery Kempe *was* informed about conflicts, controversies and debates, both at home and abroad, especially those which touched upon her spiritual life. In the Middle Ages, religious matters *were* political and vice versa, and in no time or place was this more true than in early fifteenth-century England. Kempe's prophetic interventions, however veiled and cautiously described in the *Book*, reveal her real interest and involvement in political events and current affairs. Ultimately, the historical events underpinning Kempe's *Book*, and occasionally alluded to within it, are not irrelevant or incidental to the meaning of the text; they are central to the fashioning of Kempe's prophetic identity.

9

Margery's Bodies: Piety, Work and Penance[*]

SARAH SALIH

> This Soul neither longs for nor despises poverty or tribu-
> lation, Mass or sermon, fasting or prayer; and gives to
> Nature all that it requires. (Marguerite Porete, *Mirror*)[1]
>
> And, dowtyr, þu hast an hayr vp-on þi bakke. I wyl þu do
> it a-way, & I schal ȝiue þe an hayr in þin hert þat schal lyke
> me much bettyr þan al þe hayres in þe world (5: 17).

The Book of Margery Kempe is not often read alongside the beguine Marguerite
Porete's *Mirror of Simple Souls*, which survived its author's execution for heresy
in 1310 to become an anonymous classic of negative mysticism. Nevertheless,
both texts belonged to the English Carthusians' collection of mystical writings,
and though there are very many differences between their understandings of
mysticism and piety, there is also at least this one similarity, in the idea shared
by the passages quoted above, that renunciation (of food, comfort, leisure) must
itself be renounced in the search for knowledge of God. Both texts are thus knowingly disruptive of the expectation that women should perform such pieties of
the body. Activities such as fasting and prayer are really only 'good for ȝong be-
gynnars' (36: 89), Christ tells Margery; are to be relinquished at the third of seven
stages of enlightenment, argues Porete.[2] Porete's inquisitors read this abandonment of the virtues as evidence of antinomianism, one of the charges on which
she was condemned.[3] Even after her authorship was forgotten, such passages
provoked flurries of anxiety in her English translator, who protests (too much)
'this which Love says, that these souls do not desire Masses or sermons, fastings
or prayers – this should be understood not as recommending them to neglect
such things'.[4] Margery too describes encountering resistance to her reinterpretation

---

[*] This chapter revisits some material which I have previously treated in *Versions of Virginity in Late Medieval England* (Cambridge, 2001). Thanks to John Arnold and Katherine Lewis for their constructive and attentive readings of drafts of this chapter.

[1] Margaret Porete, *The Mirror of Simple Souls*, trans. Edmund Colledge, J. C. Marler and Judith Grant (Notre Dame, 1999), p. 20. Although this edition refers to her as 'Porette', the modern spelling is employed in this article.

[2] Porete, *Mirror*, p. 142.

[3] Robert E. Lerner, *The Heresy of the Free Spirit in the Later Middle Ages* (Notre Dame, 1972), pp. 75–6.

[4] Porete, *Mirror*, p. 186; see Nicholas Watson, 'Melting into God in the English Way: Deification in the Middle English Version of Marguerite Porete's *Mirouer des simples âmes anienties*', in Rosalynn Voaden, ed., *Prophets Abroad: The Reception of Continental Holy Women in Late-Medieval England* (Cambridge, 1996), pp. 19–50 for further discussion of this translation.

of pieties of the body. To read her alongside Porete is to bring into focus some overlapping perspectives on women's performances of bodily pieties and their refusals of them.

Before considering *The Book of Margery Kempe* in more detail, it is necessary to clarify what is meant by 'physical piety' and to survey recent debates about what is at stake in our histories of it. Since the publication of Caroline Walker Bynum's hugely influential *Holy Feast and Holy Fast*, much scholarship on medieval women's piety has given privileged attention to bodily devotion as a route by which women could attain access to the divine. In such analyses physical piety consists of a cluster of practices, including often extreme asceticism, somatic paramystical phenomena, affective devotion to the human, suffering Christ and eucharistic piety, all often informed by a profound sense of penitence. Such a form of piety does not require much in the way of theological education, and would thus be open to lay and religious women, although some men, especially members of the mendicant orders, also adopted these behaviours.[5] Bynum argues that such bodily pieties, though not exclusively female, were especially and significantly favoured by women. Her analysis rehabilitates such practices, previously regarded as symptoms of the sickness and strangeness of medieval women, medieval Catholicism or indeed of the Middle Ages in its entirety. Women were themselves already identified with the physical and so were well placed to explore a central preoccupation of medieval Christianity:

> late medieval asceticism was an effort to plumb and realize all the possibilities of the flesh. It was a profound expression of the doctrine of the Incarnation: the doctrine that Christ, by becoming human, saves *all* that the human being is.[6]

In a critique of some of the implications of such arguments, Sarah Beckwith maintains the identification of women's piety as bodily, but interrogates the constructions of women and of the flesh. Her re-examination of *The Book of Margery Kempe* warns against uncritical celebration of women's bodily visions and practices:

> It is clear that women's access to the visionary, far from deriving from their place outside representation, in patriarchy derives instead from the very specific representative function given to them in medieval culture, the specific representation of themselves as associated with the debased matter of the flesh, which they see valorised and redeemed in Christ's torture on the cross, a redemption through physicality.[7]

We should thus note that women's performance of bodily pieties frequently suited orthodox clerical categories and agendas. Their unschooled access to the

---

5 André Vauchez, *Sainthood in the Later Middle Ages*, trans. Jean Birrell (Cambridge, 1997), pp. 338–40.
6 Caroline Walker Bynum, *Holy Feast and Holy Fast: The Religious Significance of Food to Medieval Women* (Berkeley, 1987), p. 294.
7 Sarah Beckwith, 'A Very Material Mysticism: The Medieval Mysticism of Margery Kempe', in David Aers, ed., *Medieval Literature: Criticism, Ideology and History* (Brighton, 1986), pp. 34–57 (p. 47).

divine might be a valuable spectacle for men.[8] Women's affective piety might also be used to counter Cathar dualism or, later, Lollard scepticism.[9] One of the most influential texts of affective devotion in England was the translation of the pseudo-Bonaventuran *Mediationes Vitae Christi* by Nicholas Love, the prior of the Mount Grace charterhouse which would later house the only surviving copy of *The Book of Margery Kempe. The Mirror of the Blessed Life of Jesus Christ* was planned by Love and received by Archbishop Arundel 'for the edification of the faithful and the confutation of heretics or Lollards': prior and archbishop must thus have agreed that this form of lay piety would indeed refute heretics.[10] As Anthony Goodman suggests, Arundel's endorsement of this style of piety may account for his respectful reception of Margery, with whom he discussed contemplation and household discipline 'tyl sterrys apperyd in þe fyrmament' (16: 37).[11]

The characterisation of women's piety as physical was ideologically informed, working to reinforce the identification of women with the flesh. It is so convenient a fit that a degree of misrecognition occurred. The gendering of bodily pieties was not, in fact, absolute. Although Love noted that his original was written for a woman reader, he addressed his translation to a wider audience: 'lewde men and women and hem þat bene of symple vndirstondyng'.[12] Holy men as well as holy women might engage in bodily asceticism: one who did so in fifteenth-century England was King Henry VI, who wore 'on his bare body a rough hair shirt' in resistance to the 'pride and vain glory' of courtly splendour.[13] Moreover, holy women were not uniformly enthusiastic: the impression that they were begins to fragment once textual genre is taken into account. As Bynum herself notes, in some cases male hagiographers emphasised somatic manifestations and extreme asceticism at the expense of less dramatic forms of female piety.[14] Amy Hollywood confirms that in some instances clerics had more invested in the physicality of women's piety than did the women themselves: she distinguishes texts by gender and genre to argue that '[w]hile ascetic and paramystical experiences may be central to medieval culture's perceptions and descriptions of female sanctity . . . their primacy in late medieval women's *lived experience* has not been proven'.[15] Traditional hagiographies of legendary female saints exuberantly exteriorise their holiness: saints blind their tormentors with their own amputated tongues, throw devils into dungheaps, live forty years in

---

8   John Coakley, 'Friars as Confidants of Holy Women in Medieval Dominican Hagiography', in Renate Blumenfeld-Kosinski and Timea Szell, eds, *Images of Sainthood in Medieval Europe* (Ithaca, NY, 1991), pp. 222–46.

9   Beckwith, 'A Very Material Mysticism', p. 45.

10 Nicholas Love, *Mirror of the Blessed Life of Jesus Christ*, ed. Michael G. Sargent (New York, 1992), p. xlvi.

11 Goodman, *World*, p. 129.

12 Love, *Mirror*, p. 10.

13 John Blacman, *Henry the Sixth*, ed. and trans. M. R. James (Cambridge, 1919), p. 36. Bodily piety is defined as an 'androgynous' type of sanctity in Donald Weinstein and Rudolph M. Bell, *Saints and Society: The Two Worlds of Western Christendom 1000–1700* (Chicago, 1982), p. 237.

14 Caroline Walker Bynum, *Fragmentation and Redemption: Essays on Gender and the Human Body in Medieval Religion* (New York, 1992), p. 75.

15 Amy Hollywood, *The Soul as Virgin Wife: Mechthild of Magdeburg, Marguerite Porete and Meister Eckhart* (Notre Dame, 1995), p. 28.

the desert on three loaves of bread and repeatedly suffer graphically recounted tortures and executions.[16] Hagiographers of contemporary women continue this external perspective, and thus emphasise the outward, especially bodily, manifestations of sanctity. Our received picture of medieval female holiness may owe as much to generic convention and clerical investment in a particular, circumscribed ideal of female holiness as to the women's own interests. To continue to gender bodily pieties as female may therefore be to over-clarify a range of discourses and practices and to reproduce the categories of medieval hagiographers. Hollywood furthermore suggests that when, in the fourteenth century, tropes of extreme asceticism appear in women's mystical writings, they are imports from hagiography at a moment when anxieties about heresy made bodily piety seem a safe option.[17] Thus women may have learnt ascetic behaviour from hagiography, and by practising it reinforced the perceived feminine gendering of bodily piety.

Although there was, then, a demonstrable clerical investment in producing the category of 'feminine bodily piety', clerical endorsement of bodily pieties was not uniform, and, it has been argued, may have been particularly susceptible to variations of location and local tradition. Hope Emily Allen's notes to the EETS edition of the *Book* consistently place Margery in an 'English tradition' of moderation in bodily practices, contrasted with the extremes of the continent. This distinction of English moderation from continental extremism continues to inform current criticism: Denise Despres, for example, comments that 'Margery Kempe's own difficulty with fasting, hairshirts and other kinds of physical penance, when she was so influenced by Continental models in general, suggests how impervious English devotionalism was to dramatic elements of Continental women's piety.'[18] Nicholas Watson notes that the English tradition was also wary of women's visions until the early fifteenth century, when the visionary writings of continental holy women began to circulate in England.[19] In early fifteenth-century Lynn, Margery was well placed to produce a pioneering synthesis of English and continental styles of devotion in her practices and her retrospective textualisation of them. Lynn had cultural and commercial links with northern Europe, the seedbed of the new feminine pieties: her own son 'passyd ouyr þe see in wey of marchawndyse' (II, 1: 222).[20] Margery's reading list of 'Hyltons boke . . . Bridis boke . . . Stimulus Amoris . . . Incendium Amoris' neatly demonstrates the inclusivity of her influences (17: 39). Allen is right that Margery's English devotional guides were on the whole not enthusiasts for extreme asceticism and that her continental role models often were. Hagiographies tell us that Marie d'Oignies cut lumps out of her flesh; Bridget

---

16 Jacobus de Voragine, *The Golden Legend: Readings on the Saints*, trans. William Granger Ryan, 2 vols (Princeton, 1993), I, pp. 387, 161, 228 and *passim*.

17 Hollywood, *Soul as Virgin Wife*, pp. 36–8.

18 Denise L. Despres, 'Ecstatic Reading and Missionary Mysticism: *The Orcherd of Syon*', in Voaden, ed., *Prophets Abroad*, pp. 141–60 (p. 159).

19 Nicholas Watson, 'The Composition of Julian of Norwich's *Revelation of Love*', *Speculum* 68 (1993): 637–83 (pp. 646, 653).

20 Gail McMurray Gibson, *Theater of Devotion: East Anglian Drama and Society in the Late Middle Ages* (Chicago, 1989), p. 22

of Sweden tied knotted cords around her body and tore up scabs which threatened to heal; Elizabeth of Hungary submitted to regular beatings from her confessor.[21] Margery herself may have made a distinction between English and continental pieties, for her more dramatic physical practices are associated with her foreign travels.

Nevertheless, extremism was not exclusively European, and moderation not exclusively English (however neatly this categorisation fits subsequent ideas of national character). On closer examination, moderation is more likely to have been a generic trait than a national one: both in England and on the continent direct instruction to perform extreme asceticism is rare, and exhortation to admire those who did more common. It is true that English pastoral and instructional texts of the thirteenth and fourteenth centuries show a consistent suspicion of extremes of physical self-deprivation. Richard Rolle advises that extreme fasting is as bad as gluttony, and that spiritual beginners should eat normally, graduating to asceticism only when they are more secure in their devotion.[22] Although modern interpreters such as Bynum argue that ascetic practices are not dualist, Rolle clearly fears that they might become so, and thus in this context explicitly defends the goodness of creation, food included. Walter Hilton also recommends a moderate diet, and comments on the limited efficacy of asceticism: 'For you can be certain that although you may watch and fast, use the scourge and do all that you can, you will never acquire purity and chastity except by the help of God and his grace of humility.'[23] *Ancrene Wisse* recommends plain but sufficient food and clothing, and bans a remarkably precise selection of extreme practices:

> Let no one put on any kind of belt unless by her confessor's leave, nor wear any iron, or hair, or hedgehog skins, not beat herself with these or with a leaded scourge, nor draw blood from herself with holly or brambles, without her confessor's leave; let her not sting herself with nettles anywhere, not beat herself on her front, nor do any cutting, nor take at one time over-harsh disciplines to extinguish temptations.[24]

The 'English tradition', then, does not advocate a Porete-style abandonment of bodily disciplines, but subordinates them to the principles of moderation and obedience. It continues to be aware of the body and to use it carefully, neither denying nor obliterating it. Physical pieties are not altogether forbidden. *Ancrene Wisse* instructs its readers to perform ritual movements during prayer, and also praises a man and a woman who practised extreme asceticism.[25] Furthermore, the very fact that all these texts deemed it necessary to instruct people not to

---

21 C. Horstmann, ed., 'Prosalegenden: Die legenden des ms. Douce 114', *Anglia* 8 (1885): 103–96
(p. 140); Roger Ellis, ed., *The Liber Celestis of St Bridget of Sweden*, EETS original series 291
(Oxford, 1987), p. 3; Osbern Bokenham, *Legendys of Hooly Wummen*, ed. Mary S. Serjeantson,
EETS original series 206 (Oxford, 1938), ll. 10329–36.
22 Richard Rolle, 'The Form of Living', *English Writings of Richard Rolle, Hermit of Hampole*, ed.
Hope Emily Allen (orig. pub. 1931; this edition Gloucester, 1988), p. 101.
23 Walter Hilton, *The Ladder of Perfection*, trans. Leo Sherley-Price (Harmondsworth, 1988), p. 92.
24 *Ancrene Wisse: Guide for Anchoresses*, trans. Hugh White (Harmondsworth, 1993), p. 193.
25 *Ancrene Wisse*, pp. 9–26, 175.

perform extreme austerities indicates that some desired to do so. *Ancrene Wisse* even becomes more moderate in its later versions: Bella Millett suggests that the author may have wished to curb his charges' enthusiasm for extremism.[26] Such enthusiasm may have been derived from reading hagiography: male and female hagiography in England had an established tradition of admiring ascetic extremism, dating at least from Thomas Becket's verminous hair shirt.[27]

Nor was continental enthusiasm for bodily extremes uniform. Porete's example shows that continental holy women did not necessarily celebrate physical pieties. The Parisian Jean Gerson, though he condemned Porete's departure from restraint, did not recommend bodily extremism to pious women. In tones very like those of the English guides, he advocated moderation and submission to authority, arguing that those who engaged in fasting, vigils and weeping without the correct attitudes of discipline and humility not only risked their physical and mental health, but also became susceptible to demonic illusions.[28] Nancy Caciola shows that the thirteenth- and fourteenth-century holy women who engaged in bodily pieties were very divisive figures in their day.[29] She also suggests that by the fifteenth century the style was on its way out, as anxiety about the similarity of divine to demonic possession produced a new validation of exterior serenity and 'a devaluation of the kinds of ecstatic trances, somatic miracles, and severe asceticism that were most often ascribed to women mystics'.[30] Bynum demonstrates that moderation was in the mainstream of pastoral teaching throughout later medieval Europe.[31] Nevertheless, bad faith was possible. Confessors might recommend moderation, while hagiographers – often the same people – nevertheless took textual pleasure in the details of women's immoderation. 'I sey not þis, preisynge þe exces, but tellynge þe feruore' writes Jacques de Vitry of Marie d'Oignies's self-mutilation, simultaneously telling and disowning it.[32] On the continent as in England, moderation and excess were constituted with reference to one another. First- and second-person texts of experience and guidance focused on the interior techniques of holiness, while third-person hagiographic texts looked at its exterior signs. If excessive performances sometimes attracted more enthusiastic audiences on the continent, this is a difference of degree rather than kind. Extreme asceticism, then, cannot be exclusively identified either with women or with the continent, and though it is more securely located in hagiography, by the early fifteenth century intertexts complicate the picture.

---

26 Bella Millett, '*Mouvance* and the Medieval Author: Re-Editing *Ancrene Wisse*', in A. J. Minnis, ed., *Late-Medieval Religious Texts and their Transmission: Essays in Honour of A. I. Doyle* (Cambridge, 1994), pp. 9–20 (p. 17).

27 Jocelyn Wogan-Browne, *Saints' Lives and Women's Literary Culture c. 1150–1300: Virginity and its Authorizations* (Oxford, 2001), pp. 178–9.

28 Jean Gerson, 'On Distinguishing True from False Revelations', *Early Works*, trans. Brian Patrick McGuire (New York, 1998), p. 343.

29 Nancy Caciola, 'Mystics, Demoniacs, and the Physiology of Spirit Possession in Medieval Europe', *Comparative Studies in Society and History* (2000): 268–306 (p. 269). On this point see also Katherine Lewis below.

30 Caciola, 'Mystics, Demoniacs, and the Physiology of Spirit Possession', p. 296.

31 Bynum, *Holy Feast*, pp. 238–43.

32 (in the Middle English translation) 'Prosalegenden', p. 136.

Margery Kempe, drawing on English and continental men's and women's texts and lives, was thus joining in an already very noisy conversation. The Proem to the *Book* blandly presents Margery as one who 'ded gret bodyly penawns' (Proem: 2), thus testifying to the intelligibility of this category and giving the initial impression that she was an uncomplicated member of it. Many critics of the *Book* remark on a tendency which is variously named 'concreteness', 'carnality', 'literalism', 'materialism' or 'corporeality'. The perception that it blurs the distinction between body and text recurs in various forms: Karma Lochrie, for example, observes that Margery 'translates body into discourse'.[33] Margery is said to have a bodily text and a textualised body; to sensualise the spiritual and find religious meaning in material things.[34] As an autohagiography, or collaborative hagiography, her *Book* combines the first-person perspective of women's mystical writings and the third-person perspective of male-authored hagiography. This-worldly and other-worldly experiences overlap, and the category of 'physical piety' is not self-evident. Prayer may be conceptualised as a bodily exercise, the 'byddyng of many bedys [prayers]' (5: 17), or weeping listed amongst the contemplative experiences of 'thynykng, wepyng, & hy contemplacyon' (36: 89). Despite such moments of uncertainty, however, the *Book*'s general principle is clear: it explicitly states that physical asceticism is an early stage on the road to holiness, which the individual is expected to surpass and leave behind. Christ's ranking of such practices is unambiguous:

> þis lyfe plesyth me mor þan weryng of þe haburion [a penitential garment] or of þe hayr [hair shirt] or fastyng of bred & water, for, ȝyf þu seydest euery day a thowsand Pater Noster, þu xuldist not plesyn me so wel as þu dost whan þu art in silens & sufferyst me to speke in thy sowle (35: 89).

The hierarchy is of forms of devotion which become less physical and more personalised as the individual progresses in her practice of holiness. Free contemplation replaces scripted prayers which replaced asceticism. Like Porete, but unlike the majority of medieval holy women, Margery aspires to a purely interior piety. She only passes through the mixed lives of worldly and pious activity, and of active and contemplative piety, on her way to the goal of pure contemplation.

Despite the clarity of this ascent, Margery nevertheless engages in all of these practices at various times and in various combinations. Contemplation may be her ideal, but her life and piety remain firmly located in the material world. Material things such as food and clothing are the means by which she proclaims her calling; material and spiritual goods are fully tradable. She continues to be a member of the communal body of her parish, and may in old age have joined Lynn's Trinity Guild.[35] She engages in outward and communal forms of devotion as well as privatised interior contemplations. Her piety is often performed in legible spaces, in her pilgrimages and processions, in the meanings and

---

[33] Lochrie, *Translations*, p. 88.
[34] Gayle Margherita, *The Romance of Origins: Language and Sexual Difference in Middle English Literature* (Philadelphia, 1994), pp. 30–1.
[35] *BMK*, Appendix III.

memories associated with each part of her parish church. In all these activities, Margery takes part in a widespread contemporary assumption that physical practices were efficacious routes to God and that ritual activity and sacred space were mutually constitutive.

Although Margery sees contemplation and bodily piety as opposite ends of a scale, her visionary experiences are often insistently vivid in physical detail. She first sees Christ 'clad in a mantyl of purpyl sylke, syttyng op-on hir beddys syde' (1: 8); later grips his feet, feeling his toes 'as it had ben very flesch and bon' (85: 208); and when she looks into her soul, she sees the Trinity seated on cushions of red velvet, white silk and cloth of gold (86: 210–11). Margery was not alone in accessing holiness through objects: some of the concrete items which feature in her visions – the Virgin's 'kerche' (31: 79), the Child's swaddling clothes – existed in the fifteenth-century present as foci of devotion.[36] Margery's pious emotions are roused by a range of physical stimuli; devotional art, for example, is an especially effective trigger of visionary experience.[37] Though she identifies contemplation as the most abstract form of life, her visions are firmly within the affective tradition taught by texts such as Love's *Mirror*. When she is unsure of how to begin a contemplation, Christ recommends the devotional exercise of thinking of the earthly life of the Virgin (6: 18). As she has been taught, Margery dwells on the body of Christ as a source of sensual pleasure and as a spectacle of suffering: her Passion visions have been described as a collage of quotations from sources such as Love's *Mirror*, the revelations of Bridget of Sweden and the English cycle plays.[38] Once Christ's body has been thoroughly visualised, it exceeds the sphere of contemplation: in Rome Margery sees infinite avatars of the Incarnation in the shape of baby boys and handsome men (35: 86).

Bodies, particularly Christ's and Margery's, are important reference points throughout the *Book*, but their uses are multiple and contextualised within the overall narrative of movement towards less embodied forms of piety. The body is not always the final answer: it may on occasion be a sign of something else. Naming ascetic practice as 'penawns', for example, means that the emphasis always falls on what the body is *for* rather than on what it *is*: it has meaning in the continuity of Margery's past sins, present repentance and future judgement. Margery is an uncomplicated performer of bodily asceticism only during the early years of her conversion, while she still shares a bed with her husband. During this period, she fasts, keeps vigil and wears a hair shirt every day (3: 12). Demanding though this regime may sound, it is at the less dramatic end of the scale. Continental hagiography offers a far more varied programme of 'wearing hair shirts, binding the flesh tightly with twisted ropes, rubbing lice into self-inflicted wounds, denying oneself sleep, adulterating food and water with ashes or salt, performing thousands of genuflections, thrusting nettles into one's

---

36 Gibson, *Theater of Devotion*, p. 52.
37 See Kathleen Kamerick, *Popular Piety and Art in the Late Middle Ages: Image Worship and Idolatry in England, 1350–1500* (New York, 2002), pp. 138–45 for further discussion of Margery's reception of visual art.
38 David Lawton, 'Voice, Authority and Blasphemy in *The Book of Margery Kempe*', in Sandra J. McEntire, ed., *Margery Kempe: A Book of Essays* (New York, 1992), pp. 93–116 (p. 99).

breasts, and praying barefoot in winter'.[39] Even when citing and critiquing her early enthusiasm for physical penance, then, Margery specifies the moderate version of the tradition. These practices are then revealed to be insufficiently demanding and ineffective:

> Sche mygth wel dure [could well endure] to fastyn, it greuyd [troubled] hir not. Sche hatyd þe joys of þe world. Sche felt no rebellyon in hyr flesch. Sche was strong, as hir thowt, þat sche dred no devylle in Helle, for sche dede so gret bodyly penawnce (3: 13).

The narrative voice unusually here ironises Margery's behaviours and self-delusion, insisting that these practices were always inadequate. Worse, her successful performance of physical asceticism is explicitly identified as the cause of her vainglory. This vainglory exposes her to psychologically agonising sexual temptations, which her ascetic regime is powerless to dispel. This vivid little narrative might have been deliberately written to prove Hilton's point that bodily practices alone cannot produce purity. The *Book* has already established that the practice of bodily penance may itself be demonically inspired (1: 7); here Margery also learns that it cannot protect her against the Devil. Her response to this failure of asceticism is not to intensify it with more dramatic and bizarre practices, but to begin the process of abandoning it in favour of less physical forms of piety.

Such abandonment is not a simple refusal of the pieties of the body, but a reinterpretation of them. Margery continues to refer to the idea of asceticism whilst not performing it. Perhaps the simplest form of this reinterpretation is found in the idea that the contemplation of physical pain may be substituted for its actuality. Margery, fearing her ability to withstand pain, imagines herself undergoing decapitation as 'þe most soft deth'. Christ approves:

> "I thank þe, dowtyr, þat þow woldyst <suffer deth> for my lofe, for, as oftyn as þow thynkyst so, þow schalt haue þe same mede [reward] in Heuyn as þow þu suffredyst þe same deth. & ʒet schal no man sle the [slay thee], ne fyer bren [burn] þe, ne water drynch þe, ne wynd deryn [harm] þe" (14: 30).

That is, thinking about physical suffering is not only an acceptable substitute for experiencing it, but even inoculates against it. Margery also makes conceptual uses of asceticism by positing bodily suffering as a gold standard, against which the value of other forms of spiritual credit may be estimated. Writing of her fear of demonic deceit, for example, she claims that 'Sche had leuar a [would rather have] sufferyd any bodyly penawns þan þes felyngys' (23: 54); the idea of bodily penance is invoked to convey the intensity of her spiritual suffering.

Margery eschews, then, the pursuit of physical piety, and even evades, as far as possible, involuntary suffering. The patient endurance of evils of all kinds, including physical pain, was a well-established form of piety which enabled the sufferer to display submission to God's will and identify with the suffering

---

[39] Bynum, *Holy Feast*, p. 210.

Christ.[40] Margery is aware of this tradition: she advises leper women that 'þei xulde not grutchyn [complain] wyth her sekenes [sickness] but hyly thankyn God þerfor' (74: 177). For her own illness, however, she is less grateful: she perceives it as punishment and bargains to be rid of it (56: 137–8). When a piece of masonry falls on her back as she is at prayer, the event is shown to be miraculous because her pain is relieved as soon as she calls on Christ (9: 22). She does patient suffering only when no trade-off presents itself. To submit to unwanted marital sex may be 'mede & meryte', but release from it is still an overall spiritual improvement, bringing 'gret gladnes of spyryt' (11: 25). Most characteristically, she notes that enduring reproof is to be preferred to enduring physical pain and thus offers to exchange her illness for social ostracism, explaining to Christ that ' "schrewyd [sharp] wordys to suffyr for þi lofe it hirte me ryth nowt" ' (56: 138). This comparison between pain and slander is not unique to Margery, and parallels can be found in both local and foreign sources. Alexandra Barratt suggests that Margery's source for what Gibson terms 'martyrdom by slander' may be the *Revelations* of Elizabeth of Toess.[41] The equivalence also appears in the East Anglian morality play of *Wisdom*:

> Gode sethe, 'Suffyr pacyenly for my loue
> Off þi neyboure a worde of repreve,
> Ande þat to mercy mor dothe me move
> Than þou dyscyplynyde þi body wyth peynys grewe.[42]

The late fifteenth-century dating of the play means that it cannot be claimed as a source for Margery, but both are perhaps part of the same (remarkably pessimistic) conversation about whether it is possible to live a religious life in the world. Margery builds on the logic of the exchange by finding ways to transform bodily into social suffering.

Margery's well-known engagement in the spiritual marketplace enables her to profit from her original investment in asceticism. After she has fasted for many years, Christ and the Virgin instruct her to eat normally again. Ending the fast is more valuable than prolonging it, because ending it enables Margery to concentrate on other forms of piety. She needs to eat meat in order to have the bodily strength to 'beryn hir gostly labowrys'. Changing her long-standing practice exposes her to 'many a scorne and meche reprefe', which are more valuable spiritual commodities than fasting. The fast is negotiable currency, and by trading it in Margery makes a shrewd exchange. Furthermore, she takes paradoxical credit: 'hir grace was not discresyd but raþar encresyd, for sche had leuar a fastyd þan an etyn ȝyf it had ben þe wyl of God' (66: 162): she is thus able to have her fast and eat it, so to speak, as renouncing renunciation becomes a test of her obedience.

40 Richard Kieckhefer, *Unquiet Souls: Fourteenth-Century Saints and their Religious Milieu* (Chicago, 1984), pp. 50–88.
41 Gibson, *Theater of Devotion*, p. 47; Alexandra Barratt, 'Margery Kempe and the King's Daughter of Hungary', in McEntire, ed., *Margery Kempe*, pp. 189–201 (p. 194).
42 Mark Eccles, ed., *The Macro Plays: The Castle of Perseverance, Wisdom, Mankind*, EETS original series 262 (Oxford, 1969), p. 147, ll. 1013–16: the source of this passage is *Novem Virtutes*, formerly attributed to Richard Rolle, p. 215.

In this use of paradox Margery reverses Rolle's narrative of spiritual develop-ment and exceeds the observance of moderation. This paradox is recognised, and mocked, by some of her observers, who taunt her with the phrase ' "fals flesch, þu xalt ete non heryng" ' (II, 9: 244). The *Book* emphatically disowns the tale and the imputation of hypocrisy: however, though the words may not be Margery's, the logic – that if you would prefer to fast, then eating meat and good pike is the truer asceticism – certainly is. Margery thus shifts the site of the production of holiness from the discipline of the individual body to social interaction as she gains further credit by her meek endurance of mockery. The *Book* indicates a gen-eral expectation amongst the laity (there is no indication that clerics joined in this particular persecution) that a holy woman would observe at least the basic aus-terities of prayer and fasting. It thus claims that the spectacle of a holy woman refusing the pieties of the body is disquieting for many contemporaries. Even if, as the example of *Wisdom* suggests, the idea that scorn was a more valuable suf-fering than bodily penance was well-known to pious East Anglians, it would be necessary for the *Book* to suppress awareness of this knowledge. If Margery is to be properly slandered, then the exchange must appear to be her idiosyncracy, shocking to a public which likes its holy women bodily and suffering and which will thereby unknowingly constitute Margery's sanctity precisely by refusing to recognise it.

Margery thus substitutes slander for bodily suffering. For isolated periods, another comparable substitution is what might be termed 'social asceticism', that is, the renunciation of her class privileges to perform menial work. She does this first in visions in which she serves St Anne and the Virgin. Perhaps mind-ful of the instruction of Love's *Mirror* to 'beþenk þe and haue in mynde þe grete pouert [poverty] of [the Virgin] . . . she sal neþere fynde brede nor wyne nor oþer necessaries, & þerwiþ she hade neþere possessiones nor money', Margery begs food and clothing for the Virgin and Child (6: 19).[43] It should not be assumed that in taking part in childcare and domestic service she is naturally projecting her woman's work into the sphere of the sacred, or sanctifying the duties of her worldly life. Rather, this is an exercise in humility: she does the work which a woman of her status would normally assign to servants. Her inti-mate care for the infant Christ and young Mary, for example, is in sharp con-trast to her response to her own pregnancy, which is automatically to delegate childcare, wondering ' "how xal I þan do for kepyng of my chylde?" ' (21: 48). Devotional texts which use domestic work as spiritual allegory do not neces-sarily sanctify the work itself: when Bridget of Sweden wrote that 'God is a nobill lawnder, þat puttis a clothe þat is noȝt clene in swilke place of þe water whare, thrugh mouinge of þe water, it mai be clenner and whitter', she did not suggest that laundresses should thereby think of their work as a sign of the cleansing of faithful souls.[44]

Margery, however, could be said to concretise and realise such devotional metaphors. Having rehearsed service in her visions, Margery plays it out in reality, at first in Rome as an experiment in obedience and humility, and again, it seems

---

[43] Love, *Mirror*, p. 32.
[44] *Liber Celestis*, p. 244. Thanks to Christiania Whitehead for letting me know of this passage.

out of necessity, to care for her aged husband. In Rome her confessor ordered her to serve a poor old woman:

> Also sche fet hom watyr [fetched home water] & stykkys in her nekke [on her neck/back] for þe poure woman and beggyd mete and wyn bothyn for hir. And, whan þe pour womans wyn was sowr [sour], þis creatur hir-self drank þat sowr wyn & yaf þe powr woman good wyn þat sche had bowt for hir owyn self (35: 86).

It is no longer possible to recapture the precise degree of transgressive thrill produced by the image of the daughter of the mayor of Lynn carrying firewood on her neck, though it may help to remember that one indicator of Elizabeth of Hungary's sanctity was that 'She dysshys in þe kechyn ful oftyn also / Wolde wasshyn & wypyn.'[45] In both cases it is the gratuitous nature of the activity which makes it holy: even in her poverty Elizabeth retained servants, and Margery, although she begs on behalf of her charge, can afford to buy good wine for herself. This service is not primarily a practical charity, any more than is her search for lepers to kiss, and the protesting old woman is abandoned once the spiritual exercise is complete (38: 93). Margery's care for the woman is a performance of 'obediens' and 'penawns' (34: 85), which thus replaces the superseded practice of 'gret bodily penawns'. It is significant that she experiments with this behaviour abroad, doing in Rome, indeed, as the Romans do, or at least as Bridget of Sweden had done. It has often been remarked that Margery followed in Bridget's footsteps in Rome, visiting her former maid for first-hand testimony of the saint: Rome is thus the appropriate locale for her to imitate Bridget, a noblewoman who experimented with begging: 'Oft times when sho had full gret nede, sho wold aske for oþir þat had noght so grete nede as sho had hirselfe.'[46] Margery adopted a foreign style of piety in a foreign land, where she could perform it without risk to her social position back home in Lynn.

Her care for John Kempe in his old age is also marked as penitential, and undertaken with some reluctance. Slander having forced them to live apart, it now forces her to take him back into her house in his infirmity. Though Margery is evidently not destitute, for she has a house of her own, her financial circumstances appear to be much reduced, as for the first time in the *Book*, she has to take responsibility for domestic work:

> And þerfor was hir labowr meche þe mor in waschyng & wryngyng & hir costage in fyryng [expenses in maintaining a hearth] & lettyd [hindered] hir ful meche fro hir contemplacyon þat many tymys sche xuld an yrkyrd [disliked] hir labowr saf [except] sche bethowt hir how sche in her ȝong age had ful many delectabyl thowtys, fleschly lustys, & inordinat louys to hys persone. & þerfor sche was glad to be ponischyd wyth þe same persone & toke it mech þe mor esily & seruyd hym & helpyd hym, as hir thowt, as sche wolde a don Crist hym-self (76: 181).

---

45 Bokenham, *Legendys of Hooly Wummen*, ll. 10353–4.
46 *Liber Celestis*, p. 4.

The interior perspective is necessary here to distinguish this activity from ordinary, unsanctified domestic work. Margery makes the experience meaningful by spiritualising it, but to do so has to revert to her now long-abandoned practice of physical penance for sins of the flesh. Christ, meanwhile, has to reverse the earlier exchange to allow Margery to substitute physical labour for contemplation. Given the *Book*'s overall movement to less bodily observance, this is an unmistakably retrograde interruption of her progress.

The final forms of 'physical piety' I shall consider are Margery's involuntary somatic manifestations, which, as paramystical phenomena, are also part of the standard picture of female bodily devotions. These are initially celebrated. Following Margery's mystic marriage to the Godhead, her body becomes a screen which registers the signs of God's presence:

> Sum-tyme sche felt swet smellys wyth hir nose . . . Sum-tyme sche herd wyth hir bodily erys [ears] sweche sowndys & melodijs . . . Sche sey wyth hir bodily eyne many white thyngys flying al a-boute hir on euery syde . . . sche felt þe hete brennyng in hir brest & at hir hert, as verily as a man schuld felyn þe material fyer ȝyf he put hys hand or hys fynger þerin (35: 87–8).

Like all Margery's physical pieties, such bodily signs are not self-evident, but need the textual supplement which identifies the white things as tokens of angels and the heat as that of the Holy Ghost. The language of the body always requires glossing. As an autohagiographer, Margery gives both exterior and interior perspectives on her bodily manifestations of saintliness. There may also be here an assimilation of her body to Christ's in the invitation to the sceptical to put their fingers into her heart. In such passages Margery is at her closest to the received picture of medieval women's bodily piety.

Of these somatic manifestations, the most dramatic and most discussed are the cryings, during which Margery involuntarily falls, writhes and screams in witness of her contemplation of the Passion. The locations of the cryings may bear witness to Margery's identification of them with continental piety: they are acquired abroad, beginning in response to a Passion vision on Mount Calvary, and brought home like a souvenir, or, as Terence N. Bowers suggests, like a pilgrim badge.[47] It was not unusual for pilgrims, especially women, to display extreme emotional reactions to the sight of Holy Places, but less usual then to carry that reaction back home again.[48] The cryings are certainly emphatically physical: it takes two men to hold Margery when they are fully underway (56: 138) during which she may turn as blue as lead (28: 69). They erupt from within her body: 'sche kept it in as long as sche mygth . . . & euyr it xuld labowryn in her mende mor and mor in-to þe tyme þat it broke owte' (28: 69). She responds to the symbolic, liturgical spectacle of 'prestys . . . & oþer worschepful men . . . devowtly representyng þe lamentabyl deth and doolful berying of owr Lord Ihesu Crist' by 'spredyng hir armys a-brood, seyd wyth lowd voys, "I dey, I dey"', thus supplementing the ceremony with her own mimetic and bodily representation of his death (57: 140).

---

[47] Terence N. Bowers, 'Margery Kempe as Traveler', *Studies in Philology* 97.1 (2000): 1–28 (pp. 25–6).
[48] Dee Dyas, *Pilgrimage in Medieval English Literature, 700–1500* (Cambridge, 2001), pp. 140–1.

The *Book* devotes much attention to the reactions to the cryings, exaggerating rather than trying to obscure how controversial they were: even Margery's scribe was sceptical until he was convinced by the *Life* of Marie d'Oignies that uncontrollable crying was behaviour proper to holy women (62: 153). The trouble with the cryings is the difficulty of interpreting them: while readers of the *Book* know them to be commemorations of the Passion, observers see the less coherent spectacle of a woman collapsing and screaming. Hence many conclude that Margery is either ill or possessed by a demon (17: 40): a hostile Franciscan preacher challenges her to admit that the cryings are symptoms of a bodily sickness (61: 151). The laity are especially suspicious of the cryings, prepared to tolerate them only in emergencies such as the fire in the church (67: 163). Clerics, with the exception of the Franciscan, are generally more sympathetic.[49] One 'worschepful clerk' remarks ' "I had leuyr þan xx pownde þat I myth han swech a sorwe for owr Lordys Passyon" ' (67: 164); 'a worshepful doctowr of diuinite' and 'a bacheler of lawe' argue that the cryings are involuntary and divinely granted (61: 150); other clerics tolerate interruptions to their sermons or even take the opportunity to extemporise in support of her devotion (68: 166–7), thus making space in the service for a dialogue with the crying. The *Book* clearly implies that crying is something of a specialist piety, distrusted by the laity but recognised by the more learned amongst the clergy. The annotations on the manuscript confirm at least the latter part of this perception: the Carthusian red-ink annotator remarks 'so dyd prior Nort in hys excesse' against the account of the first crying (44: 105, n. 4), and defends Margery against the Franciscan's suspicion that the cryings are voluntary (61: 149, n. 4).[50] The cryings are thus acknowledged and performed by learned clerics as well as holy women; modern analyses which see them as a subversive disruption of the patriarchal word by feminine bodily emotion oversimplify the *Book*'s mapping of their reception. As Julian of Norwich assured Margery, there were biblical and patristic authorisations of tears (18: 43). The cryings are intelligible and negotiable spiritual currency which can be subdivided and allotted to Margery's own sins, souls in purgatory, the conversion of heathens, and so on (57: 140–141). They are tied to the liturgical year, recurring on Good Fridays and Palm Sundays, and so can themselves be seen as liturgical elements (57: 140, 78: 184). Though the Franciscan who wants her removed from church sees the crying as a disruption of his sermon, Margery experiences it as a supportive complement, testifying to the efficacy of his evocation of the Passion. From her point of view, both of them are engaged in the same project of affective devotion (61: 149).

Nevertheless, even the cryings are eventually minimised in a coherent movement towards a less embodied devotion. Imposing narrative order on Margery's life, the *Book* once more restates its hierarchy:

> Sche . . . suffryd mech despite & repref for hir wepyng & hir criyng, owr Lord of hys hy mercy drow [drew] hir affeccyon in-to his Godhed, & þat was more

---

[49] Santha Bhattacharji, *God is an Earthquake: The Spirituality of Margery Kempe* (London, 1997), pp. 43–5.

[50] See Lochrie, *Translations*, pp. 212–19 on the similarities between Margery's behaviour and that of some Carthusians.

feruent in lofe and desyr & mor sotyl [subtle] in vndirstondyng þan was þe
Manhod. And neuyr-þe-lesse þe fyr of loue encresyd in hir, & hir vndirstan-
dyng was mor illumynyd . . . ȝet had sche not þat maner of werkyng [behav-
iour] in crying as sche had be-for, but it was mor sotyl & mor soft (85: 209).

Margery here shows herself to be aware of hierarchies of mysticism such as that
of *The Cloud of Unknowing*: 'it behoueþ man or a womman, þat haþ longe tyme
ben usid in þeese meditacions [on the Passion], algates leue hem, & put hem &
holde hem fer doun vnder þe cloude of forȝetyng'.[51] As far as one can tell, however, her mysticism remained focused on narratives and images: if she did
engage in negative mysticism, she did not articulate it. However, the reduction
in the cryings can stand as an external sign of her progress to more abstract
pieties. In the course of the *Book*, Margery one by one discards the bodily practices so often associated with affective mysticism.[52] Asceticism and routine
prayer were long abandoned; by this stage in the *Book* Margery is taking leave of
the somatic counterparts to her contemplation, as she transferred it all to text.

Finally, to return to the comparison with which I began, Porete goes on to take
the renunciation of asceticism as one of her basic models, and to dissolve will and
identity in a desire for divine union so absolute as to lead to accusations of
autotheism. By these terms, Margery remains stuck at an earlier stage, and never
comes close to Porete's uncompromising rejection of any activity, even loving
God, as a trace of individuality and therefore of imperfection. Margery's practices continue to be founded in the idea, vehemently rejected by Porete, that
actions, thoughts and desires can be exchanged for spiritual credit. She looks
harder into the *Mirror of the Blessed Life of Christ* than into the *Mirror of Simple
Souls*. She never abandons the world or the body as points of reference, but continues to rely on social interaction for both affirmation and rejection. To that
extent then, Margery's is a bodily and material piety. But it is not purely, or
naively so. As David Aers argues in relation to Margery's contemporary and
advisor, Julian of Norwich, it is possible to refer to bodily pieties without being
subjected to (and by) them.[53] Nicholas Watson argues that Margery and Julian
shared a devotion to Christ's humanity which was complex and self-aware: if
they engaged in typically feminine devotions, they did so knowingly.[54]
'Feminine bodily piety' was never a monolithic phenomenon. *The Book of Margery
Kempe* is not a celebration of the sanctification of permeable female flesh in its
identity with the suffering Christ, or of the pleasures of bodily mortification. It
refers to these processes, but also revises and recontextualises them. Margery is
aware of a model of piety which consists of affective devotion, chastity, charity
and extreme asceticism; she may even have believed that this combination was
characteristic of the continental holy women whom she considered her role

---

[51] *The Cloud of Unknowing and the Book of Privy Counselling*, ed. Phyllis Hodgson, EETS original
series 218 (London, 1944), pp. 27–8.
[52] Similarly P. H. Cullum notes below that Margery apparently ceases to perform acts of physical charity in the latter stages of her spiritual development.
[53] David Aers and Lynn Staley, *The Powers of the Holy: Religion, Politics and Gender in Late
Medieval English Culture* (University Park, PA, 1996), pp. 77–104.
[54] Nicholas Watson, 'Desire for the Past', *Studies in the Age of Chaucer* 21 (1999): 59–97 (p. 84).

models. However, despite her admiration for and appropriation of women such as Bridget and Elizabeth, she is capable of disaggregating the elements of this package to assess their efficacy separately. Picking from a menu of practices, she transforms them in performance. With her sins forgiven and her salvation assured, she has finally no need of 'penawns'. Her autohagiographical self-textualisation privileges the inner certainty of contemplation, to which it subordinates the body and its pieties.

10

'Yf lak of charyte be not ower hynderawnce': Margery Kempe, Lynn, and the Practice of the Spiritual and Bodily Works of Mercy

P. H. CULLUM

The purpose of this chapter is to place Margery Kempe in the context of contemporary ideas about the practice of charity as a part of religious observance; a part that was often considered to be particularly important for lay people. Charity was judged to be one of the more important ways in which lay people could express the active rather than contemplative form of piety, usually considered to be both more appropriate for and accessible to them. In this respect Margery was not entirely typical of fifteenth-century English lay people for much of her piety was contemplative in form. However at various points in her life Margery was not just a giver of charity but, particularly on her pilgrimages, a recipient of it as well. Moreover during her life attitudes to charity were contested: for some charity was central to a Christocentric piety, for others the poor were a threatening and even deceitful group best treated with suspicion. Margery herself reflects something of this ambivalence. Although she appears to have been familiar with contemporary continental practice in female contemplative spirituality, it may not have been until she went to Rome that she encountered the more radical practice of female charity espoused by several continental holy women and it is likely that Margery did not fully adopt it.[1] Margery's attitude to the practice of charity was thus rather different from her attitude to spirituality, and more distinctively local than continental in focus.

Charity was not just a form of active piety. Two kinds of charity were understood: the physical and the spiritual. These were referred to as Works of Mercy, and there were Seven Spiritual Works and Seven Corporal, or Bodily or Comfortable Works of Mercy. The Seven Corporal Acts of Mercy were to: feed the hungry, give drink to the thirsty, clothe the naked, shelter the stranger, visit the sick, relieve the prisoners and bury the dead.[2] The Seven Spiritual Works were to: instruct the ignorant, counsel the doubtful, admonish sinners, bear

---

[1] See Caroline Walker Bynum, *Holy Feast and Holy Fast: The Religious Significance of Food to Medieval Women* (Berkeley and London, 1987) for the classic discussion of women's relationships with food and their charitable practices in this respect.

[2] This scheme often appears in visual media within churches, either in glass or as wall paintings, such as the surviving examples at Pickering church in North Yorkshire – see http://www.paintedchurch.org/7wksintr.htm (site updated 21 December 2003; consulted 16 June 2004) for this and other extant wall painting examples.

wrongs patiently, forgive injuries, comfort the sorrowful, and pray for the living and the dead.

Both the Corporal and Spiritual Works of Mercy were taught to lay people in a variety of didactic works produced for the use of parochial clergy in the fourteenth and fifteenth centuries, such as the *Lay Folks' Catechism* and John Mirk's *Instructions for Parish Priests*. Margery herself advised a widow who had asked her to pray for her dead husband's soul, to 'don almes for hym iij [3] pownd er iiij [4] in m[essys] [masses] & almes ȝeuyng to powyr folke' (19: 46–7). The Corporal Works of Mercy were based on Christ's own injunctions in Matthew 25: 41 ('For I was hungry, and you gave me not to eat; I was thirsty, and you gave me not to drink. I was a stranger, and you took me not in; naked, and you covered me not; sick and in prison, and you did not visit me'); and the Book of Tobit which enjoined burial of the dead. In York the mystery plays culminated in the Mercers' Play of the Judgement, where the good and bad souls were separated on the basis of whether they had performed the Corporal Works of Mercy, and the bad souls were dispatched into a hell mouth with God's words ringing in their ears

> Ye cursed kaitiffis [wretches], fro me yoe flee,
> In helle to dwelle with-outen ende,
> Ther ye schall nevere butt [anything but] sorowe see
> And sitte be Satanas the fende [fiend].[3]

Plays such as this taught ordinary lay people the necessity of performing the Seven Works of Mercy. This text was taken to mean that the performance of these works to the poor would be equivalent to doing them for Christ, and the punishment for failure to do them was eternal damnation. Margery certainly understood the first of these as Christ said to her:

> "whan þu dost any seruyse to þe & to þin husband in mete or drynke er any oþer thyng þat is nedful to ȝow, to þi gostly fadirs, er to any oþer þat þu receyuyst in my name, þu xalt han þe same mede in Heuyn as thow þu dedist it to myn owyn persone" (84: 203).

The origins of the Spiritual Works of Mercy are less clear, but some of them, such as forgiving injuries and correcting sinners, can also be traced back to Matthew (6: 14 and 18: 15). They were certainly already traditional by the time they were enumerated and discussed by Thomas Aquinas (d. 1273) in his *Summa Theologiæ*.[4] In works for lay people it is the Corporal Works of Mercy which tend to receive more emphasis, and as practical activities were probably easier for the majority of the laity to perform.

Despite the apparent regularity of the formula there was, however, room for a certain amount of manoeuvre in different accounts of the Works. For example,

3   *English Mystery Plays*, ed. Peter Happé (Harmondsworth, 1975), p. 645, ll. 369–72. See pp. 643–5 for Christ's account of the ways in which the good souls had performed the Works and the bad souls had not.
4   Aquinas, St Thomas, *Summa Theologiæ*, ed. and trans. Thomas Gilby, 60 vols (Blackfriars, 1964), 2a2ae, 32, 8.

The Book of Vices and Virtues, a mid-fourteenth-century Midlands text, has variants for both Corporal and Spiritual Works. Under Corporal Works it leaves out drink (implicitly assimilating it under food), and adds a need to lend to the poor (although the loan must be interest-free) and to forgive their debts, while the Spiritual Works varied significantly in their emphases, but perhaps most obviously in seeing the sick as being those who should receive comfort, and in pitying the sinful and unfortunate. The patient bearing of wrongs is reworked as the bearing of tribulation, which the sick must do. The sick thus feature under both Corporal and Spiritual Works. Throughout, this version stresses the necessity of almsgiving and the needs of the poor.[5] It is therefore important to remember that there might be local deviations and emphases in understanding and practice of the various works. For example, in England generally, burial of the dead seems not to have had the same importance as the other works, and was probably understood primarily in terms of attending the funerals of family and peers, saying prayers for them, and including all the faithful dead, or a similar formulation, in masses for the deceased; whereas it was originally understood in terms of the decent physical disposal of corpses, and indeed it remained an important practice in parts of Italy where guilds were dedicated to this activity.[6]

What means were available to people in Margery's society who wished to put these theories of charity into practice and actually provide for the less fortunate? In aristocratic households the practice of charity was often formalised with the distribution of waste food at the end of each meal. Some households even had almsdishes into which a portion of food, and the first carving from the meat, was placed at the beginning of the meal.[7] Margery observed that the bishop of Lincoln, Philip Repingdon, gave 13d and thirteen loaves and other food to thirteen poor men, with his own hands before he sat down to his dinner, and that this was a daily occurrence (15: 34). In Repingdon's household, as in some other episcopal and aristocratic ones, the numbers chosen to receive charity were symbolic, here of Christ and the twelve apostles, but elsewhere perhaps five for the Wounds of Christ. This number symbolism indicates the way in which the poor were indeed identified with Christ, and feeding or relieving them as doing these works to Christ himself. While Repingdon provided on a daily basis, others sometimes maintained a small number of almsfolk within the household, and from there it was but a brief step to the establishment of a hospital. There was therefore a continuum from informal and occasional provision at the door or gate to institutional provision.

Hospitals and almshouses were a common feature of medieval urban life. 'Hospital' is a term mainly used of the twelfth- and thirteenth-century foundations, whereas 'almshouse' is only used of fourteenth-century and later institutions. Hospitals tended to have a staff and some sort of communal life, which almshouses did also have sometimes, but the latter could also simply take

---

[5] *The Book of Vices and Virtues*, ed. W. Nelson Francis, EETS original series 217 (1942), pp. 199–211.
[6] John Henderson, *Piety and Charity in Late Medieval Florence* (Oxford, 1994), p. 299.
[7] Felicity Heal, *Hospitality in Early Modern England* (Oxford, 1990), p. 34.

the form of free housing and some amount of pension.[8] These places were unlike modern hospitals in that they did not provide medical care or treatment. They were places which received the sick, poor and infirm, and in some cases also travellers and pilgrims. Hospitals can be found throughout Catholic Europe, (and indeed within both the Byzantine and medieval Islamic worlds). They were often popular with townspeople, who saw donations to them as a way to fulfil all of the Corporal Works of Mercy in one go. As many of them also had chapels, and their inhabitants often lived an at least partly religious life, frequently being expected to say fixed numbers of prayers every day, they could also be a route to the performance of some of the Spiritual Works of Mercy as well. Lynn had a number of hospitals in the town and nearby. Most of these were twelfth-century foundations, as was usual. There had been a great number of hospitals established in the twelfth century and into the early thirteenth century, fuelled by the great emphasis on the identification of Christ with the poor which produced (among others) St Francis. The hospital of St John the Baptist, founded in the early twelfth century lay in the north part of the town on Damgate. There was also a hospital nearby at Gaywood dedicated to St Mary Magdalene, for three lepers and nine healthy inmates. There were apparently dedicated leperhouses at Setchey, West Lynn, Cowgate, and perhaps also another at Gaywood.[9] These were in existence by 1232, but their precise foundation dates are unknown. In many cases the absence of information about the origin of leperhouses is an indication that they were not so much founded, as came into being, as the customary dwelling place of local lepers.

Margery's references to seeing lepers in the streets indicate that segregation was not always enforced by this date. The idea, found in older studies, that lepers were forced to leave their homes, and subjected to a rite in which they were given a funeral mass after which they were treated as legally dead and forbidden to come into contact with the healthy, has been shown to derive from a service in one, very late, French service book, and there is no evidence that it was used in England.[10] Margery's desire to kiss lepers 'for þe lofe of Ihesu' is a reflection of a rather old-fashioned piety, found more typically in the twelfth than the fifteenth century. Leprosy was in decline by the early fifteenth century, with some leperhouses unable to find a full complement of lepers, some disappearing, and others converting to support other needy groups. Nevertheless lepers were evidently still a fairly common sight, and leprosy itself feared and hated.

---

8   For further discussions of hospitals, almshouses and charity see N. Orme and M. Webster, *The English Hospital, 1070–1570* (New Haven and London, 1995); Carole Rawcliffe, *The Hospitals of Medieval Norwich*, Studies in East Anglian History 2 (Norwich, 1995); Carole Rawcliffe, *Medicine for the Soul: the Life, Death and Resurrection of an English Medieval Hospital, St Giles, Norwich c.1249–1550* (Stroud, 1999); P. H. Cullum, ' "For Poor people harberles": What Was the Function of the Maisondieu?', in D. J. Clayton, R. C. Davies and P. McNiven (eds), *Trade, Devotion and Governance* (Stroud, 1994) pp. 36–54. Miri Rubin, *Charity and Community in Medieval Cambridge* (Cambridge, 1987).

9   D. Knowles and R. N. Hadcock, *Medieval Religious Houses: England and Wales*, 2nd edn (London, 1971), pp. 324–5 (p. 367); Rotha Mary Clay, *The Mediaeval Hospitals of England* (London, 1909), p. 307. It is possible that the leper hospital at Gaywood was St Mary Magdalene's.

10 Orme and Webster, *The English Hospital, 1070–1570*, pp. 29–31.

As a young woman Margery had seen lepers as 'lothful' and 'abhomynabyl'. Leprosy was also often thought to be a punishment which God visited on sinners and Margery evidently took this view of it. On one occasion Christ commended her weeping, saying

> "It is my-self, al-mythy God, þat make þe to wepyn euery day for thyn own synnes . . . and whan þu seest any laʒerys [lepers] þu hast gret compassyon of hem, ʒeldyng me thankyngys & preysyngys þat I am mor fauorabyl to þe þan I am to hem" (65: 159–60).

The implication here appears to be that God did not look favourably on lepers, perhaps because their sins were even greater than Margery's own.

In Lynn, as was also a common pattern elsewhere, there appear to have been no further foundations until the middle of the fourteenth century. At least one almshouse was established in Margery's day, that near St James's chapel, founded by the Guild of St Giles and St Julian, supporting seven men and six women.[11] It is slightly surprising that there were not more; by comparison with equivalent Yorkshire towns such as Hull, Beverley or Scarborough this was a rather limited provision. The loss of the vast majority of Lynn wills is here particularly unfortunate, as in other towns wills often provide the major, sometimes the only, information about hospitals and especially these newer, smaller, and often ephemeral foundations. It is therefore possible that there were more but no records have survived, or that Lynn citizens were indeed reluctant to make new foundations. Guild hospitals were characteristic of the post-Black Death period. They usually provided principally for guild members who were no longer able to support themselves. Almshouses, founded by guilds, or wealthy individuals, were fairly common features of this period, although not always intended to be perpetual foundations in the way that the older hospitals were.

On major pilgrim routes hospitals which specifically received pilgrims and assisted them on their way could often be found and Margery was a guest at the St Thomas hospital in Rome, which was one of two which catered particularly for English travellers. St Thomas of Canterbury was the larger and wealthier of the hospices, having been founded by the English guild in 1362. In 1463 its rules were confirmed, stating that rich pilgrims were to be sheltered for three nights, poor ones for eight, and the sick until recovery or death. By Margery's time the hospital had its own chapel and a chaplain with the right to hear confessions, as Margery made hers.[12] The fact that Margery referred to being 'howselyd euery Sonday' at the hospital (32: 80), before she was put out, must indicate that she was there for at least eight days, and probably significantly longer, and perhaps that the 1463 rules were either stricter than had been the case in Margery's day, or that they were not heavily enforced. The time limit put on stays at St Thomas's, even if not rigorously enforced, indicates that pilgrims were expected to find

---

[11] Knowles and Hadcock, pp. 324, 367; D. M. Owen, ed., *The Making of Kings Lynn* (Oxford, 1984), p. 61; Stephen Alsford, 'History of Medieval Lynn', http://www.trytel.com/~tristan/towns/lynnmap1.html (created 15 May 1999; consulted 16 June 2004).

[12] Margaret Harvey, *England, Rome and the Papacy, 1417–1464* (Manchester, 1993), pp. 52–4.

other lodging for themselves if they planned a longer stay in the city as Margery did. On her travels Margery seems to have used a variety of lodging places. In Jerusalem she was able to stay in a pilgrims' hostel; at other places she seems to have used a mixture of inns and hostels which had to be paid for, and the homes of local people who took her in out of charity.

In Lynn guilds seem usually to have performed the Works of Mercy, both Spiritual and Corporal, through non-institutional forms.[13] Of these the most common and most important were the services to the dead, both in the funeral, with guild members attending and often contributing to the occasion either through help with the cost of burial, or more commonly by providing 'a good send off' with a procession and candles, but also through the guild's annual mass for all members living and dead. In the 1389 guild returns all of Lynn's guilds required guild members to attend the funeral of a dead brother or sister if they possibly could, and to make an offering, typically of a halfpenny.[14] The offering was sometimes divided, half for the soul of the dead, half in alms. Guilds sometimes supported poor people, mainly members of the guild, without actually establishing a hospital. The Trinity Guild to which Margery probably belonged towards the end of her life, also distributed bread and shoes to the poor.[15] Of twenty-six Lynn guilds whose 1389 returns are preserved fifteen aided members who had fallen into poverty, and five provided drink to members too sick to attend the annual drinking.

Another point of note is the fact that the practice of the Corporal Works of Mercy was regarded as especially suitable to laywomen. After all, they were the ones who had control of the household resources such as food and drink and clothing.[16] When beggars came to the door, particularly the kitchen door, it was most likely to be the housewife who dealt with them. Nevertheless a wife's independence was to a degree circumscribed, the goods that she gave away were not necessarily hers, but her husband's. Thinkers like Thomas Aquinas put limits on the extent to which the housewife could dispose of property not her own. In practice, theological theory was probably interpreted differently in different parts of Europe. In English towns like Lynn, where wives often had a degree of economic autonomy, their right to make decisions about household goods was probably more accepted than in Aquinas's or Bernardino of Siena's Italy.[17] Margery herself was often the recipient of women's charitable endeavours during her travels, from Dame Margaret Florentyne who took Margery into her own company on the way back to Rome and fed her herself (38: 93), to the Swiss and Italian women who let her sleep in their own beds on her journey from Constance to Bologna and Venice (27: 65), or the good woman in Calais

13 Goodman, *World*, pp. 93–8 for the religious guilds in Lynn.
14 *English Guilds* ed. J. and L. T. S. Toulmin Smith, EETS original series 40 (1870), pp. 45–109 for an edition of the surviving Lynn guild returns in English.
15 Owen, *Making of King's Lynn*, p. 61.
16 See P. H. Cullum, ' "And hir name was charity": Charitable Giving By and For Women in Late Medieval Yorkshire', in P. J. P. Goldberg, ed., *Woman is a Worthy Wight: Women in English Society c.1200–1500*, 2nd edn (Stroud, 1997), pp. 182–211; Bynum, *Holy Feast Holy Fast*, pp. 189–92.
17 For the economic independence of some women in Lynn see Kate Parker above, pp. 67–8.

who took her home, cleaned her up, gave her a new smock and made her feel better (II, 8: 241).

Medieval people therefore had various means at their disposal both to give and to receive charity, depending on their inclination and social background. However, underlying this is evidence that attitudes to charity and to the poor were contested and ambivalent during Margery's lifetime. This ambivalence is expressed within the *Book*. On the one hand religious ideology strongly emphasised the necessity of charity to the poor and needy, and the widespread acknowledgement of this is to be found in many contemporary wills. While those from Lynn have largely been lost, wills from both Norwich and the diocese of York with which Lynn and Margery had such close connections, show that bequests to the poor, sick and needy, both as individuals and in hospitals, were a common concern.[18] In Lollard texts and practices of the late fourteenth and early fifteenth century there is also a considerable concern for the poor, but it differs in some respects from the orthodox norm as it is often expressed as a preference for giving alms over false worship of saints or images or going on pilgrimage. In 1395 the *Twelve Conclusions of the Lollards* were pinned to the doors of Westminster Hall in London during a session of Parliament and makes much use of the language of charity and of the preference for almsdeeds. 'God openly schewith, comanding to don almesse dede [almsgiving] to men þat ben [are] nedy, for þei ben þe ymage of God in a more likenesse [a better likeness] þan þe stok [stick] or þe ston [stone].'[19] The reference to 'stok' and 'ston' here is an argument that it is better to give alms to the poor than to images of saints or the Trinity, carved from wood or stone. The Lollard Disendowment Bill of c.1410 also argued for the seizure of the temporalities or bishops and religious houses out of which the king might support more lords and knights and also a hundred almshouses.[20] Margery's own parish priest, William Sawtre, tried for heresy in 1399 and again in 1401 when he was executed, had maintained among a larger body of issues more concerned with the nature of the Eucharist and the worship due to the cross, that anybody who vowed to go on pilgrimage could instead disburse the money they had gathered as alms.[21] So conspicuous concern for the needy could have heretical overtones in some settings.

Awareness of the precariousness of life and prosperity fostered a concern for but also about the poor. Margery herself went from wealth to poverty during the course of her life, and in the absence of insurance or state welfare, accident, illness or fire could reduce the most prosperous to beggary literally overnight. Aiding the needy was both a meritorious act and an acknowledgement of mutual dependence, helping another now set up reciprocal bonds which could be called on later. However, on the other hand developments since the Black Death had

---

[18] N. P. Tanner, *The Church in Late Medieval Norwich, 1370–1532* (Toronto, 1984), pp. 227–36 (transcripts of wills); P. H. Cullum and P. J. P. Goldberg, 'Charitable Provision in late medieval York: "In Praise of God and to the Use of the Poor"', *Northern History* 29 (1993): 24–39; for connections between Lynn and Yorkshire see Parker above, p. 61.

[19] Anne Hudson, ed., *Selections from English Wycliffite Writings* (Cambridge, 1978), p. 27.

[20] Ibid., pp. 135–7.

[21] Peter McNiven, *Heresy and Politics in the Reign of Henry IV: the Burning of John Badby* (Woodbridge, 1987), pp. 81–91.

produced a scarcity of labour and a suspicion on the part of some, particularly those who were employers, that the poor were both more demanding than was their due and inclined to idleness and even to the faking of illness or injury to avoid work and illicitly obtain alms. Such fears are dramatised in William Langland's *Vision of Piers Plowman*. Piers has a half-acre of land to be worked and receives a lot of help in this from some dedicated pilgrims. However, others do not exert themselves in the same way:

> Thanne seten somme and songen ate nale,
> And holpen ere this half acre with "How trolly lolly!"
> 'Now, by the peril of my soule!' quod Piers al in pure tene,
> 'but ye arise the rather and rape yow to werche,
> Shal no greyn that here growth glade yow at need,
> And though ye deye for doel, the devel have that recche!'
> Thow were faitours afered, and feyned hem blynde;
> Somme leide hir legges aliry, as swiche losels konneth,
> And made hir [pleynt] to Piers and preide hym of grace:
> 'For we have no lymes to laboure with, lord, ygraced be ye!'[22]

[Some of the people he found were sitting down and singing songs over their ale; their sole contribution to ploughing the half-acre field 'Fol-de-rol and fiddle-de-dee'! 'Now, by my soul's peril!' Piers swore in sheer rage, 'unless you get up right away and set to work, not a single wheat-grain that sprouts in this place will ever help to brighten your looks when your stomachs start to feel the pinch. You can die of starvation for all I care – and the devil take anyone who sheds a tear for it!' At this, the scrimshankers took fright, and they began to pretend their sight was defective, or they twisted their legs to look as if they were maimed – layabouts of this ilk know all the little tricks! – and started moaning to Piers and begging him to let them off. 'Oh, bless you sir', they whined, 'our poor arms and legs aren't fit for working.'][23]

Similar fears may have been particularly strong in East Anglia where the 1381 Peasants' Revolt had taken lives, and where Bishop Despenser of Norwich had been notably enthusiastic in the putting down of the revolt. Such concerns were perhaps also fuelled especially in Lynn by a terrible story which confirmed contemporary prejudice. In 1417, the St Albans chronicler recorded, beggars had kidnapped three Lynn children, mutilated them, and taken them to London, where their injuries might bring increased alms. Fortunately, one of the children saw his merchant father on a London street and was rescued.[24] A number of historians have argued that there was an increasing hostility to the poor during this period, and a greater concern to discriminate between the worthy and unworthy recipients of alms.[25]

All of these institutions and issues provide a backdrop against which to read the descriptions of charity in *The Book of Margery Kempe*. Within the *Book*, Margery

22 William Langland, *The Visions of Piers Plowman: A Complete Edition of the B-Text*, ed. A. V. C. Schmidt (London and Melbourne, 1987), pp. 69–70, ll. 115–24.
23 William Langland, *Piers Plowman*, trans. A. V. C. Schmidt (Oxford etc., 1992), p. 67–8.
24 Goodman, *World*, p. 18.
25 Diana Wood, *Medieval Economic Thought* (Cambridge, 2002), pp. 42–68.

clearly distinguishes (as did many contemporaries) between 'charity', which she understood as a spiritual feeling, and 'almsgiving', one of a variety of good works that included the Corporal Works of Mercy among other forms of spiritual practice such as prayers and fasting. For her, charity derived from the Latin term *caritas*, which can be translated as charity, but more accurately as love. It is found for example in the New Testament in one of St Paul's epistles, 1 Corinthians 13: 13, where it is traditionally rendered 'And now abideth faith, hope, charity, these three; but the greatest of these is charity', where in modern editions 'charity' is often translated 'love'. She expresses her understanding of 'charity' early on in the *Book* in the Proem, where she sets out what she (or her amanuensis) thinks is the purpose of the book.

Alle þe werkys of ower Saviowr ben for ower exampyl & instruccyon, and what grace þat he werkyth in any creatur is ower [our] profyth yf lak of charyte be not ower hynderawnce [a hindrance to us]. And þerfor, be þe leue [leave] of ower mercyful Lord Cryst Ihesu, to þe magnyfying of hys holy name, Ihesu, þis lytyl tretys schal tretyn sumdeel in parcel [to some extent] of hys wonderful werkys, how mercyfully, how benyngly [benignly], & how charytefully he meued & stered [stirred] a synful caytyf [sinful wretch] vn-to hys love.

(Proem: 1)

Christ steered her to love him through his charity, and only lack of charity prevents understanding of the works that God does for our instruction. God has charity, but so did the neighbour who pulled her out when a roofbeam fell on her head while she was at her prayers in church. 'Þe creatur al hol [whole] & sownd [sound] thankyd hym of hys cher & hys charyte' (9: 22).

Obviously the *Book* is not designed specifically as a handbook of or guide to the various Works of Mercy, Spiritual and Corporal. But it is important to note that it does give a particular message about the relative merits of different kinds of charity and almsgiving, for its accounts of charitable acts implicitly (and occasionally explicitly) serve to show the superiority of the Spiritual over the Corporal Works of Mercy. The relationship between, and relative importance of, Corporal as opposed to Spiritual Works of Mercy are discussed on a number of occasions in the *Book*. While in Rome, Christ approved her form of devotion saying:

"Fastyng, dowtyr, is good for ȝong be-gynnars & discrete [discreet] penawns, namly þat her [their] gostly fadyr ȝeuyth hem [them] er inioyneth [enjoins] hem for to do. And for to byddyn [pray] many bedys it is good to hem þat can no bettyr do, & ȝet it is not parfyte. But it is a good wey to-perfeccyon-ward. For I telle þe, dowtyr, þei þat arn gret fastarys [fasters] & gret doers of penawnce þei wold þat it schuld ben holdyn þe best lyfe; also þei þat ȝevyn hem to sey many deuocyons þei wold han þat þe best lyfe; and þei þat ȝeuyn mech almes þei wold þat þat wer holdyn þe best lyfe. And I haue oftyn-tymes, dowtyr, teld þe þat thynkyng, wepyng, & hy contemplacyon is þe best lyfe in erthe."

(36: 89)

Here almsgiving was commended, alongside a number of other forms of active forms of devotion, but was clearly subordinated to contemplation. Elsewhere the doing of deeds spiritually, in contemplation, was commended as being of

equivalent value to doing them physically. ' "Dowtyr, þow xalt han as gret mede
& as gret reward wyth me in Heuyn for þi good seruyse & þe good dedys þat
þu hast don in þi mynde & meditacyon as ʒyf þu haddyst don þo same dedys
with thy bodily wittys " ' (84: 203). The context of this passage makes it clear that
the Corporal Works of Mercy were intended, for the discussion then moves onto
provision of food and drink for her husband (' ". . . whan þu dost any seruyse
to þe and to þin husbond in mete or drynke er any oþer thyng þat is nedful to
ʒow" '), presumably in the last years of his life, when she was nursing him. For
Margery then, the actual doing of the Corporal Works of Mercy was always an
inferior form of religious practice, and one that she was often ambivalent about.

Furthermore, Margery's ambivalence about the practice of charity is signalled
very early on in the *Book*. On recovery from her madness she asked her husband
for the keys to the buttery. Her husband's return of them recognised her ability
to resume control of the household.[26] Her maidens and keepers however advised
him not to do this 'for þei seyd sche wold but [only] ʒeue awey swech good
[goods] as þer was, for sche wyst not what sche seyde'. (1: 8) This account is principally about the superior perception of John Kempe compared with the socially
or spiritually inferior servants (for he does return the keys to his wife), but it also
tells us about contemporary Lynn attitudes. Whatever Margery's own views at
this time, she could not behave like an Elizabeth of Hungary or Frances of Rome,
two examples of continental holy women who did make extravagant almsgiving
gestures, as this would have made her servants think, not that she was holy, but
that she was mad (fig. 2).[27] In practice it seems unlikely that she was actually
trapped between charity and madness. The lack of reference to heroic acts of
charity of this nature performed by her within the *Book* suggest that she probably acquiesced in this conservative and bourgeois attitude to helping the genuinely needy, in which one provided what could be afforded out of one's own
goods, rather than giving them all away.

This contention is also supported by Margery's famous comment that 'þei haddyn many powyr neybowrys whech þei knewyn wel a-now [enough] hadyn gret
nede to ben holpyn [helped] & relevyd [relieved], & it was mor [better] almes to
helpyn hem þat þei knewyn wel for [to be] wel dysposyd folke [people who try
to do the right thing] & her owyn neybowrys þan oþer strawngerys which þei
knew not' (24: 56) which, while ostensibly about charity, was again much more
about spiritual discernment and moral judgement than about almsgiving per se.
The full story of chapter 24 is about the priest who wrote the book, his desire to
test her prophetic abilities, and his lack of faith in her. A young man, whom the
priest did not know, came to him, complaining of poverty and asking for help.
The young man claimed to have taken priestly orders but had in self-defence
struck a man or two who might as a result be dead. The young man, afraid of

---

26 As Sarah Salih has also argued. Sarah Salih, 'At home; out of the house', in Carolyn Dinshaw
    and David Wallace, eds, *The Cambridge Companion to Medieval Women's Writing* (Cambridge,
    2003), pp. 124–40 (p. 124).
27 For further discussion of charitable practices in both female and male saints' lives see P. H.
    Cullum, 'Gendering Charity in medieval hagiography', in Samantha J. E. Riches and Sarah
    Salih, eds, *Gender and Holiness: Men, Women and Saints in Late Medieval Europe* (London and
    New York, 2002), pp. 135–51.

Figure 2. St Elizabeth of Hungary, fifteenth-century rood screen, Barnham Broom church, Norfolk. Here charity (specifically the provision of food and drink) is used as the emblem of Elizabeth's sanctity – she is shown carrying a covered cup in one hand and bread in the other. Photograph taken by Katherine J. Lewis.

arrest, had fled rather than contact his friends for help. He asked money in order to contact other friends who would help and who would then repay the priest. The priest takes this request to a very ill alderman and his wife, where Margery happened to be present. Margery argues against giving alms, on the grounds above, and also because she has privileged knowledge of his future conduct, prophesying that the young man would deceive the priest. The alderman and his wife agree with her and refuse to help him. The priest, however, was taken in by the young man because he was 'an amyabyl persone, fayr feturyd, wel faueryd in cher & in cuntenawns, sad [sober] in hys langage and dalyawns, prestly in hys gestur and vestur' (24: 56). Lacking faith in Margery's warning, the priest gives the young man some money, and Margery is proved right, for that is the last they see of him. In a subsequent, similar case, when an old man tries to sell the priest a book, the priest is seen to have learned his lesson and this time listens to Margery's warning and is much more wary in his conduct, so does not lose out again (24: 57–8). The story is thus primarily about Margery's ability to prophesy and to discern spirits, even of people she had not met, rather than being specifically about charity. However, it does serve to make a point about the superiority of Spiritual Works over Corporal ones – perhaps, on a prosaic level, this is in part because Spiritual Works do not involve the handover of money which could be used in ways which the giver did not intend. The behaviour of the young man involved certainly serves to illustrate contemporary anxieties about the unworthy poor and the fine line that there could be between beggars and criminals, who were quite prepared to take advantage of the foolishly charitable. The episode is also, and perhaps more surprisingly, about the parochialism of attitudes to charity, in contrast to the continental influences on her spiritual practice. The preference for poor *neighbours* is a preference for the known against the unknown, for those of good character against those of bad character, a preference which the pious alderman and his wife found persuasive (even though they did not share Margery's divinely inspired intuition). All of this suggests a conservative and discriminatory approach to the practice of charity; there is nothing at all radical in Margery's attitude or conduct here, and in this respect her behaviour is very much seen to be in concert with the 'haves' of the Lynn bourgeoisie.

Indeed, perhaps as a result of this, Margery's marked preference in doing the Works of Mercy was to do them spiritually and directly to the person of Christ or his mother. An early vision (or at least one placed early in the text) was of St Anne and of the births of the Virgin and Christ. In the vision Margery took the Virgin and raised her until she was of marriageable age 'wyth good mete & drynke, with fayr whyte clothys & whyte kerchys' (6: 18). The vision then allowed Margery to accompany the Virgin as a servant to the house of Elizabeth and then to Bethlehem, on the way buying her lodging at night and providing bedding once Christ was born. She also begged for swaddling clothes for the infant and food for mother and child (6: 18–19). If, as Sarah Salih argues, this vision is an act of humility, it is not altogether a successful enactment.[28]

---

[28] See above, p. 171.

Margery presents herself as the Virgin's servant and yet is unable to let go of her status; indeed, as Kim Phillips points out in this volume, servants were not necessarily of lowly social status in this period, and the fact that Margery has herself taking care of the arrangements for securing the Virgin's lodgings is significant in this respect – she fulfils the contemporary role of servant as companion of similar status to her mistress rather than servant as inferior.[29] In the next chapter the vision then elides seamlessly into a discussion first of weeping and then into Christ's order to her 'to knele be-for þe Trynyte for to prey for al þe world, for many hundryd thowsand sowlys schal be sauyd be þi prayers' (7: 20). Thus the spiritual enactment of a Corporal Work of Mercy is completed by the performance of a more important Spiritual Work: prayer for the living and the dead, with the strong sense of the efficacious nature of Margery's intercession.[30]

It may well be that it was not until Margery visited Rome that she encountered a more radical practice of charity, perhaps influenced by that of St Frances or Francesca of Rome (1384–1440).[31] The two women were contemporaries, and Frances would have been active at the time of Margery's visit, though she is not mentioned in the *Book* and there is therefore no evidence that they met. Frances was regarded as a saint during her lifetime and there were processes for her canonisation immediately on her death in 1440, continued in the succeeding decade, though she was not formally canonised until 1608. Nevertheless there was an immediate cult and this had spread to England by the end of the fifteenth century: in Sandringham church, less than ten miles north-east of Lynn, she is depicted in the glass.[32] St Frances was, like Margery, a married woman with children. Her family, like the Brunhams, was well (if newly) established in the urban hierarchy.[33] Like Margery she had visions, and in the latter part of her married life practised continence. But unlike Margery she also practised a radical charity, which sometimes left her family not knowing where their next meal was coming from, and this was the occasion of food-multiplication miracles. In acts of humility Frances constantly undercut her own social status, addressing her servants as brother and sister, carrying firewood on her own shoulders and collecting money at the church door like the street beggars (as St Francis of Assisi had once done). Susan Dickman has argued that the two were 'spiritual sister(s)', but although there are significant similarities between the two, and especially when we

---

[29] See above, p. 23.

[30] On the importance of the *Book*'s presentation of Margery as intercessor see also Katherine Lewis's essay below.

[31] For discussion of St Frances and a brief account of her life see Donald Weinstein and Rudolph M. Bell, *Saints and Society: The Two Worlds of Western Christendom, 1000–1700* (Chicago and London, 1982), pp. 39–40, also pp. 42–3, 231 for visual representations of her life; also Guy Boanas and Lyndal Roper, 'Feminine Piety in Fifteenth-Century Rome: Santa Francesca Romana', in Jim Obelkevich, Lyndal Roper and Raphael Samuel, eds, *Disciplines of Faith: Studies in Religion, Politics and Patriarchy* (London, 1987), pp. 177–93 and Cullum, 'Gendering Charity'.

[32] Charles E. Keyser, 'Notes on some ancient stained glass in Sandringham Church, Norfolk', *Norfolk Archaeology* 19 (1917): 122–32 (129). I am very grateful to Katherine Lewis for drawing this to my attention.

[33] Although Frances was of noble descent rather than bourgeoise; whereas the aristocracy in England largely lived in the country, Italian nobles were much more likely to live in towns and cities.

consider the *Book*'s account of Margery's charitable activities in Rome, there are also some clear differences.[34]

What is notable about Margery's Roman charity is that it was not voluntary. It was imposed on her as a penance. In this respect she was distinctively different from Frances. Margery's Dutch confessor, Wenceslas, imposed service to an old woman as a combination of penance and test of obedience. The test aspect was inspired by the English priest who was her enemy, and thus presumably doubly unwelcome (33: 84). Margery is not specific about what the penance was for, but it was probably a general penance subsequent to the complete confession she had recently made to her confessor of 'alle hir synnes as ner as hir mende wold seruyn hir fro hir childhode vn-to þat owre & receyued hir penawns ful joyfully' (33: 83). This confession to a good priest who understood her and could impose an appropriate penance is implicitly contrasted to the failed confession of her childbed, which tipped her into madness and began her spiritual journey (1: 6–7). The penance involved serving a poor old woman and an explicit comparison is drawn with the service she did to the Virgin; Margery worked as the woman's servant, she slept on the floor wrapped in her cloak, carried water and firewood on her neck (a precise parallel with Frances), and begged the woman's food and drink. When the poor woman's wine was sour, the depths of Margery's abnegation are indicated by the fact that she gave up the good wine she had bought for herself, and drank the sour. Any tendency to play-act this service was evidently squashed by Wenceslas (34: 85–6). Why he imposed this particular penance is not clear. Perhaps he felt that the vision of her service to the Virgin smacked too much of spiritual pride, for there are very clear parallels between the two episodes. A clue may lie in Christ's later words to Margery after she had given away her money ' "thow hast cownseld oþer men to ben powr for my sake, & þerfor þu must folwyn thyn owyn cownsel" ' (37: 92). Again this demonstrates Margery's sense that this is appropriate behaviour for those less spiritually advanced (and perhaps less socially important) than herself. If Wenceslas (and Christ) sought to re-engage Margery with the humble bodily charity of ordinary lay folk they signally failed.

Just as the failed confession led to the assaults of the Devil, so the successful confession with its associated penance and obedience led her to the reward of marriage with the Godhead (chapter 35). In the state of exaltation produced by the marriage, smelling sweet scents, hearing sweet melodies, feeling the fire of love and surrounded by angels (again the reversal of her experience of madness) Margery was reassured that it was not her Works of Corporal Mercy that had produced these results. This is when Christ tells her, as quoted above, that fasting is only for beginners and that contemplation is far superior to this. She was emboldened to return to Wenceslas and insist that she return to her white clothing (37: 91–2). When he agreed, she evidently felt that the penance was complete for she told the poor woman that she must leave her. And then she embarked upon her most radically extravagant act, the giving away not only of

---

34 Susan Dickman, 'Margery Kempe and the Continental Tradition of the Pious Woman', in Marion Glasscoe, ed., *The Medieval Mystical Tradition in England* (Cambridge, 1984), pp. 150–68 (p. 157).

all her goods, but also those of Richard the broken-backed man (37: 92). This act is, however, different from that of St Frances; whereas St Frances had sought to be both donor and recipient at the same time, obliterating the hierarchy of rich and poor, just as she did that of mistress and servant, Margery replaced one with the other. She had found a way in which being poor gave her superior status, good men and women took her home and served her with their own hands (this is when she meets Margaret Florentyne), and then in a vision the Virgin begged for Margery, in a reversal of their previous roles (38: 92–3). It is difficult to imagine how anybody could top this. Once again Margery's acts of bodily piety elided into a greater spiritual act; what starts off looking conventional becomes something rather different. For after this the *Book* shows Margery much more usually (and certainly more importantly) as a recipient of bodily aid rather than as its giver.

Dickman argues that Margery's giving away of all her money in Rome 'was consciously conceived as an experiment, limited in time and space and carefully insulated from her life in Lynn'.[35] It could thus be argued to be a liminal practice, an out-of-place and excessive piety conducted only in the liminal (to Lynn) space of Rome, while her return home reincorporated her into the conventions of Lynn itself. This is certainly possible. Margery does not indicate continuance of this practice after her return. However there is another possibility, that after her return she had neither the resources, nor perhaps the secure social status to risk this kind of practice. When she was back in Lynn and wanting to set off again to St James's she described herself as 'powr and awt [owing] meche dette' (44: 105). Radical charity, like Margery's own public weeping, was spectacular, but in order to provide a spectacle there had to be a superfluity or abundance of giving. The small charity of the poor was by definition not spectacular, and Margery may not have been able to afford to alienate her supporters by this practice.

Nor can we be certain that the *Book* accurately presents the entire range of Margery's charitable activities. The *Book* is designed to show her extraordinary gifts, and to highlight the special experiences of her life. It thus probably underplays her more conventional and low-key forms of charitable practice, as essentially beneath noticing. For example, in the prelude to her period of madness when she was troubled by an unconfessed sin, she performed other good works which she hoped would be a sufficient substitute. 'And þerfor þis creatur oftyntymes dede greet penawns in fasting bred & watyr, *& oþer dedys of almes* wyth devowt preyers' (1: 7, my italics). Similarly, there are relatively few specific accounts of her visiting the sick, and yet looking back on her spiritual life she could say 'þe sayd creatur had continuyd hir lyfe þorw þe preseruyng of owr Sauyowr Crist Ihesu mor þan xxv ʒer [twenty-five years] whan þis tretys was wretyn weke [week] by weke & day by day, les þan [unless] sche wer ocupijd [occupied] with seke [sick] folke er ellys [or else] were lettyd [prevented] with oþer needful occupasyon' (87: 214). This suggests that visiting the sick took up a significant part of her time, and yet was not considered to be sufficiently distinctive

---

[35] Ibid., p. 163.

of her particular spirituality to be worth much attention. Indeed, it is noticeable that almsgiving tends to drop out of the list of her pious works at later stages in her account. Almsgiving may therefore be characterised as the kind of thing that she did as an unregenerate soul, in her earlier and more conventional life.[36]

Despite this downplaying, the *Book* gives the sense that in Margery's later years she was evidently in demand for the efficacy of her prayers at sick beds, and perhaps also for her personal care. When the good priest who read to her fell sick she organised necessaries for him and went on a pilgrimage for him to the tomb of the popular saint Richard Caistor of St Stephen's, Norwich, after which he recovered (60: 147). Master Aleyn too fell sick, and Margery was not permitted to visit him, but after she prayed for him he recovered (70: 169–70). The woman who had fallen into madness after the birth of a child, may have had a particular significance for Margery, and she visited her daily, talking with her, as well as praying for her.[37] This probably went on for some time, as when the woman's husband asked for help she was 'newly delyueryd' and Margery continued to visit until she was fit to be churched, which did not usually happen until six weeks after the birth, and might have been longer delayed by the woman's condition (75). The power of Margery's prayers for the sick, and particularly the dying, is indicated on the occasion of her visit to Denney. Margery went to see one of her 'regulars', the wife of a burgess who lay sick, to tell her that that she would be going away. The wife was distressed: ' "I wolde not . . . þat myn husbond deyid whil ȝe wer owt for xls [40 shillings]" ', but was assured by Margery that ' "he xulde leuyn [live] & faryn ryth wel & þat he xulde not dey ȝet" ' (84: 202).

Sometimes Margery went voluntarily to visit the sick, partly for their sake, but often for her own spiritual benefit. It was presumably to one of the Lynn leperhouses, perhaps St Mary Magdalene, that Margery went when she wanted to kiss the leperwomen (chapter 74). She was also able to help one of these women who was close to a state of despair through sexual temptations (74: 177). Here she was performing Works of Spiritual Mercy in comforting the sorrowful and counselling the doubtful. Margery also helped another sexually troubled person: her own son. She saw the illness which afflicted him, in which 'hys colowr chawngyd, hys face wex ful of whelys [welts] and bloberys [pustules] as it had ben a lepyr [leper]' (II, 1: 222), as a punishment for sin, specifically sexual sin. She never stated that the disease was leprosy, just that it looked like it, but claimed that the boy's master threw him out because he thought it might be leprosy. The miraculous cure of the disease was a result of the son promising amendment and Margery's intercession 'askyd forȝeuenes of hys synne & relesyng of þe sekenes þat owr Lord had ȝouyn hym' (II, 1: 223). Once again Margery's acts of bodily charity were outshone by the importance of her Spiritual Works.

It is a commonplace of discussions of Margery's piety that it was strongly influenced by continental patterns of female piety, but this essay has argued for the ways in which her charitable practice seems much more shaped by the

---

36 See Sarah Salih's essay in this collection which similarly argues for a development from bodily to more contemplative forms of piety, over the course of Margery's life.

37 For discussion of this episode see also Katherine J. Lewis below, pp. 203–4.

concerns of her Lynn community. It is more parochial and conformist than her spiritual practice. Nevertheless she conceived as appropriate to other lay people the Corporal Works of Mercy, and her own acts of devotion, particularly on pilgrimage, would have come to a premature end had it not been for the charitable activity of many lay people who assisted her on her travels. To provide a final example, Margery was only able to get to St James's shrine in Compostella through the financial aid of Thomas Marchale, the man from Newcastle, who gave her ten marks to pay for the trip. Moreover, Margery apparently instructed him to give further money to the poor and he obeyed: '"what þat ȝe byd me ȝeuyn to any powr man er woman I wyl do ȝowr byddyng"' (45: 108). In her own conduct Margery reveals a strong prioritising of the Spiritual over the Corporal Works of Mercy; she obviously regarded the latter as more appropriate to ordinary lay people, not to someone such as herself, the beloved of Christ, who was anything but ordinary.

11

Margery Kempe and Saint Making in Later Medieval England[1]

KATHERINE J. LEWIS

> And so, as sche went with þe forseyd men, sche teld hem
> good talys [tales] tyl on of þe Dukys [the duke of Bedford's]
> men whech had a-restyd hir seyd vn-to hir, "Me ouyr-
> thynkyth [regret] þat I met with þe, for me semyth [it seems
> to me] þat þu seyst ryth good wordys." Than seyd sche vn-
> to hym, "Ser, ouyrthynkyth ne repentith ȝow not þat ȝe met
> with me. Doth ȝowr Lordys wille, & I trust al schal be for
> þe best, for I am ryth wel plesyd þat ȝe met with me." He
> seyd a-ȝen, "Damsel, yf euyr þu be seynt in Heuyn, prey
> for me.' 'Sir, I hope ȝe xal be a seynt ȝowr-selfe & euery man
> þat xal come to Heuyn" (53: 130).

The inclusion of this incident in *The Book of Margery Kempe* provides one of the most explicit indications within the text that Margery Kempe is deliberately presented to the reader as a potential saint and, moreover, that she was actually recognised as such by others during her lifetime. This hagiographical purpose has long been acknowledged by scholars as fundamental to the meaning and intended function of the text, for it shapes both the representation of Margery's experiences and the form of the *Book* itself. For example, Lynn Staley has discussed the ways in which the tropes of female sacred biography provided authorisation for the *Book*, arguing that it is 'Written in English about an English "saint"', while Gail McMurray Gibson describes the *Book* as a 'calculated hagiographic text, a kind of autobiographical saint's life' or autohagiography as others often term it.[2] Much attention has been paid to the models upon which Margery and/or her scribe apparently drew in constructing their picture of Margery, the trainee saint.[3]

---

[1] I am grateful to John Arnold for some very helpful comments on an earlier draft of this essay and to P. H. Cullum and Joanna Huntington for discussion of the general issues which it considers.

[2] Staley, *Dissenting Fictions*, p. 38; Gail McMurray Gibson, *The Theatre of Devotion: East Anglian Drama and Society in the Late Middle Ages* (Chicago and London, 1989), p. 47; for discussion of the deliberate hagiographical organisation of the *Book* see Samuel Fanous, 'Measuring the Pilgrim's Progress: Internal Emphases in *The Book of Margery Kempe*', in Denis Renevey and Christina Whitehead, eds, *Writing Religious Women: Female Spiritual and Textual Practices in Late Medieval England* (Cardiff, 2000), pp. 157–76.

[3] In what follows I assume that the *Book* is based to some extent on the experiences and reminiscences of a woman called Margery Kempe from Lynn, but that its construction of Margery as a saint was a cooperative production in which her clerical scribe/s also played a role. However, I do not intend to speculate further on the precise degree of their relative input, hence use of the 'and/or' formula here and elsewhere.

St Bridget of Sweden (1303–1373), canonised in 1391, has often been cited as the key model for Margery Kempe, both in terms of her life experiences and in her production of visionary literature.[4] Hope Emily Allen's notes to the EETS edition demonstrate the ways in which the presentation of Margery bears close comparison to the presentation of other continental female mystics too, such as Dorothea of Montau and Angela of Foligno, while others have traced similarities between Margery and Catherine of Siena.[5] This aspect of the *Book* intersects with studies of the dissemination and reception of female visionary literature, for the writings of such women were popular reading matter among lay people of a certain status, perhaps particularly women, in later medieval England.[6] However, no one female saint provided the blueprint for St Margery, for, as Timea Szell notes, four different models of holy women apparently influenced the *Book*: widows, virgin-martyrs, penitent prostitutes and cross-dressers.[7] Sarah Salih has rightly suggested that virgin-martyrs provided the most significant of these, arguing in particular that 'Margery's pursuit of sanctity is to a large extent an *imitatio Margaretae*': the virgin-martyr Margaret of Antioch; while she and others have also traced the ways in which Margery's conduct is clearly modelled on that of Katherine of Alexandria, the most popular virgin-martyr of all (fig. 3).[8] Susan Eberly has emphasised the paradigm of Mary Magdalene, the non-virginal repentant sinner, who shared a unique relationship with Christ (fig. 4).[9] However, not all of Margery's models were female; Salih has explored the ways in which St Paul, as both penitent and apostle, also informs the *Book*'s presentation of its protagonist.[10]

As these issues have already received much attention they will not be considered here; rather, I want to move from a consideration of the form of Margery's sanctity to its function. As others have also suggested, it seems entirely likely that the intention was not simply for Margery to be seen as a saint in abstract, exemplary terms, but for her to be concretely venerated as such by

---

4   e.g. Clarissa W. Atkinson, *Mystic and Pilgrim: The Book and the World of Margery Kempe* (Ithaca, NY and London, 1983), pp. 168–79; see also Diane Watt above, pp. 153–6.

5   *BMK*, pp. liii–lxviii and *passim*; also e.g. Susan Dickman, 'Margery Kempe and the Continental Tradition of the Pious Woman', in Marion Glasscoe, ed., *The Medieval Mystical Tradition in England* 3 (Cambridge, 1984), pp. 150–68; Atkinson, *Mystic and Pilgrim*, pp. 157–94.

6   For the most recent survey see Alexandra Barratt, 'Continental Women Mystics and English Readers', in Carolyn Dinshaw and David Wallace, eds, *The Cambridge Companion to Medieval Women's Writing* (Cambridge, 2003), pp. 240–55.

7   Timea K. Szell, 'From Woe to Weal and Weal to Woe: Notes on the Structure of *The Book of Margery Kempe*', in Sandra J. McEntire, ed., *Margery Kempe: A Book of Essays* (New York and London, 1992), pp. 73–91.

8   Sarah Salih, *Versions of Virginity in Late Medieval England* (Cambridge, 2001), pp. 195–201 (pp. 196–7); Katherine J. Lewis, *The Cult of St Katherine of Alexandria in Late Medieval England* (Woodbridge, 2000), pp. 242–56; Naoë Kukita Yoshikawa, 'Veneration of Virgin Martyrs in Margery Kempe's Meditation: Influence of the Sarum Liturgy and Hagiography', in Renevey and Whitehead, eds, *Writing Religious Women*, pp. 177–95.

9   Susan Eberly, 'Margery Kempe, St Mary Magdalene, and Patterns of Contemplation', *Downside Review* 107 (1989): 209–223; see also Claire Sponsler above, pp. 136–7.

10 Sarah Salih, 'Staging Conversion: The Digby Saint Plays and *The Book of Margery Kempe*', in Samantha J. E. Riches and Sarah Salih, eds, *Gender and Holiness: Men, Women and Saints in Late Medieval Europe* (London and New York, 2002), pp. 121–34.

Figure 3. St Katherine of Alexandria, early sixteenth-century rood screen, North Tuddenham church, Norfolk. Katherine is shown carrying the distinctive emblems of her martyrdom, the sword and spiked wheel. Photograph taken by Katherine J. Lewis

devotees. Indeed, this prospect is underlined by the promise of Christ himself when he tells her:

"In þis chirche [St Margaret's, Lynn] þu hast suffyrd meche schame and reprefe for þe ȝyftys þat I haue ȝowyn þe & for þe grace and goodnes þat I haue wrowt

Figure 4. St Mary Magdalene, early sixteenth-century rood screen, Wiggenhall
St Mary church, Norfolk. Mary carries the pot of ointment with which she anointed
Christ's feet. Photograph taken by Katherine J. Lewis

in þe, and þerfore in þis cherche and in þis place I xal ben worschepyd in þe.
Many a man & woman xal seyn it is wel sene þat God louyd [loved] hir wel.
Dowtyr, I xal werkyn so mech grace for þe þat al þe werld xal wondreyn
& meruelyn of my goodness" (53: 156).

This seems a clear indication that some sort of shrine to Margery would be established at St Margaret's, most likely focused on her tomb.[11] Indeed, Carol Meale has suggested (as have others) that 'the unwritten agenda on the part of Margery and/or her confessors was canonization'.[12] As will become apparent, I am not sure that canonisation would have been seen as a realistic possibility by them. But that is not to say that they didn't think Margery could and would come to be seen as a saint, and in this respect Christ's identification of St Margaret's as the place where Margery will be venerated is crucial (fig. 5). In elucidating these contentions this chapter will not examine the *Book* and its presentation of Margery as a saint in terms of hagiography and textual models, or in terms of generalised ideas about what makes someone 'saintly'.[13] Instead the *Book* will be placed within the specific setting of saints' cults and saint making in late medieval England.[14] In this way I hope to shed a different light on why the *Book* presents Margery as a saint and why it did not succeed in fostering the posthumous cult which Christ envisaged (or at least, not one that has left any trace in documentary records). As will be seen, this failure arguably has less to do with any perceived deficiencies in Margery Kempe or her *Book* (as is often assumed) and more to do with the nature of the saints which late medieval English people favoured and the dynamics of their cults.[15]

' "*Dowtyr, I xal makyn al þe werld to wondryn of þe, & many man & many woman xal spekyn of me for lofe of þe & worshepyn me in þe*" ' (29: 73).

I shall begin by revisiting the ways in which the *Book* presents Margery herself as a saint. Others have already illustrated at length the ways in which Margery's conduct as described in the *Book*, and its similarities to the lives of other saints,

---

[11] Margery's burial place is unknown, but the parish church at Lynn seems the most likely candidate for it.

[12] Carol M. Meale, ' "This is a Deed Bok, the Tother a Quick": Theatre and the Drama of Salvation in *The Book of Margery Kempe*', in Jocelyn Wogan-Browne et al., eds, *Medieval Women: Texts and Contexts in Late Medieval Britain. Essays for Felicity Riddy* (Turnhout, 2000), pp. 49–68 (p. 64).

[13] See Anneke B. Mulder-Bakker, 'The Invention of Saintliness: Texts and Contexts', in *eadem*, ed., *The Invention of Saintliness* (London and New York, 2002), pp. 3–23 for a lucid discussion of the problems of applying post-medieval and ahistorical standards to saints' cults.

[14] I shall use the term saint to signify someone around whom a posthumous cult grows, regardless of whether or not they have been canonised. I follow Ronald Finucane's definition of a cult as 'the belief in the sanctity and miraculous powers of a particular dead individual, the group of people who believe, and their actions consequent upon that belief – particularly pilgrimage or devotion to his [*sic*] shrine or tomb, and the attribution of specific miracles to him [*sic*]'; *Miracles and Pilgrims: Popular Beliefs in Medieval England* (London etc., 1977), p. 11, n. 2. In addition, I shall not make use of an 'official'/'unofficial' distinction in referring to cults that received papal approval as opposed to those which did not.

[15] For instance Richard Kieckhefer offers several explanations as to why Margery failed to be recognised as a saint: first that she may not have had the 'charismatic spark' which would have convinced those around her that she was truly holy; second that she did not have enough clerical support; third that the final part of her 'actual' life (after the *Book* was written) may not have been conducted in as ultra-religious a fashion as the *Book* describes; see *Unquiet Souls: Fourteenth-Century Saints and their Religious Milieu* (Chicago, 1984), pp. 188–9. While not absolutely denying that such considerations may have played a part, this chapter proposes that they would not have been foremost in the minds of most of Margery's contemporaries in their assessment of whether or not she was a saint.

Figure 5. The west front of St Margaret's church, Lynn. This is the only parish church in the country to have two towers at its west end. Photograph taken by John Lewis.

qualifies her for sainthood, focusing on such elements as her visions, her interrogations, her pilgrimages, her suffering at the hands of others, her preoccupation with virginity, her social criticism and her charity. Instead, I want to consider the ways in which the *Book* establishes that Margery also meets that other essential saintly criterion: the ability to perform miracles, to intercede with God for the benefit of devotees.

The *Book* makes reference to several incidents in Margery's life which are held to be miraculous. In chapter 9 while she is sitting quietly at mass a nine-pound weight

of stone and wood falls from the ceiling onto her head and back and Margery
fears for her life – but after calling on Christ the pain vanishes. Such miraculous
events in saints' lives needed the eye-witness of a third party to be verified and
thus it is significant that this is one of the rare occasions in the book when an
attendant layman is identified by name: 'Iohn of Wyreham', a Lynn mercer, is
cited as an onlooker to 'þis wondyr'. The spirit of God confirms this, telling her
' "Helde þis for a *gret myracle*, &, ȝyf þe pepyl wyl not leuyn [believe] þis, I schal
werkyn meche mor" ' (9: 22, my italics). Further proof of the genuinely miraculous nature of this event is provided by another witness, Master Aleyn, who
carefully examines the stone and beam in question (the two having apparently
become separated – the latter ending up on a fire): 'And þis worschepful doctowr
seyd it was a *gret myracle* & ower Lord was heyly [highly] to be magnified for þe
preseruyng of þis creatur a-ȝen the malice of hir enmy, and told it mech pepyl &
mych pepyl magnified mech God in þis creatur.' (9: 22, my italics). We are
told that some people preferred to believe that this was an indication of God's
wrath rather than his pleasure, but the event is clearly presented as evidence
that Margery has been singled out as God's vessel through his performance of
something twice identified as a 'gret myracle' and confirmed as such by two witnesses. Like the early martyrs, Margery has emerged unscathed from an incident
which should, at the least, have paralysed her, if not killed her.[16] This demonstration over, Christ proceeds to hand over the powers of protection and patronage to Margery herself. The key chapters here are 22 and 23.

Margery has been lamenting the loss of her virginity and, to comfort her,
Christ addresses her as follows:

> "A, dowtyr, how oftyn tymes haue I teld þe þat thy synnes arn forȝoue þe & þat
> we ben onyd [joined] to-gedyr with-owtyn ende? Þu art to me a synguler lofe,
> dowtyr, & þerfor I behote þe þu schalt haue a synguler grace in Hevyn, dowtyr,
> & I be-hest þe <þat I shal> come to þin ende at þi deyng with my blyssed Modyr
> & myn holy awngelys & twelve apostelys, Seynt Kateryne, Seynt Margarete,
> Seynt Mary Mawdelyn, & many oþer seyntys þat ben in Hevyn, whech ȝevyn
> gret worship to me for þe grace þat I ȝeue to þe, God, þi Lord Ihesu" (22: 50–1).

Not only will Margery be collected from her death bed by some of the most
important saints in the Christian pantheon, but she is also reassured that ' "þu
xuldyst noon oþer purgatory han þan slawndyr & speche of þe world" ' (22: 51);
a promise that he reiterates later (63: 157). Only the truly blessed could expect to
get straight to heaven without any time in Purgatory, so this underlines Margery's
sanctity. Christ then proceeds to explain what Margery's role in Heaven will be:

> "Dowtyr, I be-hote [promise] þe þat same grace þat I be-hyte Seynt Kateryne,
> Seynt Margarete, Seynt Barbara, & Seynt Powle, in so mech þat what creatur

---

[16] This incident also bears clear similarities to an episode in the posthumous miracles of
St William of York in which a stone falls onto a man while he's hanging up a tapestry, but
doesn't injure him, and he carries the stone to St William's tomb in thanks for this escape.
A stone identified by inscription as the very stone in question is still on display in York
Minster undercroft. The incident is illustrated in three lights of the St William window in the
north choir transept of the Minster. It was built 1415–20 so would have been under construction when Margery visited York in 1417.

in erth vn-to þe Day of Dom aske þe any bone [boon] & beleuyth þat God
louyth þe he xal haue hys bone or ellys a bettyr thing . . . & men in erth schal
iojn [rejoice] in God for þe, for he xal werkyn meche grace for þe & makyn al
þe world to knowyn þat God louyth þe. Þu hast be despised for my lofe,
& þerfor þu xalt be worshepyd for my lofe. Dowtyr, whan þu art in Heuyn,
þu xalt mown [be able to] askyn what þu wylt, & I xal grawnte þe al þi desyr".

(22: 52)

The text could not be more explicit. After her death Margery will be worshipped and she will be able to ask anything she wants of Christ on behalf of
her grateful devotees. It is significant that this is couched not simply in general
terms, but by specifically granting Margery the same intercessory powers
already enjoyed by four of the so-called universal saints; those who were venerated across medieval Europe. These long established saints, drawn from the
Bible or the early centuries of Christianity, were perceived as figures of great
importance and power and the *Book* here strives to present Margery as one of
their number, both in terms of her intimacy with Christ and her abilities. This
is confirmed in a later chapter when Margery tells Christ that she wishes she
was as worthy to be secure in Christ's love as Mary Magdalene was. Christ
replies: ' "I loue þe as wel, & þe same pes þat I ʒaf to hir þe same pes I ʒeue to
þe." ' Lest Margery fear that the Magdalene, or any of the other saints might be
jealous of Margery's special status, Christ continues: ' "For, dowtyr, þer is no
seynt in Heuyn displesyd thow I loue a creatur in erde [on earth] as mech as
I do hem" ' (74: 176).

In order to demonstrate the reliability of Christ's promise, and underline
Margery's saintly status, chapter 23 is entirely given over to an illustration of
her God-given powers. Various incidents are recounted where people ask for
Margery's help and she provides relief and solace to them. For example,
a priest asks her to pray for a dying woman and, on hearing from Christ that
the woman will be damned, Margery begs tearfully that the woman be saved,
and Christ grants her request. Another woman, a particular friend of
Margery's, is apparently dying and Margery prays for her. Christ promises that
the woman will recover and live another ten years. She is also given prophetic
information about the fate of various other sick and dying people. In a later
chapter it transpires that Margery's prayers at the deathbed are in great
demand, even by those who couldn't stand her weeping and crying during
their lifetime. Finding themselves at the point of death, they are happy for her
to do both, having evident belief in the value of her prayers (72: 172–3). We are
told that this is only a sample of the many revelations which Margery experienced and, in order to add authority to the preceding narrative, the chapter
ends by emphasising that Margery continually worried that her visions were
in fact 'illusyons & deceytys of hir gostly enmys' (23: 54). But her confessor is
always on hand to ensure that this is not the case, and the fact of these two
chapters and their extraordinary claims about Margery's powers being
included is proof in itself of their veracity.

Margery's intercessory powers are demonstrated even more dramatically in
chapter 67, when a terrible fire threatens to engulf St Margaret's church. This
event is attested to in contemporary sources and happened on 23 January

1420/1421.[17] The chapter begins by telling us that the 'solempne place' and indeed the whole town would have burned down 'ne had grace ne myracle ne ben' (67: 162), serving at the outset to place subsequent events within a register of the miraculous. Margery is distraught, crying and weeping outside the burning church, and we are told that even those who 'myth not enduryn hir to cryen & wepyn' now not only tolerated it, but encouraged her to do so 'for eschewing of her bodily perel' and, significantly, 'ful trustyng & beleuyng þat thorw hir cry-ing & wepyng owr Lord wolde takyn hem to mercy' (67: 163). She has been appointed to intercede for the town with God. We are given a vivid description of 'þe sparkys of þe fyer fleyn a-bowte þe Cherch . . . þe hedows [hideous] flawme of þe fyr' and Margery prays that ' "sum reyn er sum wedyr" ' may be sent to quench these flames. Shortly thereafter three men come to her covered in snow and proclaim that God has indeed sent a snowstorm and the fire is out. Margery gives thanks for this 'myrakyl & special grace' (67: 163) and her confessor offers the following assessment:

> he beleuyd þat *God grawntyd hem for hir preyerys to be delyueryd owt of her great perellys*, for it myth not be, wyth-owtyn deuowt preyerys, þat þe eyr [air] being brygth & cler xulde be so sone chongyd in-to clowdys & derkys [darkness] & sendyn down gret flakys of snow (67: 164, my italics).

Thus the church and town's miraculous deliverance is attributed directly to Margery's prayers, despite the fact that some people, once the danger is over, revert to criticising her for her cries. It seems that many people (like those *in extremis* in chapter 72) are only prepared to believe in Margery's holiness when they find themselves in dire straits.

Another example of Margery's abilities is provided in chapter 75, and, import-antly, the events of this chapter serves to underline Christ's earlier assimilation of her into the ranks of the universal saints.[18] While Margery is praying in St Margaret's she encounters a distressed man who tells her that his wife, after giving birth, has apparently gone mad; she doesn't recognise any of her friends, she emits terrifying roars and cries and has to be physically restrained in order to prevent her biting and striking people. Margery goes with the man to help his wife. She is partly qualified to do this by her own similar experiences in chapter 1. But it can be no coincidence that Margery explicitly gives the name of her church on this occasion (75: 177). St Margaret was held to be the special protectress of women in childbirth and here Margery assumes her role, moving from the space dedicated to the saint, into the arena in which her intercession was believed to be most efficacious. Margery stands in for St Margaret, the implication being that her intercession with God will be just as effective as that of the virgin-martyr. And indeed, Margery's daily prayers for the woman's recovery are answered, as God restores her wits and her mind (75: 178). As with previous examples of

---

[17] See *BMK*, p. 327, n.162, 29–31.

[18] Both Gibson and Salih have also commented on the ways in which this chapter serves to make explicit the similarities between St Margaret and Margery; *Theater of Devotion*, pp. 64–5; *Versions of Virginity*, pp. 196–7.

Margery's intercession, a witness is on hand to vouch for its miraculous truth; in
this case the scribe himself:

> It was, as hem thowt þat knewyn it, a ryth gret myrakyl, for he þat wrot þis boke
> had neuyr be-for tyme sey man ne woman, as hym thowt, so fer owt of hir-self
> as þis woman was ne so euyl [difficult] to rewlyn ne to gouernyn, & sithyn he
> sey hir sad [well behaved] & sobyr a-now, worschip & preysyng be to owr Lord
> with-owtyn ende for hys hy mercy & hys goodnes þat euyr helpith at need.
>
> (75: 178–9)

The *Book* also stresses that Margery's intercession is not restricted to specific,
local incidents, but extends much further than that. Chapter 57 contains a passage which explains that, as Margery has had all her sins forgiven, she feels great
sorrow for the sins and misfortunes of others: the souls in purgatory, the poor,
those in trouble, Jews, Muslims and heretics, and all sinners (57: 140–1). In chapter 84 we hear also of her prayers for lepers, prisoners, and lecherous men and
women, whom she implores Christ to treat as kindly as he treated Mary
Magdalene (84: 186). The efficacy of her intercessions is confirmed by Christ
when he tells her:

> "Dowtyr, þu hast a good ȝele [zeal] of charite in þat þou woldist alle men wer
> sauyd, & so wolde I. . . . I haue many tymys seyd to þe þat many thowsand
> sowlys xal be sauyd thorw þi preyerys, & sum þat lyn in point of deth xal han
> grace thorw þi merytys & þi preyerys, for þi terys & þi preyerys arn ful swet
> & acceptabil to me" (78: 186).

In chapter 64 Christ tells Margery that there is so much sinfulness in the world that
he is tempted to destroy it – but he desists ' "for þe lofe" ', and because she weeps
every day and pleads with him to have mercy on his people (64: 158). Christ notes
that there are some who, as we have seen, ' "wil not . . . beleuyn þe goodnes þat
I werke in þe for hem" ', but goes on to promise, darkly, that there will be a time,
after death, when these people will be very glad to believe in her, and any who
don't will be punished (64: 159). Margery, like a good saint, asks mercy even for
them; however, intriguingly, the chapter ends with her words – Christ does not
reply to confirm whether or not her detractors will be punished. Perhaps an admon-
ition to those reading the text who may not be entirely convinced themselves?

By describing the ways in which Margery is able to intercede for devotees and
invoke the power of God both spiritually and physically during her lifetime the
Book lays the foundations for a posthumous cult of St Margery, when she will be
able to continue this work without being bound either spatially or temporally.
This is also anticipated in the words of Christ:

> "& so schal I ben worschepyd in erth for þi lofe, dowtyr, for I wyl haue þe grace
> þat I haue shewyd to þe in erth knowyn to þe worlde þat þe pepil may won-
> deryn in my goodnes & meruylyn of my gret goodnes þat I haue schewyd to
> þe þat hast ben synful" (84: 206).

This is one of four occasions on which Christ tells Margery that the whole world
will know of her, and wonder at her, thus anticipating a widespread devotion to

her.[19] Indeed, even within her lifetime there are suggestions that she had a reputation of holiness, for example when a native of Boston states that in his town she is known to be ' "an holy woman & a blissid woman" ' (46: 112) and when people in Rome welcome her 'for hir perfeccyon & hir holynes' (31: 78). These are consonant with the duke of Bedford's man identifying her as a future saint, quoted at the outset. By imitating various hagiographic models, the *Book* establishes that Margery's sainthood derives, in part, from the holiness of her life. But its descriptions of Margery's intercessions and miracles are not mere incidental details or corroborative evidence; they are a crucial aspect of her performance of sanctity. Because in order to generate a cult to her in late medieval England, miracles, not a reputation for holy living, would be the decisive factor, as will be seen.

> . . . *Honoure Theyse Glorious Seyntes þat haue Laboured in this Countrey for þe Helthe of þe People.*[20]

Let us now consider the circumstances of saints and saint making in later medieval England to suggest why Margery Kempe was presented as a saint. A key aspect of this which has received comparatively little attention is that the fifteenth century in particular saw a rise of interest in the lives and cults of native English saints. I have argued elsewhere that this development owes much to conceptions of such saints as representatives of English national identity and focuses on English pride.[21] One obvious example of this phenomenon is the establishment of St George as patron of England; another is Henry V's attribution of his victory at Agincourt to the intercession of saints John of Bridlington and John of Beverley.[22] We know that the cults of native saints were also very popular; the Italian visitor who recorded his impressions in around 1500 mentions that the tombs of English saints were very splendid, and documentary records of the shrines of saints such as Edmund of East Anglia and Ætheldreda bear this out.[23]

It is possible that, in this environment of renewed interest in English saints, combined with an interest in new forms of religiosity from the Continent, *The Book of Margery Kempe* constitutes, in part, an attempt to introduce a new kind of saint's cult to medieval England. André Vauchez has established that there were marked differences between northern and southern European countries with respect to the canonised saints which they produced, and the other cults which

---

[19] See also 29: 73, quoted at the beginning of the section; 56: 138–9; 63: 156.
[20] *The Kalendre of the Newe Legende of Englande*, ed. Manfred Görlach (Heidelberg, 1994), pp. 45–6.
[21] Katherine J. Lewis, 'Anglo-Saxon Saints' Lives, History and National Identity in Late Medieval England', in Helen Brocklehurst and Robert Phillips, eds, *History, Nationhood and the Question of Britain* (Houndmills, 2003), pp. 160–70.
[22] Jonathan Bengston, 'St George and the Form of English Nationalism', *Journal of Medieval and Early Modern Studies* 27 (1997), pp. 317–40; David Hugh Farmer, *The Oxford Dictionary of Saints* (second edition; Oxford and New York, 1987), p. 231.
[23] *A Relation, or Rather a True Account of the Island of England; About the Year 1500*, trans. Charlotte Augusta Sneyd, Camden Society, 1 series 37 (1847), pp. 29–30. The *Book* does not mention any local East Anglian saints such as Edmund.

they followed.[24] The Mediterranean countries, especially Italy, showed a particular preference for the cults of lay saints who had led exemplary lives of charity, labour and asceticism.[25] An increasing number of these saints were female in the later Middle Ages, and the mendicant orders, especially the Dominicans, were closely involved in their promotion. A close comparison to Margery from among their ranks is provided by Frances of Rome for instance.[26] The growth in numbers of female holy women on the continent is linked to the rise of affective piety, visionary literature and the rehabilitation of the lay religious life, and, as was noted at the outset, this brand of sanctity clearly provides an important model for Margery.[27] So, perhaps the *Book* was intended to create a saint who tapped into contemporary interest in these sorts of women, but, given the concurrent interest in home-grown saints, one who also had the attraction of being English into the bargain. In attempting to have Margery recognised as a saint the *Book* faced an uphill struggle however, for it is remarkable that, since Anglo-Saxon times, no medieval English woman had been the focus of any sizeable cult that has left its mark in documentary sources. The exemplars of specifically English sanctity were all royal abbesses and nuns such as Ætheldreda, Frideswide, Werburga and Withburga (who had a particular East Anglian connection). Apart from Christina of Markyate in the twelfth century and Margaret and Alice, the sisters of St Edmund of Abingdon, in the thirteenth, later nuns, anchoresses and other holy women do not seem to have enjoyed a conspicuous reputation of sanctity, whether in life or after death. As we shall see, the general picture of English saints post-Conquest, both in terms of cults recognised by the papacy, and others which were not, is almost entirely male. And this becomes even more marked in the later medieval period.[28]

Eleven English saints were canonised between 1161 and 1457; all male, and all ecclesiastics, largely bishops or archbishops.[29] Two of these are mentioned in the *Book*: William of York (canonised in 1226, 51: 122) and John of Bridlington (canonised in 1401 – Margery refers to him as being ' "now canonysed" ', 52: 125). Other candidates were put forward to the papal curia for canonisation but they too were all high-status men.[30] Two of these were high status laymen: Thomas of Lancaster and Edward II, testament to the fact that fourteenth- and fifteenth-century England was particularly interested in high-status martyr-saints. Cults of varying size also grew up around Simon Sudbury (murdered by the rebels in 1381), Archbishop Richard Scrope, Henry VI and even an embryonic one around

---

[24] André Vauchez, *Sainthood in the Later Middle Ages*, trans. Jean Birrell (Cambridge, 1997), pp. 135, 155.

[25] Ibid., pp. 207–18.

[26] See P. H. Cullum's essay above pp. 189–90.

[27] Much has been written on the rise of female sanctity; see for example Donald Weinstein and Rudolph M. Bell, *Saints and Society: The Two Worlds of Western Christendom 1000–1700* (Chicago and London, 1982), esp. pp. 220–38. This book also contains useful tables comparing numbers and types of male and female canonised saints, e.g. pp. 221–2.

[28] With thanks to Diana Webb for confirming this point and for general discussion of the issue.

[29] Margaret of Scotland was the only woman in the British Isles to be canonised (in 1249) before Margaret Clitheroe, Margaret Ward and Anne Line (the Elizabethan martyrs) in 1970.

[30] Diana Webb, *Pilgrimage in Medieval England* (London and New York, 2000), p. 64.

Henry's son Edward.[31] This brand of political martyr-saint is exclusively male, as is another sort of saint who was particularly popular in England: the martyred child, for example William of Norwich (fig. 6), Little St Hugh of Lincoln and Robert of Bury. Diana Webb has traced the cults (generally of small scale) which grew up around a variety of other people who died violently; again, all male.[32] These are lay saints, but of a very different kind to the continental model, for perceptions of their sanctity had very little or nothing to do with their manner of life and everything to do with their violent manner of death, which was reinterpreted as martyrdom. Vauchez suggests that the popularity of these sorts of saints in England as opposed to the kinds of lay saints who were popular on the continent may be linked to it being a much less urbanised country. Consequently the friars had less influence on perceptions of sanctity, meaning that they were less able to disseminate the sorts of cults with which they were associated on the continent, in particular the cult of the devout lay person.[33] Although this does not explain why all of the identified English martyrs in question seem to have been male.

The other very popular kind of saint in England in this period was male by definition: the holy and miracle-working parish priest.[34] The most prominent of these was John Schorne, parish priest of North Marston.[35] He died in 1313 and a cult developed at his tomb, as surviving pilgrim badges demonstrate. A clear indication of his popularity comes in 1478 when his shrine was moved (with papal permission) to the newly built chapel of St George at Windsor, in order to stimulate pilgrimage and offerings.[36] Once Henry VI's body was also reburied in the chapel in 1483 Windsor was lucky enough to have the monopoly on what were probably the two most popular cults in fifteenth-century England; all the more popular for being new.[37] Another example of a cult developing around a parish priest is Richard Caister, who appears in the *Book* and acted as Margery's confessor and supporter in the last years of his life. He died in 1420 and a cult grew up around his tomb; there are surviving examples of pilgrim badges representing Caister and devotion to him seems to have been reasonably widespread.[38] The *Book* provides evidence of the nascent cult when Margery goes to give thanks at Caister's tomb for the recovery of her reading priest from illness (60: 47).

---

[31] Most scholarship on these figures and their cults stresses political motives in their veneration, e.g. Simon Walker, 'Political saints in later medieval England', in R. H. Britnell and A. J. Pollard, eds, *The McFarlane Legacy: Studies in Late Medieval Politics and Society* (Stroud, 1995), pp. 77–106. For an interpretation which stresses devotional motives instead see Webb, *Pilgrimage*, pp. 164–79. Anthony Goodman suggests that Margery may have venerated Scrope as well as St William at York, *World*, p. 136.

[32] Webb, *Pilgrimage*, pp. 154–63.

[33] Vauchez, *Sainthood*, p. 135.

[34] Webb, *Pilgrimage*, pp. 153–6.

[35] Brian Spencer, *Pilgrim Souvenirs and Secular Badges* (London, 1998), pp. 192–5.

[36] Ibid., p. 193.

[37] Ibid., pp. 189–92. See also J. W. McKenna, 'Piety and propaganda: the cult of King Henry VI', in Beryl Rowland, ed., *Chaucer and Middle English Studies in Honour of Rossell Hope Robbins* (London, 1974), pp. 72–88. Neither of these cults was papally recognised, but it makes little sense to describe either as 'unofficial' given the location of their shrines and the support they received from both high-ranking clerics and royalty.

[38] Spencer, *Pilgrim Souvenirs*, pp. 196–8.

Figure 6. The martyrdom of St William of Norwich, late fifteenth-century rood screen, Loddon church, Norfolk. William is shown strung up on a scaffold by Jews, one of whom cuts out his heart. Photograph taken by Katherine J. Lewis.

All of this suggests that although some people in medieval England were very interested in the visionary writings of continental holy women, they were not really interested in the cults of lay people whose claim to sanctity was their holy way of life. It is perhaps for this reason that the *Book* adopts a hybrid of saintly models in its presentation of Margery; making some use of the example of the continental holy woman, but also drawing on the paradigms of the virgin-martyr and penitent saints who had a proven track record in England of inspiring cults and devotion. Moreover, English people were particularly interested in holy bishops and clerics. Self-evidently Margery could not be included among their number, but she could at least receive the approval of a saintly priest (Richard Caister) and have her way of life approved by top-ranking ecclesiastics. Bridget of Sweden had been recently canonised but patriotic English people could be proud that, in Margery, they had a saint who Christ himself says enjoys even more intimacy with him than Bridget did (20: 47). The *Book* can therefore be seen as an extremely brave attempt to stimulate the first successful cult of an English woman since the Conquest. But those writing it would have been well aware of the patterns of saint making around them and consequently have known that, without posthumous miracles, any attempt to have Margery recognised as a saint in this context would be doomed to failure. We know, of course, that this attempt did fail; but the final question is why?

Bi the Prayer of Thes Seyntis Alle, / Iesu, haue Mercy Whan We to the Calle[39]

On one level we could say that Margery's attempt to become a saint obviously failed because she was not canonised. However, canonisation was not necessarily a prerequisite for an individual to become a saint. Technically canonisation does not create a saint, for only God can do that. Instead it publicly acknowledges that a person is saintly, and provides papal authorisation of the cult. Canonisation only became a regularised process from about the twelfth century onwards in any case, so most of the saints who lived before this period never went through it.[40] The papacy was concerned to control the mechanisms and politics of saint making for a variety of reasons, but chiefly to ensure that the 'right' sort of saints were being recognised and honoured. As the Middle Ages progressed the church became less keen on recognising the sanctity of individuals who had died a violent death and performed posthumous miracles, and much more determined to promote those who demonstrated different signs of sanctity through living a thoroughly spiritual and devout life. Miracles did remain extremely important to the canonisation process, but the papacy sought to downgrade them to proof not of the individual's sanctity per se, but of the physical range of their holy reputation.[41] The problem with this is that canonisation in itself couldn't necessarily guarantee that a saint or his/her cult would become popular. Cults could not be manufactured, or imposed without genuine devotional interest being present, and, as the examples

---

[39] From John Lydgate's prayer to saints Katherine, Margaret and Mary Magdalene, *The Minor Poems of John Lydgate: Part I*, ed. Henry Noble MacCracken, EETS extra series 107 (London, 1911), pp. 134–5 (p. 135).

[40] Vauchez, *Sainthood*, provides the most comprehensive account of the development of the process.

[41] Ibid., pp. 414–8, 531, 536–7.

drawn from medieval England illustrate, there could be rather a gulf between the sorts of saints which the papacy offered to the people, and the sorts of saints which the people themselves chose and created.[42]

This is not to say that canonisation held no importance, or that the texts of saints' lives were of no interest to devotees. The literate or those who, like Margery, could be read to, would have had access to written saints' lives, of which there are many surviving examples from fifteenth-century England, in both Latin and Middle English. Saints' lives could also be encountered as sermons; John Mirk's *Festial* provides an example of a very popular collection of short saints' lives in English which were explicitly intended for use by priests as sermons on feast days.[43] Saints' lives also existed in the form of visual narratives, such as wall paintings, stained glass and altarpieces too. But in terms of documentary evidence for saint making in later medieval England, neither canonisation nor saints' lives seem to be the crucial factor. Indeed, Anneke Mulder-Bakker puts the case that historians 'spend far too much time examining the life story for an explanation of a saint's popularity'.[44] As already noted, for medieval English people the decisive form of evidence that would convince them that an individual was a saint was not their life story at all, but rather some palpable demonstration of his or her intercession in the form of miracles, and, more particularly, in the form of healing miracles.[45] Most of the men discussed above who were perceived as saints were not canonised; the key to their identification as saintly was a shrine at which miracles were performed, often, but not always, preceded by a brutal and untimely death. It was the spread of miracle stories (generally by word of mouth) and the subsequent attraction of others to the shrine on hopeful pilgrimage which would stimulate growth of a cult around a person.[46] This is what I believe is being envisaged in Christ's promise to Margery that he will be worshipped through her in St Margaret's; the way in which ' "Many a man & woman xal seyn it is wel sene þat God lauyd hir wel" ' within this setting would be through the report of miracles at her tomb.

The dossier of miracles which Henry VI was believed to have performed at Windsor, alongside liturgical poems and prayers, and images of him alongside other saints on rood screens (fig. 7) provide ample evidence that he was both addressed and appealed to as a saint in the late fifteenth century, despite the fact that Tudor attempts to have him canonised came to nothing.[47] There is also

---

42 Cf. Andrew Brown, *Church and Society in England, 1000–1500* (Basingstoke and New York, 2003), p. 62.

43 *Mirk's Festial*, ed. Theodor Erbe, EETS extra series 96 (London, 1905).

44 Mulder-Bakker, 'Invention', p. 11.

45 Brown, *Church and Society*, pp. 79–80. Eamon Duffy argues very strongly that intercession was the most important aspect of saints' cults in late medieval England: *The Stripping of the Altars: Traditional Religion in England c.1400–c.1580* (New Haven and London, 1992), pp. 155–205.

46 Detailed explorations of this phenomenon are provided by Webb, *Pilgrimage* and Finucane, *Miracles and Pilgrims*.

47 *The Miracles of Henry VI*, eds, Ronald Knox and Shane Leslie (Cambridge, 1923) provides a translated selection. For a recent discussion of Henry's cult which emphasises its intercessory dimension see Leigh Ann Craig, 'Royalty, Virtue and Adversity: The Cult of King Henry VI', *Albion* 35 (2003): 187–209.

Figure 7. Henry VI, 1493 rood screen, Ludham church, Norfolk. Despite being uncanonised, Henry VI is here identified as a saint, both by his inclusion on the screen, and by his halo. Photograph taken by Katherine J. Lewis.

a hagiographical account of Henry VI's saintly life extant, written by a member of his spiritual entourage, John Blacman.[48] However, this life seems to have had nothing to do with the spread and popularity of Henry's cult (which began almost immediately after his death in 1471) and, indeed, the fact that there is no surviving record of any life of John Schorne was absolutely no hindrance to the popularity of his cult. Similarly Walstan of Bawburgh, with whose East Anglian cult Margery Kempe must have been familiar (although it is not mentioned in the *Book*) only gained a Middle English life in the early sixteenth century, as something of an afterthought to the popular cult which was well established at his shrine a century before this.[49] Conversely, other figures who did have a written life were not the focus of a posthumous cult of this nature after their deaths.[50]

Coming back to Margery Kempe, the point is that she or those involved in her *Book* may not have seen canonisation as an obvious goal because it was possible to achieve sanctity (in terms of being at the centre of a cult) without it. There are further considerations that would have rendered Margery's canonisation unlikely too; on a practical level it was a lengthy and expensive process which could involve political as well as religious considerations, and canonisation was actually becoming less common in the later Middle Ages too.[51] Besides, the *Book* is in English, and the *vitae* and miracle accounts associated with canonisations were always written in Latin, so it would need to be translated in any case. Moreover, despite the rising number of female saints in this period there were still far fewer canonised women than men, so it may not have been seen as a realistic possibility for Margery on those grounds either. In fact, there is evidence to suggest that, despite the canonisation of Bridget of Sweden, and the interest shown by many in female visionary literature, others were extremely suspicious of the identification of such women as saints.[52] Werner Williams-Krapp argues that the fourteenth and fifteenth centuries were a time of increasing intolerance for female mystics among certain theologians; famously Jean Gerson felt that the canonisation of Bridget was setting a dangerous precedent and it is notable that the only other female mystic to enjoy a substantial cult and canonisation in the period was Catherine of Siena (canonised in 1461).[53] Dorothea of Montau, for instance (to whom Margery is often compared) was only canonised in 1976 and in the fifteenth century remained a localised saint.[54] In addition, Bridget and

---

48 John Blacman, *Henry the Sixth*, ed. and trans. M. R. James (Cambridge, 1919).

49 Eamon Duffy, 'The Dynamics of Pilgrimage in Late Medieval England', in Colin Morris and Peter Roberts, eds, *Pilgrimage: The English Experience from Becket to Bunyan* (Cambridge, 2002), pp. 164–77.

50 Mulder-Bakker, p. 10. She notes that this is true of several of the later medieval female visionaries commonly identified as 'saints' because of their way of life, but who did not garner a posthumous cult of this nature.

51 Vauchez, *Sainthood*, 419.

52 On this point see also Sarah Salih above, p. 166.

53 Werner Williams-Krapp, 'Literary Genre and Degrees of Saintliness: The Perception of Holiness in Writings By and About Female Mystics', in Mulder-Bakker, *Invention of Saintliness*, pp. 206–18 (pp. 206–7); on the same point see also André Vauchez, 'The Reaction of the Church to Late-Medieval Mysticism and Prophecy', in *idem*, *The Laity in the Middle Ages: Religious Beliefs and Devotional Practices*, ed. and introduced by Daniel E. Bornstein, trans. Margaret J. Schneider (Notre Dame and London, 1993), pp. 243–54.

54 Williams-Krapp, 'Literary Genre', p. 212.

Catherine were only able to achieve canonisation because their causes were supported by powerful sponsors.

Although the writings of Bridget and Catherine and accounts of their lives were popular in late medieval England it is important to note that there is much less evidence for cultic devotion to them. Their writings were valued for the spiritual insights which they contained and the devotional musings which they could inspire, but this would not be enough to make either woman a saint in the eyes of some. Besides, it is debatable to what extent mystical writings such as these percolated down to the parish level at which many saints' cults actually operated.[55] Moreover, Williams-Krapp argues that the lives of female mystics do not contain miracles, and only rarely recount miracles which the mystic performed for others; the holiness of mystics was seen instead to derive largely from their communication with God, and this was problematic because of its intangible nature.[56] The question of whether visions came from God or the Devil was an extremely vexed one, as the *Book* demonstrates, so to assign sainthood to an individual on those grounds alone was seen as problematic. It is significant that, although Bridget was canonised, the grounds for this was her virtuous way of life, supported by some documented miracles, *not* her visionary experiences and writings.[57] On a more prosaic level, having audiences with Christ was all very well, but what the average devotee in late medieval England wanted to know of the putative saint was whether she or he could mend damaged limbs, cure blindness, banish insanity or restore apparently dead children to life, so they were perhaps unsure of purely visionary figures on this account too. Williams-Krapp's contention that the lives of female mystics do not contain miracles makes the explicitly miraculous episodes in Margery Kempe's life all the more unusual and significant. I would argue that this demonstrates an attempt to tailor the figure of the continental female visionary for an English audience who were more accustomed to using the miraculous as a standard by which to judge and make saints. Margery has visions of Christ, but she can also intercede with him for the protection and healing of others.

Yet, despite this tailoring, and the effort to present her as a miracle worker, Margery still did not come to be seen as a saint. Is it perhaps purely a question of gender? That medieval English people were more interested in male saints than female ones? Patently not for while they may not have been particularly interested in the cults of women who lived more recently, the cults of some of the universal female saints, particularly the virgin-martyrs, were hugely popular in England in this period. There are more Middle English lives of St Katherine and more surviving representations of her in church wall paintings than there are of any other saint for example. It could be argued that the popularity of saints such

---

[55] Christine Peters, *Patterns of Piety: Women, Gender and Religion in Late Medieval and Reformation England* (Cambridge, 2003), p. 88.

[56] Williams-Krapp, 'Literary Genre', pp. 210–1.

[57] Farmer, *Dictionary of Saints*, p. 62; this stands in opposition to Kathleen Ashley's claim that visions were 'the requisite sign of sanctity' in the fourteenth and fifteenth centuries: 'Historicizing Margery: *The Book of Margery Kempe* as Social Text', *Journal of Medieval and Early Modern Studies* 28 (1998): 371–88 (387, n. 34).

as Katherine, Margaret, Mary Magdalene and, perhaps most significantly, the Virgin Mary, means that the gender imbalance we perceive between the numbers of men and women created as saints in the Middle Ages was not held to exist in the same way by contemporaries.[58] The status of these women as saints was unequivocal in a way that the sanctity even of Bridget of Sweden was not, and this may be why they are referred to in the *Book* so much more frequently than the female visionaries who may seem to share more in common with Margery's experiences. The universal female saints provide much better character references for Margery than any recent saint could.

But this is also a problem for Margery and the *Book*, for perhaps another reason why it did not succeed in having her recognised as a saint was because English people were already well supplied with female saints who could work miracles for them.[59] And crucially, the cults of some of the most important and powerful of these had been localised through particular images or relics, and some of them had even been appropriated as native saints, fitting in with the patriotic strand to English devotions discussed above.[60] This point is illustrated by Southwell Minster MS 7, a copy of Mirk's *Festial* which contains as an appendix seven additional saints' lives taken from the early fifteenth-century translation of the *Legenda Aurea* known as the *Gilte Legende*.[61] As a group, these lives constitute something of a mini Anglo-British legendary supplementing the *Festial* (which, in this copy, only contains two native saints: Thomas Becket and Winifred). There are four Anglo-Saxon saints: Oswald the Bishop, Dunstan, Edmund of East Anglia and Edward the Martyr, as well as a later English saint, Edmund of Abingdon. There are also the lives of three legendary virgin-martyrs: Ursula, Katherine and Faith. The life of St Katherine is already in the *Festial*, but the scribe has chosen to include a longer version in the appendix, which tells the story of her genealogy, upbringing and mystical marriage to Christ, before going on to the more familiar events of her martyrdom. For our purposes it is significant that by this period St Katherine had been appropriated as 'British', because of her relationship to the Emperor Constantine (her genealogy establishes Constantine as her half-uncle).[62] Similarly, the life of St Ursula describes her as being the daughter of the king of Britain, and she is espoused to the son of the king of England – and she too was understood as being 'British' in later medieval England.[63] However, to be 'British' in this period was to be English as the subsuming of 'Britain' into 'England' – 'British' into 'English' – was a common formulation, also occurring

---

58 A point also made by Mulder-Bakker, 'Invention', p. 16.

59 For a discussion of the intercessory appeal of these saints see Eamon Duffy, 'Holy Maydens, Holy Wyfes: The Cult of Women Saints in Fifteenth and Sixteenth Century England', *Studies in Church History* 23 (1990): 175–96.

60 Nancy Bradley Warren has pointed out the important ways in which holy women and their revelations were also used to create political capital and to support propaganda by both Lancastrians and Yorkists in fifteenth-century England: *Spiritual Economies: Female Monasticism in Later Medieval England* (Philadelphia, 2001), pp. 111–33.

61 I am grateful to Laurence Craik, the librarian at Southwell Minster, for permission to consult this manuscript. For discussion of the *Gilte Legende* see Manfred Görlach, *Studies in Middle English Saints' Legends* (Tübingen, 1998).

62 Lewis, *Cult of St Katherine*, pp. 45–6, 74–5.

63 Ibid., pp. 74–5.

in Arthurian literature.[64] So, although Katherine and Ursula lived and died before 'England' even existed, the fact of their being British means that they, like the male saints alongside whom they appear here, are also English, or at the very least they somehow 'belong' to England.[65] The same was presumably also felt to be true of Faith, in order to make sense of her appearance here.[66] The scribe's addition of this group of lives certainly suggests that he is responding to contemporary interest in native saints alongside universal ones.

The fact that the scribe of the Southwell Minster manuscript did not include the lives of any 'real' (i.e. non-legendary) or any more recent British/English female saints serves to illustrate the point made above about the lack of such figures; it was a much better option to include a universally venerated figure such as Katherine as a sort-of-English female saint. Perhaps there was also a devotional and emotional need to have a purchase on female saints of stature that were somehow 'one of us'. It may be that the *Book* and its presentation of Margery was therefore intended to plug a perceived gap in female English sanctity by providing a saint who was Katherine, Bridget, Mary Magdalene and others all rolled into one – thus providing something for everyone. But equally, if St Katherine and St Ursula could be thought of as part of England then perhaps there was no gap for the *Book* to fill after all, so no need for a St Margery.

In the end the *Book* did achieve part of its purpose, for the annotations in its manuscript and the history of the printed extracts from Margery's book indicate that she did at least enjoy some posthumous reputation as a visionary.[67] The *Book* does everything it possibly can to present Margery as a saint, both in terms of her way of life and her intercessory powers. But the *Book* alone (and in its vernacular form) was never going to gain her more general recognition as a saint, no matter how well written it was, and I suspect that both Margery and her scribe knew this. Margery could become a saint without canonisation, but holiness in life simply wasn't enough to achieve sanctity in late medieval England. As with everything else in Margery's life there is no evidence outside of the *Book* to corroborate what she or it may or may not have hoped to achieve in this respect. But for once that silence speaks volumes, for there is absolutely no record of any cult to her memory; no shrine in St Margaret's (despite Christ's promises) and no posthumous miracles. Margery did her very best, but without these she could never hope to be recognised and venerated as a saint in late medieval England.

---

[64] This point is explored at length by Patricia Clare Ingham, *Sovereign Fantasies: Arthurian Romances and the Making of Britain* (Philadelphia, 2001).

[65] The shrine of the Virgin at Walsingham, and the representation of her house which it contained, provides a further example of the means by which a universally popular cult could be locally and nationally appropriated.

[66] Although admittedly the life of St Faith doesn't contain any explicit links to Britain as the lives of Katherine and Ursula do.

[67] As discussed by Allyson Foster in this volume.

12

Afterword

JOHN H. ARNOLD AND KATHERINE J. LEWIS

This is not, by any means, the last word: who would attempt to claim such a thing when dealing with Margery Kempe? But it seems useful to look back over the collection of essays gathered here, to draw out a few threads and themes that have struck us as editors; and to point to some issues and directions that continue to present themselves in the study of this extraordinary text. We draw upon our contributors in this conclusion, but do not claim to speak for them. We have sole responsibility for the thoughts and concerns presented here, which we have extrapolated both from the preceding analyses of the *Book* and its settings, and from our own wider reading of the text and understanding of its representations.

All of the essays in this volume *historicise* Margery. This is perhaps unsurprising, in a book edited, as was stated at the outset, by two historians. It is a point, however, that we would like to emphasise, and to gloss a little. There is plenty of comment contained herein on Kempe (or Kempe-and-scribe, or scribe-via-Kempe, and so forth) as author of the *Book*. All of the contributors are aware that we deal with a text, not a mirror which directly and uncomplicatedly reproduces late fourteenth- and early fifteenth-century England to our gaze. Nonetheless, we have shared a sense of the wider world surrounding that text, and the complex ways in which it reflects, refracts, illumines and (of course) conceals elements of its setting. Historicising Margery, as we see it, is not a means of silencing her astonishing voice by dissipating it into a normalised landscape, as some have argued, by way of explaining a conscious decision *not* to historicise her. On the contrary we see this approach as a way of examining simultaneously the forces surrounding the constitution of the *Book*, the import and meaning of the events it purports to describe, and the wider social, cultural and political currents through which Margery cut a swathe. Therefore, to make a larger claim that may not sit well with some literary critics, we would argue that historicising Margery provides a *better* reading of the *Book*. Our claim is, for example, that our understanding of Margery's tactics in her encounters with authority is deepened having read Kate Parker's evocation of the socio-political milieu in which she grew up; or that the degree to which we read the *Book* as 'autobiography' is better informed after Kim Phillips's examination of life cycle; or that interpreting Margery's particular brand of somatic and post-somatic experiences is enriched by Sarah Salih's analysis of bodily piety and asceticism. In each of these accounts Margery does not stand utterly alone, nor is she automatically assumed to be an extraordinary 'creature' with reference to every aspect of her conduct or experiences.

There are many reasons why she has so often been seen not just as our heroine, but our *unique* heroine. As Barry Windeatt shows, these range from the uncommon nature of the source itself – the memoirs of a little old lady, as they were initially seen – to the rich character of Margery's voice, to the insistent claims that the *Book* makes for Margery's difference from her fellows and for the unprecedented nature of her relationship with Christ. But we should not make the mistake of assuming that, because the *Book* itself is a unique survival from late medieval England, it follows that all that Margery Kempe said and did (both as protagonist and putative author) is also necessarily singular. Indeed, within the *Book* William Southfield, the Carmelite friar, makes explicit reference to other 'good creatures' who are like her, and it has been pointed out before that Margery's attempted way of life was likely something that many others also tried to lead, albeit none of them have left behind a book detailing their experience of this.

There are valid reasons, particularly in opposition to the rather patronising reactions her text initially engendered, for treating the claim to originality, authenticity and uniqueness with great sympathy. It is in this respect that Margery is sometimes to be found functioning as a symbol or representative of various marginal positions and political declarations. But we should be wary also of what such readings occlude or displace. For instance, within the *Book*, we may develop curiosity (some of which is explored in this collection) about those characters beyond the central figure: Margery's husband John, so often a silent presence; her travelling companions upon her pilgrimage adventures; even the apparently nasty and repressive secular officials who harassed her in England, for one can still be curious about what is represented as nasty and repressive. Indeed, such curiosity may save one from making too many assumptions about the extent of power and control, as John Arnold's essay here explores. Beyond the pages of the *Book*, after many years of developments in social history, the dismissive lament that medieval 'old ladies did not write their reminiscences' no longer falls into a silent vacuum. There are few other female memoirs, it is true, but historians have grown far more adept at reading recalcitrant sources such as court records, petitions, manor court rolls and so on for female voices and evidence of female experiences. Not to relate Kempe's *Book* to these other voices seems to us to constitute a failure of the historical project itself. Margery Kempe need not be *subsumed* by such a relation – indeed, it is quite hard to imagine such a thing – but equally these other voices should not be forgotten or silenced by Kempe's high visibility and audibility.

Margery's attitudes and thoughts and the conversations with Christ which provide the rationale for the *Book*'s creation, are born of the cultural milieu she inhabited. Even if, and sometimes especially when, these are expressed in reaction against that milieu they can nonetheless tell us something more about the currents of cultural discourse in the period. Concomitant to this is the degree to which Margery Kempe's particular social position needs to be considered and incorporated into future analyses of the *Book*. We have always known her to be the daughter of someone who was five times mayor of Lynn, because she makes a point of telling us so. What has perhaps been less clear until now is really quite how high up the social scale this places her. As Parker makes clear in her essay, in the fifteenth century Lynn was very far indeed from the rather small and isolated town it is today. The civic oligarchy in medieval Lynn were closely connected by trade to other parts of England, and to Europe as well. Moreover, as Parker demonstrates, these men (and John Brunham in particular) were players on the stage of national as well as local politics. This was Margery's background, and it is one of which she makes us acutely aware at various stages in the text.

Several points follow from this. One is that we must think very hard about what we mean if we describe Kempe as 'marginal'. Another is that we must recognise that Kempe's ability to travel, and particularly to travel abroad; her interest in continental models of mystical comportment; her ability to read; her willingness to debate (to a degree) with bishops and civic officials; all of these elements that contribute to the wonder and excitement of the *Book* are grounded not purely in Margery's individual emotional and interior resources, but also upon the economic and cultural resources that come from social status. The very mechanisms of her particular piety – the 'penances' that she undergoes, the opprobrium she thus occasions – only make sense, only *work* as cultural acts, by dint of her elite social position. Women from much lower social backgrounds would not occasion comment in the same way when giving aid to a lowly old lady in Rome, nor be asked to perform this role as a penance. They would also likely not have gained the same sense of penance from caring bodily for an aged husband, nor quite definitely would they have got into trouble for advising aristocratic ladies to leave their husbands – as they would simply never have had that chance. They were also, we would argue, less likely to find the strength, the cultural resources, to act publicly in the many ways that Margery did; to 'perform', as Clare Sponsler demonstrates, in an ongoing work of public theatre. This is not to deny Kempe the virtues of female empowerment or to denigrate the importance of hearing such a strong female voice from a strongly misogynist era. But it is to insist upon the importance of recognising the social and political framework that facilitated this voice; and it is to note that, in this respect, Margery is not Everywoman.

Of course in a different way one of the driving purposes of the *Book* is precisely to emphasise that Margery is not representative but exceptional. Her identity is fashioned in ways that draw on established models of female piety and sanctity but which do so in order to underline her uniquely privileged access to Christ, for even Bridget of Sweden (we are very pointedly told) did not see or experience him as Margery did. Jacqueline Jenkins's, Diane Watt's and Sponsler's essays all explore various dimensions of this which point to the conclusion that while there are similarities between Margery and women such as Bridget, Angela of Foligno, Dorothea of Montau and the universal saints such as Mary Magdalene, Katherine of Alexandria and the Virgin Mary, her imitation of them is not slavish and her own claims to sanctity are founded on a patchwork derived from aspects of all of these rather than deriving essentially from any one. Indeed, Allyson Foster's comparison of the writings of Catherine of Siena and Margery Kempe shows that, while working together as companion pieces in a devotional anthology, there are also some important differences in emphasis between them. Moreover, as Sarah Salih and P. H. Cullum show, we need to beware of imposing the so-called continental model of female piety upon

Margery and making her experiences fit seamlessly with these, rather than noticing the ways in which her pious practices diverge from them to change and develop throughout the *Book*. For the end result that it produces arguably places much more of a premium on contemplative forms of piety than on bodily ones, and this is not something that has generally been acknowledged. Related to this is the observation that it is very important to recognise and explore the similar religious and cultural trends which linked England (and particularly East Anglia) to the continent, but it is equally important to remember that these similarities may not apply equally to all aspects of life, nor to all groups within society. As Katherine Lewis shows, there were some marked differences between the sorts of people identified as saints in England, as opposed to those on the continent; moreover, there is the whole question of whether East Anglia's rich tradition of religious representation and re-enactment should be seen as illustrative of what we have lost from elsewhere in England, or something that, even in the later Middle Ages, was regionally distinct. Answers to this question could also have ramifications for our understanding of Margery's experiences in the various parts of England which she visited.

Issues of gender have played an extremely important role in many analyses of the *Book*. For instance, there is much evidence to suggest that the writings of holy women were of great interest to a female audience, a point that informs both Jenkins's account of the immediate literate context for the *Book* and Foster's exploration of its early modern reception. Indeed, Margery has often (although certainly not universally) been claimed as a representative of feminism or a proto-feminist icon and her book therefore seen as a text of particular relevance to female readers, both then and now. However, it is less often noted that the only direct evidence we have for a readership of Margery's *Book* in the fifteenth and sixteenth centuries is provided by the male readers and annotators of Mount Grace. This fact in itself problematises readings of the *Book* which argue that it speaks chiefly, even solely, to the experiences of women. There are undoubtedly instances in which Margery's gender plays a key part in the problems she faces at certain points in the text. Indeed, her clashes with male authority figures are often presented as evidence for her status as a woman striving to resist the oppressive control of men and particularly of clerics. However, this is to ignore the obvious point that she receives far more approval than opprobrium from clerical figures within the *Book*, and is evidently very keen to receive it, which (as Arnold notes) undercuts identification of her as an embodiment of radical dissent. The *Book* presents a more complex picture of her relationship with clerics than a straightforward male v. female confrontational model can allow for and in this respect Isabel Davis's application of theories of masculinity to the text helps us to gain a much more nuanced sense of the way in which gender operates as both ideology and practice within it. Just as Margery cannot necessarily 'stand in' for all medieval women, so the men whom she encounters are not all identical ciphers but embody various roles and occupy different places within a patriarchal gender hierarchy.

For example, could the clerics whom Margery criticises for their wordly conduct and lascivious lifestyle be linked to the men who emerge from other sources, struggling to settle into a social identity of masculinity which did not, or rather should not, include the traditional male markers of fornication and fighting? Moreover, despite frequent identification of Margery's devotional and somatic experiences as intrinsically female/feminine, it should also be noted that the only characters within the *Book* who share these experiences are men: the scribe who is overtaken with tears as proof that hers are holy, and the layman Thomas Marchale, who also finds himself weeping for hours and falling down in the fields moved by devotional compunction. In chapters 18 and 19 there is a widow from Lynn who apparently wants to share Margery's experiences, but she receives a rather curt letter from Margery telling her that she will never have the same grace, which is hardly encouragement. Perhaps Margery simply didn't want the competition. The *Book* therefore provides us with the opportunity to rethink issues of gender and devotion. Did the monks observing that Richard Methley acted in the same way as Margery Kempe therefore perceive that he was acting in a feminine way? Or that Margery was acting in a masculine one? (Especially as she actually eschews the bodily practices so often identified as feminine, as Salih and Cullum note.) Or did the conduct of both people make them similar in allowing them to transcend a simple gender binary? These are questions that beg further analysis in relation to wider patterns of devotional behaviour and the ways in which both women and men identified and appropriated models. While much scholarship has been devoted to issues of gender and devotion with respect to medieval women (both lay and religious), the same certainly cannot be said with respect to men.

The *Book* has a difficult job to perform in its presentation of Margery as conventional and comprehensible yet exceptional and otherworldly at the same time. This is the problem faced by any account of a saint's life: how can she be both part of a paradigm and yet depart from it too? A similar conundrum faces those who read and rewrite Margery Kempe now. Is she one among many? Does she stand on her own? Or do the answers to such questions depend on which aspect of her presentation or experience we choose to prioritise and the methods that we use in order to analyse these? We have made our own priorities and methods clear and leave it up to others to decide for themselves how best to approach this captivating and challenging woman.

Bibliography

Manuscripts

British Library Additional MS 27376.
British Library Cotton MS Julius D.vii.
British Library MS Royal 17 D.v.
Corporation of London Record Office, Miscellaneous MSS 1863.
King's Lynn Corporation Archives:
  Series 6 no. 3.
  Series 10 nos 2 & 6.
  Series 39 nos 36, 43, 45–6, 48.
Lambeth Palace Library MS 472.
Norfolk Record Office, Hare MSS 2091.
Public Record Office E 210/1176.
Public Record Office KB 27/580.
Southwell Minster MS 7.
Westminster Abbey Muniments 5966.

Editions of The Book of Margery Kempe

The Book of Margery Kempe, ed. S. B. Leech, EETS original series 212 (London, 1940).
Lynn Staley, ed., *The Book of Margery Kempe*, TEAMS Medieval Institute Publications (Kalamazoo, MI, 1996).
Barry Windeatt, ed., *The Book of Margery Kempe*, Longmans Annotated Texts (Harlow, 2000).
Lynn Staley, ed., *The Book of Margery Kempe*, Norton Critical Editions (New York, 2001).

Translations of The Book of Margery Kempe

The Book of Margery Kempe 1436, A Modern Version, ed. and trans. W. Butler-Bowdon (London, 1936).
The Book of Margery Kempe, abridged trans. Liz Herbert McAvoy (Cambridge, 2003).
The Book of Margery Kempe, trans. Barry Windeatt (Harmondsworth, 1985).

General Primary Works

Ancrene Wisse: Guide for Anchoresses, trans. Hugh White (Harmondsworth, 1993).
Aquinas, St Thomas, *Summa Theologiæ*, ed. and trans. Thomas Gilby, 60 vols (Blackfriars, 1964).
St Augustine, *Confessions*, trans. R. S. Pine-Coffin (Harmondsworth, 1961).

Blacman, John, *Henry the Sixth*, ed. and trans. M. R. James (Cambridge, 1919).

Bokenham, Osbern, *Legendys of Hooly Wummen*, ed. Mary Serjeantson, EETS original series 206 (London, 1938).

The Book of Vices and Virtues, ed. W. Nelson Francis, EETS original series 217 (London, 1942).

Borough Customs, ed. Mary Bateson, 2 vols, Selden Society 18, 21 (London, 1904–6).

Brown, Carleton, ed., *English Lyrics of the XIIIth Century* (Oxford, 1932).

Calendar of Close Rolls.

Calendar of Inquisition Miscellaneous.

Calendar of Patent Rolls.

Catherine of Siena, *The Orcherd of Syon*, ed. P. Hodgson and G. M. Liegey, EETS original series 258 (London, 1966).

The Cell of Self-Knowledge: Seven Early English Mystical Treatises Printed by Henry Pepwell in 1521, ed. Edmund G. Gardner (orig. pub. 1910, this ed., New York, 1966).

The Cell of Self-Knowledge, ed. John Griffiths (New York, 1981).

Chaucer, Geoffrey, *The Riverside Chaucer*, ed. Larry D. Benson et al., 3rd edn (Oxford, 1987).

The Cloud of Unknowing and the Book of Privy Counselling, ed. Phyllis Hodgson, EETS original series 218 (London, 1944).

The Cloud of Unknowing and Related Treatises on Contemplative Prayer, ed. Phyllis Hodgson (Salzburg, 1982).

Cronica Monasterii St Albani, ed. H. T. Riley (Rolls Series, London, 1886).

Deonise Hid Diuinite, and Other Treatises on Contemplative Prayer Related to The Cloud of Unknowing, ed. Phyllis Hodgson, EETS original series 231 (London, 1955).

Emden, A. B., *A Biographical Register of the University of Oxford to A.D. 1500* (Oxford, 1957).

English Gilds, ed. J. and L. T. S. Toulmin Smith, EETS original series 40 (London, 1870).

English Historical Documents 1327–1485, ed. A. R. Myers (London, 1969).

Fasciculus Morum, ed. S. Wenzel (Philadelphia, 1989).

Foxe, John, *Acts and Monuments*, ed. J. Pratt, 8 vols, 4th edn (London, 1877), 3.

Gerson, Jean, 'On Distinguishing True from False Revelations', *Early Works*, trans. Brian Patrick McGuire (New York, 1998).

The Good Wife Taught her Daughter, The Good Wyfe wold a Pylgremage, The Thewis of Gud Women, ed. Tauno F. Mustanoja, Annales Academiae Scientarum Fennicae B 61/2 (Helsinki, 1948).

The Great Chronicle of London, eds A. H. Thomas and I. D. Thornley (1938; repr., Gloucester, 1983).

Greene, Richard Leighton, ed., *The Early English Carols*, 2nd edn (Oxford, 1977).

Heresy Trials in the Diocese of Norwich, 1428–31, ed. Norman P. Tanner (London, 1977).

Hilton, Walter, *The Ladder of Perfection*, trans. Leo Sherley-Price (Harmondsworth, 1988).

——, *The Scale of Perfection*, ed. Thomas H. Bestul (Kalamazoo, 2000).

Historical Manuscripts Commission Report XI, Appx. iii.

Hoccleve, Thomas, *Hoccleve's Works: The Minor Poems*, ed. F. J. Furnivall and I. Gollancz, rev. J. Mitchell and A. I. Doyle, EETS extra series 61and 73 (Oxford, 1970).

A. D. Hope: Selected Poems, ed. Ruth Morse (Manchester, 1986).

Horstmann, C., ed., 'Prosalegenden: Die legenden des ms. Douce 114', *Anglia* 8 (1885): 103–96.

Idley, Peter, *Instructions to His Son*, ed. Charlotte d'Evelyn (London, 1935).

The Kalendre of the Newe Legende of Englande, ed. Manfred Görlach (Heidelberg, 1994).

Langland, William, *The Visions of Piers Plowman: A Complete Edition of the B-Text*, ed. A. V. C. Schmidt (London and Melbourne, 1987).

——, *Piers Plowman*, trans. A. V. C. Schmidt (Oxford etc, 1992).

The Late Medieval Religious Plays of Bodleian MSS Digby 133 and e Museo 160, ed. Donald C. Baker, John L. Murphy and Louis B. Hall, Jr., EETS original series 283 (Oxford, 1982).

The Liber Celestis of St Bridget of Sweden, ed. Roger Ellis, EETS original series 291 (Oxford, 1987), vol. 1.

The Life of Saint Birgitta, ed. Birger Gregersson and Thomas Gascoigne, trans. Julia Bolton Holloway (Toronto, 1991).

Love, Nicholas, *Mirror of the Blessed Life of Jesus Christ*, ed. Michael G. Sargent (New York, 1992).

The Minor Poems of John Lydgate: Part I, ed. Henry Noble MacCracken, EETS extra series 107 (London, 1911).

The Macro Plays: The Castle of Perseverance, Wisdom, Mankind, ed. Mark Eccles, EETS original series 262 (Oxford, 1969).

Marienwerder, Johannes von, *The Life of Dorothea von Montau, a Fourteenth-Century Recluse*, trans. Ute Stargardt (Lewiston, 1997).

Middle English Dictionary, ed. H. Kurath *et al.* (Ann Arbour, 1956–2001).

The Miracles of Henry VI, ed. Ronald Knox and Shane Leslie (Cambridge, 1923).

Mirk's Festial, ed. Theodor Erbe, EETS extra series 96 (London, 1905).

Norwich Consistory Court Depositions, ed. E. D. Stone and B. Cozens-Hardy, Norwich Record Society 10 (1938).

North Country Wills, ed. J. W. Clay, Surtees Society 116 (Durham, 1908).

Porete, Margaret, *The Mirror of Simple Souls*, trans. Edmund Colledge, J. C. Marler and Judith Grant (Notre Dame, 1999).

On the Properties of Things: John Trevisa's Translation of Bartholomaeus Anglicus De Proprietatibus Rerum; a Critical Text, ed. M. C. Seymour, 3 vols (Oxford, 1975–88).

Proverbs, Sentences, and Proverbial Phrases from English Writers mainly before 1500, ed. B. J. Whiting (Cambridge, MA, 1968).

Die Recesse und andere Akten der Hansetage von 1256–1430, ed. K. Koppmann, 8 vols (Leipzig, 1870–97).

The Red Register of Lynn, ed. H. Ingleby, 2 vols (King's Lynn, 1919–22), 2.

Register of Nicholas Bubwith, bishop of Bath and Wells 1407–1424, ed. T. S. Holmes, 2 vols, Somerset Record Society 29 and 30 (1914).

Register of Bishop Philip Repingdon, 1405–1419, ed. Margaret Archer, 3 vols, Lincoln Record Society 57 (Lincoln, 1963), 58 (Lincoln, 1964), 74 (Lincoln, 1982).

Register of John Waltham, Bishop of Salisbury 1388–1395, ed. T. C. B. Timmins, Canterbury & York Society (London, 1994).

A Relation, or Rather a True Account of the Island of England; About the Year 1500, trans. Charlotte Augusta Sneyd, Camden Society, first series 37 (1847).

Richard of St Victor's Treatise of the Study of Wisdom that Men Call Benjamin, trans. and ed. Dick Barnes (New York, 1986).

Rolle, Richard, 'The Form of Living', *English Writings of Richard Rolle, Hermit of Hampole*, ed. Hope Emily Allen (orig. pub. 1931; this edition, Gloucester, 1988).

Rotuli Parliamentorum III, IV.

The St Albans Chronicle 1406–1420, ed. V. H. Galbraith (Manchester, 1927).

The Scale of Perfection, ed. and trans. J. P. H. Clark and R. Dorward (Mahwah, NJ, 1991).

Secretum Secretorum: Nine English Versions, ed. M. A. Manzaloui, EETS original series 276 (Oxford, 1977).

Selections from English Wycliffite Writings, ed. Anne Hudson (Cambridge, 1978).

Statutes of the Realm, II.

The Towneley Plays, ed. Martin Stevens and A. C. Cawley, 2 vols, EETS supplementary series 13 and 14 (Oxford, 1994).

A Tretise of Miraclis Pleyinge, ed. Clifford Davidson (Kalamazoo, MI, 1993).

Two Wycliffite Texts: the Sermon of William Taylor 1406; the Testament of William Thorpe 1407, ed. Anne Hudson, EETS original series 301 (Oxford, 1993).

Vitry, Jacques de, *The Life of Marie d'Oignies*, trans. Margot H. King (Toronto, 1993).

Voragine, Jacobus de, *The Golden Legend: Readings on the Saints*, trans. William Granger Ryan, 2 vols (Princeton, 1993).

The York Plays, ed. Richard Beadle (London, 1982).

Secondary Works on Margery Kempe

Aers, David, *Community, Gender and Individual Identity: English Writing 1360–1430* (London, 1988).

Aers, David and Lynn Staley, *The Powers of the Holy: Religion, Politics and Gender in Late Medieval English Culture* (University Park, PA, 1996).

Akel, Catherine S., 'Familial Structure in the Religious Relationships and Visionary Experiences of Margery Kempe', *Studia Mystica* 16 (1995): 116–32.

Ashley, Kathleen, 'Historicizing Margery: *The Book of Margery Kempe* as Social Text', *Journal of Medieval and Early Modern Studies* 28 (1998): 371–88.

Atkinson, Clarissa W., *Mystic and Pilgrim: The Book and the World of Margery Kempe* (Ithaca, NY, 1983).

Barratt, Alexandra, 'Margery Kempe and the King's Daughter of Hungary', in Sandra J. McEntire, ed., *Margery Kempe: A Book of Essays* (New York, 1992), pp. 189–201.

Beckwith, Sarah, 'A Very Material Mysticism: The Medieval Mysticism of Margery Kempe', in David Aers, ed., *Medieval Literature: Criticism, Ideology and History* (Brighton, 1986), pp. 34–57.

——, 'Problems of Authority in Late Medieval English Mysticism: Language, Agency and Authority in the *Book of Margery Kempe*', *Exemplaria* 4 (1992): 171–99.

——, *Christ's Body: Identity, Culture and Society in Late Medieval Writings* (London, 1993).

Bhattacharji, Santha, *God is an Earthquake: The Spirituality of Margery Kempe* (London, 1997).

Bowers, Terence N., 'Margery Kempe as Traveler', *Studies in Philology* 97 (2000): 1–28.

Burns, George, 'Margery Kempe Reviewed', *The Month* 171 (1938): 238–44.

Cleve, Gunnel, 'Semantic Dimensions in Margery Kempe's "Whyght Clothys"', *Mystics Quarterly* 12 (1986): 162–70.

——, 'Margery Kempe: A Scandinavian Influence on Medieval England', in Marion Glasscoe, ed., *The Medieval Mystical Tradition in England 5* (Cambridge, 1992), pp. 163–78.

Cohen, Jeffrey J., 'The Becoming Liquid of Margery Kempe', in *idem, Medieval Identity Machines* (Minneapolis, 2003), pp. 154–87.

Colledge, Edmund, 'Margery Kempe', in J. Walsh, ed., *Pre-Reformation English Spirituality* (Bronx, NY, 1965), pp. 210–23.

Craun, Edwin D., '*Fama* and Pastoral Constraints on Rebuking Sinners: *The Book of Margery Kempe*', in T. Fenster and D. L. Smail, eds, *Fama: The Politics of Talk and Reputation in Medieval Europe* (Ithaca, NY, 2003), pp. 187–209.

Dickman, Susan, 'Margery Kempe and the continental Tradition of the Pious Woman' in Marion Glasscoe, ed., *The Medieval Mystical Tradtion in England: Papers read at Dartington Hall, July 1984* (Cambridge, 1984), pp. 150–68.

Dillon, J., 'The Making of Desire in *The Book of Margery Kempe*', *Leeds Studies in English*, new series 26 (1995): 114–44.

——, 'Margery Kempe's Sharp Confessors', *Leeds Studies in English*, new series 27 (1996): 131–8.

Dinshaw, Carloyn, 'Margery Kempe Answers Back', in *eadem, Getting Medieval: Sexualities and Communities, Pre- and Postmodern* (Durham, NC, 1999), pp. 143–82.

——, 'Margery Kempe', in Carolyn Dinshaw and David Wallace, eds, *The Cambridge Companion to Medieval Women's Writing* (Cambridge, 2003), pp. 222–39.

Eberly, Susan, 'Margery Kempe, St Mary Magdalene, and Patterns of Contemplation', *Downside Review* 107, no. 368 (July 1989): 209–23.

Elliott, Dyan, 'Dress as Mediator Between Inner and Outer Self: The Pious Matron of the High and Later Middle Ages', *Mediaeval Studies* 53 (1991): 279–308.

Ellis, Deborah S., 'The Merchant's Wife's Tale: Language, Sex, and Commerce in Margery Kempe and in Chaucer', *Exemplaria* 2 (1990): 595–626.

——, 'Margery Kempe and King's Lynn', in Sandra J. McEntire, ed., *Margery Kempe: A Book of Essays* (New York, 1992), pp. 139–63.

Ellis, Roger, 'Margery Kempe's Scribe and the Miraculous Books', in Helen Phillips, ed., *Langland, the Mystics and the Medieval Religious Tradition* (Cambridge, 1990), pp. 161–75.

Erler, Mary, 'Margery Kempe's White Clothes', *Medium Aevum* 62 (1993): 78–83.

Fanous, Samuel, 'Measuring the Pilgrim's Progress: Internal Emphases in *The Book of Margery Kempe*', in Denis Renevey and Christina Whitehead, eds, *Writing Religious Women: Female Spiritual and Textual Practices in Late Medieval England* (Cardiff, 2000), pp. 157–76.

Farley, Mary Hardiman, 'Her Own Creature: Religion, Feminist Criticism, and the Functional Eccentricity of Margery Kempe', *Exemplaria* 11 (1999): 1–21.

Fienberg, Nona, 'Thematics of Value in *The Book of Margery Kempe*', *Modern Philology* 87 (1989): 132–41.

Fredell, Joel, 'Margery Kempe: Spectacle and Spiritual Governance', *Philological Quarterly* 75 (1996): 137–66.

Gibson, Gail McMurray, *The Theater of Devotion: East Anglian Drama and Society in the Late Middle Ages* (Chicago, 1989).

Glenn, Cheryl, 'Author, Audience and Autobiography: Rhetorical Technique in *The Book of Margery Kempe*', *College English* 54 (1992): 540–53.

Goodman, Anthony, 'The Piety of John Brunham's Daughter of Lynn', in Derek Baker, ed., *Medieval Women*, Studies in Church History subsidia 1 (Oxford, 1987), pp. 347–58.

——, *Margery Kempe and Her World* (Harlow, 2002).

Hanna III, Ralph, 'Some Norfolk Women and Their Books', in June Hall McCash, ed., *The Cultural Patronage of Medieval Women* (Athens, GA, 1996), pp. 288–305.

Harding, Wendy, 'Body into Text: *The Book of Margery Kempe*', in Linda Lomperis and Sarah Stanbury, eds, *Feminist Approaches to the Body in Medieval Literature* (Philadelphia, 1993), pp. 168–87.

Harvey, N. L., 'Margery Kempe: Writer as Creature', *Philological Quarterly* 71 (1992): 173–84.

Higgs, Laquita, 'Margery Kempe: "Whete-Breed" or Barley-Breed?', *Mystics Quarterly* 13.2 (1987): 57–64.

Hirsh, John, C., 'Author and Scribe in *The Book of Margery Kempe*', *Medium Aevum* 44 (1975): 145–50.

——, 'Margery Kempe', in A. S. G. Edwards, ed., *Middle English Prose: A Critical Guide to Major Authors and Genres* (New Brunswick, 1984), pp. 109–19.

——, *The Revelations of Margery Kempe: Paramystical Practices in Late Medieval England* (Leiden, 1989).

Ho, Cynthia, 'Margery Reads Exempla', *Medieval Perspectives* 13 (1993): 143–52.

Holbrook, Sue Ellen, 'Order and Coherence in *The Book of Margery Kempe*', in Constance H. Berman, Charles W. Connell and Judith Rice Rothschild, eds, *The Worlds of Medieval Women: Creativity, Influence, Imagination* (Morgantown, 1985), pp. 91–110.

——, 'Margery Kempe and Wynkyn de Worde', in Marion Glasscoe, ed., *The Medieval Mystical Tradition in England: Exeter Symposium IV* (Cambridge, 1987), pp. 27–46.

——, ' "About Her": Margery Kempe's Book of Feeling and Writing', in James M. Dean and Christian K. Zacher, eds, *The Idea of Medieval Literature: New Essays on Chaucer and Medieval Culture in Honor of Donald R. Howard* (Newark, NJ, 1992), pp. 265–84.

Holloway, Julia Bolton, 'Bride, Margery, Julian, and Alice: Bridget of Sweden's Textual Community in Medieval England', in Sandra J. McEntire, ed., *Margery Kempe: A Book of Essays* (New York, 1992), pp. 203–22.

Hoppenwasser, M., 'The Human Burden of the Prophet: St Birgitta's Revelations and *The Book of Margery Kempe*', *Medieval Perspectives* 8 (1993): 153–62.

Howes, L. L., 'On the Birth of Margery Kempe's Last Child', *Modern Philology* 90 (1992): 220–5.

Hussey, Stanley, 'The Rehabilitation of Margery Kempe', *Leeds Studies in English*, new series 32 (2001): 171–94.

Johnson, Ian, '*Auctricitas*: Holy Women and their Middle English Texts', in Rosalynn Voaden, ed., *Prophets Abroad: The Reception of Continental Holy Women in Late-Medieval England* (Cambridge, 1996), pp. 177–97.

Jones, Sarah Rees, ' "A Peler of Holy Cherch": Margery Kempe and the Bishops', in Jocelyn Wogan-Browne et al., eds, *Medieval Women: Texts and Contexts in Late Medieval Britain. Essays for Felicity Riddy* (Turnhout, 2000), pp. 377–91.

Kamerick, Kathleen, *Popular Piety and Art in the Late Middle Ages: Image Worship and Idolatry in England, 1350–1500* (New York, 2002).

Kelliher, H., 'The Rediscovery of Margery Kempe: A Footnote', *British Library Journal* 23 (1997): 259–63.

Landman, James H., 'The Laws of Community, Margery Kempe, and the "Canon's Yeoman's Tale" ', *Journal of Medieval and Early Modern Studies* 28 (1998): 389–425.

Lavezzo, Kathryn, 'Sobs and Sighs between Women: The Homoerotics of Compassion in The Book of Margery Kempe', in L. O. Aranye Fradenburg and Carla Freccero, eds, *Premodern Sexualities* (London, 1996), pp. 175–98.

Lawton, David, 'Voice, Authority and Blasphemy in *The Book of Margery Kempe*', in Sandra J. McEntire, ed., *Margery Kempe: A Book of Essays* (New York, 1992), pp. 93–116.

Lewis, Katherine J., *The Cult of St Katherine of Alexandria in Late Medieval England* (Woodbridge, 2000).

Lochrie, Karma, '*The Book of Margery Kempe*: The Marginal Woman's Quest for Literary Authority', *Journal of Medieval and Renaissance Studies* 16 (1986): 33–55.

——, *Margery Kempe and Translations of the Flesh* (Philadelphia, 1991).

Long, J., 'Mysticism and Hysteria: The Histories of Margery Kempe and Anna O.', in Ruth Evans and Leslie Johnson, eds, *Feminist Readings in Middle English Literature* (London, 1994), pp. 88–111.

Manter, Lisa, 'The Savior of Her Desire: Margery Kempe's Passionate Gaze', *Exemplaria* 13 (2001): 39–66.

McCann, Justin, 'The Book of Margery Kempe', *Dublin Review* 200 (1937): 103–16.

McEntire, Sandra J., ed., *Margery Kempe: A Book of Essays* (New York, 1992).

Meale, Carol M., ' "This is a Deed Bok, the Tother a Quick": Theatre and the Drama of Salvation in *The Book of Margery Kempe*', in Jocelyn Wogan-Browne et al., eds, *Medieval Women: Texts and Contexts in Late Medieval Britain. Essays for Felicity Riddy* (Turnhout, 2000), pp. 49–68.

Mueller, Janel M., 'Autobiography of a New "Creatur": Female Spirituality, Selfhood and Authorship in *The Book of Margery Kempe*', in Donna C. Stanton, ed., *The Female Autograph: Theory and Practice of Autobiography from the 10th to the 20th Century* (Chicago, 1984), pp. 57–69.

Myers, Michael D., 'A Fictional-True Self: Margery Kempe and the Social Reality of the Merchant Elite of King's Lynn', *Albion* 31 (1999): 377–94.

Partner, Nancy F., 'Reading *The Book of Margery Kempe*', *Exemplaria* 3 (1991): 29–66.

Renevey, Denis, 'Margery's Performing Body: The Translation of Late Medieval Discursive Religious Practices', in Denis Renevey and Christiania Whitehead, eds, *Writing Religious Women: Female Spiritual and Textual Practices in Late Medieval England* (Toronto, 2000), pp. 197–216.

Riddy, Felicity, 'Looking Closely: Authority and Intimacy in the Late Medieval Urban Home', in Mary C. Erler and Maryanne Kowaleski, eds, *Gendering the Master Narrative: Women and Power in the Middle Ages* (Ithaca, 2003), pp. 212–28.

Ross, Ellen M., 'Spiritual Experience and Women's Autobiography: The Rhetoric of Selfhood in *The Book of Margery Kempe*', *Journal of the American Academy of Religion* 59 (1991): 527–46.

Ross, R. C., 'Oral Life, Written Text: The Genesis of *The Book of Margery Kempe*', *Yearbook of English Studies* 22 (1992): 226–37.

Salih Sarah, *Versions of Virginity in Late Medieval England* (Cambridge, 2001).

——, 'Staging Conversion: The Digby Saint Plays and *The Book of Margery Kempe*', in Samantha J. E. Riches and Sarah Salih, eds, *Gender and Holiness: Men, Women and Saints in Late Medieval Europe* (London and New York, 2002), pp. 121–34.

——, 'At home; out of the house', in Carolyn Dinshaw and David Wallace, eds, *The Cambridge Companion to Medieval Women's Writing* (Cambridge, 2003), pp. 124–40.

Shklar, Ruth [Nissé], 'Cobham's Daughter: *The Book of Margery Kempe* and the Power of Heterodox Thinking', *Modern Language Quarterly* 56.3 (1995): 277–304.

Slade, C., 'The Mystical Experience of Angela of Foligno and Margery Kempe', *Religion and Literature* 23 (1991): 109–26.

Staley, Lynn [Johnson], 'Margery Kempe: Social Critic', *Journal of Medieval and Rennaissance Studies* 22 (1992): 159–84.

Staley, Lynn [Johnson], 'The Trope of the Scribe and the Question of Literary Authority in the Works of Julian of Norwich and Margery Kempe', *Speculum* 66 (1991): 820–38.

Staley, Lynn, *Margery Kempe's Dissenting Fictions* (University Park, Pennsylvania, 1994).

Stokes, Charity Scott, 'Margery Kempe: Her Life and the Early History of Her Book', *Mystics Quarterly* 25 (1999): 9–67.

Summit, Jennifer, *Lost Property: The Woman Writer and English Literary History, 1380–1589* (Chicago, 2000).

Swanson, Robert N., *Church and Society in Late Medieval England* (Oxford, 1989).

Szell, Timea K., 'From Woe to Weal and Weal to Woe: Notes on the Structure of *The Book of Margery Kempe*', in Sandra J. McEntire, ed., *Margery Kempe: A Book of Essays* (New York and London, 1992), pp. 73–91.

Tarvers, Josephine, 'The Alleged Illiteracy of Margery Kempe', *Medieval Perspectives* 11 (1996): 113–24.

Thurston, Herbert, 'Margery the Astonishing', *The Month* 168 (1936): 446–56.

Uhlman, Diane R., 'The Comfort of Voice, the Solace of Script: Orality and Literacy in *The Book of Margery Kempe*', *Studies in Philology* 91 (1994): 50–69.

Voaden, Rosalynn, 'God's Almighty Hand: Women Co-Writing the Book', in Lesley Smith and Jane H. M. Taylor, eds, *Women, the Book and the Godly: Selected Proceedings of the St Hilda's Conference, 1993* (Cambridge, 1995), pp. 55–65.

——, *God's Words, Women's Voices: The Discernment of Spirits in the Writing of Late-Medieval Women Visionaries* (Cambridge, 1999).

Warren, M. L., *Asceticism in the Christian transformation of self in Margery Kempe, William Thorpe and John Rogers* (Lewiston, NY, 2003).

Warren, Nancy Bradley, *Spiritual Economies: Female Monasticism in Later Medieval England* (Philadelphia, 2001).

Watson Nicholas, 'The Making of *The Book of Margery Kempe*', in Katheryn Kerby-Fulton and Linda Olson, eds, *Voices in Dialogue* (forthcoming, South Bend, IN, 2004).

Watt, Diane, *Secretaries of God: Women Prophets in Late Medieval and Early Modern England* (Cambridge, 1997).

Wiethaus, Ulrike, ed., *Maps of Flesh and Light: The Religious Experience of Medieval Women Mystics* (Syracuse, NY, 1993).

Wilson, Janet, 'Communities of Dissent: The Secular and Ecclesiastical Communities of Margery Kempe's *Book*', in Diane Watt, ed., *Medieval Women in Their Communities* (Cardiff, 1997), pp. 155–85.

Wright, M. J., 'What They Said to Margery Kempe: Narrative Reliability in her Book', *Neophilologus* 79 (1995): 497–508.

Yoshikawa, Naoë Kukita, 'Veneration of Virgin Martyrs in Margery Kempe's Meditation: Influence of the Sarum Liturgy and Hagiography', in Denis Renevey and Christina Whitehead, eds, *Writing Religious Women: Female Spiritual and Textual Practices in Late Medieval England* (Cardiff, 2000), pp. 177–95.

——, 'Margery Kempe's Mystical Marriage and Roman Sojourn: Influence of St Bridget of Sweden', *Reading Medieval Studies* 28 (2002): 39–57.

General Secondary Works

Alexander, Michael Van Cleave, *The Growth of English Education 1348–1648* (University Park, PA, 1990).

Allatt, Patricia, et al., *Women and the Life Cycle: Transitions and Turning Points* (New York, 1987).

Aston, Margaret, 'Lollard Women Priests?', *Journal of Ecclesiastical History* 31 (1980): 441–63.

——, 'William White's Lollard Followers', in *eadem*, ed., *Lollards and Reformers: Images and Literacy in Late Medieval Religion* (London, 1984), pp. 71–100.

——, 'Devotional Literacy', in *eadem*, ed., *Lollards and Reformers: Images and Literacy in Late Medieval Religion* (London, 1984), pp. 101–33.

——, 'Bishops and Heresy: The Defence of the Faith', in her *Faith and Fire: Popular and Unpopular Religion, 1350–1600* (London, 1993), pp. 73–93.

——, 'Caim's Castles: Poverty, Politics and Disendowment', in her *Faith and Fire: Popular and Unpopular Religion, 1350–1600* (London, 1993), pp. 95–131.

Atherton, I., et al., eds, *Norwich Cathedral: Church, City and Diocese 1096–1996* (London, 1996).

Attreed, L., *The King's Towns* (New York, 2001).

Bartlett, Anne Clark, *Male Authors, Female Readers: Representation and Subjectivity in Middle English Devotional Literature* (Ithaca, NY and London, 1995).

Barratt, Alexandra, ed., *Women's Writing in Middle English* (London, 1992).

——, 'The Revelations of Saint Elizabeth of Hungary: Problems of Attribution', *The Library* 6th series, 14 (1992): 1–11.

——, 'Continental Women Mystics and English Readers', in Carolyn Dinshaw and David Wallace, eds, *The Cambridge Companion to Medieval Women's Writing* (Cambridge, 2003), pp. 240–55.

Barron, Caroline, 'The "Golden Age" of Women in Medieval London', *Reading Medieval Studies* 15 (1989): 35–58.

——, 'Introduction: The Widow's World', in Caroline M. Barron and Anne F. Sutton, eds, *Medieval London Widows, 1300–1500* (London, 1994), pp. xxiv–xxv.

——, 'The Education and Training of Girls in Fifteenth-Century London', in Diana E. S. Dunn, ed., *Courts, Counties and the Capital in the Later Middle Ages* (New York, 1996), pp. 139–53.

——, 'The Expansion of Education in Fifteenth-Century London', in John Blair and Brian Golding, eds, *The Cloister and the World: Essays in Honour of Barbara Harvey* (Oxford, 1996), pp. 219–45.

Bäuml, Franz H., 'Varieties and Consequences of Medieval Literacy and Illiteracy', *Speculum* 55 (1980): 237–65.

Beauroy, J., 'Family Patterns and Relations in Bishop's Lynn Will-makers in the Fourteenth Century', in L. Bonfield, R. M. Smith and K. Wrightson, eds, *The World We Have Gained* (Oxford, 1986), pp. 23–42.

Bell, Susan Groag, 'Medieval Women Book Owners: Arbiters of Lay Piety and Ambassadors of Culture', *Signs* 7 (1982): 742–68.

Bengston, Jonathan,' St George and the Form of English Nationalism', *Journal of Medieval and Early Modern Studies* 27 (1997), pp. 317–40.

Bennett, Judith M., 'Women's History: A Study in Continuity and Change', *Women's History Review* 2 (1993): 173–84.

—— and Amy M. Froide, 'A Singular Past', in *eaedem*, eds, *Singlewomen in the European Past, 1250–1800* (Philadelphia, 1999), pp. 1–37.

Benton John F., ed., *Self and Society in Medieval France: The Memoirs of Abbot Guibert of Nogent (1064? – c.1125)* (New York, 1970).

Bloch, R. H., *Medieval Misogyny and the Invention of Western Romantic Love* (Chicago, 1991).

Boanas, Guy and Lyndal Roper, 'Feminine Piety in Fifteenth-Century Rome: Santa Francesca Romana', in Jim Obelkevich, Lyndal Roper and Raphael Samuel, eds, *Disciplines of Faith: Studies in Religion, Politics and Patriarchy* (London, 1987), pp. 177–93.

Bourdieu, Pierre, *The Logic of Practice*, trans. Richard Nice (Cambridge, 1990).

Breitenberg, Mark, *Anxious Masculinity in Early Modern England* (Cambridge, 1996).

Brown, Andrew, *Church and Society in England, 1000–1500* (Basingstoke and New York, 2003).

Brundage, James, 'Rape and Seduction in the Medieval Canon Law', in V. Bullough and J. Brundage, eds, *Sexual Practices and the Medieval Church* (New York, 1982), pp. 141–8.

——, *Law, Sex and Christian Society in Medieval Europe* (Chicago, 1990).

Bryman, Alan, et al., eds, *Rethinking the Life Cycle* (Houndmills, 1987).

Burrow, J. A., *The Ages of Man: A Study in Medieval Writing and Thought* (Oxford, 1986).

Bynum, Caroline Walker, *Jesus as Mother: Studies in the Spirituality of the High Middle Ages* (Berkeley and Los Angeles, 1982).

——, *Holy Feast and Holy Fast: The Religious Significance of Food to Medieval Women* (Berkeley and Los Angeles, 1987).

——, *Fragmentation and Redemption: Essays on Gender and the Human Body in Medieval Religion* (New York, 1992).

Caciola, Nancy, 'Mystics, Demoniacs, and the Physiology of Spirit Possession in Medieval Europe', *Comparative Studies in Society and History* 42 (2000): 268–306.

Cadden, Joan, *The Meanings of Sex Difference in the Middle Ages: Medicine, Science and Culture* (Cambridge, 1993).

Cameron, H. K., 'The Fourteenth-Century Flemish Brasses at King's Lynn', *Archaeological Journal* 136 (1980): 151–72.

Cannon, Christopher, 'The Rights of Medieval English Women: Crime and the Issue of Representation', in David Wallace and Barbara Hanawalt, eds, *Medieval Crime and Social Control* (Minneapolis, 1999), pp. 156–83.

Carey, Hilary M., 'Devout Literate Laypeople and the Pursuit of the Mixed Life in Later Medieval England', *Journal of Religious History* 14 (1987): 361–81.

Chance, Jane, 'St Catherine of Siena in Late Medieval Britain: Feminizing Literary Reception Through Gender and Class', *Annali d'Italianistica: Women Mystic Writers* 13 (1995): 163–203.

Clanchy, Michael, *From Memory to Written Record*, 2nd edn (London, 1979).

Clarke, H., and A. Carter, *Excavations in King's Lynn 1963–1970*, Society for Medieval Archaeology Monograph Series 7 (London, 1977).

Clay, Rotha Mary, *The Mediaeval Hospitals of England* (London, 1909).

Clopper, Lawrence M., *Drama, Play, and Game: English Festive Culture in the Medieval and Early Modern Period* (Chicago, 2001).

Coakley, John, 'Friars as Confidants of Holy Women in Medieval Dominican Hagiography', in Renate Blumenfeld-Kosinski and Timea Szell, eds, *Images of Sainthood in Medieval Europe* (Ithaca, NY, 1991), pp. 222–46.

Cohen, J. J. and B. Wheeler, eds, *Becoming Male in the Middle Ages* (New York, 1997).

Coldewey, John C., 'The Non-cycle Plays and the East Anglian Tradition', in Richard Beadle, ed., *The Cambridge Companion to Middle English Theatre* (Cambridge, 1994), pp. 189–210.

Coleman, Joyce, *Public Reading and the Reading Public in Late Medieval England and France* (Cambridge, 1996).

Coletti, Theresa, 'Paupertas est donum Dei: Hagiography, Lay Religion, and the Economics of Salvation in the Digby Mary Magdalene', *Speculum* 76 (2001): 337–78

Connell, R. W., *Masculinities* (Cambridge, 1995).

Cooke, Jessica, 'Nice Young Girls and Wicked Old Witches: The "Rightful Age" of Women in Middle English Verse', in Evelyn Mullally and John Thompson, eds, *The Court and Cultural Diversity: Selected Papers from the Eighth Triennial Congress of the International Courtly Literature Society* (Cambridge, 1997), pp. 219–28.

Copeland, Rita, *Pedagogy, Intellectuals and Dissent in the Later Middle Ages: Lollardy and Ideas of Learning* (Cambridge, 2001).

Courtenay, W. J., *Schools and Scholars in Fourteenth Century England* (Princeton, 1987).

Craig, Leigh Ann, 'Royalty, Virtue and Adversity: The Cult of King Henry VI', *Albion* 35 (2003): 187–209.

Craig, Hardin, *English Religious Drama of the Middle Ages* (Oxford, 1955).

Cross, Claire, ' "Great Reasoners in Scripture": The Activities of Women Lollards, 1380–1530', in D. Baker, ed., *Medieval Women*, Studies in Church History subsidia 1 (Oxford, 1978), pp. 359–80.

Cullum, P. H. ' "For Poor people harberles": What Was the Function of the Maisondieu?', in D. J. Clayton, R. C. Davies and P. McNiven, eds, *Trade, Devotion and Governance* (Stroud, 1994), pp. 36–54.

——, ' "And hir name was charity": Charitable Giving By and For Women in Late Medieval Yorkshire', in P. J. P. Goldberg, ed., *Women in English Society c. 1200–1500*, 2nd edn (Stroud, 1997), pp. 182–211.

——, 'Gendering Charity in medieval hagiography', in Samantha J. E. Riches and Sarah Salih, eds, *Gender and Holiness: Men, Women and Saints in Late Medieval Europe* (London and New York, 2002), pp. 135–51.

—— and P. J. P. Goldberg, 'Charitable Provision in late medieval York: "In Praise of God and to the Use of the Poor" ', *Northern History*, 29 (1993): 24–39.

Darnton, Robert, *The Great Cat Massacre and Other Episodes in French Cultural History* (New York, 1984).

D'Avray, D. and M. Tausche, 'Marriage Sermons in *Ad Status* Collections of the Central Middle Ages', *Archives d'Histoire Doctrinale et Literaire du Moyen Age* 47 (1981): 71–119.

Davis, I., 'Consuming the Body of the Working Man', in T. Walters and L. Herbert McAvoy, eds, *Consuming Narratives: Gender and Monstrous Appetite in the Middle Ages and the Renaissance* (Cardiff, 2002), pp. 42–53.

Demaitre, Luke, 'The Care and Extension of Old Age in Medieval Medicine', in M. Sheehan, ed., *Ageing and the Aged in Medieval Europe* (1990), pp. 5–22.

Despres, Denise L., 'Ecstatic Reading and Missionary Mysticism: *The Orcherd of Syon*', in Rosalynn Voaden, ed., *Prophets Abroad: The Reception of Continental Holy Women in Late-Medieval England* (Cambridge, 1996), pp. 141–60.

Dillon, Janette, 'Holy Women and their Confessors or Confessors and their Holy Women?', in Rosalynn Voaden, ed., *Prophets Abroad: The Reception of Continental Holy Women in Late-Medieval England* (Cambridge, 1996), pp. 115–40.

Dove, Mary, *The Perfect Age of Man's Life* (Cambridge, 1986).

Duffy, Eamon, 'Holy Maydens, Holy Wyfes: The Cult of Women Saints in Fifteenth and Sixteenth Century England', *Studies in Church History* 23 (1990): 175–96.

——, *The Stripping of the Altars: Traditional Religion in England c.1400–c.1580* (New Haven and London, 1992).

——, 'The Dynamics of Pilgrimage in Late Medieval England', in Colin Morris and Peter Roberts, eds, *Pilgrimage: The English Experience from Becket to Bunyan* (Cambridge, 2002), pp. 164–77.

Dyas, Dee, *Pilgrimage in Medieval English Literature, 700–1500* (Cambridge, 2001).

Ellis, Roger, ' "Flores ad Fabricandum . . . Coronam": An Investigation into the Uses of the Revelations of St Bridget of Sweden in Fifteenth-Century England', *Medium Ævum* 51 (1982): 163–86.

Emmerson, R. K., 'The Prophetic, the Apocalyptic, and the Study of Medieval Literature', in J. Wojcik and R. J. Frontain, eds, *Poetic Prophecy in Western Literature* (London, 1984).

Erler, Mary C., *Women, Reading, and Piety in Late Medieval England* (Cambridge, 2002).

Farmer, David Hugh, *The Oxford Dictionary of Saints*, 2nd edn (Oxford and New York, 1987).

Finucane, Ronald C., *Miracles and Pilgrims: Popular Beliefs in Medieval England* (London etc, 1977).

Fleming, Peter, *Women in Late Medieval Bristol*, Bristol Branch of the Historical Association, Local History Pamphlets no. 103 (Bristol, 2001).

Fletcher, Alan J., 'The N-Town Plays', in Richard Beadle, ed., *The Cambridge Companion to Middle English Theatre* (Cambridge, 1994), pp. 163–88.

French, Katherine L., 'Maidens' Lights and Wives' Stores: Women's Parish Guilds in Late Medieval England', *Sixteenth Century Journal* 29 (1998): 399–425.

Gibson, Gail McMurray, *The Theater of Devotion: East Anglian Drama and Society in the Late Middle Ages* (Chicago, 1989).

Goddard, Richard, 'Female Apprenticeship in the West Midlands in the Later Middle Ages', *Midland History* 27 (2002): 165–81.

Goldberg, P. J. P., *Women, Work and Life Cycle in a Medieval Economy: Women in York and Yorkshire, c.1300–1520* (Oxford, 1992).

——, 'Girls Growing Up in Later Medieval England', *History Today* (June 1995): 25–32.

——, 'Household and the Organisation of Labour in Late Medieval Towns: Some English Evidence', in Myriam Carier and Tim Soens, eds, *The Household in Late Medieval Cities: Italy and Northwestern Europe Compared* (Leuven, 2001), pp. 59–70

Görlach, Manfred, *Studies in Middle English Saints' Legends* (Tübingen, 1998).

Gransden, A., 'A Fourteenth-Century Chronicle from the Grey Friars at Lynn', *English Historical Review* 72 (1957): 270–8.

Gras, N. S. B., *The Early English Customs System* (Cambridge, MA, 1918).

Grisé, C. Annette, ' "In the Blessid Vyneyerd of Oure Holy Saueour": Female Religious Readers and Textual Reception in the *Myroure of Oure Ladye* and the *Orcherd of Syon*', in Marion Glasscoe, ed., *The Medieval Mystical Tradition in England, Ireland and Wales: Exeter Symposium VI* (Cambridge, 1999), pp. 193–211.

——, 'Women's Devotional Reading in Late-Medieval England and the Gendered Reader', *Medium Ævum* 71 (2002): 209–25.

Hadley, D. M., ed., *Masculinity in Medieval Europe* (London, 1999).

Hanawalt, Barbara, 'The Widow's Mite: Provisions for Medieval London Widows', in Louise Mirrer, ed., *Upon My Husband's Death: Widows in the Literature and Histories of Medieval Europe* (Ann Arbor, 1992), pp. 21–46.

——, *Growing Up in Medieval London: The Experience of Childhood in History* (New York, 1993).

——, 'Remarriage as an Option for Urban and Rural Widows in Late Medieval England', in Sue Sheridan Walker, ed., *Wife and Widow in Medieval England* (Ann Arbor, 1993), pp. 141–64.

Harper-Bill, Christopher, 'Monastic Apostasy in late Medieval England', *Journal of Ecclesiastical History* 32 (1981): 1–18.

Harvey, Margaret, *England, Rome and the Papacy, 1417–1464* (Manchester, 1993).

Heal, Felicity, *Hospitality in Early Modern England* (Oxford, 1990).

Hearn, Jeff, *The Gender of Oppression: Men, Masculinity and the Critique of Marxism* (Brighton, 1987).

Helmholz, Richard, *Marriage Litigation in Medieval England* (Cambridge, 1974).

——, 'Crime, Compurgation and the Courts of the Medieval Church', *Law and History Review* 1 (1986): 1–26.

Henderson, John, *Piety and Charity in Late Medieval Florence* (Oxford, 1994).

Hillen, H. J., *The History of the Borough of King's Lynn*, 2 vols (Wakefield, 1978), 2.

Hollywood, Amy, *The Soul as Virgin Wife: Mechthild of Magdeburg, Marguerite Porete and Meister Eckhart* (Notre Dame, 1995).

Hudson, Anne, 'A Lollard Sect Vocabulary?', in *eadem Lollards and Their Books* (London, 1985), pp. 166–73.

——, *The Premature Reformation: Wycliffite Texts and Lollard History* (Oxford, 1988).

Hudson, Anne, 'William Thorpe and the Question of Authority' in G. R. Evans, ed., *Christian Authority: Essays in Honour of Henry Chadwick* (Oxford, 1988), pp. 127–37.

Hughes, J., *Pastors and Visionaries: Religion and Secular Life in Late Medieval Yorkshire* (Woodbridge, 1988).

Hunt, Lynn, ed., *The New Cultural History* (Berkeley, 1989).

Hutchison, Ann M., 'Devotional Reading in the Monastery and in the Late Medieval Household', in Michael G. Sargent, ed., *De Cella in Seculum: Religious and Secular Life and Devotion in Late Medieval England* (Cambridge, 1989), pp. 215–27.

——, 'What the Nuns Read: Literary Evidence from the English Bridgettine House, Syon abbey', *Mediaeval Studies* 57 (1995): 205–22.

Ingham, Patricia Clare, *Sovereign Fantasies: Arthurian Romances and the Making of Britain* (Philadelphia, 2001).

Jenks, S., *England, die Hanse und Preussen: Handel und Diplomatie, 1377–1474*, Quellen und Darstellungen zur Hansischen Geschichte NS 38, 3 vols (Cologne/Vienna 1992), 1, pp. 444–50.

——, 'Die preussischen Hansestädte und England', in Z. H. Nowak and J. Tanxeci, eds, *Die preussischen Stadte und ihre Stellung im Nord – und Ostssraum des Mittelalters*, Ordines Militares – Colloquia Torunensia Historica 8 (1998), pp. 111–29.

——, 'King's Lynn and the Hanse: Trade and Relations in the Middle Ages', in K. Friedland, ed., *Proceedings of the Hanseatic History Union; Lynn, 1998* (forthcoming).

Kamerick, Kathleen, *Popular Piety and Art in the Late Middle Ages: Image Worship and Idolatry in England, 1350–1500* (New York, 2002).

Kandiyoti, Deniz, 'Bargaining with Patriarchy', *Gender and Society* 2 (1988): 274–90.

Keiser, George R., 'The Mystics and the Early English Printers: The Economics of Devotionalism', in Marion Glasscoe, ed., *The Medieval Mystical Tradition in England: Exeter Symposium IV* (Cambridge, 1987), pp. 9–26.

Kermode, Jennifer, *Medieval Merchants: York, Beverley and Hull in the Later Middle Ages* (Cambridge, 1998).

Keyser, Charles E., 'Notes on some ancient stained glass in Sandringham Church, Norfolk', *Norfolk Archaeology* 19 (1917): 122–32.

Kieckhefer, Richard, *Unquiet Souls: Fourteenth-Century Saints and their Religious Milieu* (Chicago, 1984).

Knowles, David and R. N. Hadcock, *Medieval Religious Houses: England and Wales* (London, 1953); 2nd edn (London, 1971).

Knowles, David, *The English Mystical Tradition* (London, 1961).

Kowaleski, Maryanne, 'Women's Work in a Market Town: Exeter in the Late Fourteenth Century', in Barbara A. Hanawalt, ed., *Women and Work in Preindustrial Europe* (Bloomington, IN, 1986), pp. 145–64.

—— and Judith M. Bennett, 'Crafts, Guilds, and Women in the Middle Ages: Fifty Years after Marian K. Dale', in Judith M. Bennett et al., eds, *Sisters and Workers in the Middle Ages* (Chicago, 1989), pp. 11–25.

Krug, Rebecca, *Reading Families: Women's Literate Practice in Late Medieval England* (Ithaca, 2002).

Lees, C. A., ed., *Medieval Masculinities: Regarding Men in the Middle Ages* (Minneapolis, 1994).

Leff Gordon, 'The Apostolic Ideal in Later Medieval Ecclesiology', *Journal of Theological Studies* NS 18 (1967): 58–82.

Lerner, Gerda, *The Creation of Patriarchy* (Oxford, 1986).

Lerner, Robert E., *The Heresy of the Free Spirit in the Later Middle Ages* (Notre Dame, 1972).

Lewis, Katherine J., 'Virgin Martyrs and the Training of Young Medieval Women', in Katherine J. Lewis, Noël James Menuge and Kim M. Phillips, eds, *Young Medieval Women* (New York, 1999), pp. 25–46.

——, 'Anglo-Saxon Saints' Lives, History and National Identity in Late Medieval England', in Helen Brocklehurst and Robert Phillips, eds, *History, Nationhood and the Question of Britain* (Houndmills, 2003), pp. 160–70.

Little, A. and Stone, 'Corrodies at the Carmelite Friary of Lynn', *Journal of Ecclesiastical History* 9 (1958): 8–29.

Lloyd, T. H., *England and the German Hanse 1157–1611* (Cambridge, 1991).

Lucas, P. J., 'A Bequest to the Austin Friars in the Will of John Spycer 1439–40: John Capgrave O.S.A. (1393–1464), William Wellys O.S.A. (fl. 1434–40) and Augustinian Learning at Lynn in the Fifteenth Century', *Norfolk Archaeology* 41 (1993): 482–9.

Mackerell, B., *The History and Antiquities of the Flourishing Corporation of King's Lynn in the County of Norfolk* (London, 1738).

MacFarlane, K. B., *John Wycliffe and the Beginnings of English Non-conformity* (London, 1952).

Margherita, Gayle, *The Romance of Origins: Language and Sexual Difference in Middle English Literature* (Philadelphia, 1994).

Marshall, John, ' "O 3e Souerens þat Sytt and 3e Brothern þat stoned right wppe": Addressing the Audience of *Mankind*', *European Medieval Drama* 1 (1997): 189–202.

Mate, Mavis E., *Daughters, Wives and Widows after the Black Death: Women in Sussex, 1350–1535* (Woodbridge, 1998).

Matthew, F. D., 'The Trial of Richard Wyche', *English Historical Review* 5 (1890): 530–44.

McEntire, Sandra J., *The Doctrine of Compunction in Medieval Literature: Holy Tears* (Lewiston, NY, 1990).

McKenna, J. W., 'Piety and propaganda: the cult of King Henry VI', in Beryl Rowland, ed., *Chaucer and Middle English Studies in Honour of Rossell Hope Robbins* (London, 1974), pp. 72–88.

McKisack, M., *Parliamentary Representation of English Boroughs during the Middle Ages* (Oxford, 1932).

——, *The Fourteenth Century 1307–1399* (Oxford, 1959).

McNamara, Jo Ann, 'Chaste Marriage and Clerical Celibacy', in V. Bullough and J. Brundage, eds, *Sexual Practices and the Medieval Church* (Buffalo, 1982), pp. 22–33.

McNiven, Peter, *Heresy and Politics in the Reign of Henry IV: The Burning of John Badby* (Woodbridge, 1987).

McSheffrey, Shannon, *Gender and Heresy: Women and Men in Lollard Communities 1420–1530* (Philadelphia, 1995).

——, 'Heresy, Orthodoxy and English Vernacular Religion, 1480–1525', *Past & Present* (forthcoming).

Meale, Carol M., ' "alle the bokes that I haue of latyn, englisch, and frensch": Laywomen and Their Books in Late Medieval England', in *eadem*, ed., *Women and Literature in Britain, 1150–1500* (Cambridge, 1993), pp. 128–58.

Millett, Bella, '*Mouvance* and the Medieval Author: Re-Editing *Ancrene Wisse*', in A. J. Minnis, ed., *Late-Medieval Religious Texts and their Transmission: Essays in Honour of A. I. Doyle* (Cambridge, 1994), pp. 9–20.

Muir, Carolyn Diskant, 'Bride or Bridegroom? Masculine Identity in Mystical Marriages', in P. H. Cullum and Katherine J. Lewis, eds, *Holiness and Masculinity in Medieval Europe* (forthcoming, Cardiff, 2004).

Mulder-Bakker, Anneke B., ed., *The Invention of Saintliness* (London and New York, 2002).

Murray, Jacqueline, 'Individualism and Consensual Marriage: Some Evidence from Medieval England', in C. M. Rousseau and J. T. Rosenthal, eds, *Women, Marriage and Family in Medieval Criticism: Essays in Memory of Michael M. Sheehan* (Kalamazoo, 1998), pp. 121–51.

——, ed., *Conflicted Identities and Multiple Masculinities: Men in the Medieval West* (New York, 1999).

Musson, A., *Medieval Law in Context* (Manchester, 2001).

Nelson, Alan H., *The Medieval English Stage* (Chicago, 1974).

Nissé, Ruth, ' "Oure Fadres Olde and Modres": Gender, Heresy, and Hoccleve's Literary Politics', *Studies in the Age of Chaucer* 21 (1999): 275–99.

Nitecki, Alicia K., 'Figures of Old Age in Fourteenth-Century English Literature', in M. Sheehan, ed., *Ageing and the Aged*, pp. 107–116.

Oliva, Marilyn, *The Convent and the Community in Late Medieval England: Female Monasteries in the Diocese of Norwich, 1350–1540* (Woodbridge, 1998).

Origo, I., *The Merchant of Prato* (London, 1963).

Orme, N., *English Schools in the Middle Ages* (London, 1973).

——, *Education and Society in Medieval and Renaissance England* (London, 1989).

—— and M. Webster, *The English Hospital, 1070–1570* (New Haven and London, 1995).

Owen, D. M., 'King's Lynn: the making of a new town', *Anglo-Norman Studies* 2 (1979): 141–53.

—— ed., *The Making of King's Lynn* (Gloucester, 1984).

Owst, G. W., *Literature and Pulpit in Medieval England* (Oxford, 1966).

Parkes, M. B., 'The Literacy of the Laity', in D. Daiches and A. Throlby, eds, *The Medieval World* (London, 1973), pp. 555–77.

Payer, Pierre J., *The Bridling of Desire: Views of Sex in the Later Middle Ages* (Toronto, 1993).

Peters, Christine, *Patterns of Piety: Women, Gender and Religion in Late Medieval and Reformation England* (Cambridge, 2003).

Phillips, Kim M., 'Maidenhood as the Perfect Age of Woman's Life', in Katherine J. Lewis, Noël James Menuge and Kim M. Phillips, eds, *Young Medieval Women* (Stroud, 1999), pp. 1–24.

——, *Medieval Maidens: Young Women and Gender in England, 1270–1540* (Manchester, 2003).

——, 'Four Virgins' Tales: Sex and Power in Medieval Law', in Anke Bernau, Ruth Evans and Sarah Salih, eds, *Medieval Virginities* (Cardiff, 2003), pp. 80–101.

Phythian-Adams, Charles, *Desolation of a City: Coventry and the Urban Crisis of the Late Middle Ages* (Cambridge, 1979).

Poos, L., 'Sex, Lies and the Church Courts of Pre-Reformation England', *Journal of Interdisciplinary History* 25 (1995): 585–607.

Powell, Edward, *Kingship, Law and Society: Criminal Justice in the Reign of Henry V* (Oxford, 1989).

Power, Eileen, *Medieval English Nunneries, c.1275 to 1535* (New York, 1964).

——, *Medieval Women*, new edn (Cambridge, 1997).

Rawcliffe, Carole, *The Hospitals of Medieval Norwich*, Studies in East Anglian History 2 (Norwich, 1995).

——, *Medicine for the Soul: the Life, Death and Resurrection of an English Medieval Hospital, St Giles, Norwich c.1249–1550* (Stroud, 1999).

Rees Jones, Sarah, 'Household, Work and the Problem of Mobile Labour: The Regulation of Labour in Medieval English Towns', in James Bothwell, P. J. P. Goldberg and W. M. Ormrod, eds, *The Problem of Labour in Fourteenth-Century England* (York, 2000), pp. 133–53.

Renevey, Denis, 'Margery's Performing Body: The Translation of Late Medieval Discursive Religious Practices', in Denis Renevey and Christiania Whitehead, eds, *Writing Religious Women: Female Spiritual and Textual Practices in Late Medieval England* (Toronto, 2000), pp. 197–216.

Rex, Richard, *The Lollards* (Houndmills, 2002).

Richards, W., *History of Lynn*, 2 vols (Lynn, 1812), 2.

Richardson, H. G., 'Heresy and the Lay Power under Richard II', *English Historical Review* 51 (1936): 1–28.

Riddy, Felicity, ' "Women Talking About the Things of God": A Late Medieval Sub-culture', in Carol M. Meale, ed., *Women and Literature in Britain, 1150–1500* (Cambridge, 1993), pp. 104–27.

——, 'Mother Knows Best: Reading Social Change in a Courtesy Text', *Speculum* 71 (1996): 66–86.

Rosenthal, Joel, T., *Old Age in Late Medieval England* (Philadelphia, 1996).

Rossi, Alice, 'Life Span Theories and Women's Lives', *Signs* 6 (1980): 4–32.

Rubin, Miri, *Charity and Community in Medieval Cambridge* (Cambridge, 1987).

Russell, Josiah C., 'How Many of the Population were Aged?', in Michael M. Sheehan, ed., *Aging and the Aged in Medieval Europe* (Toronto, 1990), pp. 119–28.

Sargent, Michael, 'Walter Hilton's *Scale of Perfection*: The London Manuscript Group Reconsidered', *Medium Aevum* 52 (1983): 189–216.

Scherb, Victor I., *Staging Faith: East Anglian Drama in the Later Middle Ages* (Cranbury, NJ, 2001).

Schochet, Gordon J., *Patriarchalism in Political Thought: The Authoritarian Family and Political Speculation and Attitudes Especially in Seventeenth-Century England* (Oxford, 1975).

Sears, Elizabeth, *The Ages of Man: Medieval Interpretations of the Life Cycle* (Princeton, 1986).

Shahar, Shulamith, *Growing Old in the Middle Ages: 'Winter Clothes us in Shadow and Pain'*, trans. Yael Lotan (London, 1997).

Smith, Sidonie, *A Poetics of Women's Autobiography: Marginality and the Fictions of Self-Representation* (Bloomington, 1987).

Snape, M. G., 'Some Evidence of Lollard Activity in the Diocese of Durham in the Early Fifteenth Century', *Archaeologia Aeliana* 4th series 39 (1961): 355–61.

Spencer, Brian, *Pilgrim Souvenirs and Secular Badges* (London, 1998).

Strohm, Paul, *England's Empty Throne: Usurpation and the Language of Legitimation 1399–1422* (New Haven, 1998).

——, 'Walking Fire: Symbolization, Action, and Lollard Burning', in *idem, Theory and the Premodern Text* (Minneapolis, 2000), pp. 20–32.

Swanson, Heather, 'The Illusion of Economic Structure: Craft Guilds in Late Medieval English Towns', *Past and Present* 121 (1988): 29–48.

——, *Medieval Artisans: An Urban Class in Late Medieval England* (Oxford, 1989).

Tanner, Norman P., *The Church in Late Medieval Norwich* (Toronto, 1984).

Thrupp, Sylvia, *The Merchant Class of Medieval London, 1300–1500* (Ann Arbor, 1962).

Topenwasser, Nanda, 'A Performance Artist and her Performance Text: Margery Kempe on Tour', in Mary A. Sudyan and Joann E. Ziegler, eds, *Performance and Transformation: New Approaches to Late Medieval Spirituality* (Houndmills, 1999), pp. 97–131.

Vauchez, André, 'The Reaction of the Church to Late-Medieval Mysticism and Prophecy', in his *The Laity in the Middle Ages: Religious Beliefs and Devotional Practices*, ed. and introduced by Daniel E. Bornstein, trans. Margaret J. Schneider (Notre Dame and London, 1993), pp. 243–54.

Vauchez, André, *Sainthood in the Later Middle Ages*, trans. Jean Birrell (Cambridge, 1997).

Voaden, Rosalynn and Stephanie Volf, 'Visions of My Youth: Representations of the Childhood of Medieval Visionaries', *Gender and History* 12 (2000): 665–84.

Walker, Simon, 'Political saints in later medieval England', in R. H. Britnell and A. J. Pollard, eds, *The McFarlane Legacy: Studies in Late Medieval Politics and Society* (Stroud, 1995), pp. 77–106.

Wallace, David, 'Mystics and Followers in Siena and East Anglia: A Study in Taxonomy, Class and Cultural Mediation', in Marion Glasscoe, ed., *The Medieval Mystical Tradition in England: Exeter Symposium III* (Cambridge, 1984), pp. 169–91.

Warren, Nancy Bradley, *Spiritual Economies: Female Monasticism in Later Medieval England* (Philadelphia, 2001).

Watson, Nicholas, *Richard Rolle and the Invention of Authority* (Cambridge, 1991).

——, 'The Composition of Julian of Norwich's *Revelation of Love*', *Speculum* 68 (1993): 637–83.

——, 'Censorship and Cultural Change in Late-Medieval England: Vernacular Theology, the Oxford Translation Debate, and Arundel's Constitutions of 1409', *Speculum* 70 (1995): 822–64.

——, 'Melting into God in the English Way: Deification in the Middle English Version of Marguerite Porete's *Mirouer des simples âmes anientes*', in Rosalynn Voaden, ed., *Prophets Abroad: The Reception of Continental Holy Women in Late-Medieval England* (Cambridge, 1996), pp. 19–50.

——, 'The Middle English Mystics', in David Wallace, ed., *The Cambridge History of Medieval English Literature* (Cambridge, 1999), pp. 539–65.

Watt, Diane, 'The Prophet at Home: Elizabeth Barton and the Influence of Bridget of Sweden and Catherine of Siena', in Rosalynn Voaden, ed., *Prophets Abroad: The Reception of Continental Holy Women in Late-Medieval England* (Cambridge, 1996), pp. 161–76.

Webb, Diana, *Pilgrimage in Medieval England* (London and New York, 2000).

——, *Medieval European Pilgrimage* (Houndmills, 2002).

Weinstein, Donald and Rudolph M. Bell, *Saints and Society: The Two Worlds of Western Christendom, 1000–1700* (Chicago, 1982).

Westfall, Suzanne, *Patrons and Performance: Early Tudor Household Revels* (Oxford, 1990).

Williams-Krapp, Werner, 'Literary Genre and Degrees of Saintliness: The Perception of Holiness in Writings By and About Female Mystics', in Anneke B. Mulder-Bakker, ed., *The Invention of Saintliness* (London and New York, 2002), pp. 206–18.

Windeatt, B. A., *English Mystics of the Middle Ages* (Cambridge, 1994).

——, ' "I use but comownycacyon and good wordys": Teaching and *The Book of Margery Kempe*', in Dee Dyas and Roger Ellis, eds., *Approaching Medieval English Anchoritic and Mystical Texts* (forthcoming).

Winstead, Karen A., *Virgin Martyrs: Legends of Sainthood in Late Medieval England* (Ithaca, 1997).

Wogan-Browne, Jocelyn, *Saints' Lives and Women's Literary Culture c.1150–1300: Virginity and its Authorisations* (Oxford, 2001).

——, Nicholas Watson, Andrew Taylor and Ruth Evans, eds., *The Idea of the Vernacular: An Anthology of Middle English Literary Theory 1280–1520* (University Park, PA, 1999).

Wood, Diana, *Medieval Economic Thought* (Cambridge, 2002).

Unpublished Works

Beattie, Cordelia, 'Meanings of Singleness: The Single Woman in Late Medieval England', D.Phil. thesis, University of York (2001).

Dutton, Anne, 'Women's Use of Religious Literature in Late Medieval England', D.Phil. thesis, University of York (1995).

McSheffrey, Shannon, 'Women in Lollardy, 1420–1530: Gender and Class in Heretical Communities', Ph.D. thesis, University of Toronto (1992).

Index

Note: Works are indexed by author, where known, and otherwise by title. Names of the form 'Katherine of Alexandria' are indexed by first name; otherwise, by surname.

9 781843 842149